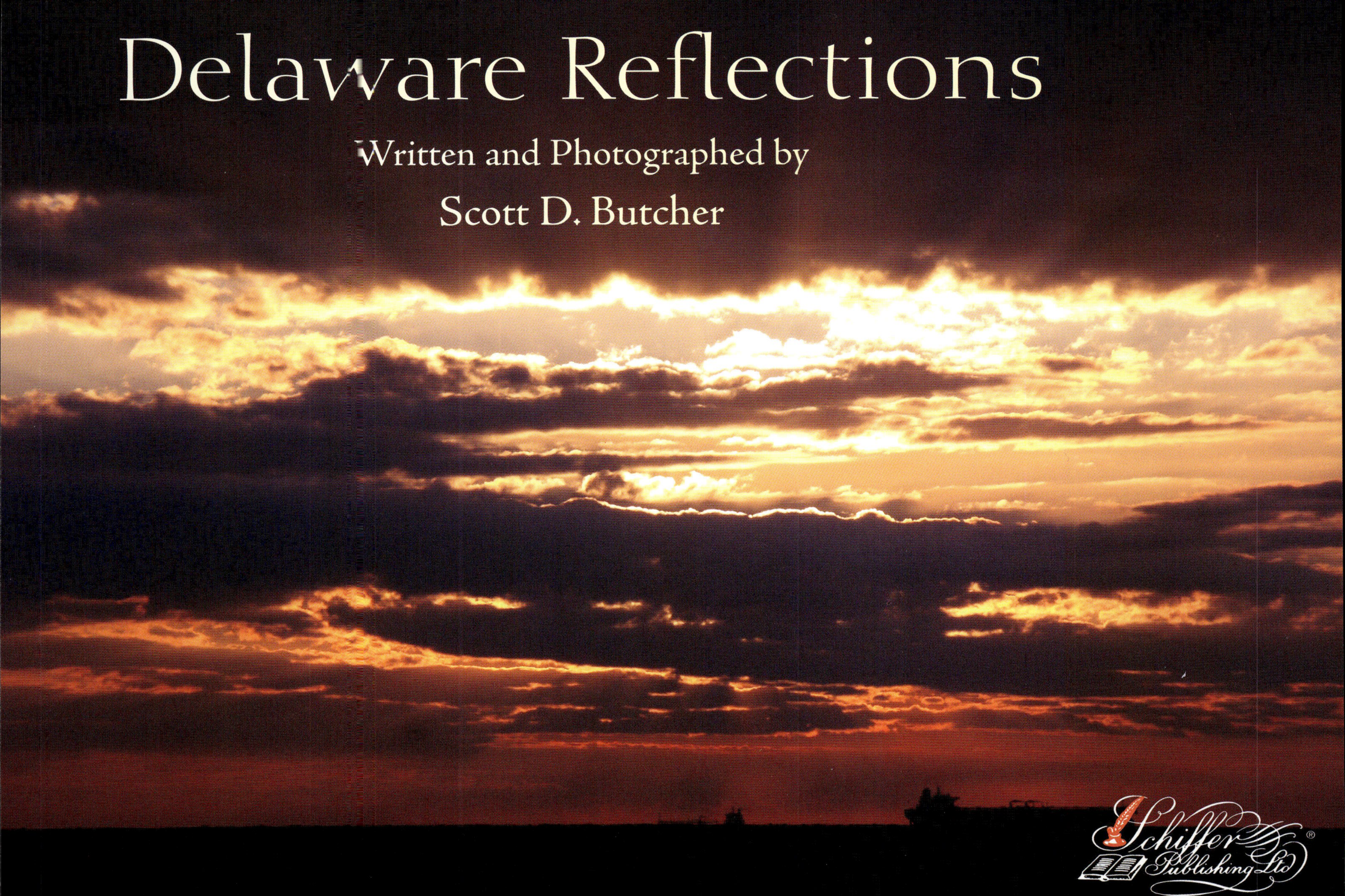

Delaware Reflections

Written and Photographed by

Scott D. Butcher

Schiffer Publishing Ltd

Library of Congress Control Number: 2008940266

Designed by John P. Cheek
Cover design by Bruce Waters
Type set in Adobe Jenson Pro/Zurich BT
ISBN: 978-0-7643-3200-5
Printed in China

Schiffer Books are available at special discounts for bulk purchases for sales promotions or premiums. Special editions, including personalized covers, corporate imprints, and excerpts can be created in large quantities for special needs. For more information contact the publisher:

Published by Schiffer Publishing Ltd.
4880 Lower Valley Road
Atglen, PA 19310
Phone: (610) 593-1777; Fax: (610) 593-2002
E-mail: Info@schifferbooks.com

For the largest selection of fine reference books on this and related subjects, please visit our web site at **www.schifferbooks.com**

We are always looking for people to write books on new and related subjects. If you have an idea for a book please contact us at the above address.

This book may be purchased from the publisher.
Include $5.00 for shipping.
Please try your bookstore first.
You may write for a free catalog.

In Europe, Schiffer books are distributed by
Bushwood Books
6 Marksbury Ave.
Kew Gardens
Surrey TW9 4JF England
Phone: 44 (0) 20 8392-8585; Fax: 44 (0) 20 8392-9876
E-mail: info@bushwoodbooks.co.uk
Website: www.bushwoodbooks.co.uk
Free postage in the U.K., Europe; air mail at cost.

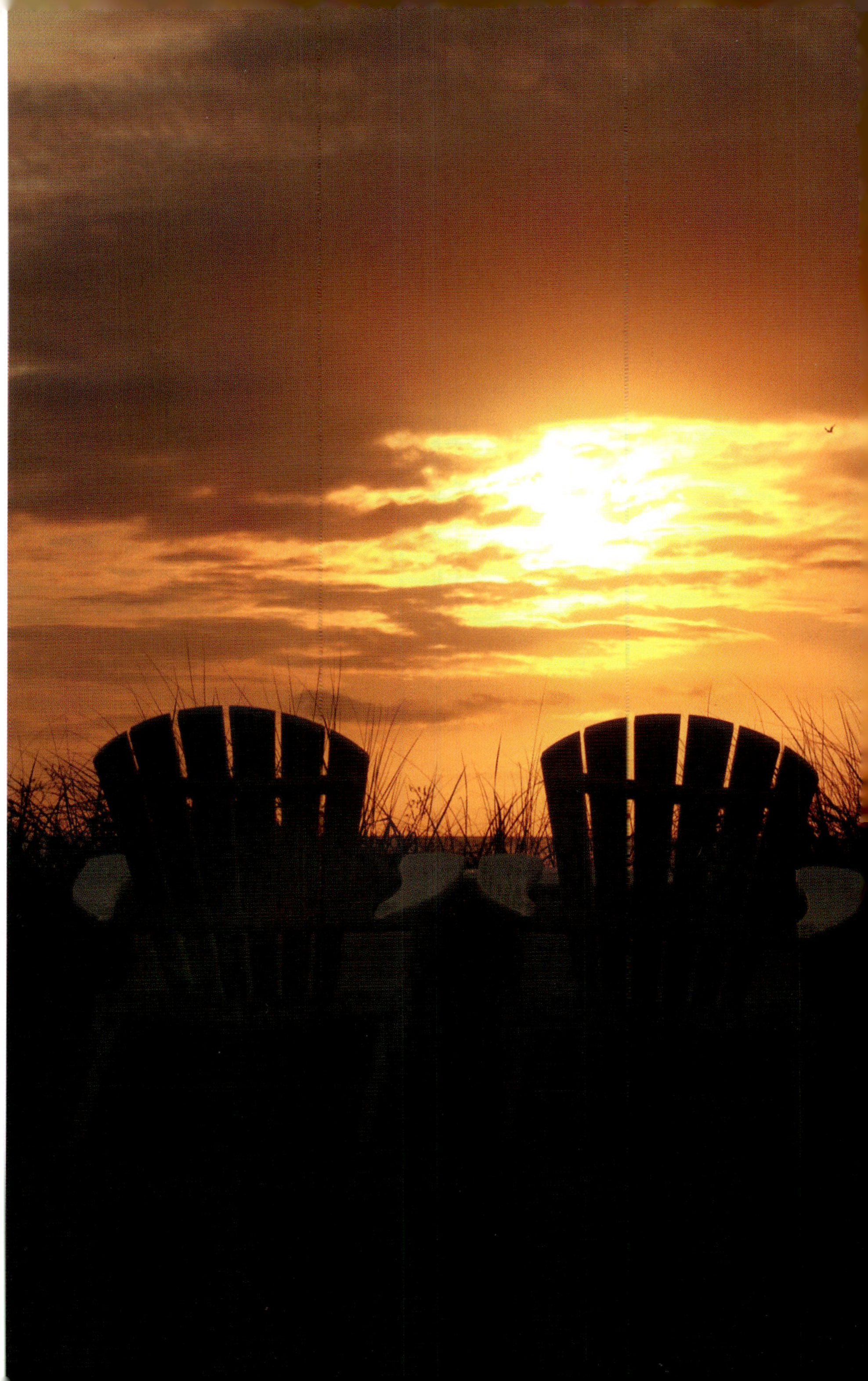

Dedication

For my parents, Marla and Don Butcher. Not only have you always offered words of encouragement, but you also introduced me to the Delaware coast through many summer vacations at Bethany Beach. Thank you.

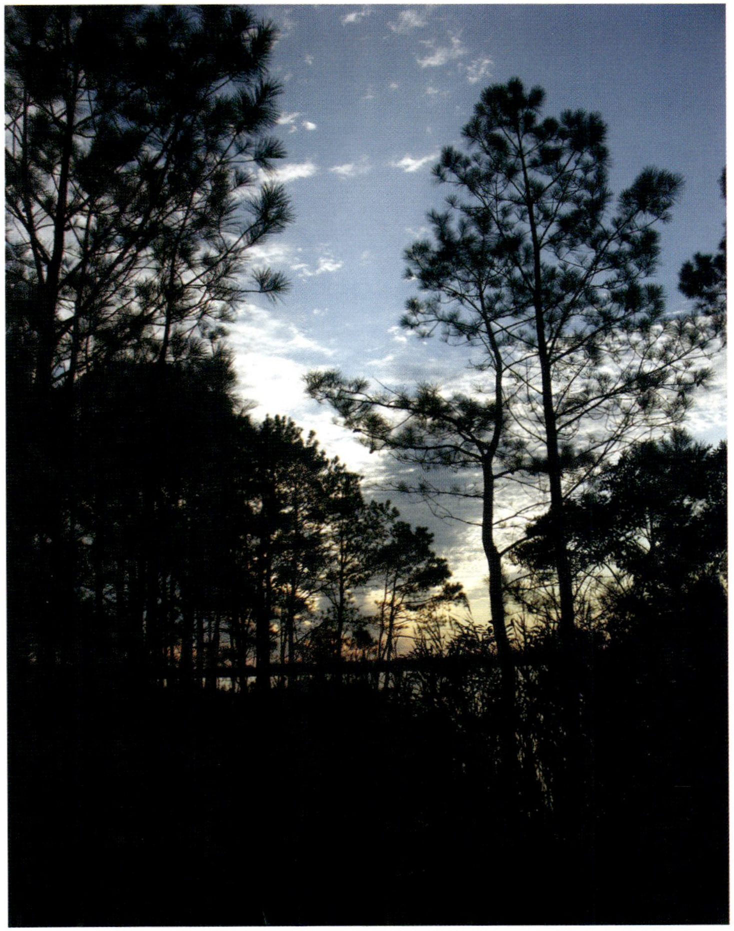

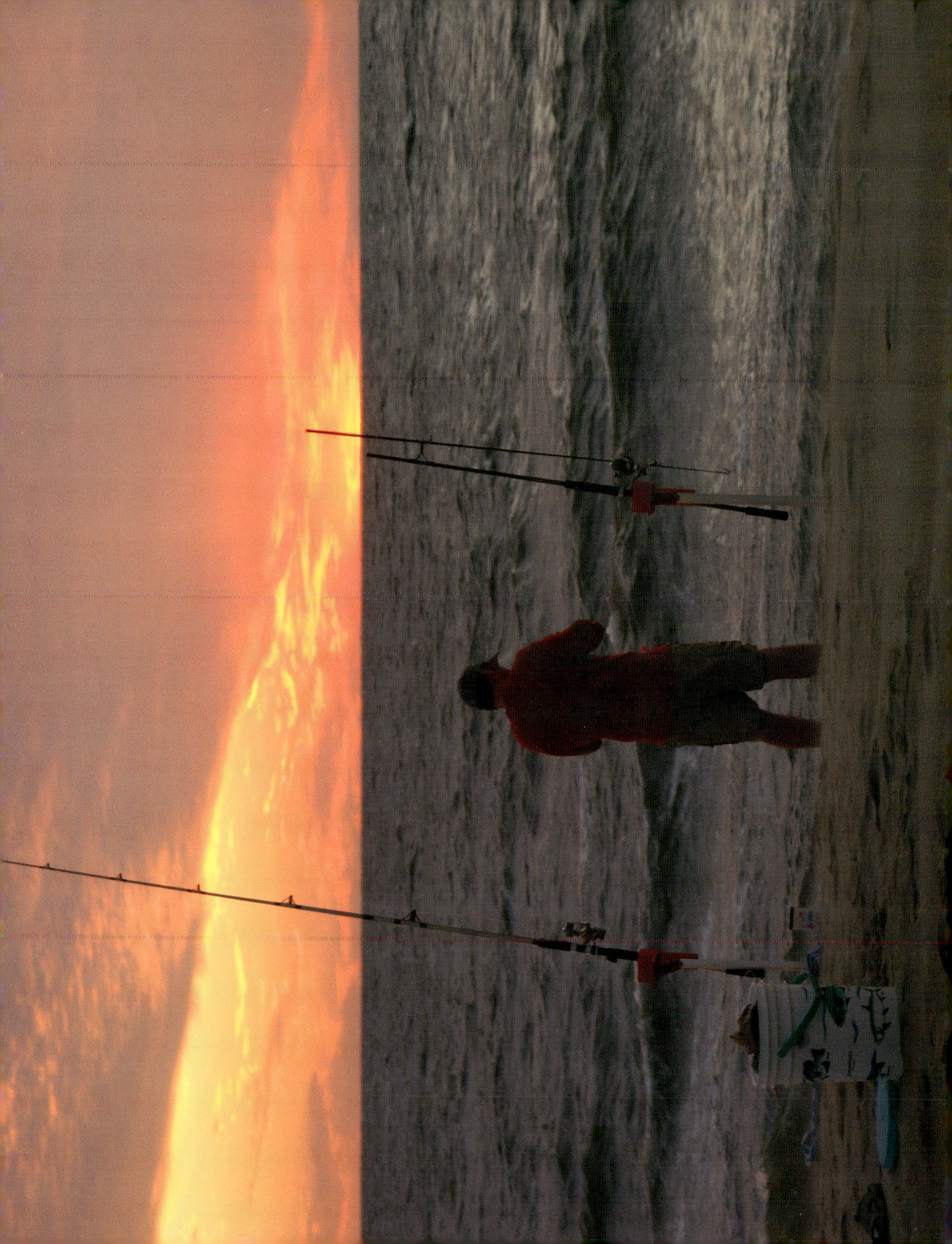

Contents

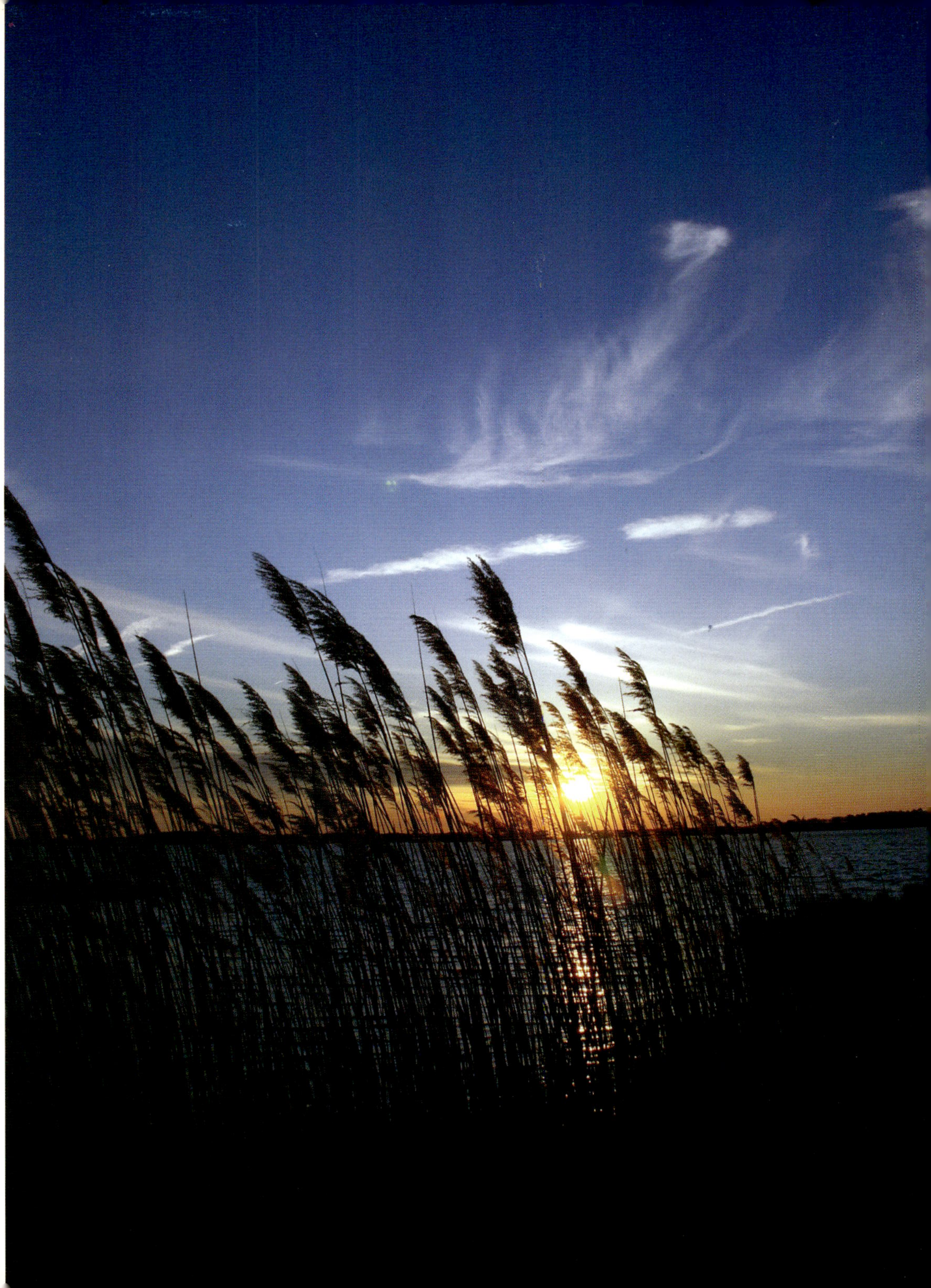

Introduction

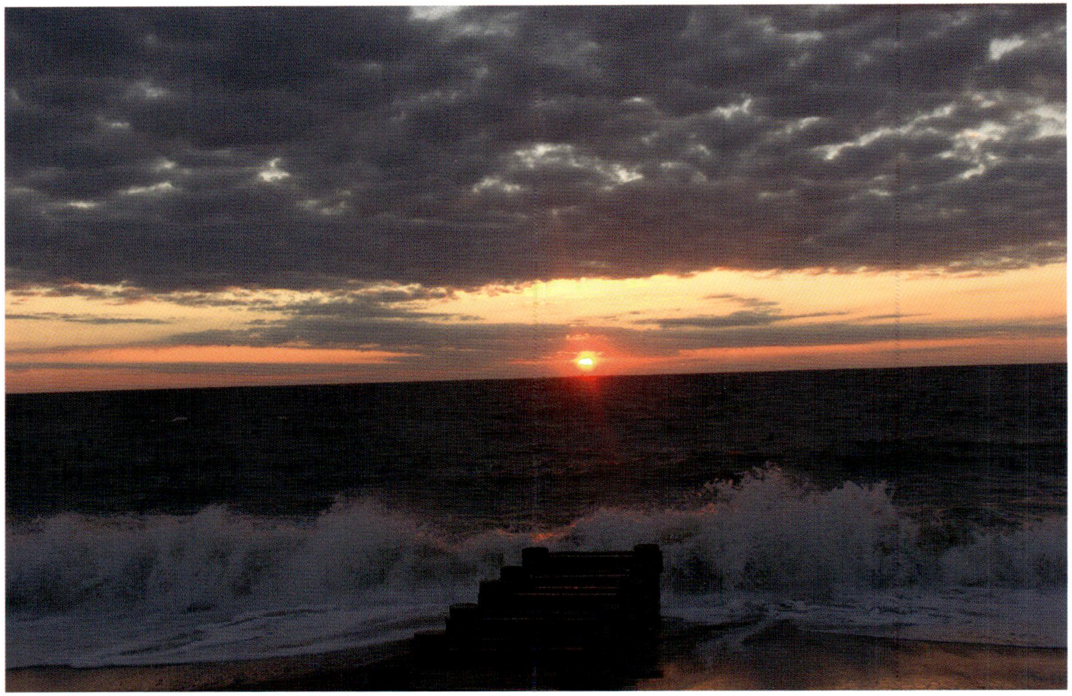

A drive along the Delaware coast is a study in contrasts. From the north, travelers on Route 1/Coastal Highway first encounter signs to Lewes, the Cape May-Lewes Ferry, and Cape Henlopen State Park. The unassuming markers do little to reveal the rich history of Delaware's first town or an important World War II defense system among a great dune.

Travelers next encounter the outlets and commercial centers of Rehoboth Beach, which obscure the historic beachfront community known as "The Nation's Summer Capital" – home of a nationally-recognized boardwalk.

Then, suddenly, they find themselves in a small planned community, surrounded by hotels, condominiums and nightclubs. But as soon as they arrive in Dewey Beach, they see it in their rearview mirror.

An open road awaits – unadulterated coastline to one side, open bay to the other – Delaware Seashore State Park heralds a break from development and commercialism. Concrete sentinels from World War II silently guard over the ocean. A bridge rises in the distance, and soon a panoramic view of the Atlantic Ocean and Indian River Bay can be seen in all directions.

Beyond the inlet, condominiums grow from the sands, and shorefront communities with large homes and private entrances pass one by one beyond the side windows. And soon there's a stoplight, adjacent to a large Native American face and eagle carved from Alaskan red cedar. The refrained bustle of Bethany Beach can be seen looking toward the boardwalk. Further south, massive tan sandcastles reach toward the sky along the coast. Beyond Sea Colony the character of South Bethany turns residential, with commercial offerings along the west side of Route 1.

But soon the openness returns as travelers enter Fenwick Island State Park. A smattering of condominiums dot the highway to the east and to the west, but there are no crowds, no stoplights, and no strip centers. A lighthouse rises in the distance, announcing the town of Fenwick Island and the sort of yesteryear charm devoid of the majority of the amenities found today in most seaside resorts. In the distance mountains of steel, glass and neon appear, heralding the end of the Delaware coastline and the beginning of Ocean City, Maryland.

The journey is through.

The stretch of Delaware's Atlantic Coast is less than one-quarter the length of New York's Long Island. The coastline of Ocean City, Maryland itself is over one-third the length of the Delaware coast between Lewes and Fenwick Island.

But within this relatively small stretch of land is an eclectic collection of seaside resorts and quaint towns, beaches and bays, and over 375 years of history – whaling colonies, pirates, British bombardments, and Nazi submarines.

There is not just something for everyone, but many things for everyone. Each community along the coast has its own distinctive personality – and they are all just a short drive from one-another. Where else can you find a National Trust for Historic Preservation "Distinctive Destination," AARP "Best Place to Retire," *Tennis Magazine* "Top 50 Tennis Community," and golf destination with championship courses designed by some of the best in the business? Where else can you begin your day watching a pastel sunrise over a turquoise ocean, then end it while viewing a vivid sunset over a platinum bay – only a few hundred yards from where you started?

The Delaware Coast is a treat for the senses – pristine tan beaches, grass-covered dunes, and sparkling water delight the eyes. Salt air, Old Bay, and caramel popcorn tease the nose. Live bands, children laughing, and the crash of the surf provide music to the ears. Beach fries, salt water taffy, and seafood galore tempt the taste buds. The squish of sand between the toes, sun dancing upon the skin, and a wooden crab mallet in the hand touch you both physically and emotionally, providing a final movement in this symphony of the senses.

The Delaware coast has beckoned generations of visitors and residents to her shores, lighting the way with beacons reaching into the night sky.

The memories of time spent along the Delaware coast are reflected in the stories passed from generation to generation – ever changing yet as consistent and reliable as a golden sunrise reflected across a silky smooth ocean or bay.

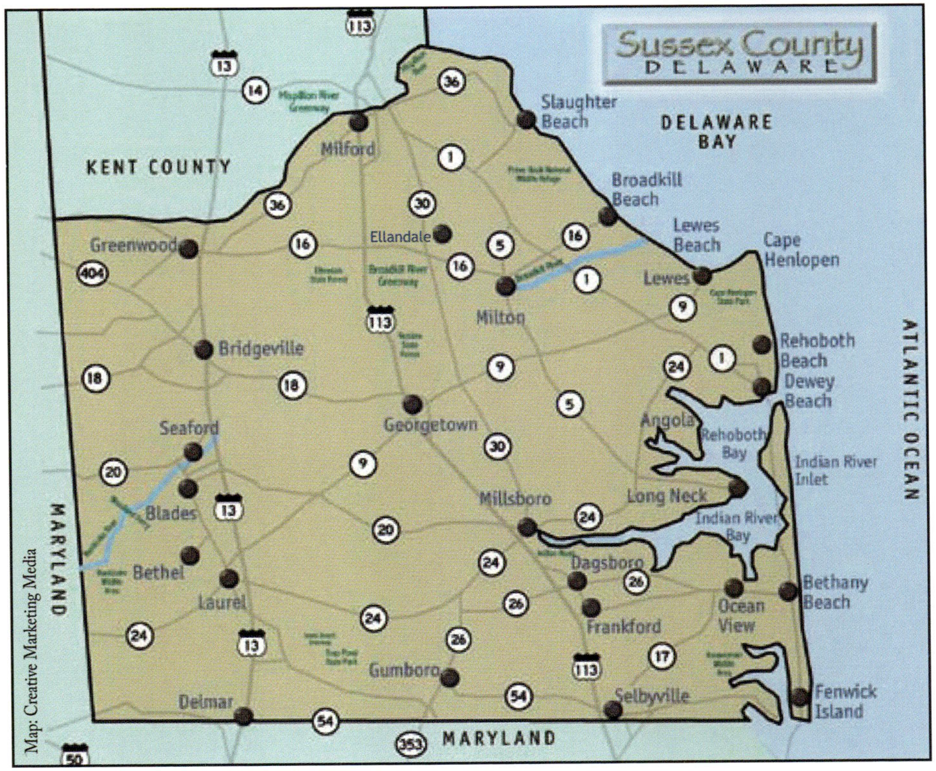

Map: Creative Marketing Media

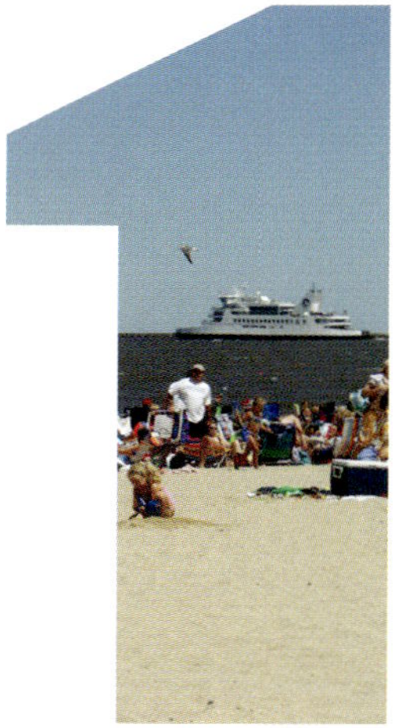

Lewes: *The First Town in the First State*

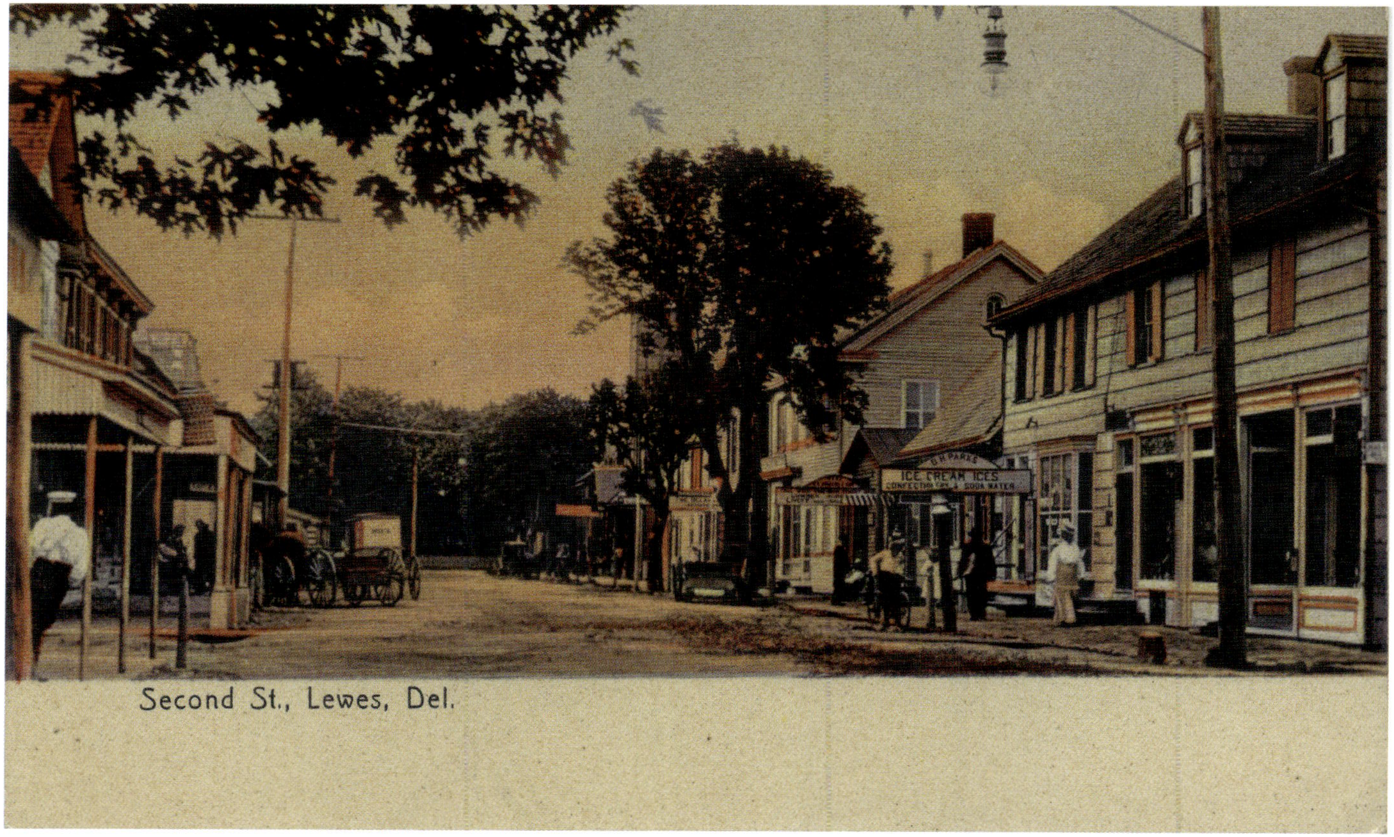

University of Delaware Library Postcard Collection, University of Delaware, Newark, Delaware

The inviting, tree-lined streets of Lewes take residents and visitors to another era. While its claim to fame may be as "The First Town in the First State," Lewes exudes a Victorian charm rarely found in towns today. In fact, the *Washington Post* dubbed Lewes as "a miniature San Francisco lined with 'painted lady' Victorian and Queen Anne houses."

In 1631, Dutch settlers came to the area and established a whaling station which they called Swanendael, which means "valley of the swans." It didn't last long. One year later, Siconese Indians massacred the inhabitants of the tiny colony, also burning their buildings and supplies. A lone survivor escaped to New Amsterdam (New York). In 1659, the Dutch returned and resettled the area, naming it Hoerenkill. The town was also known as Whorekill and Deale.

The land was eventually conveyed to William Penn, and he personally named the town Lewes, after a town in Sussex County, England. Visitors to Lewes today are easy to pick out, because they frequently pronounce the town "lews"; the correct pronunciation, however, is "loo-iss."

For a town of about 3,000 year-round residents, Lewes is rich in history. Pirates, including Captain Kidd, are known to have visited her shores. The town was ransacked by French pirates in 1698. Kidd actually anchored his boat, the Saint Antonio, offshore and invited residents of Lewes on board; they were astonished at the riches, and some are known to have made purchases from the pirates.

In April 1813, a British frigate unleashed a torrent of cannonballs on the town during the War of 1812. The aptly named Cannonball House bares a symbol of the bombardment: a cannonball in its foundation. By 1869, the railroad had arrived. With the Junction and Breakwater Railroad, and subsequent arrival of Queen Anne's Railroad, Lewes was able to grow and prosper. The multitude of high-style Victorian architecture is testament to the town's success. The Lewes & Rehoboth Canal was authorized in 1912, and by 1916 boats were using the new canal. However, tragedy struck in 1920 when much of the business district was destroyed by fire.

But the town with humble beginnings as a Dutch whaling colony rebuilt, and today is a destination for residents and visitors seeking a different kind of shore experience. Lewes Beach is located along the Delaware Bay, and the calm, glistening waters are an apt metaphor for the town itself. While neighbors Rehoboth Beach and Dewey Beach are filled with high energy, a lively boardwalk, and myriad nightlife, Lewes is content to treasure its history and low-key lifestyle.

Historic sites abound, and a quaint shopping district provides antique stores and boutiques, while also offering up a smorgasbord of unique dining opportunities. Lewes has even been recognized as one of the nation's "Dozen Distinctive Destinations" by the National Trust for Historic Preservation.

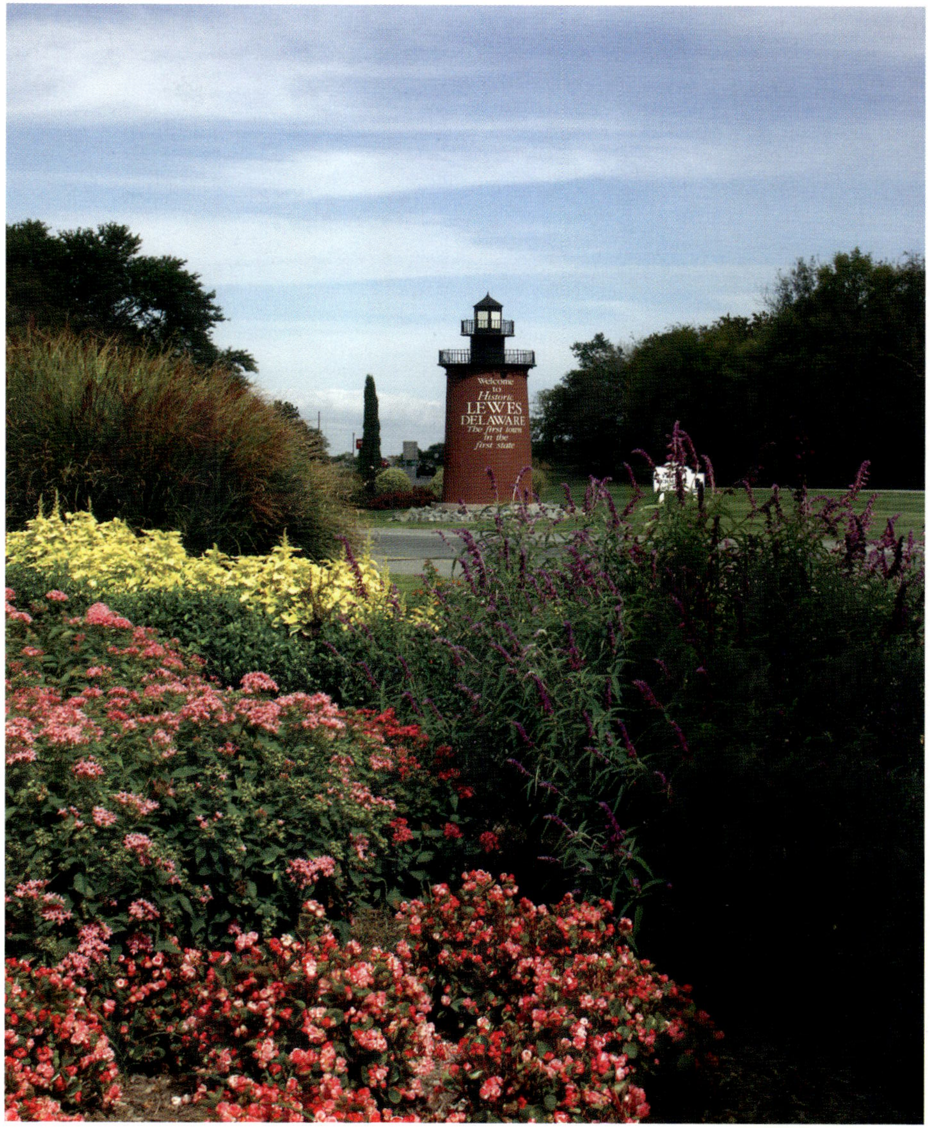

A rich palette of color and small lighthouse greets visitors to "The First Town in the First State."

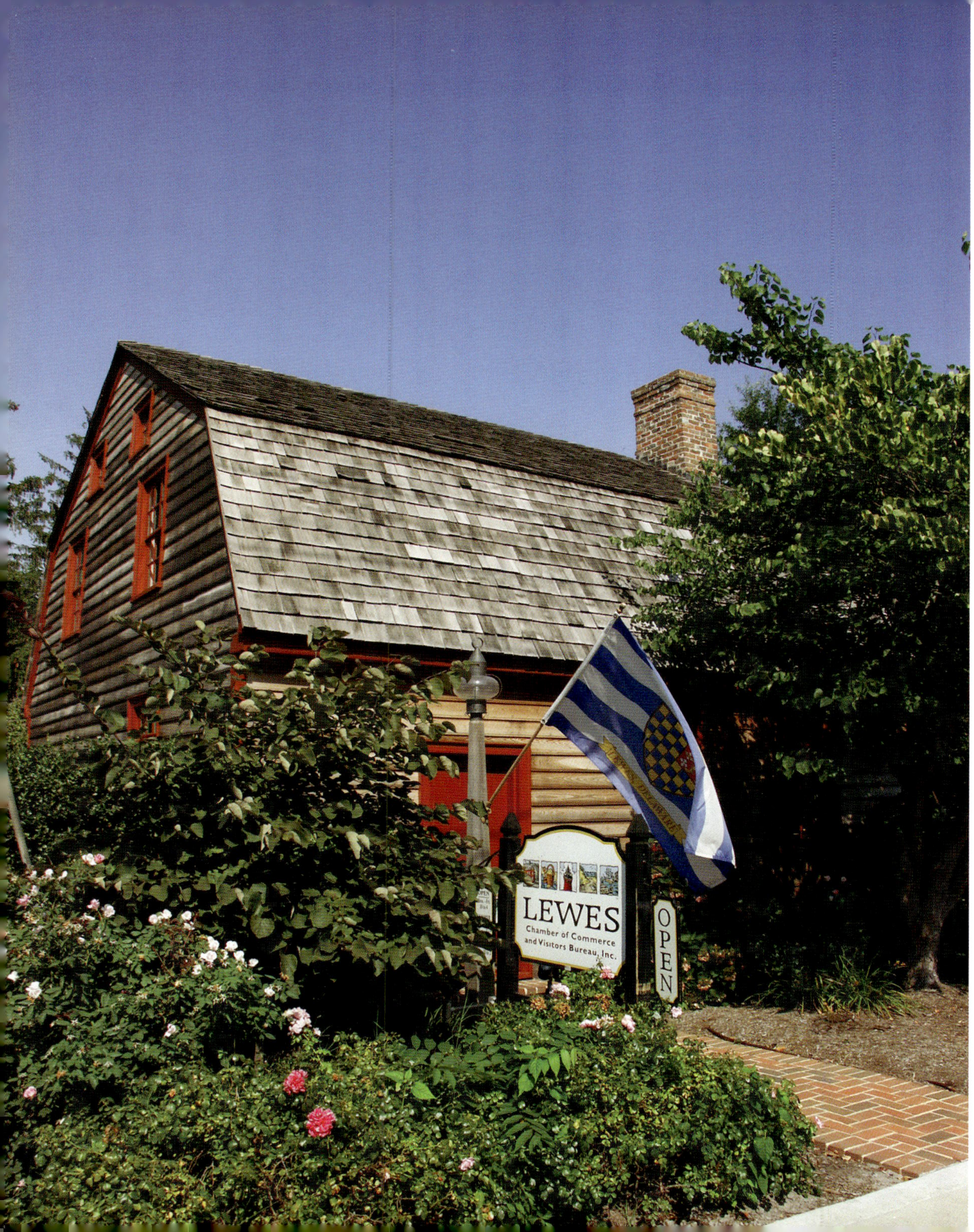

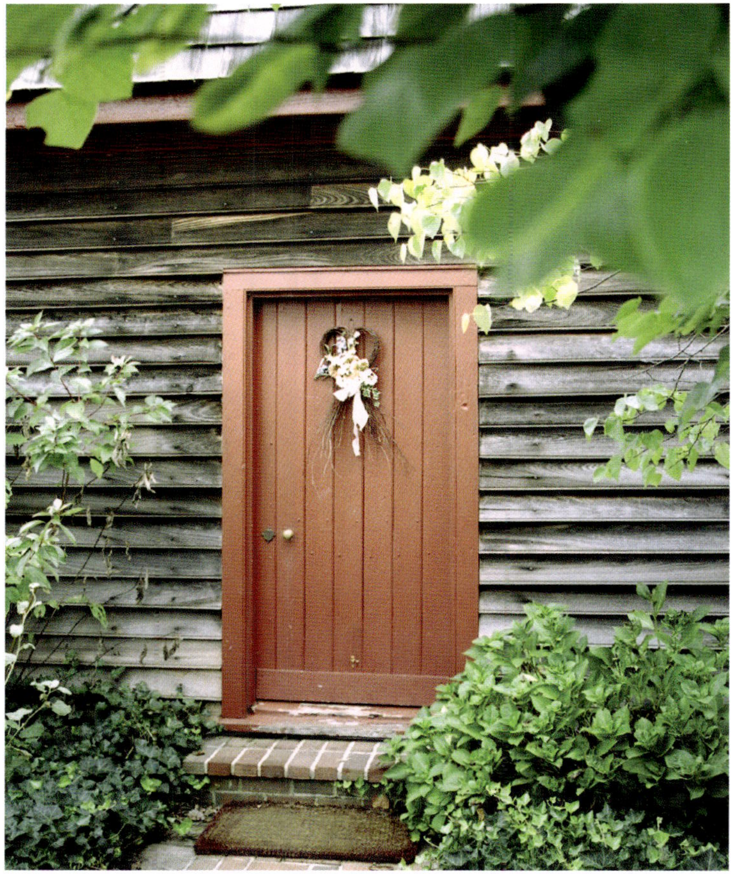

The Fisher-Martin House dates from around 1730 and was moved to its current location in 1980. It is named for Thomas and Joshua Fisher, who owned the land upon which the building once stood, and Rev. James Martin, a local minister who owned the house. It remained in his family for over 200 years. Today, the Fisher-Martin House hosts the Lewes Chamber of Commerce Information Center. Its gambrel roof is a defining feature of Dutch architecture.

Zwaanendael Museum is a unique example of Dutch architecture. Its design is based upon the old town hall in Hoorn, Holland. The building was constructed in 1931 in celebration of the 300th anniversary of the first European settlement in Delaware. Today, the museum is home to a collection of artifacts and exhibits interpreting the history of Lewes and Sussex County, from the original settlement to the War of 1812 to the Cape Henlopen Lighthouse.

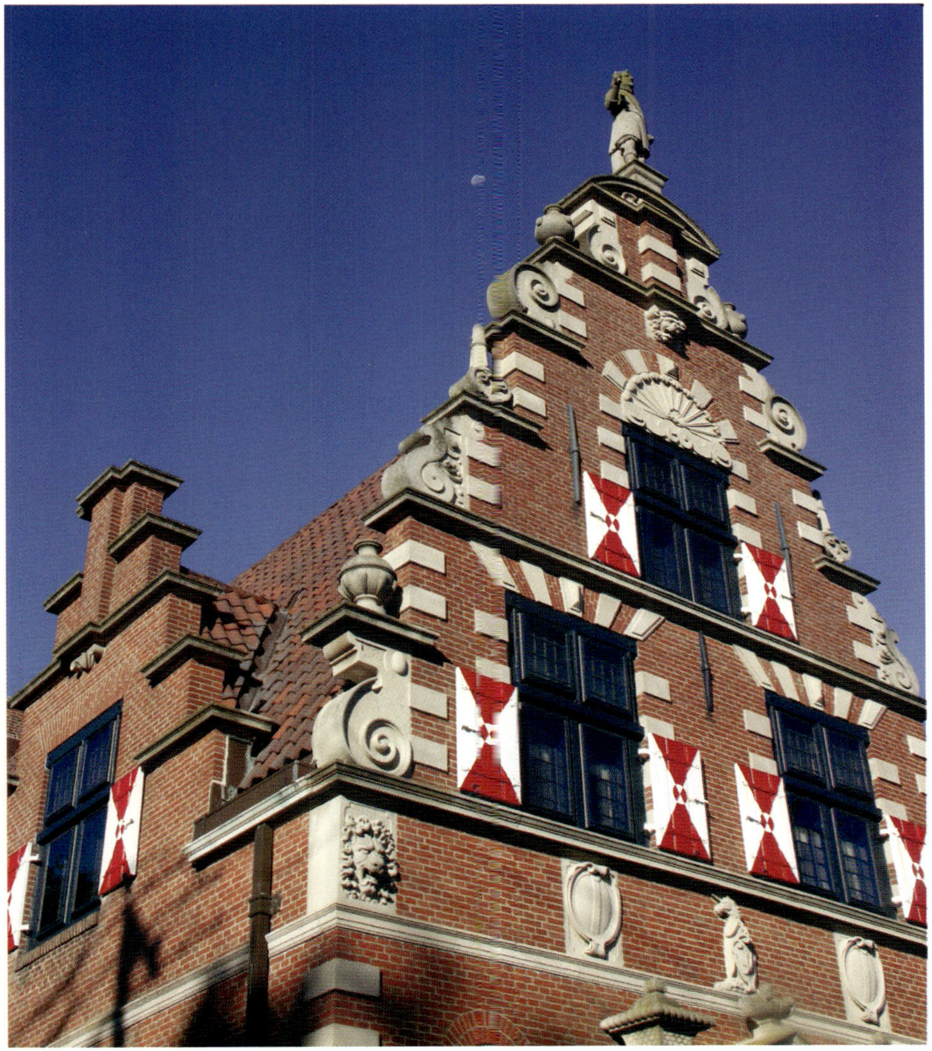

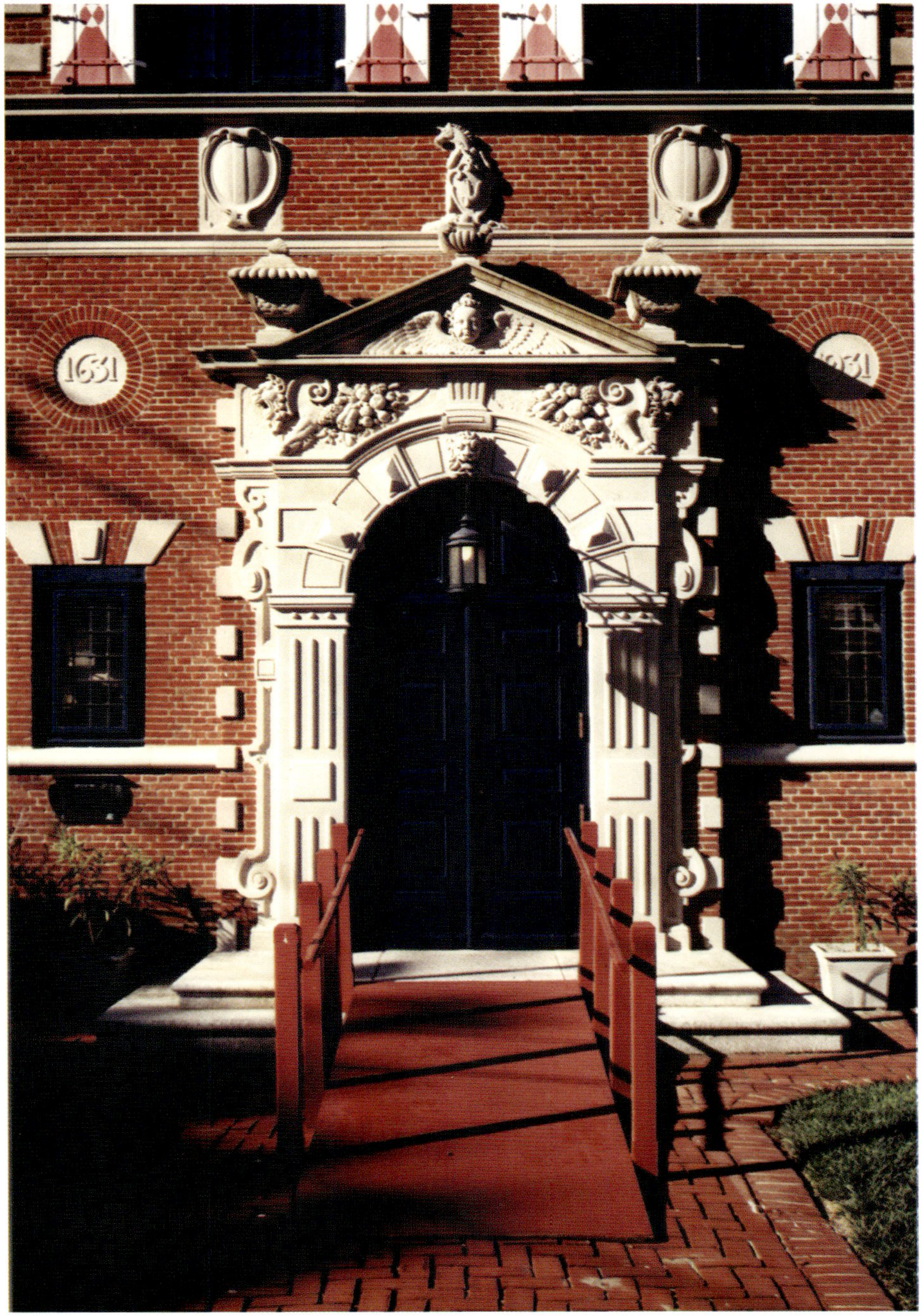

The Lewes Historical Society Complex can be found at the intersection of Shipcarpenter Square and Third Street. Most of the buildings located in the complex were relocated there in the 1960s. Buildings include an 1850 Greek Revival Doctor's Office, Swedish style Plank House, 1785 Federal Burton-Ingram House, and 1800 Thompson Country Store. The Rabbits Ferry House, a farmhouse dating from the 18th century, serves as the visitors center. The oldest portion of the Hiram Burton House dates from around 1720 and is constructed of hand-hewn timbers and cypress shingles. Dr. Hiram Burton was a Lewes physician and director of the Queen Anne's Railroad.

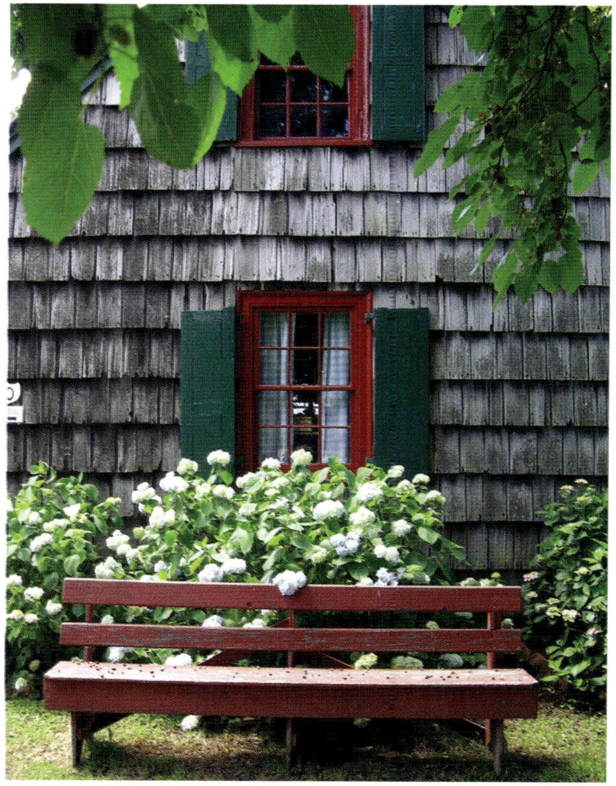

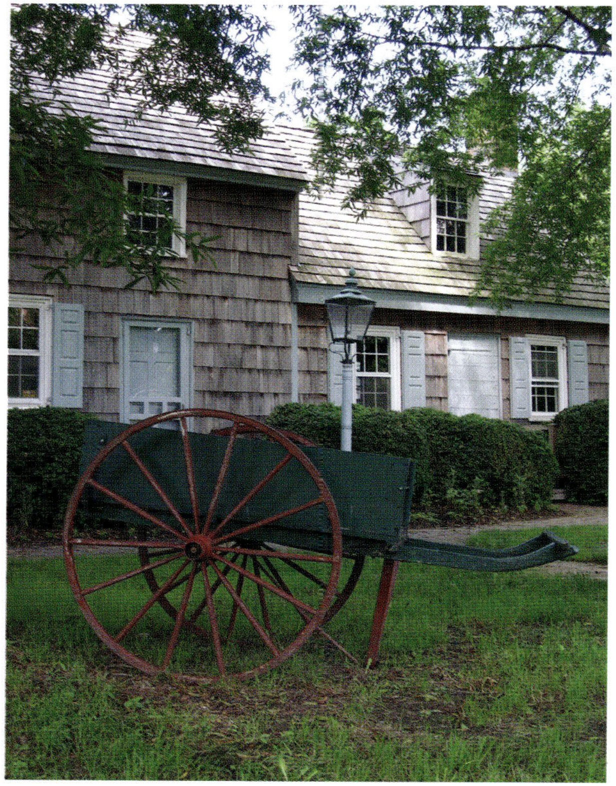

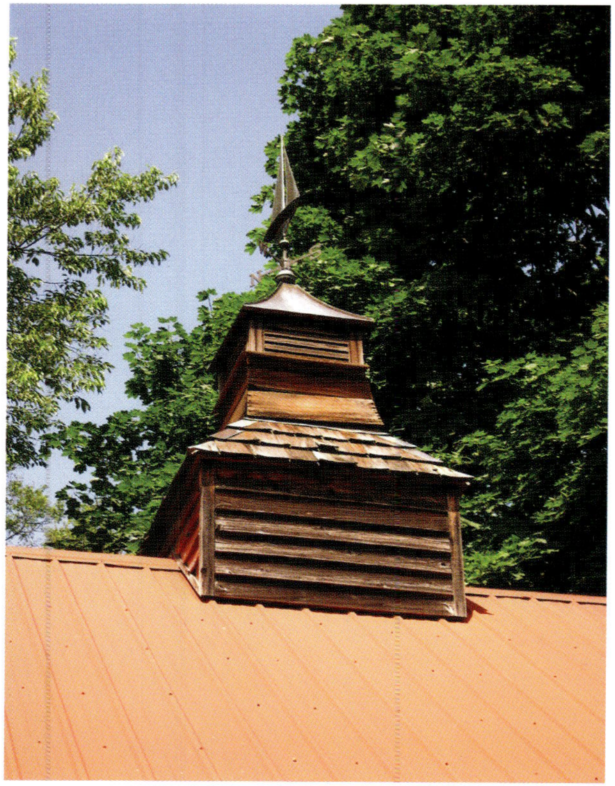

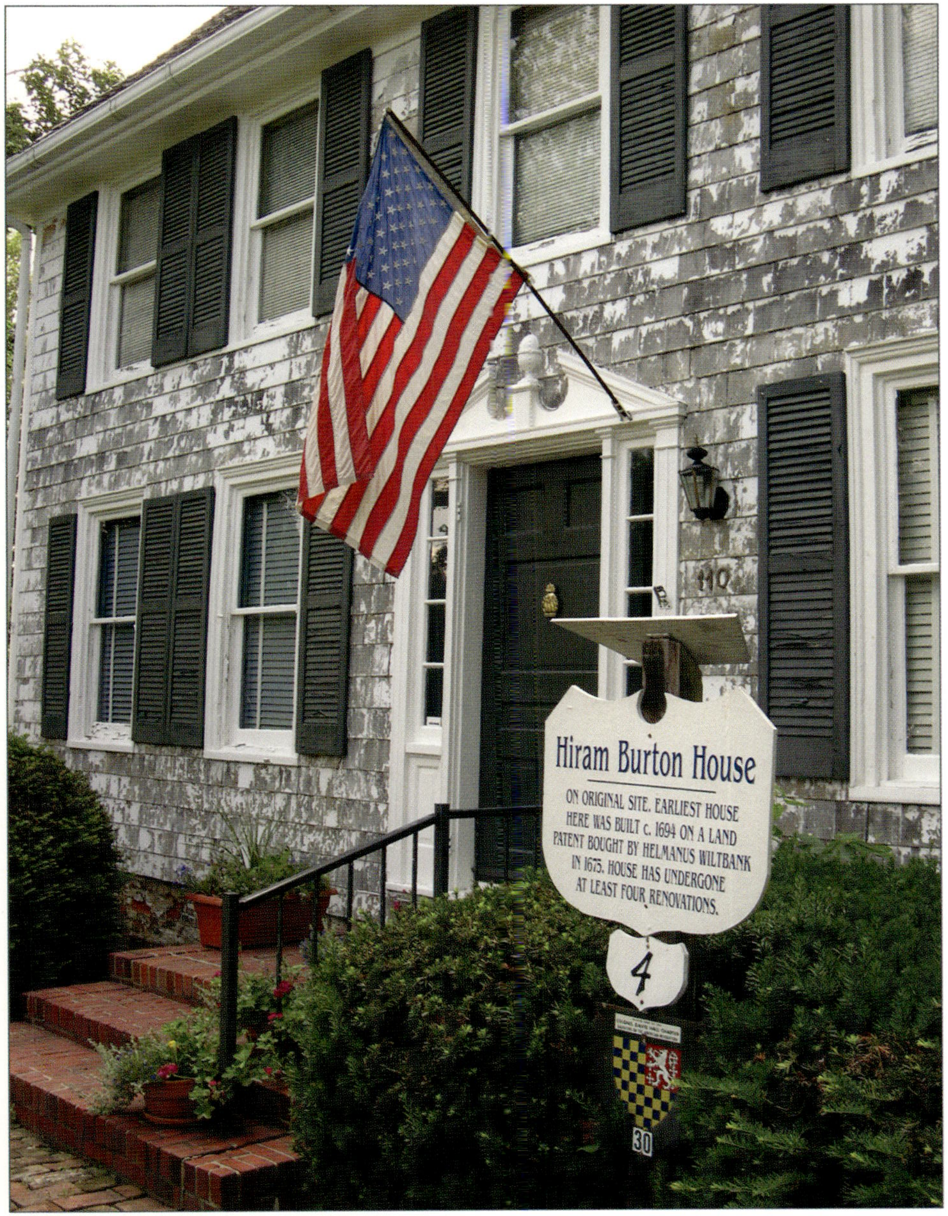
Hiram Burton House
ON ORIGINAL SITE. EARLIEST HOUSE HERE WAS BUILT c. 1694 ON A LAND PATENT BOUGHT BY HELMANUS WILTBANK IN 1675. HOUSE HAS UNDERGONE AT LEAST FOUR RENOVATIONS.
4
110
30

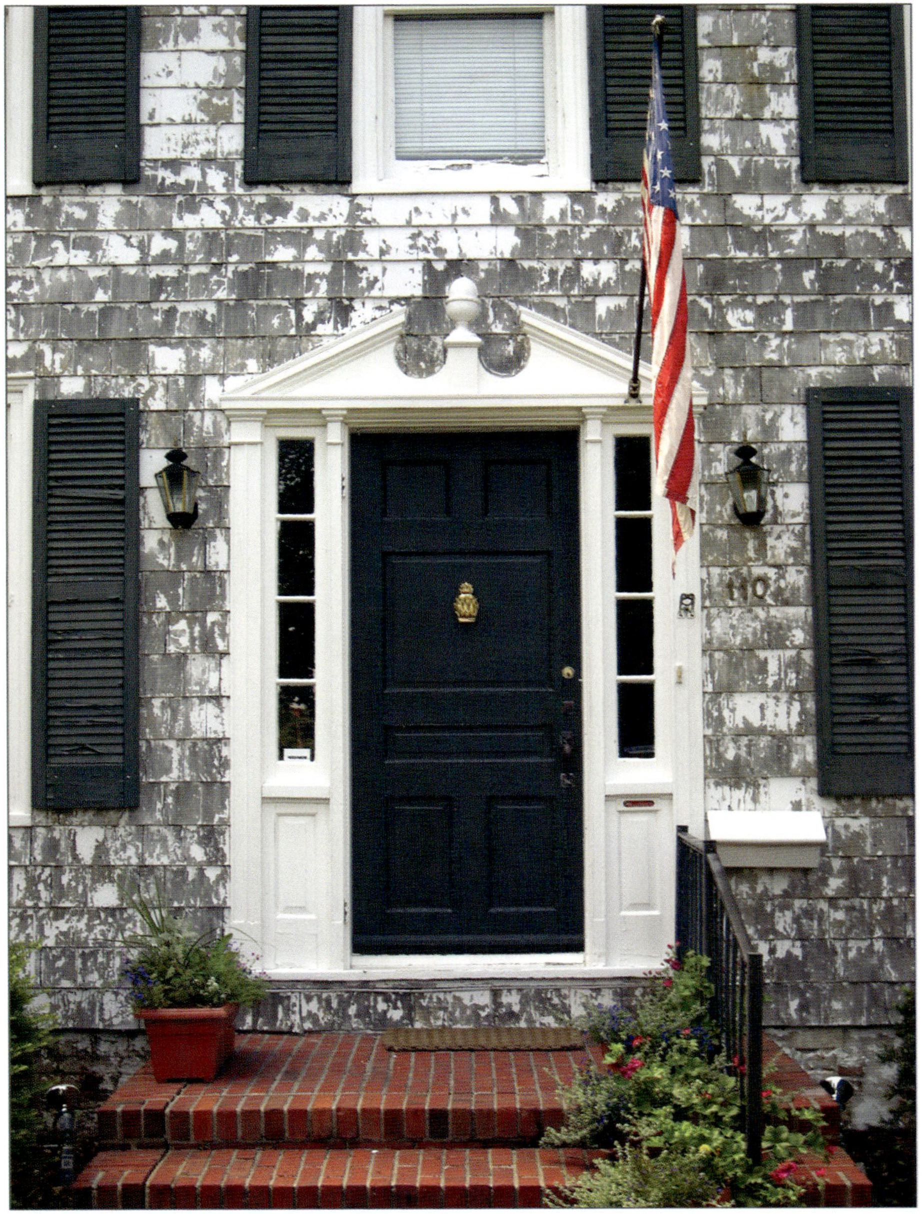
110

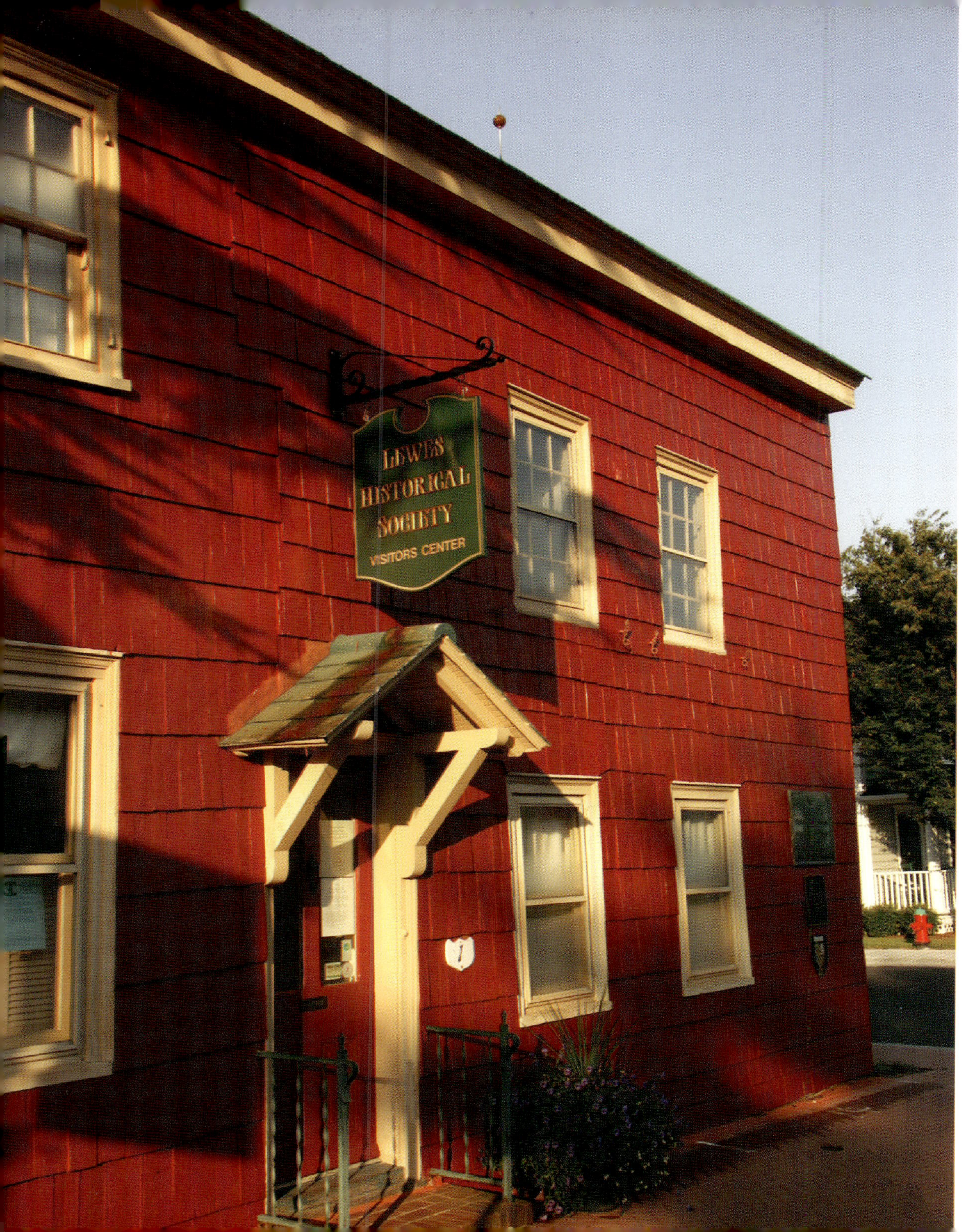

The Ryves Holt House is believed to be the oldest house in Delaware. It is constructed of shingles and has been dated to 1665. Ryves Holt served as Naval Officer of Port Lewes and High Sheriff of Sussex County. He later served as Chief Justice of the Supreme Court in the "Three Lower Counties on the Delaware River and Bay" – part of William Penn's province known today as the State of Delaware.

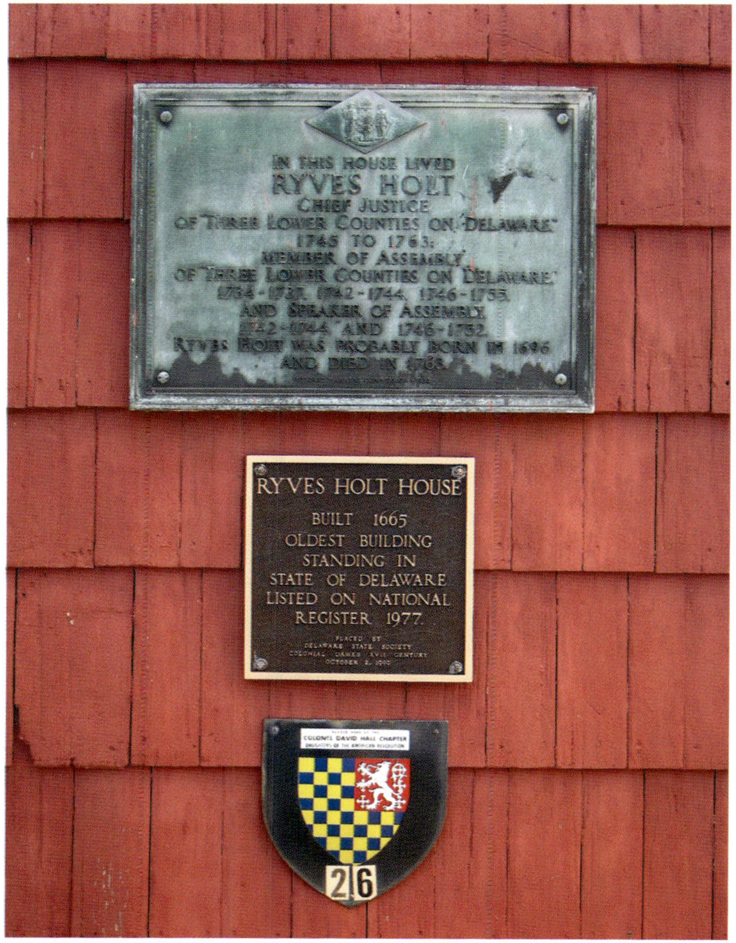

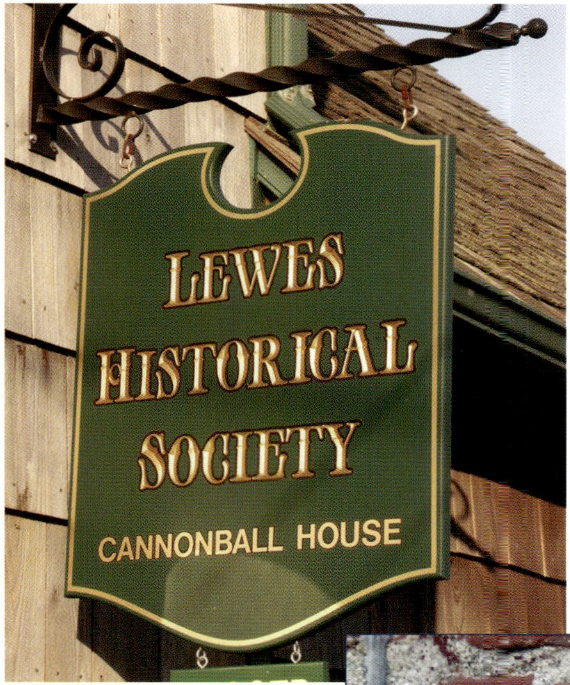

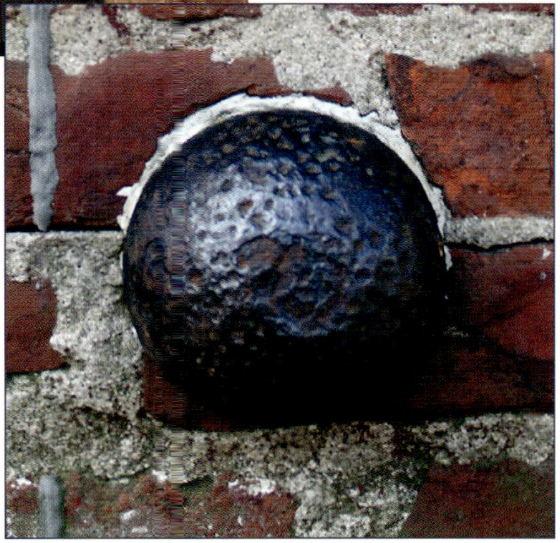

The cedar-shingled Cannonball House Marine Museum is located in a house that was constructed in the late 18th century. During the War of 1812, the building was struck by a cannonball during a two-day British bombardment that occurred in April 1813. Nautical themed exhibits are housed in the museum, which is part of the Lewes Historical Society.

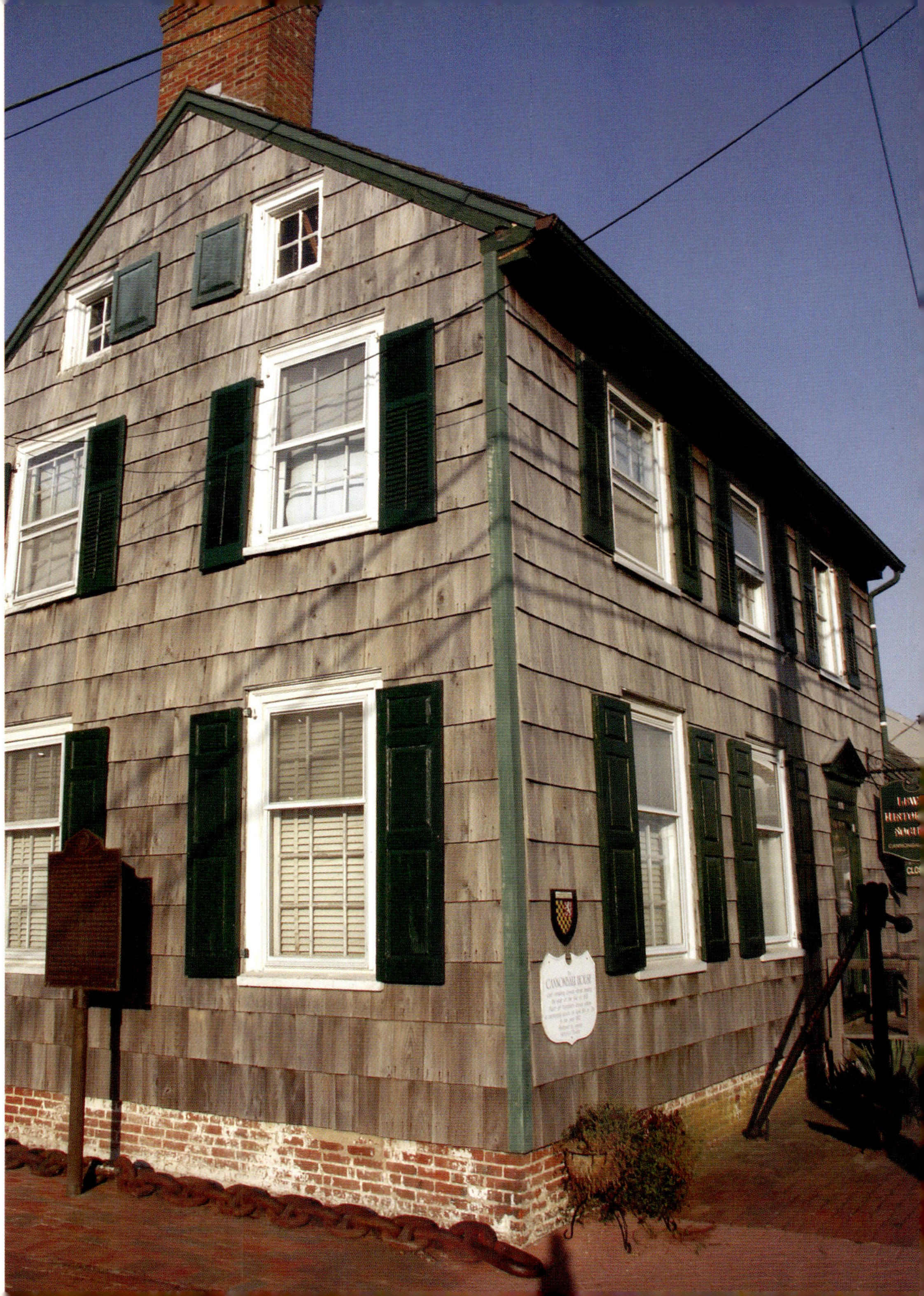

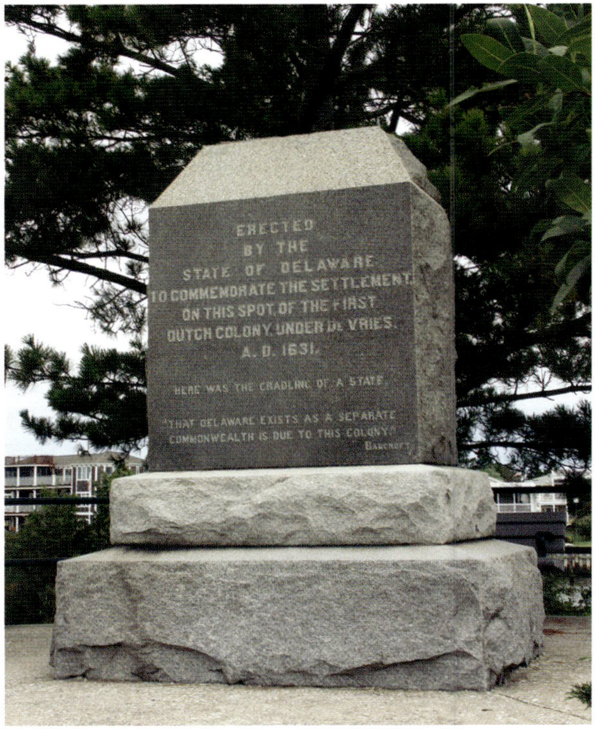

The DeVries Monument marks the spot where Dutch settlers established a whaling colony in 1631, naming is Swanendael. A small fort was erected here. Tragedy occurred soon thereafter, however, when the Siconese Indians annihilated the settlement. Captain David Pieterson DeVries arrived here in December 1632 and found everything destroyed. The monument was dedicated in 1909.

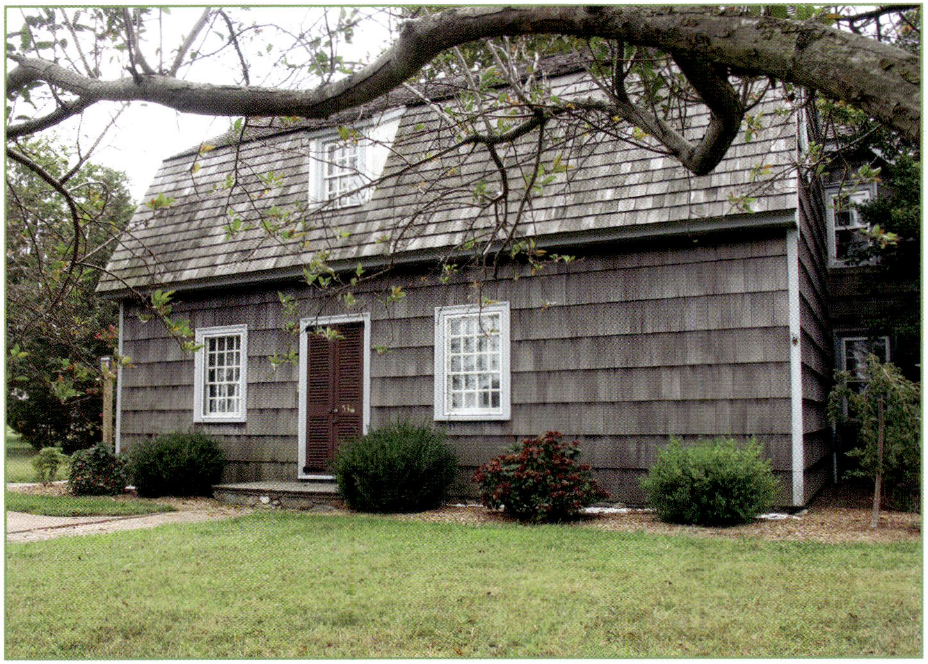

The Maull House on Pilottown Road was constructed around 1739 in the Dutch Colonial style of architecture. It is named for the Maull family, who owned the home for over 120 years. Local legend tells of a visit to the house by Jerome Bonaparte, Napoleon's brother, who found refuge here with his wife on a stormy night in 1803. The house is today owned by the Colonel David Hall Chapter, National Society Daughters of the American Revolution.

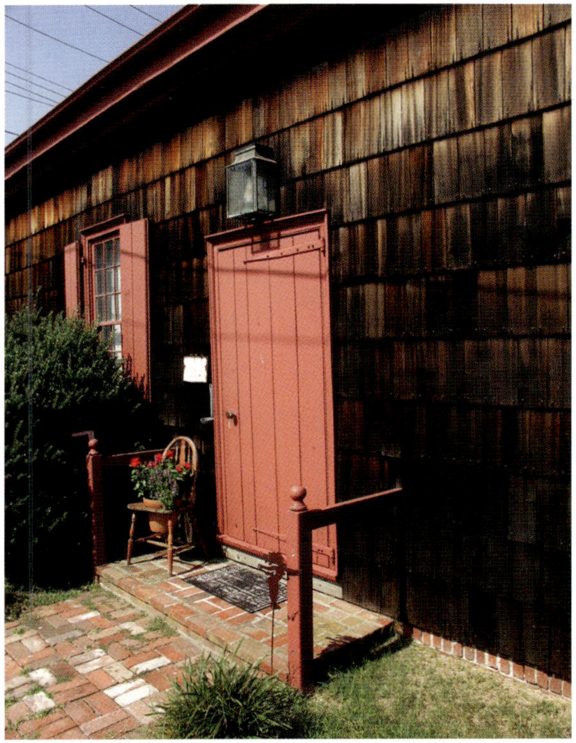

Old Bethel Church, a Methodist meeting house, dates from 1790. It was relocated several times, earning the nickname "The Traveling Meeting House."

The War of 1812 came to Lewes on April 6-7, 1813, when the British fleet arrived and demanded fresh provisions. Col. Samuel Boyer Davis, who commanded the American troops in Lewes, refused, and a bombardment ensued, led by the Poictiers, a 74-gun frigate. Fortunately for Lewes, trees blocked the view from the British ships, and there was minimal damage, with no loss of human life. The 1812 Memorial Park commemorates the bombardment and defense of Lewes.

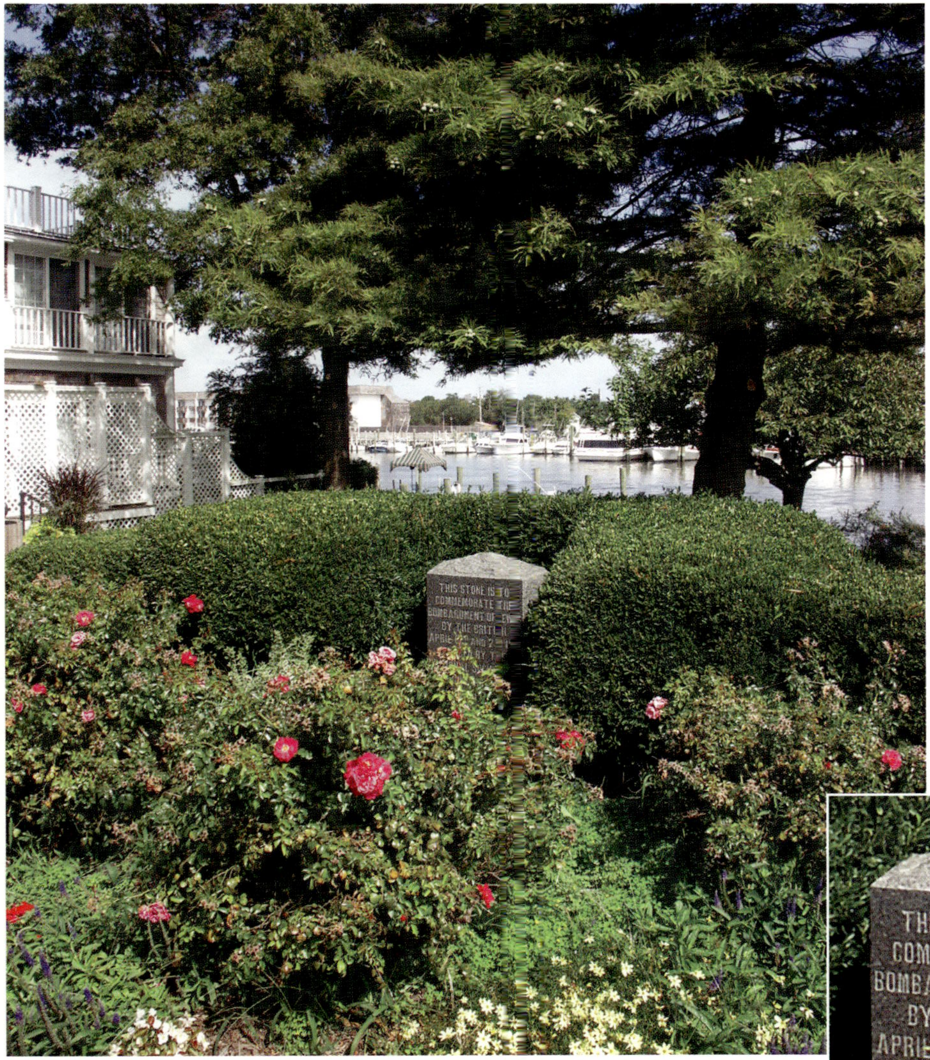

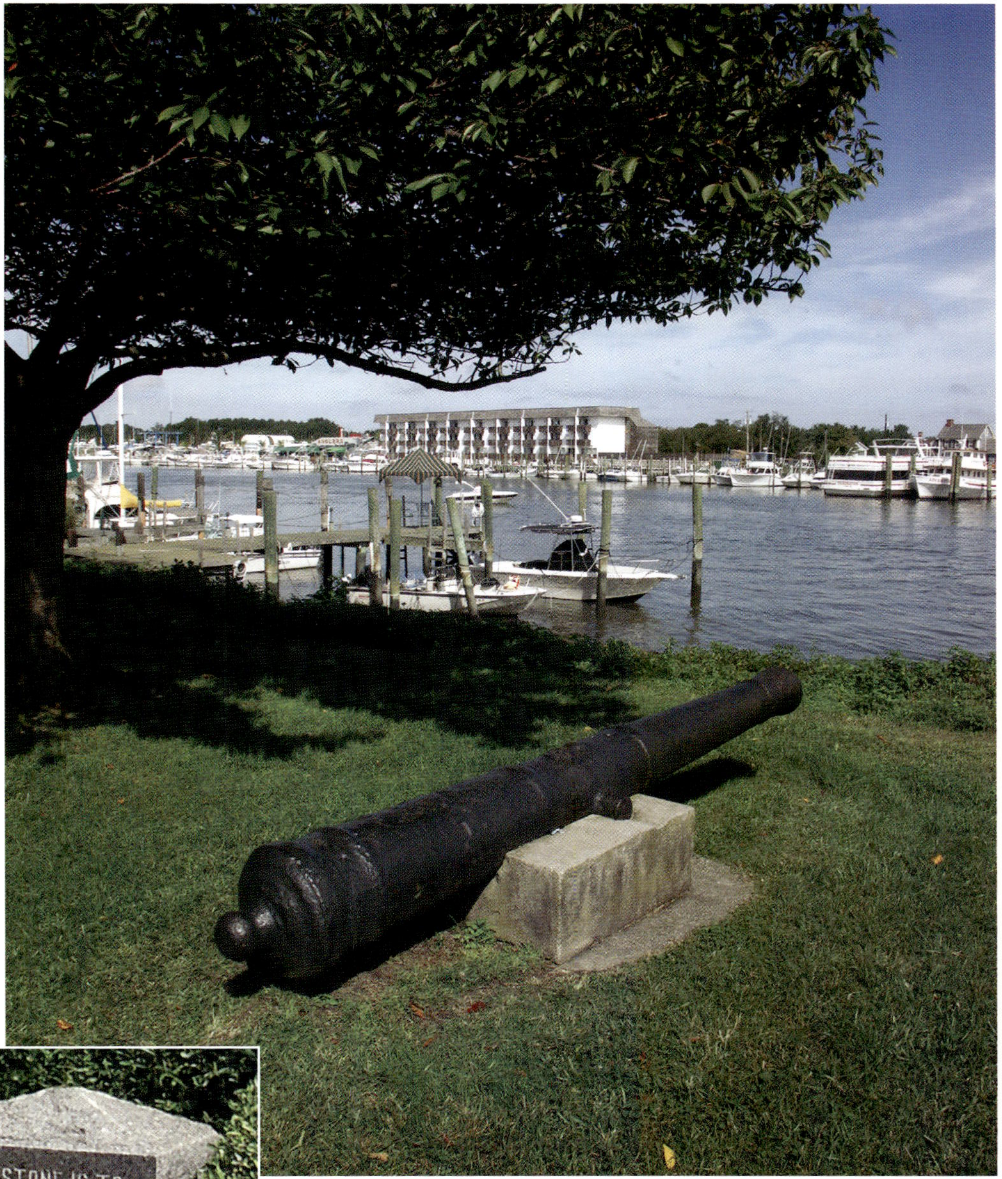

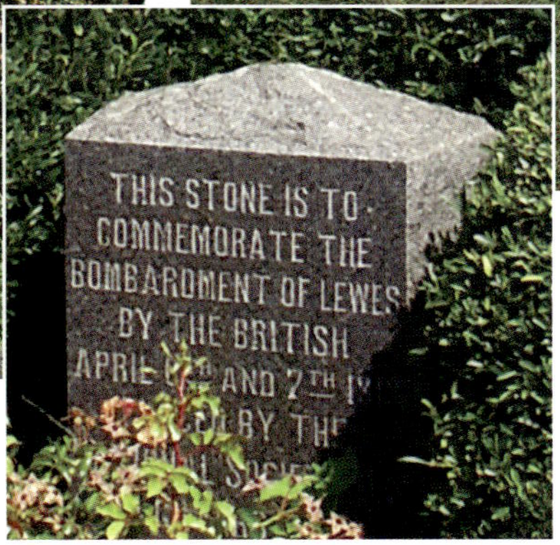

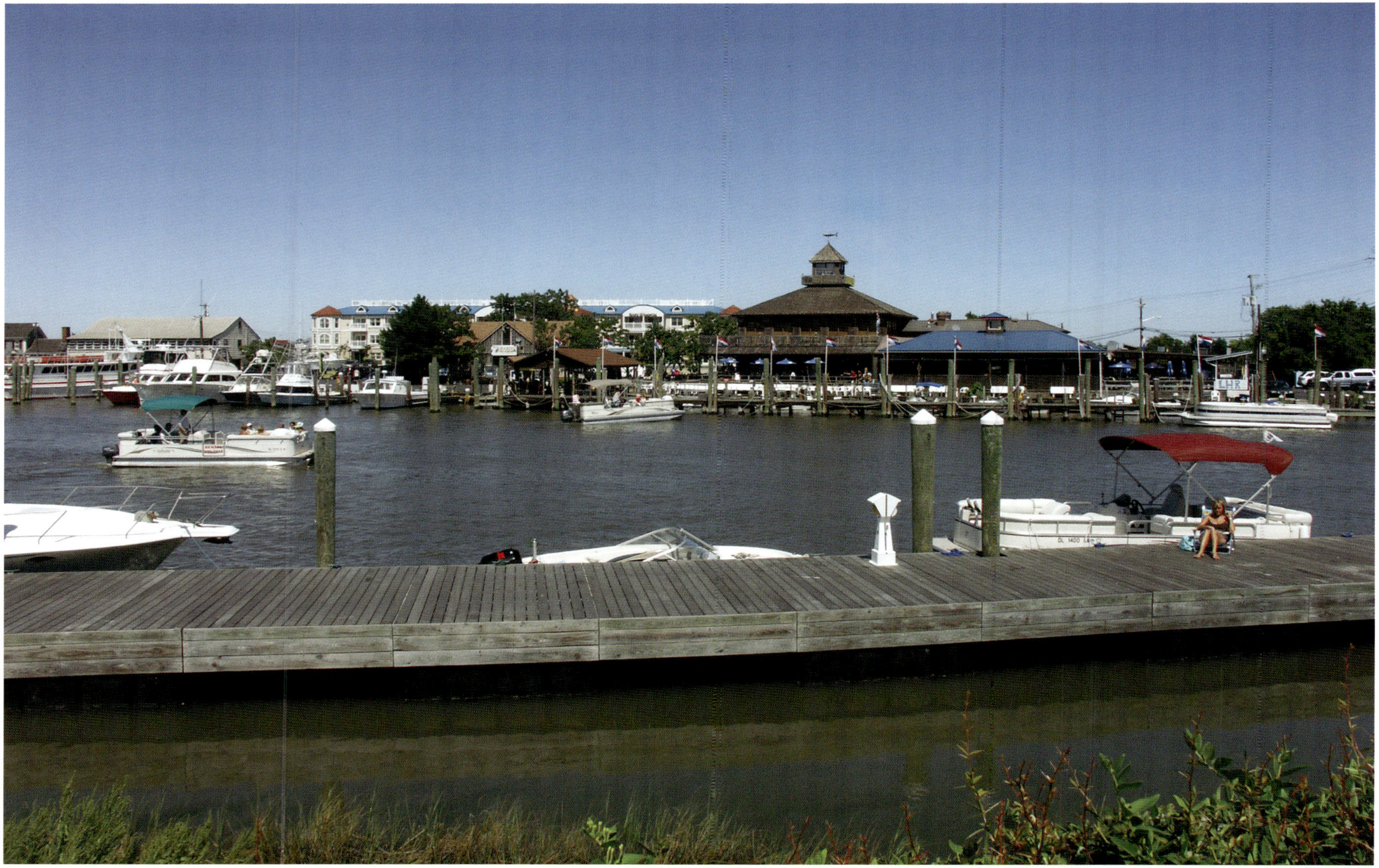

Fisherman's Wharf is located along the Lewes & Rehoboth Canal, next to the drawbridge. Here head boats, deep sea charter boats, and sightseeing vessels head out to sea daily, while the Lighthouse Restaurant provides local cuisine and a unique setting to watch the boats coming and going.

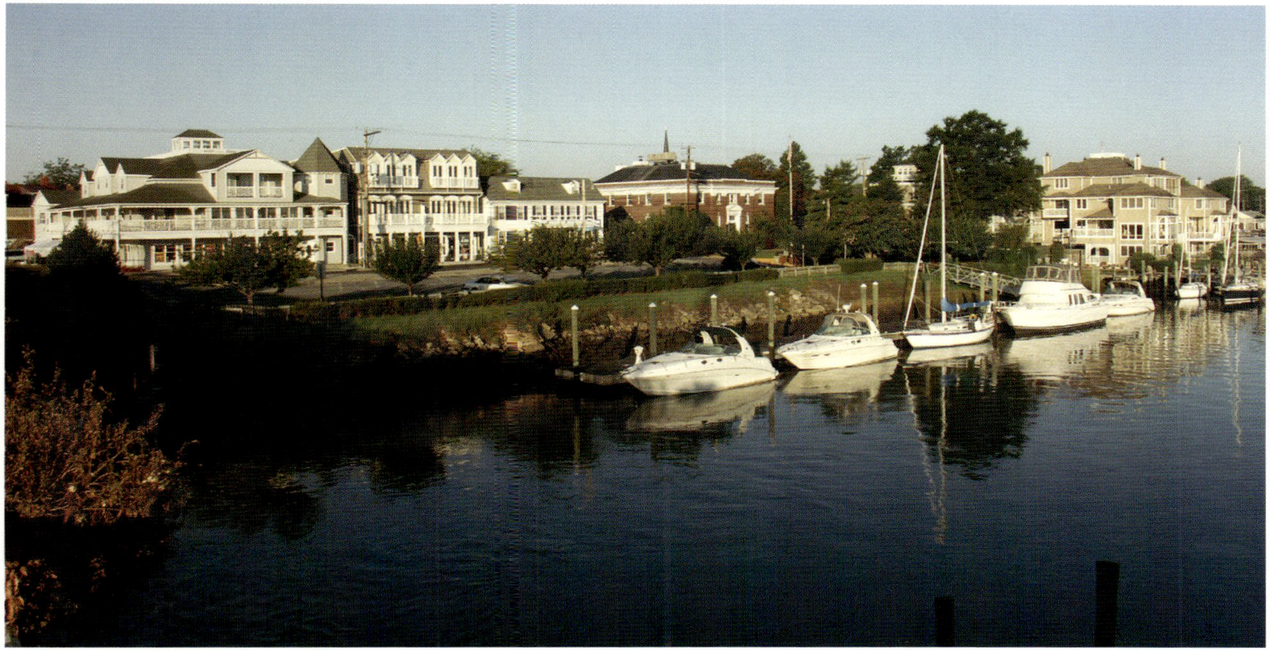

The Lewes & Rehoboth Canal was authorized by the U.S. River and Harbor Act of 1912, with digging beginning one year later. The first boat passed through the canal in 1916.

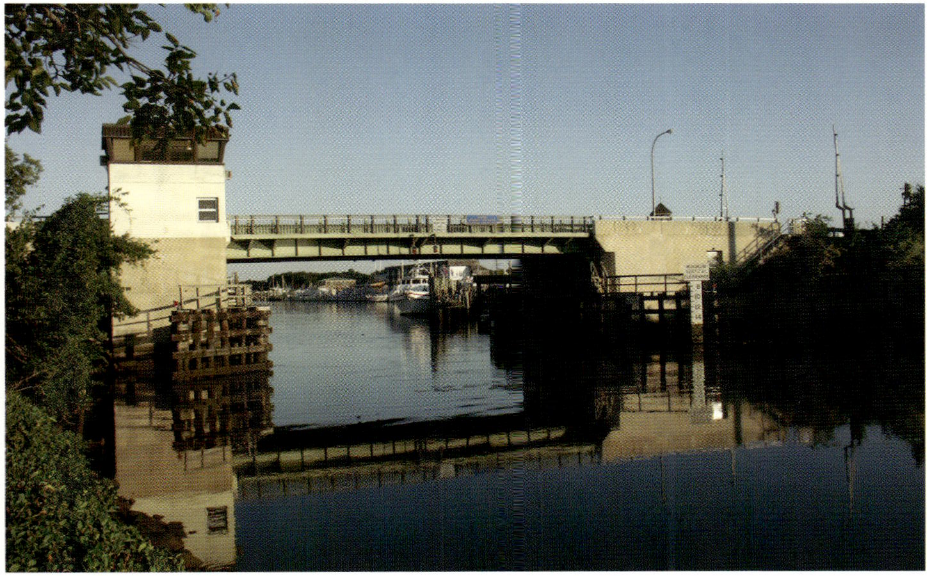

The drawbridge over the Lewes & Rehoboth Canal connects the business district with the beaches.

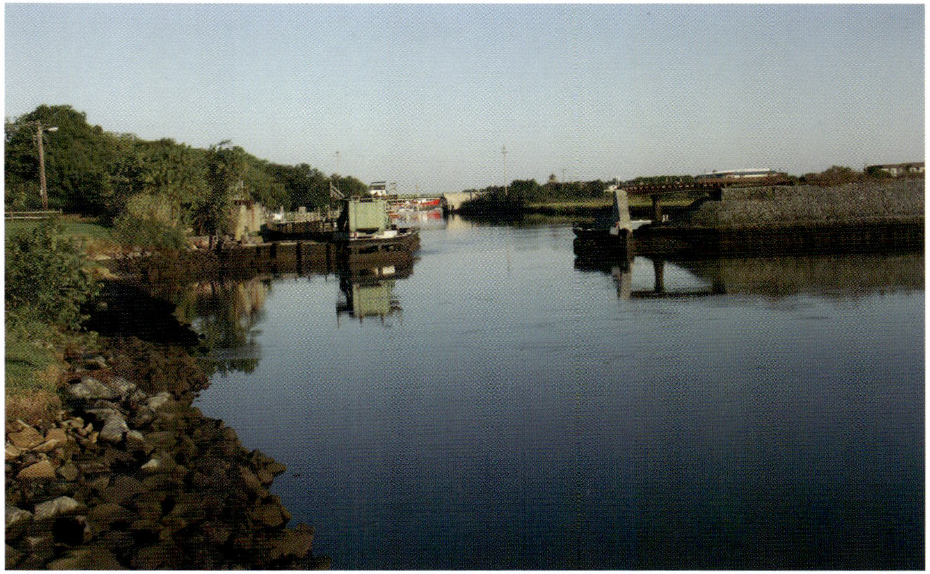

The moveable swing-bridge along the Lewes & Rehoboth Canal was used by the railroad. Today, few of this type of bridge still exist.

Second Street – Views of the main commercial area in Lewes, Second Street. A fire erupted on December 6, 1920, destroying many of the businesses located on the west side of the street. Today, Second Street is home to galleries, charming antique stores and boutiques, and eateries.

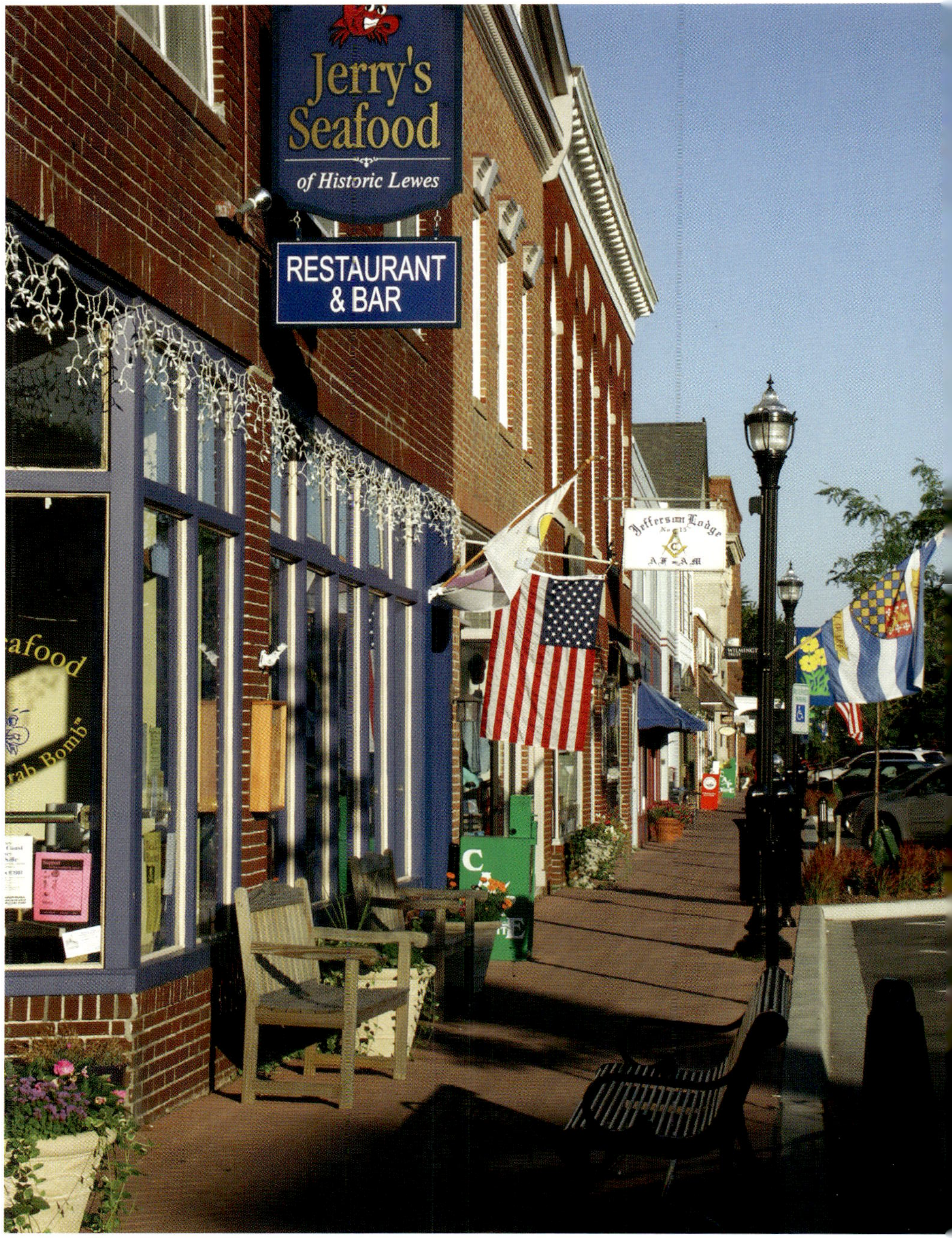

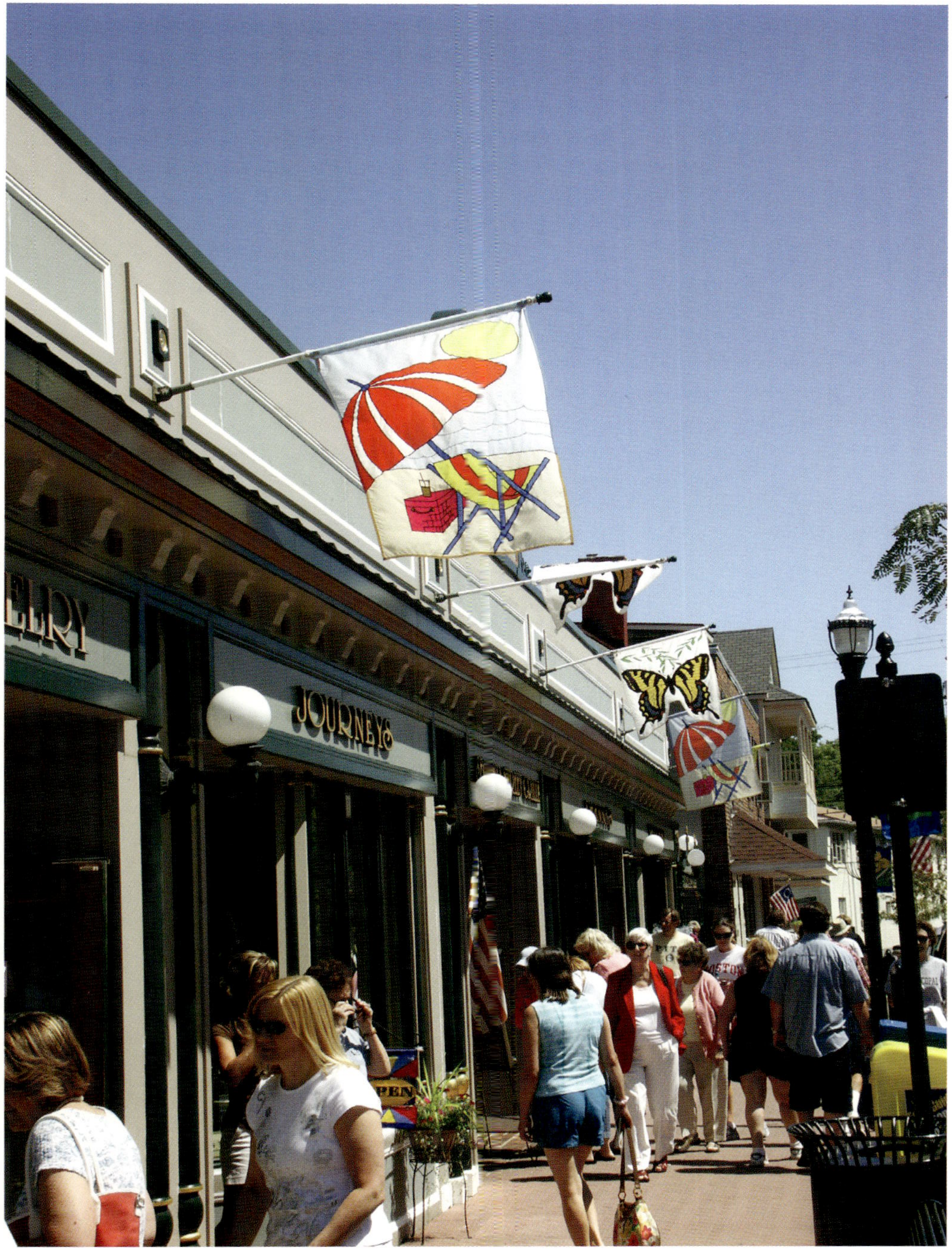
JOURNEYS

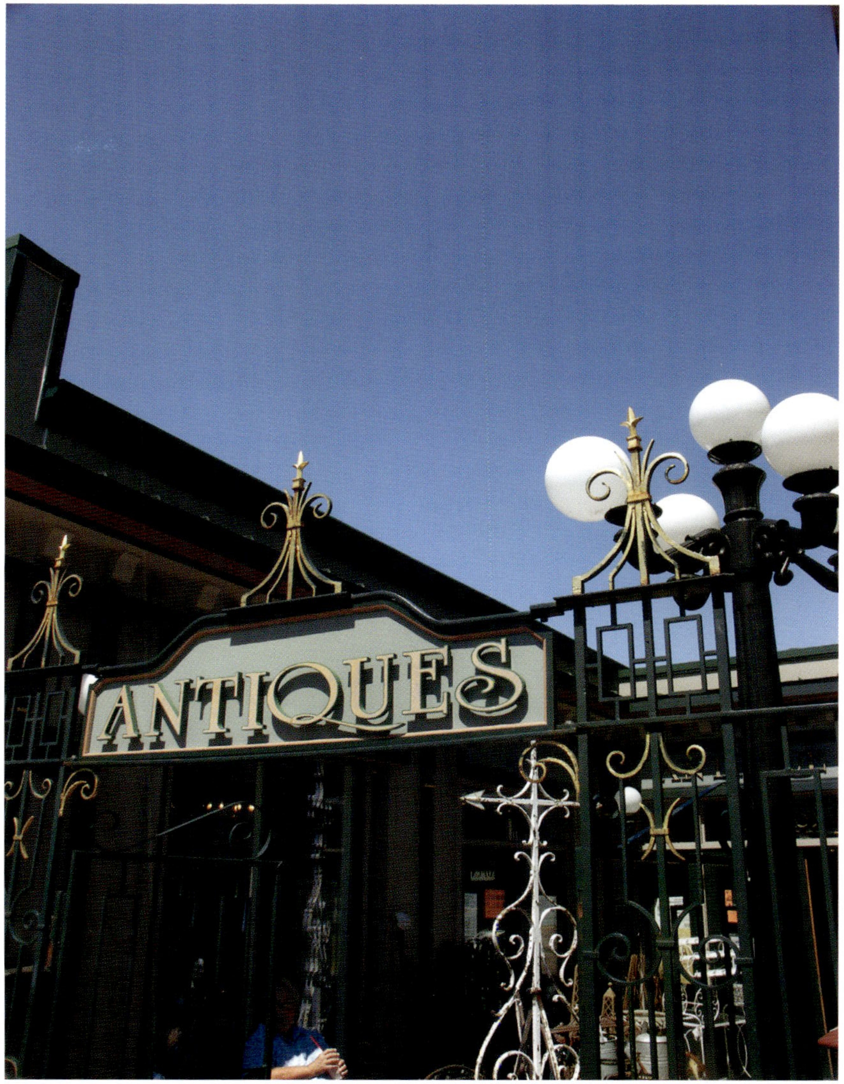
ANTIQUES

The original Maritime Exchange was used from 1884 to 1928. Look-out towers atop the building had a purpose: employees stationed there would use telescopes to identify ships, then contact the ships via telegraph.

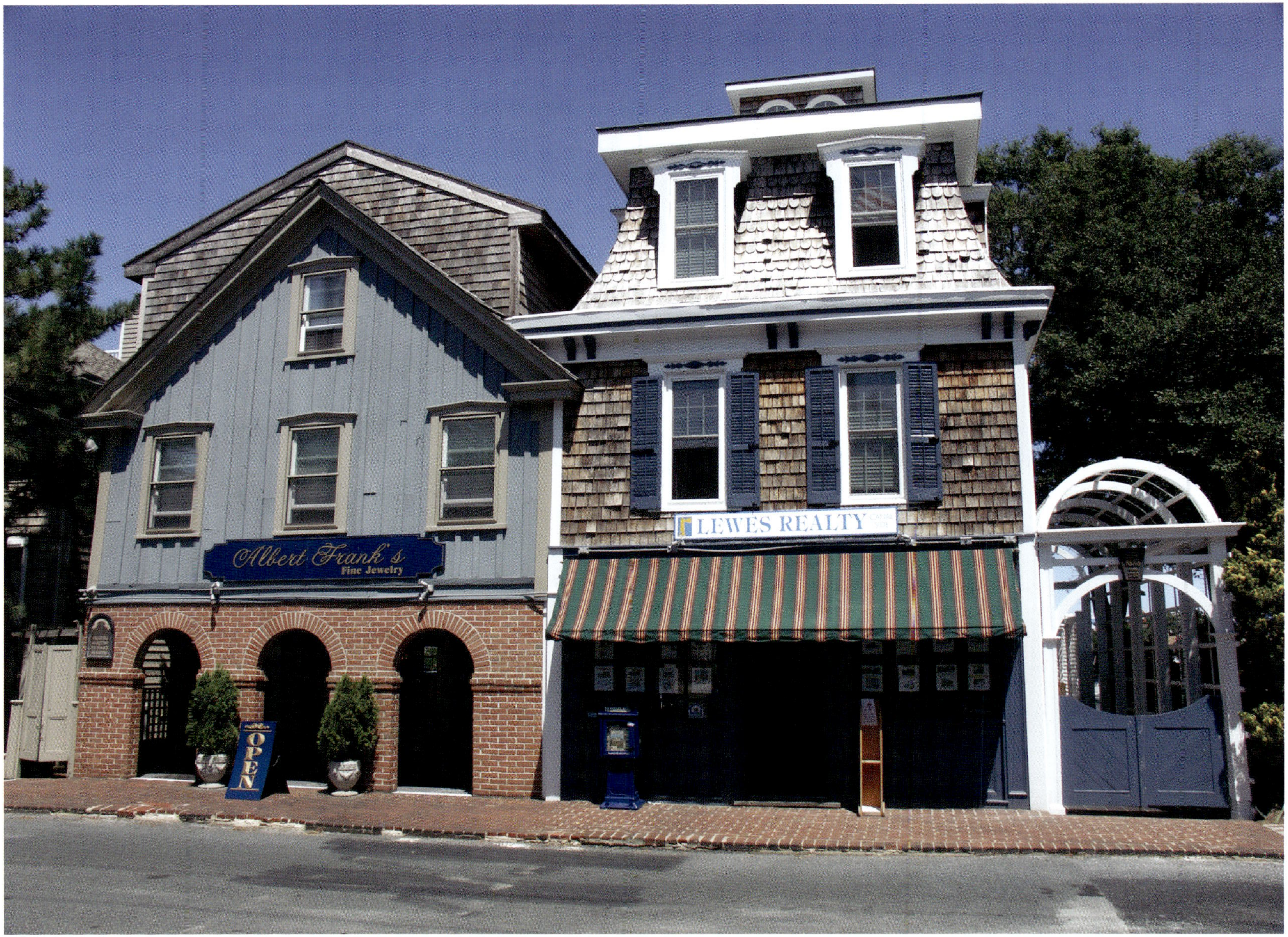

Second Street provides treats for the eyes – eclectic architecture, and treats for the stomach – an ice cream cone from King's Homemade Ice Cream Shop.

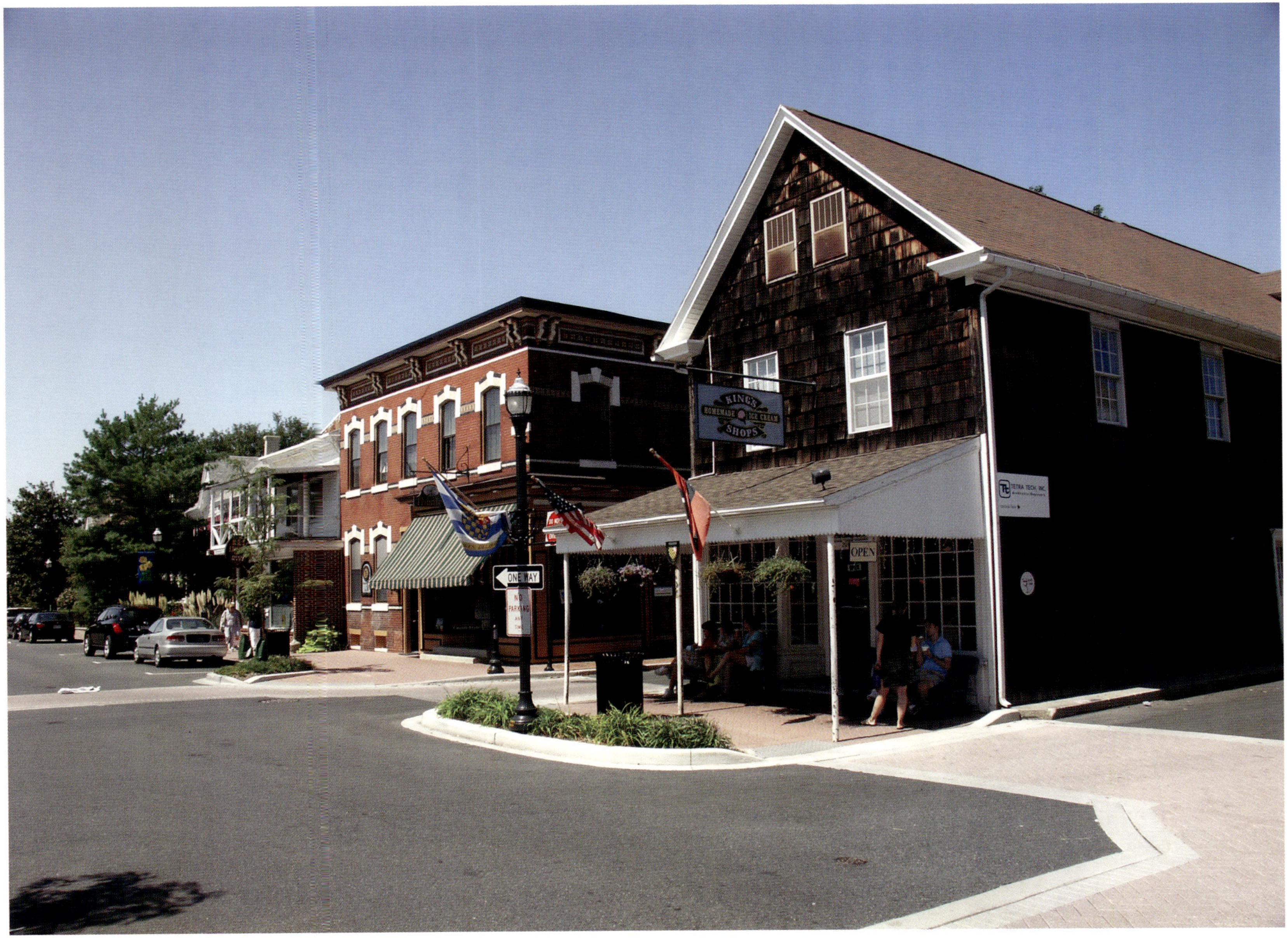

The Cape Artists Gallery is located on 3rd Street and provides a one-stop shop for high-quality art.

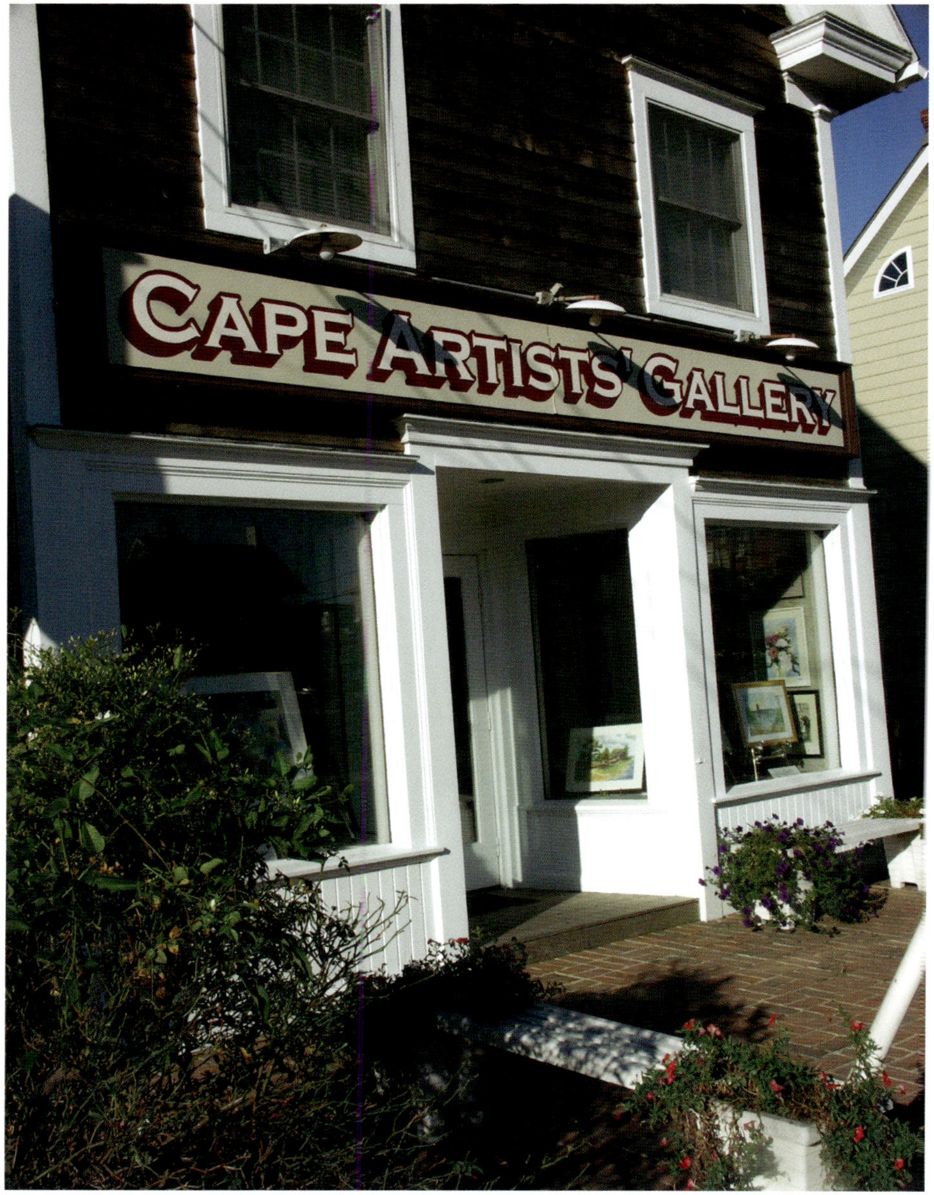

Preservation Forge is a working blacksmith forge and museum, with handcrafted ironwork available for purchase.

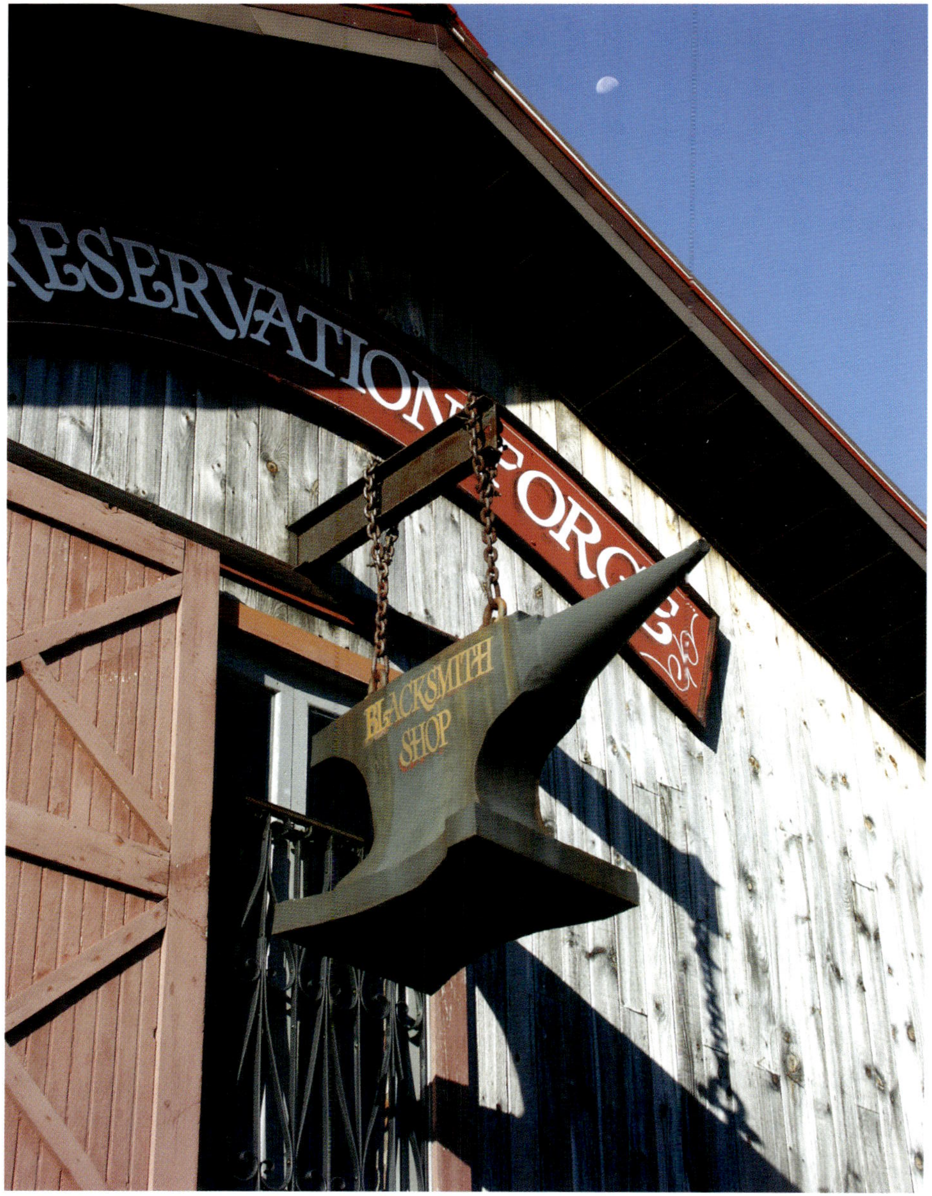

The Inn at Canal Square provides a Nantucket-like feel and views of Lewes Harbor from 22 lavish rooms and two VIP suites.

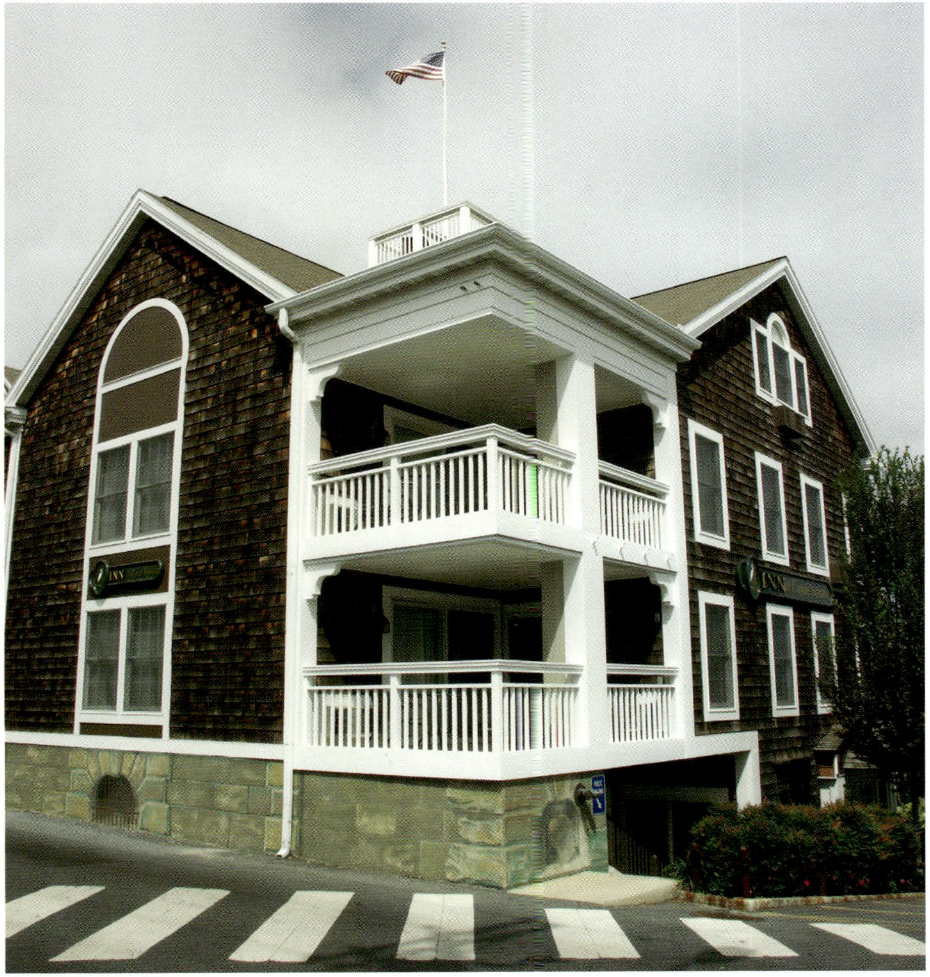

The eclectic Auntie M's Emporium is located at the site of the old Lewes Fire House, which was built in 1897.

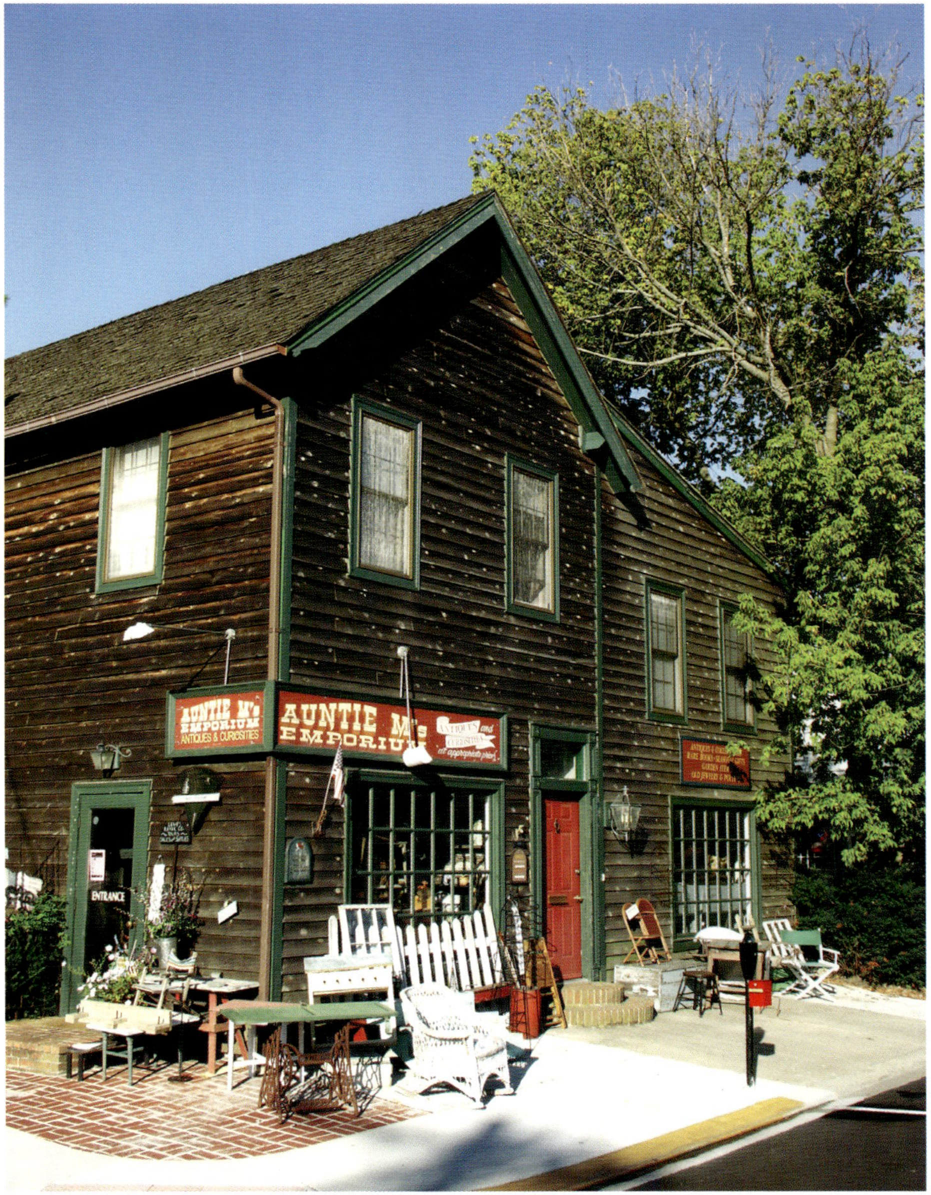

The Junction & Breakwater Railroad was extended to Lewes in 1869, and Queen Anne's Railroad arrived 29 years later. This building was the train station for Queen Anne's Railroad.

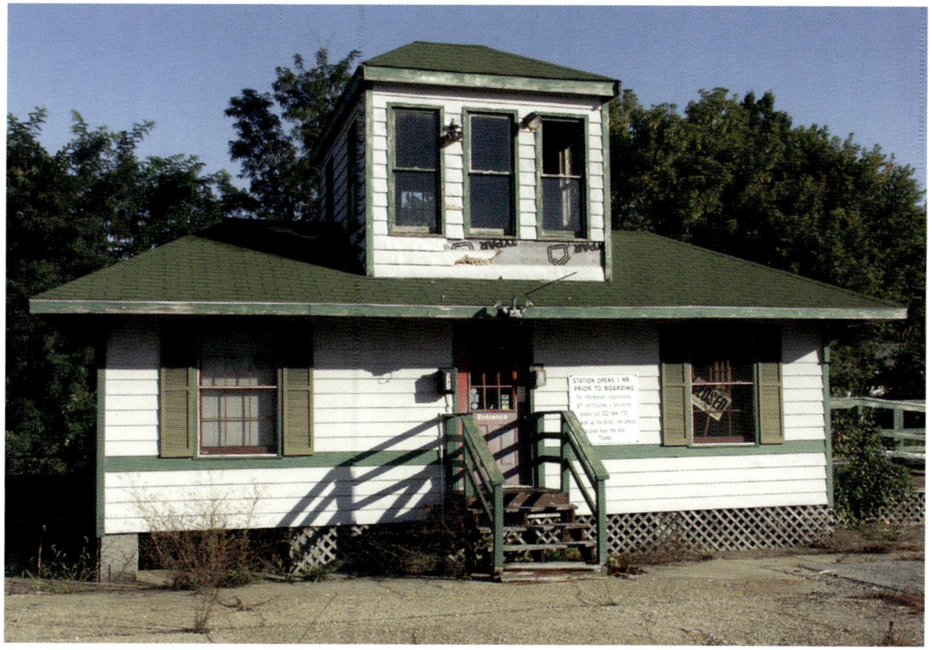

The Zwaanendael Women's Club was organized in 1905 by a group of women seeking to promote volunteer service to create a better community. This building was donated to the club in 1929; it had been originally constructed in 1898 by the Sussex Trust Title and Safe Deposit Company. When the Zwaanendael Club first occupied the building, they set up a lending library and opened the building to community groups.

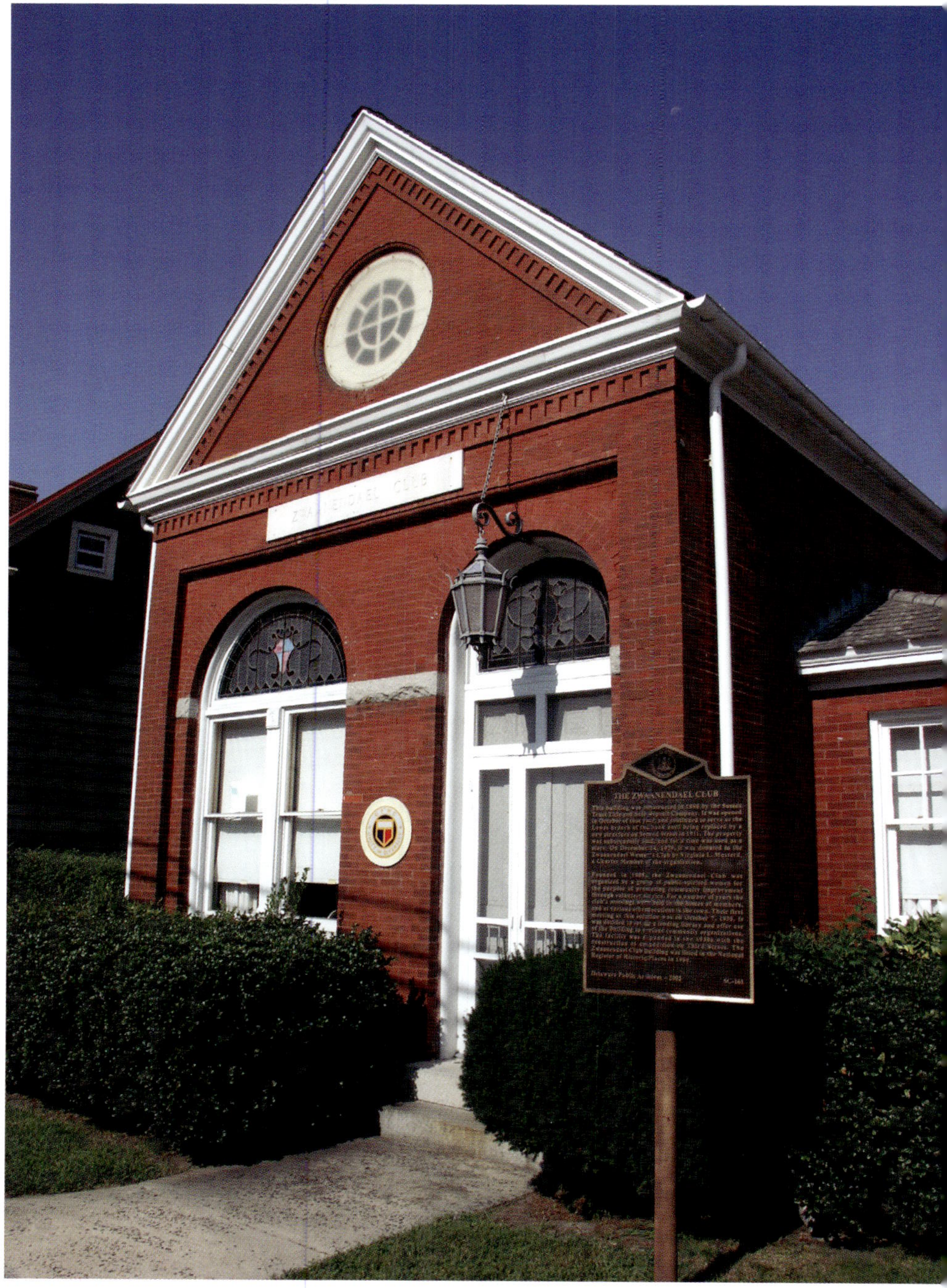

The congregation of Lewes Presbyterian Church dates from 1692 and was established by Scots and Scots-Irish settlers. They constructed a wooden building in 1707 and a brick church in 1727. This building was constructed in 1832 and has been enlarged several times.

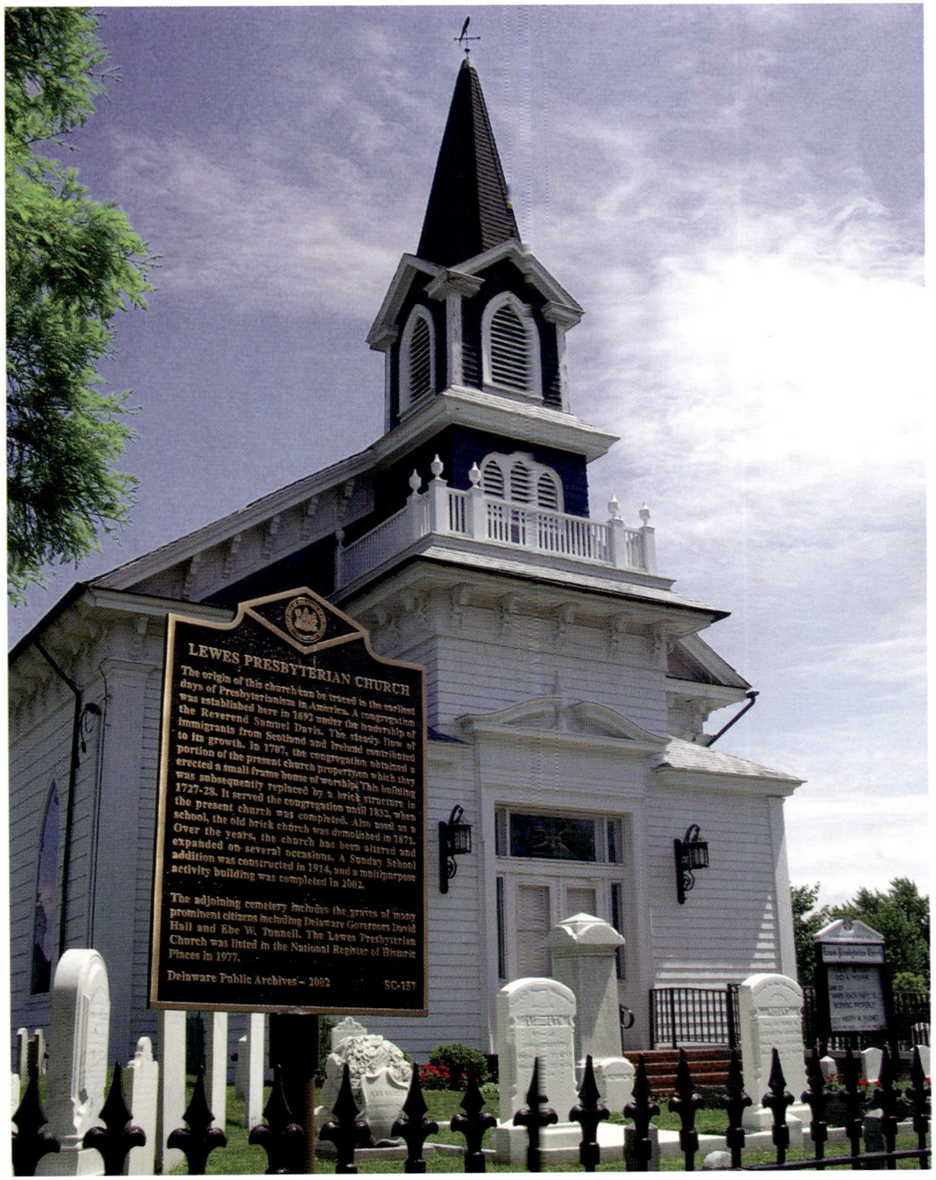

St. Peters Episcopal Church was constructed in the 1850s, replacing structures built in the early 1700s and 1808. The 1808 church was relocated to make room for the new brick church, which was consecrated in 1858. The steeple was added in 1870. Many early settlers of Lewes were members of the Church of England, and the congregation of this church traces its beginnings to 1680.

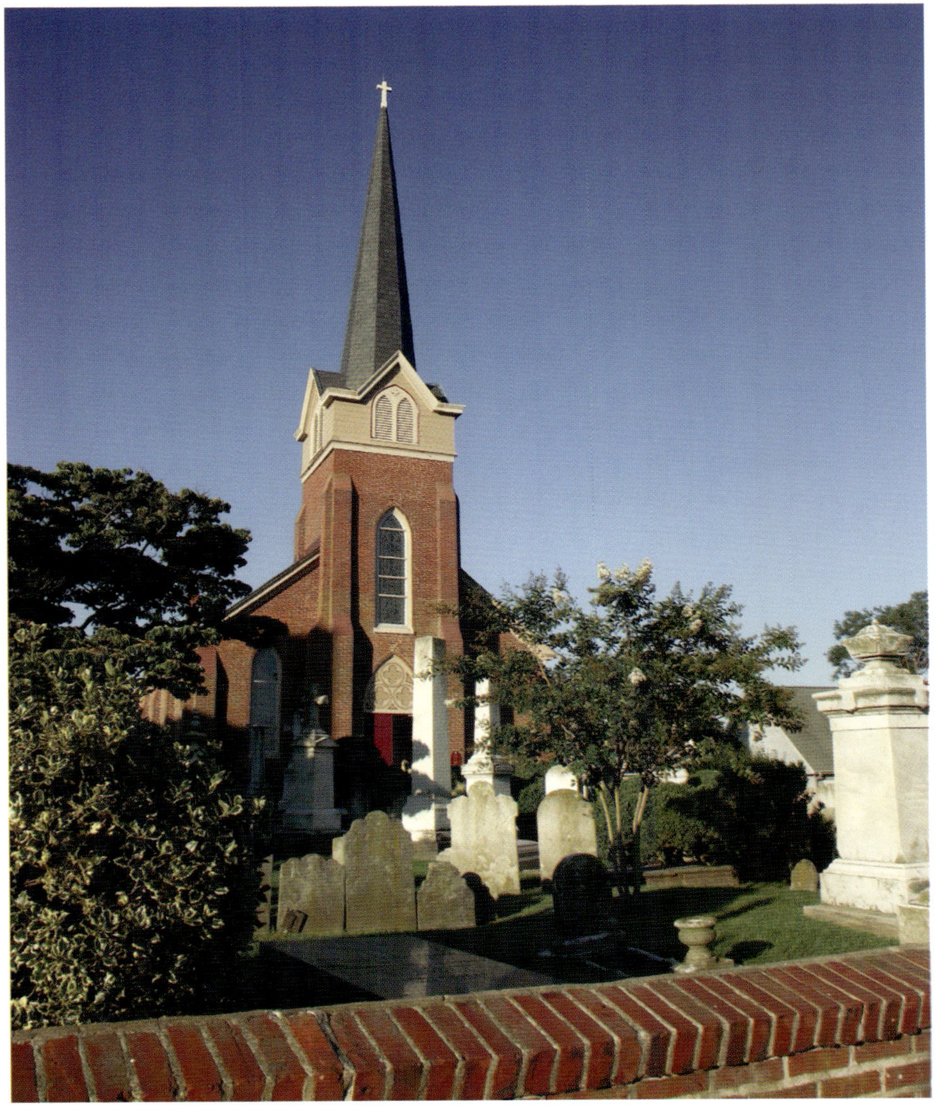

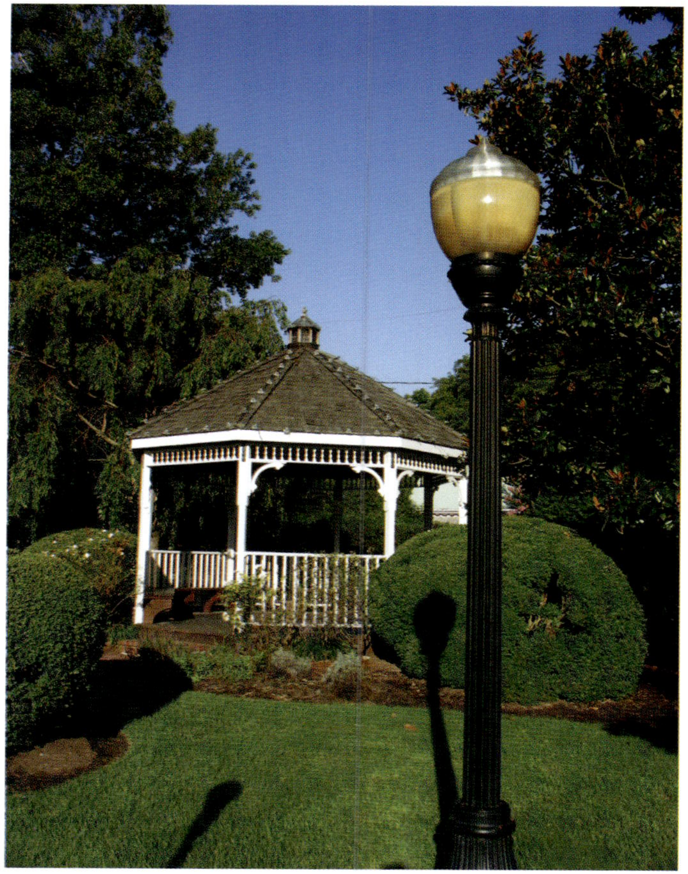

The gazebo in Mary Vessels Park on Market Street is surrounded by attractive plantings throughout the seasons.

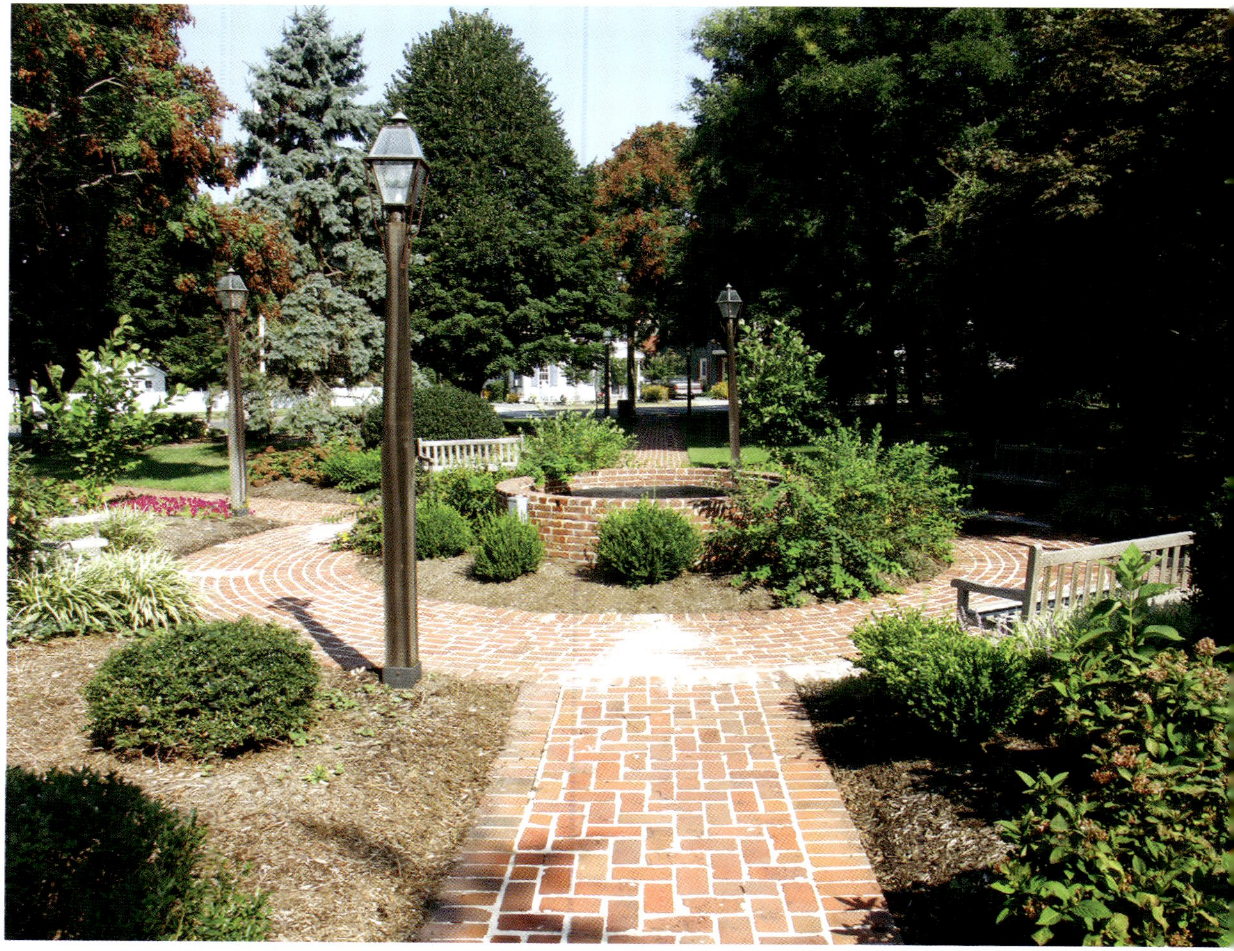

Picturesque Zwaanendael Park is located behind the Fisher-Martin House.

The Buttery Restaurant promises exquisite dining in an elegant Victorian setting. The charming Queen Anne building also serves as an entrance to the commercial district.

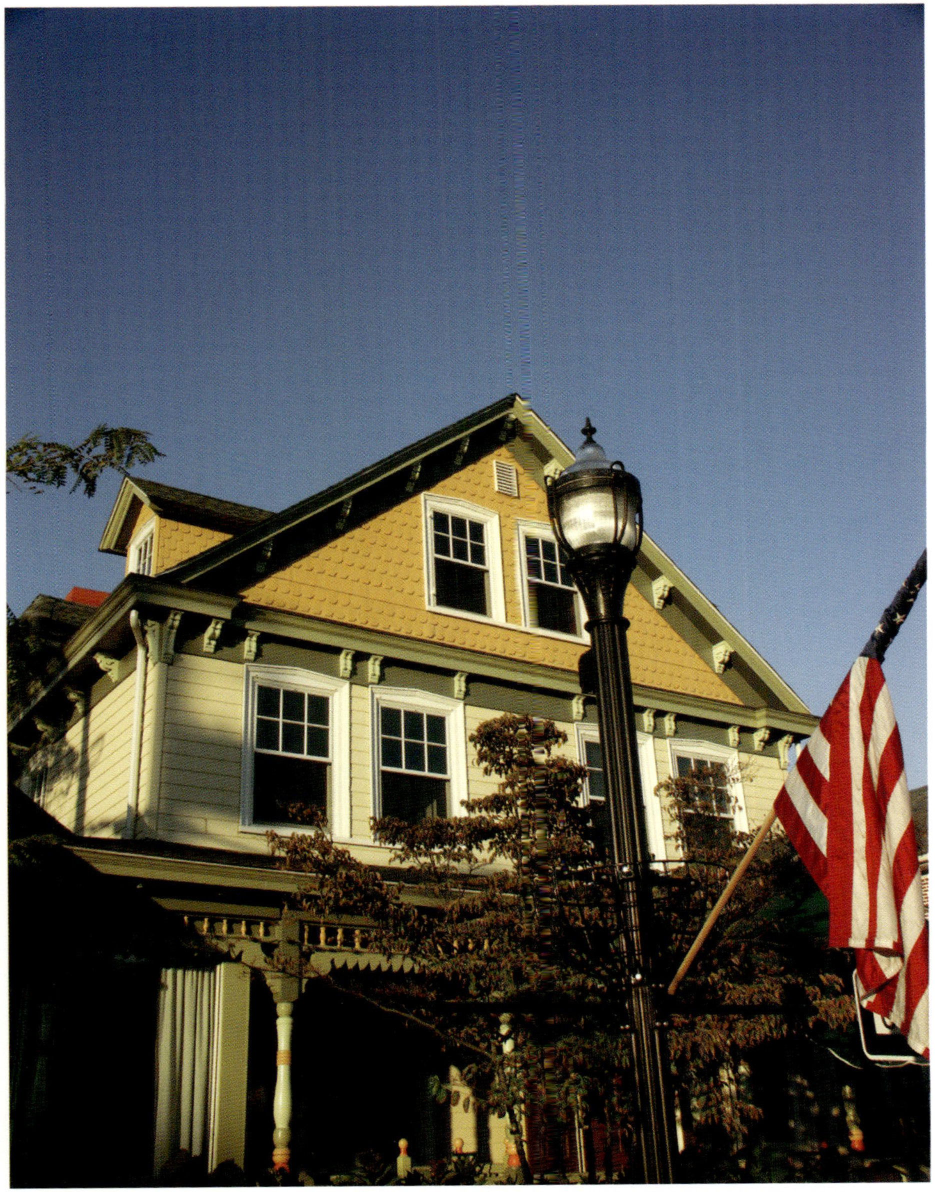

The Ocean Retreat Day Spa & Hair Studio is located in a beautifully-restored Queen Anne house on Savannah Road. It was constructed in 1899 for Captain Charles Johnston, a contractor involved with construction of Cape Henlopen's Harbor of Refuge. The building is known locally as "Harvard House."

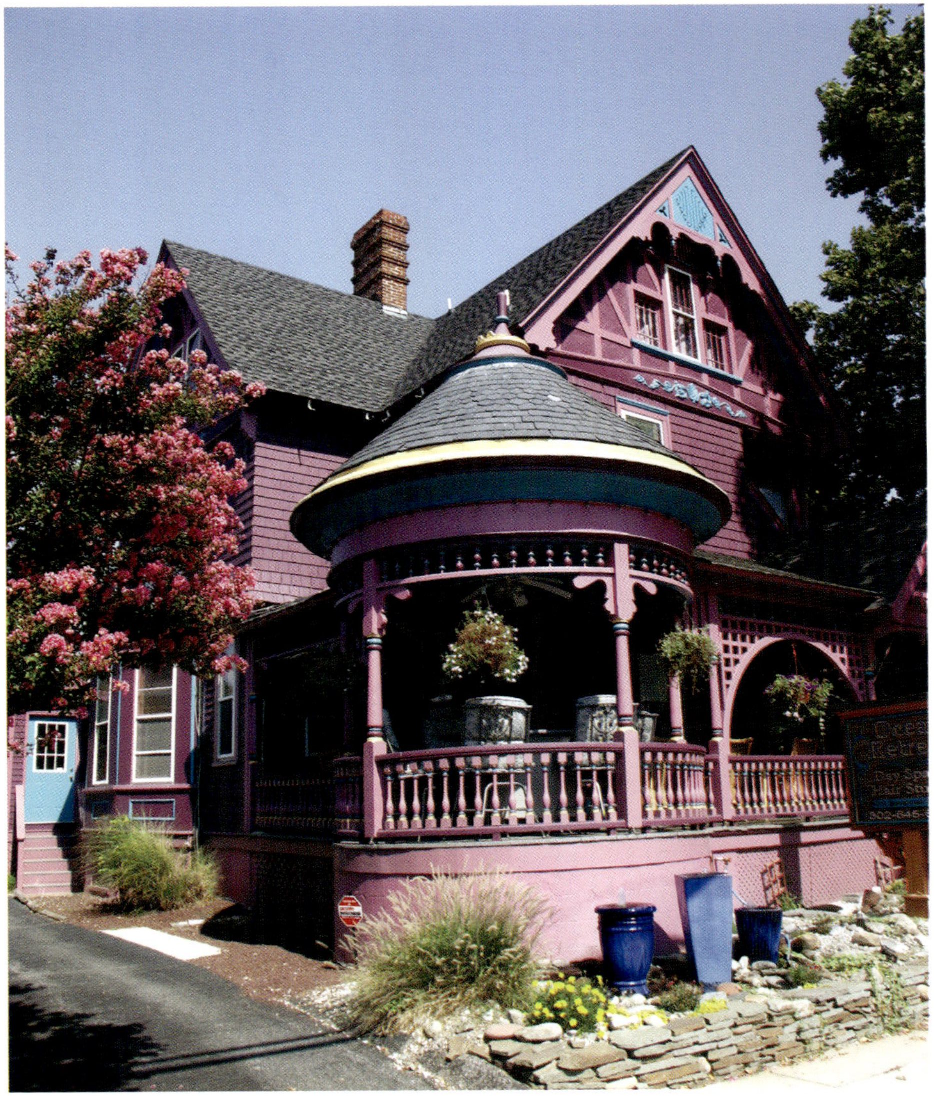

Many first-time visitors are astounded at the architectural variety found in Lewes. From shingled 17th century Dutch Colonial buildings to high-style Victorian era homes dressed in gingerbread, Lewes is a highly walkable town with a breadth of architectural styles.

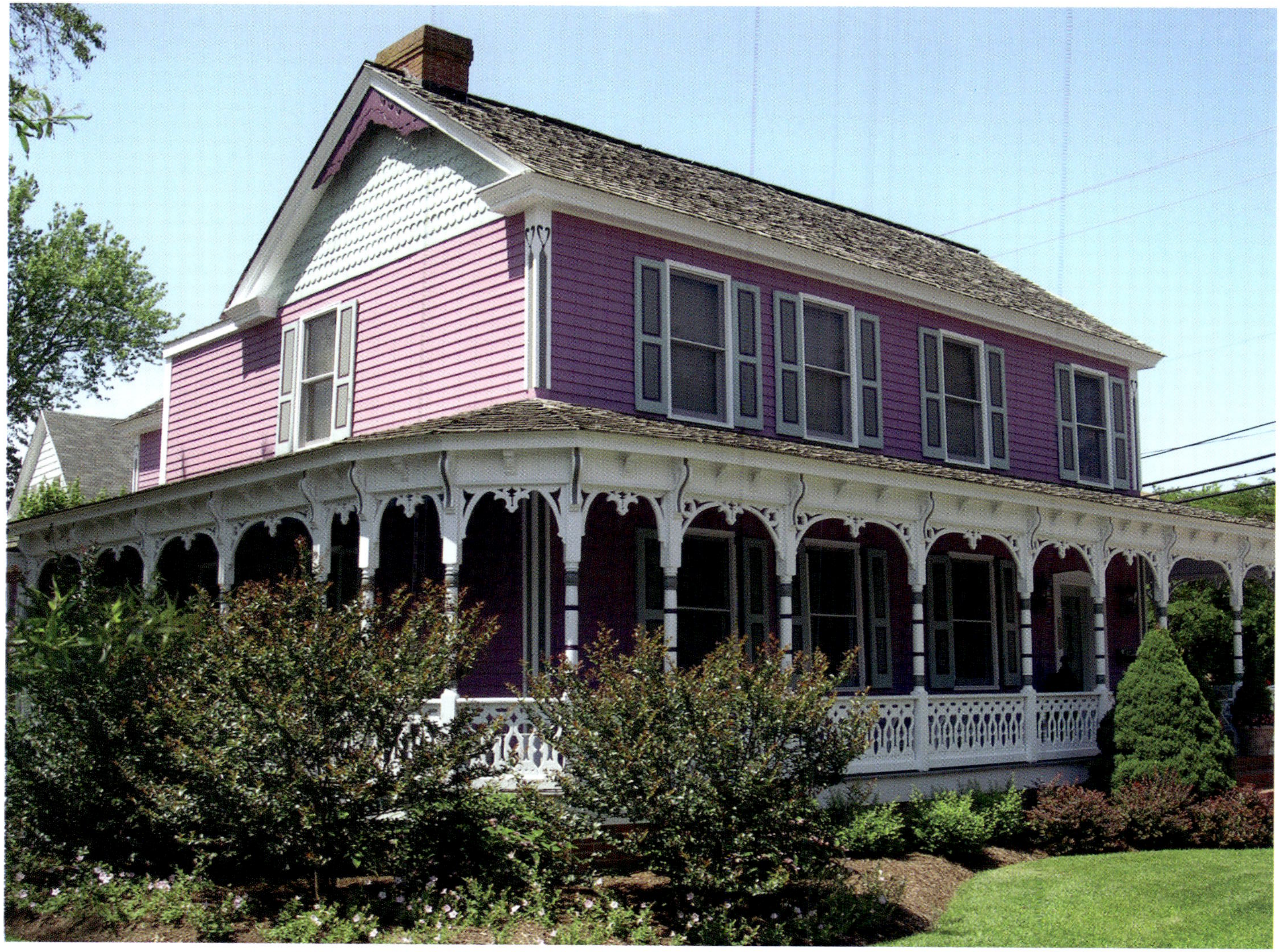

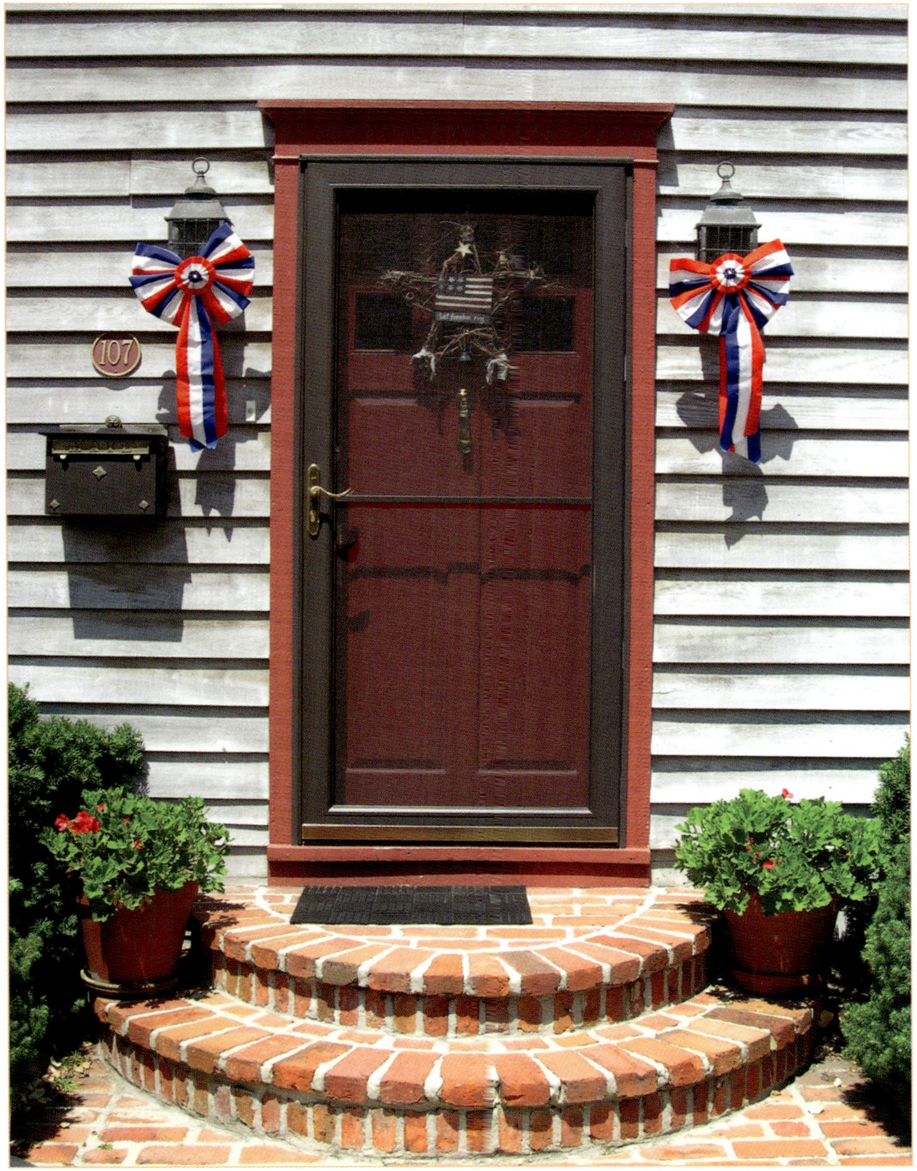
107

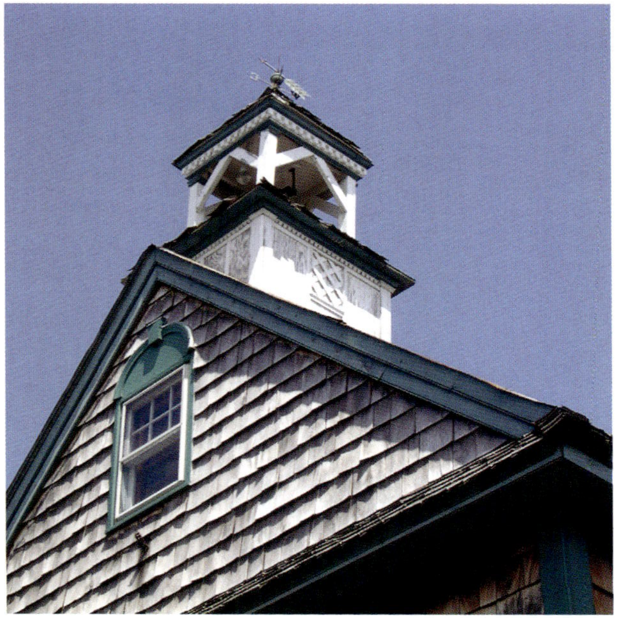

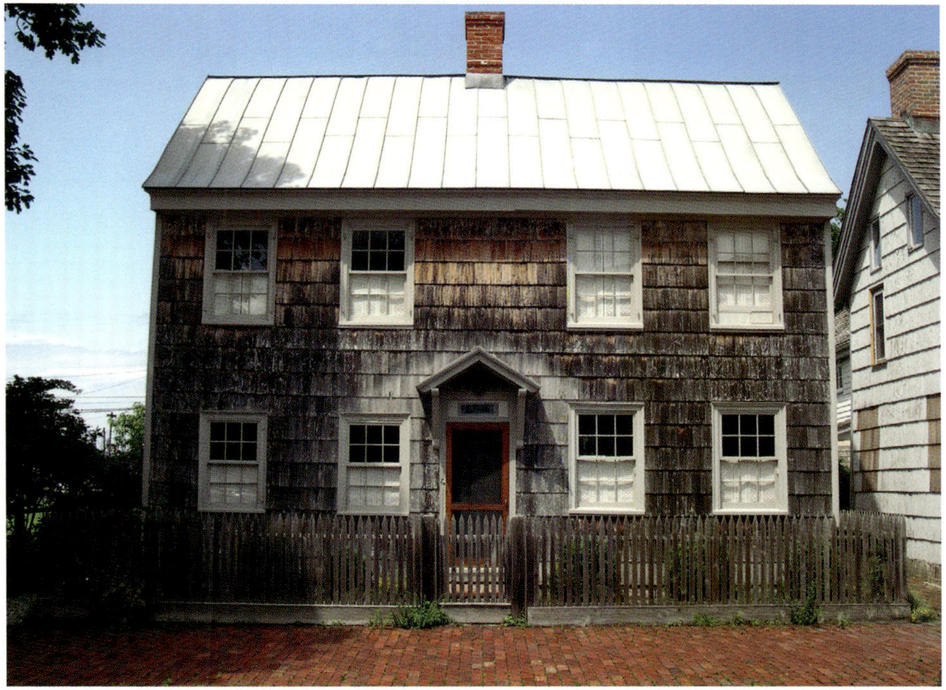

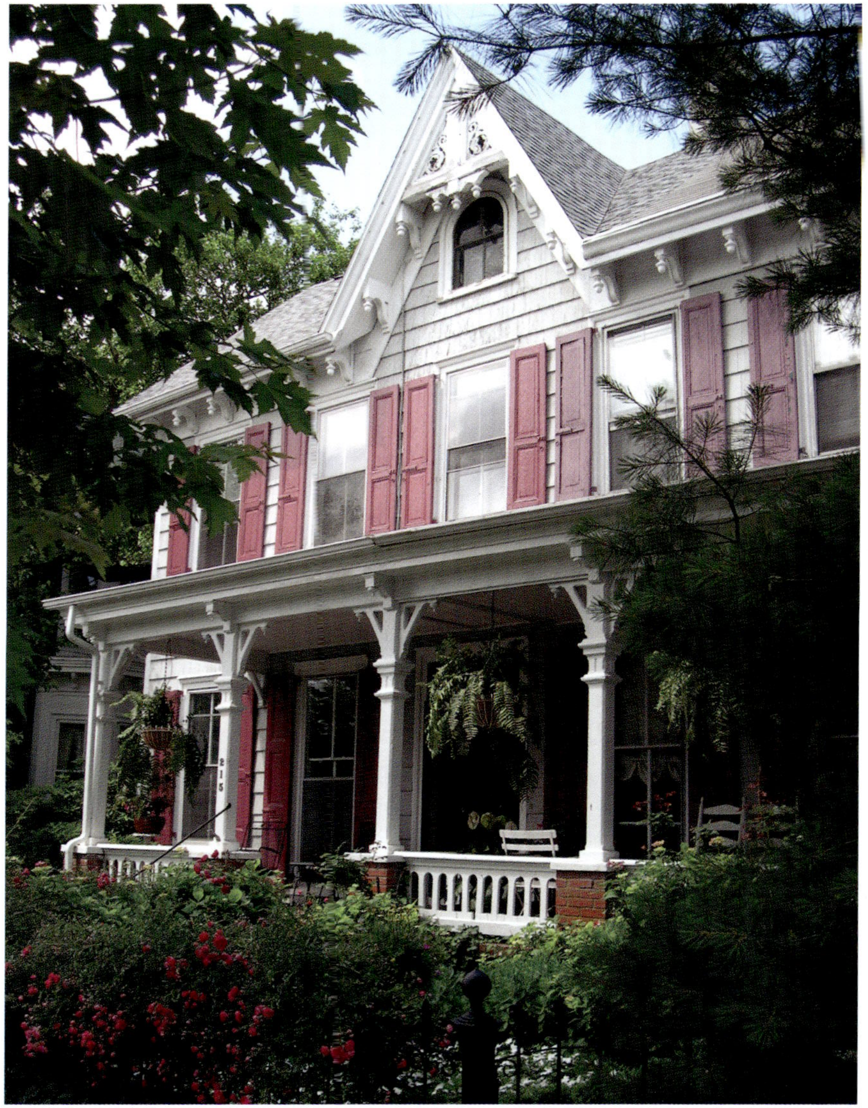

215

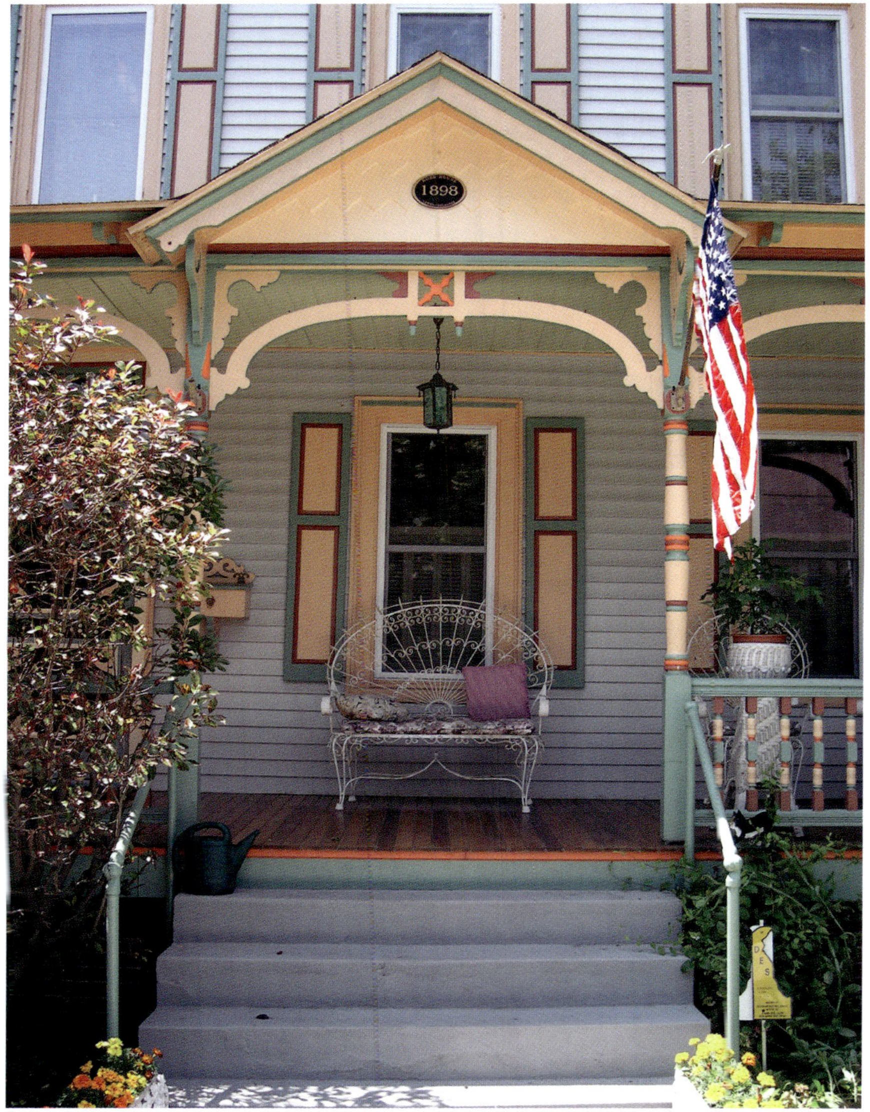

1898

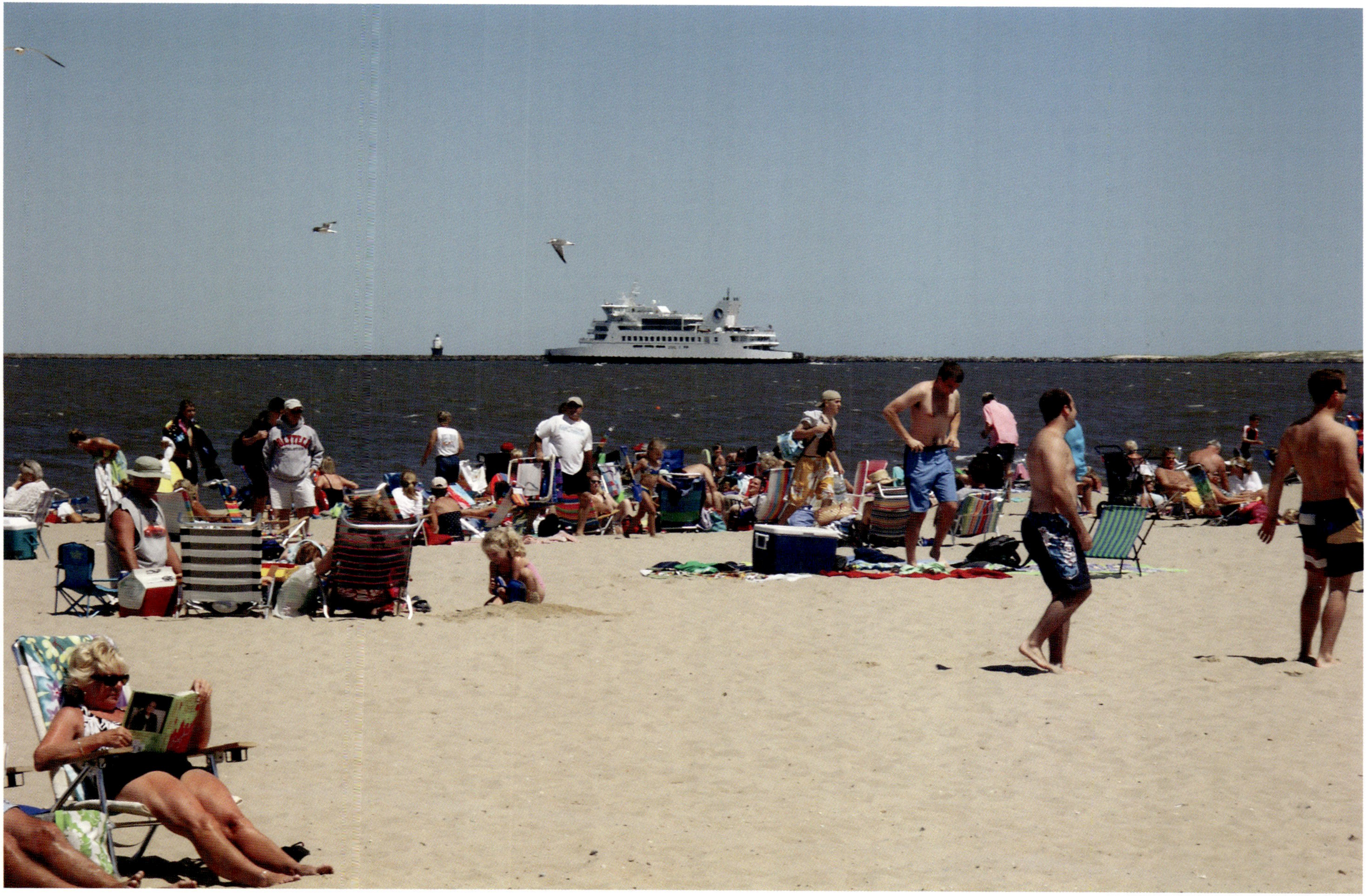

Lewes Beach offers an alternative to the crowded Atlantic Ocean beaches. Located on the Delaware Bay, the beach provides access to calm, shimmering water and views of the Cape May-Lewes Ferry.

The Lightship Overfalls was the last lightship built by the U.S. Lighthouse Service. It was commissioned in 1938 and spent time stationed at various locations off the New England coast, including Cape Cod's Boston Station. A 1970 storm caused major damage, and the boat was taken out of service one year later. In 1973, the U.S. Coast Guard donated the boat to the Lewes Historical Society; ownership has since been transferred to the Overfalls Maritime Museum Foundation. Of 179 lightships constructed between 1820 and 1952, only 17 are known to still survive.

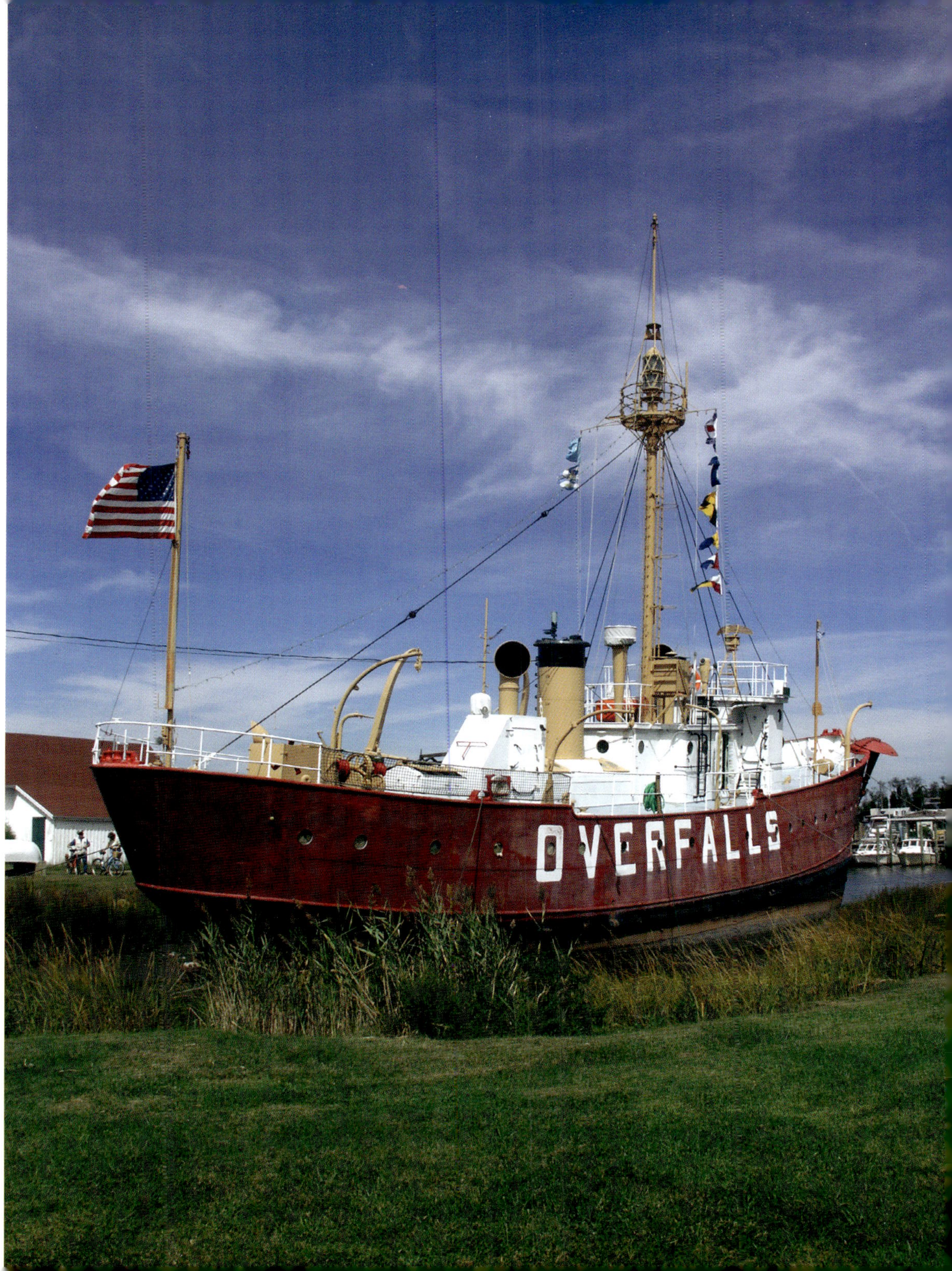

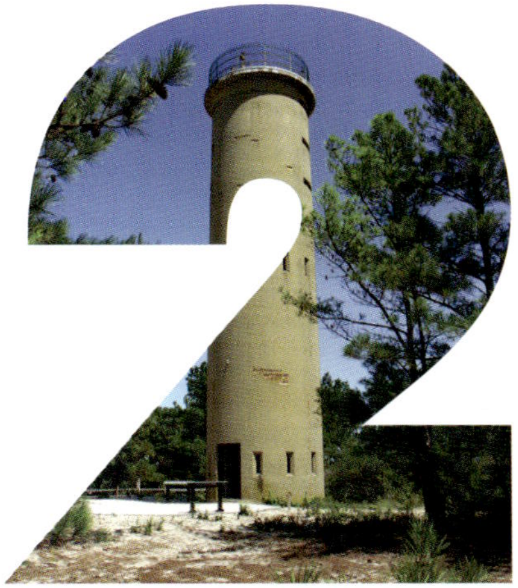

2 Cape Henlopen: *Dunes, Beach & Bay*

Cape Henlopen was "discovered" in 1609 by English Explorer Henry Hudson, who was hired by the Dutch East India Company to find an easterly passage to Asia. Over twenty years later, the Dutch established a whaling colony at what is today Lewes. The name Henlopen comes from a prominent Dutch trader, Thijmen Jacobsz Hinlopen.

William Penn created the nation's first public lands in 1682 when he proclaimed that Cape Henlopen was for the common usage of the citizens of Lewes and Sussex County. The sixth lighthouse in the country was constructed at Cape Henlopen in 1765-1767, only to be gutted by fire ten years after completion. In 1784 it was repaired and returned to duty. Funding for construction came from the merchants of Philadelphia.

A breakwater was constructed in 1828 to provide refuge from rough seas, the only such breakwater between Sandy Hook, NJ and Cape Charles, VA. It took 835,000 tons of stone and over $2.1 million to construct the 2,586-ft. breakwater. A lighthouse was eventually constructed on the west end in 1849.

The Cape Henlopen Beacon was constructed in 1825 to mark the tip of the cape. It was replaced in 1864 by a screwpile lighthouse, and discontinued in 1884.

In 1920, the Cape Henlopen Lighthouse was damaged by a storm. Four years later it was lit for the final time. Sadly, movement of the Great Dune caused the picturesque lighthouse to collapse in 1926.

Many visitors to the Delaware Coast and Cape Henlopen State Park don't know the history of Fort Miles. They may be familiar with the concrete observation towers that line the coast, but perhaps not of their purpose. Fort Miles was established at Cape Henlopen in 1941 to defend the Delaware Bay, Wilmington, and Philadelphia. Observation towers were constructed, as were underground bunkers to store ammunition. Large guns were strategically placed, with a corresponding tower to mark the distance of the gun; these sand and concrete sentinels served as artillery control towers while providing a lookout for the stealthy Nazi U-boats and submarines that patrolled the coast, sinking commercial vessels. A mine from a German submarine destroyed a tugboat off the shores of Cape Henlopen. Fort Miles included a hospital, theater, gymnasium, fire hall, warehouse, mess facilities, barracks, club houses, and more. A pier was constructed to lay mines in the Delaware Bay. In 1945, Fort Miles served as headquarters for German and Italian Prisoners of War. During the Korean War, the base was used for training. The Army post closed in 1958.

Cape Henlopen State Park was dedicated in 1964, and today provides 5,193-acres of outdoor activity and recreation space, including both ocean and bay beaches. The park includes the Gordon's Pond Wildlife Area, which features many species of birds, as well as the Great Dune, which rises 80-ft. above sea level and is the highest dune between Cape Cod and Cape Hatteras. The pier originally built to lay mines is now known as the Fishing Pier. The park also includes two lighthouses – Delaware Breakwater, which was constructed of brick in 1885 and features a 49-ft tower, and Harbor of Refuge, which was built in 1926 of cast iron and features a 76-ft. tower.

Cape Henlopen is unique in that visitors can watch a sunrise over the ocean, then watch the sun set over the bay after an action-packed day of hiking and swimming.

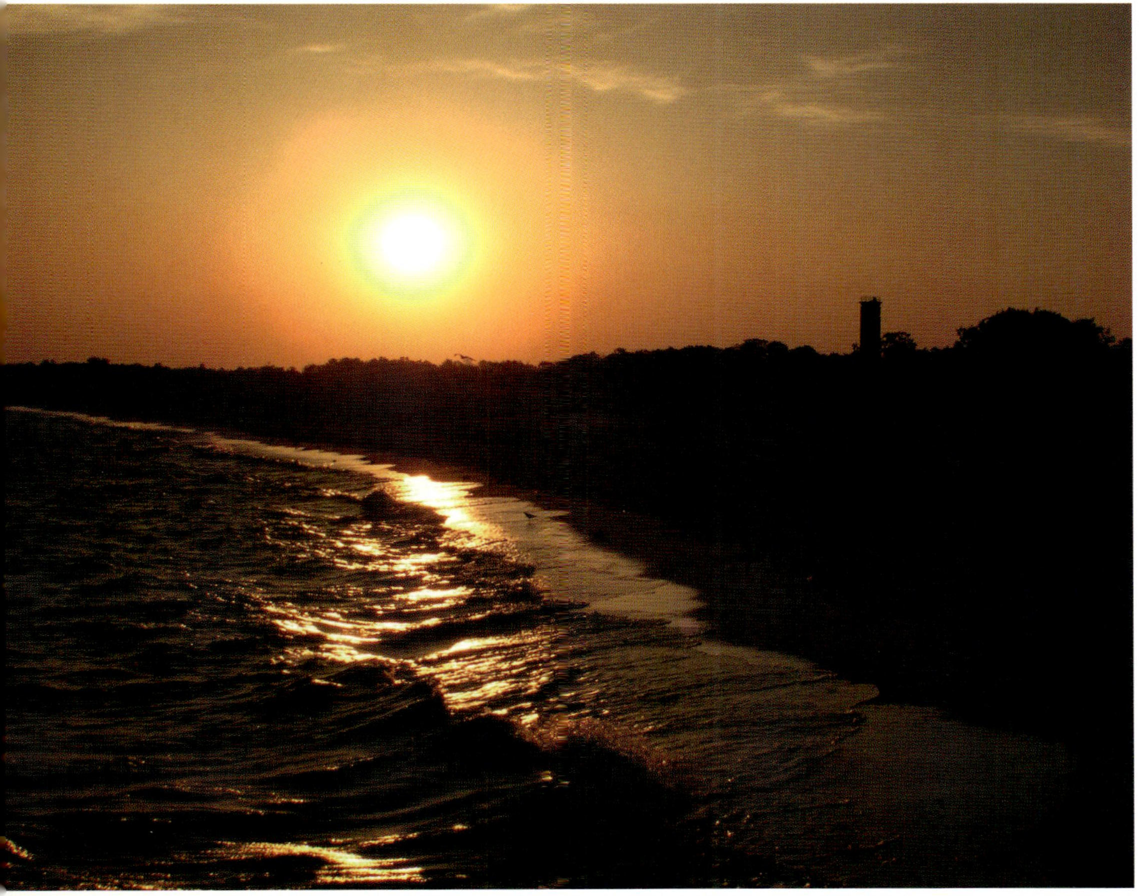

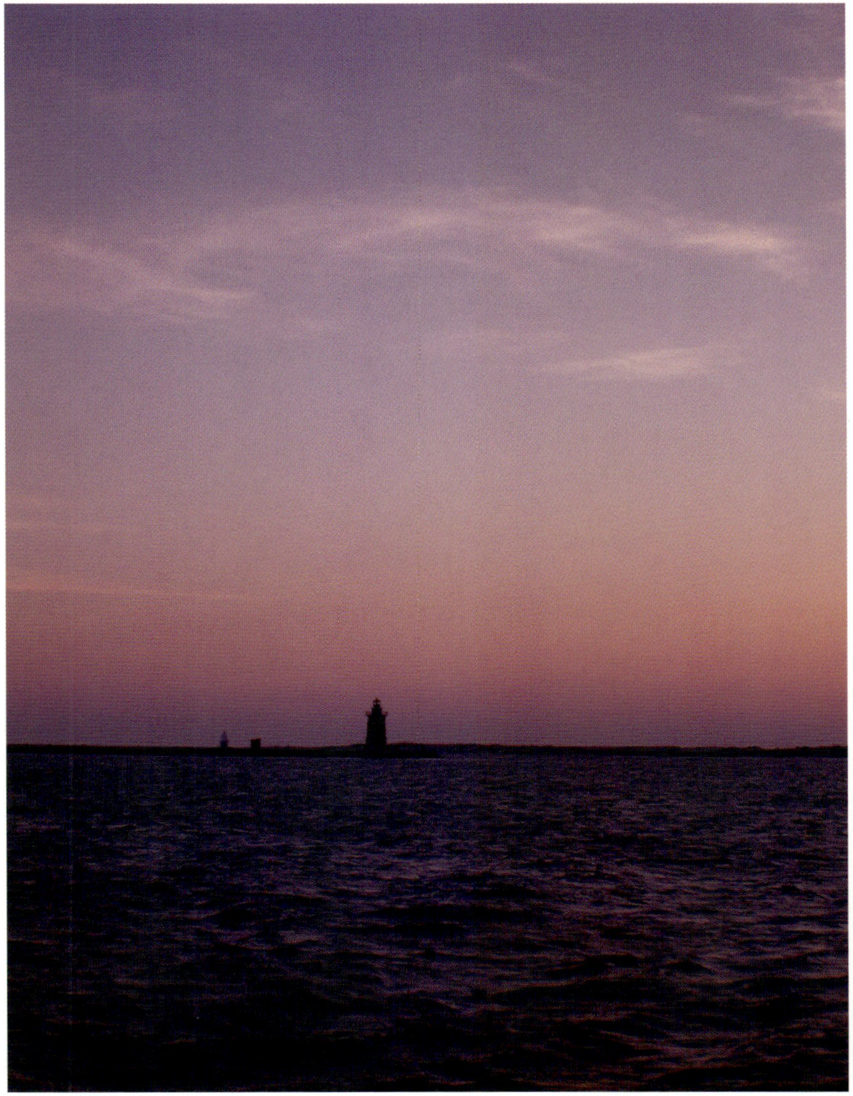

The artillery control towers are easily Cape Henlopen's most notable manmade features. One is open to the pubic while another serves as the base for the Delaware River & Bay Pilot's Ship Reporting Station.

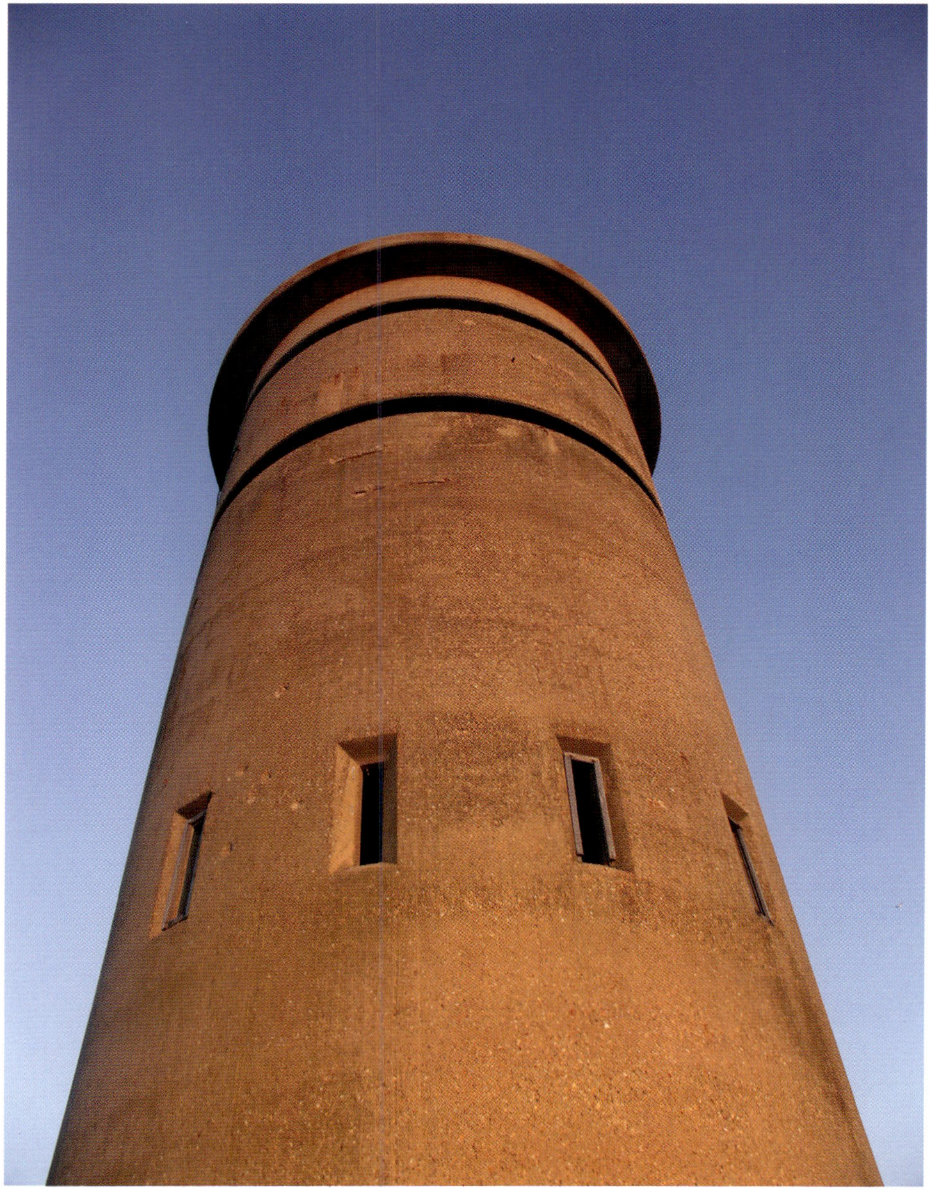

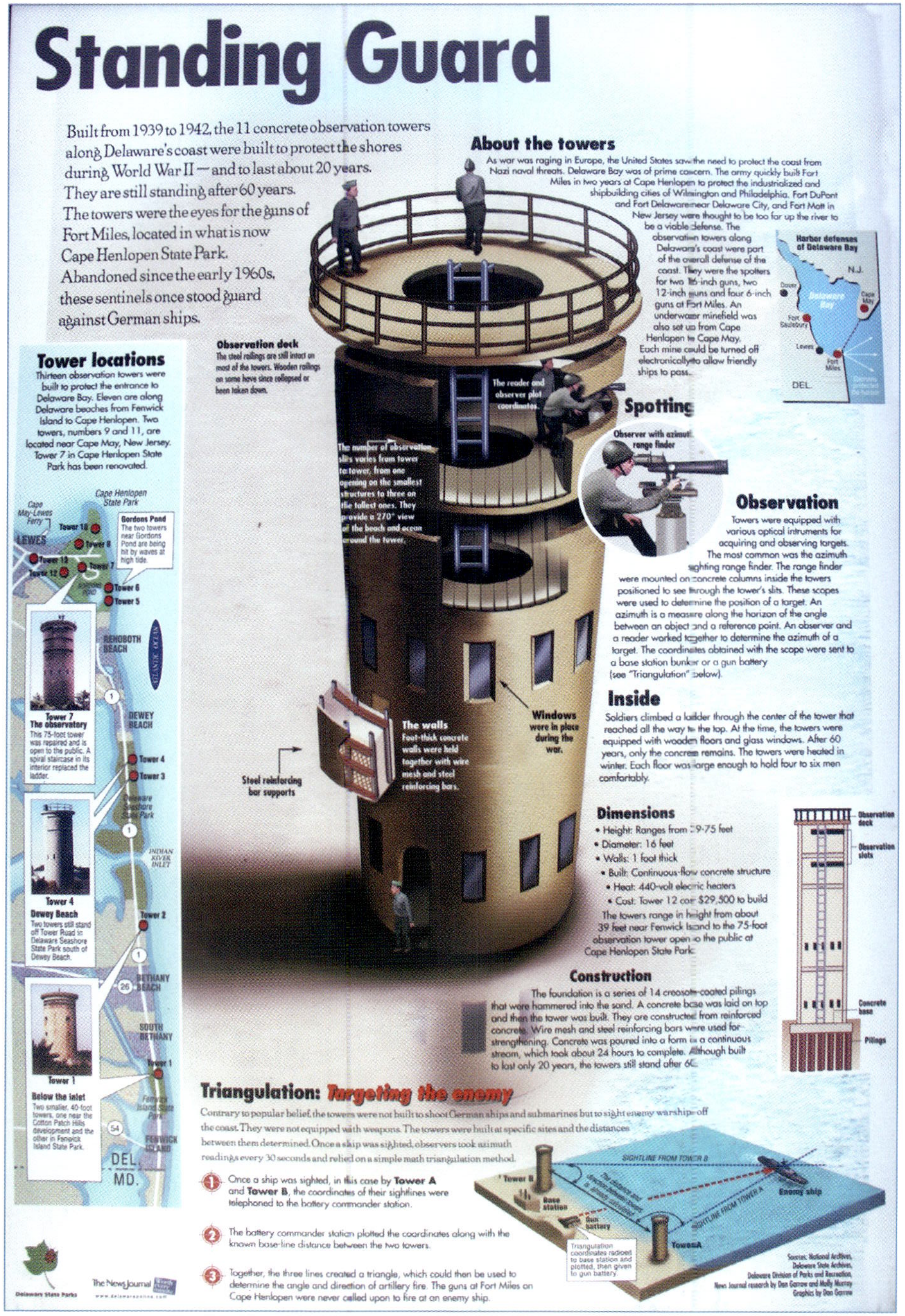

Standing Guard

Built from 1939 to 1942, the 11 concrete observation towers along Delaware's coast were built to protect the shores during World War II — and to last about 20 years. They are still standing after 60 years. The towers were the eyes for the guns of Fort Miles, located in what is now Cape Henlopen State Park. Abandoned since the early 1960s, these sentinels once stood guard against German ships.

About the towers

As war was raging in Europe, the United States saw the need to protect the coast from Nazi naval threats. Delaware Bay was of prime concern. The army quickly built Fort Miles in two years at Cape Henlopen to protect the industrialized and shipbuilding cities of Wilmington and Philadelphia. Fort DuPont and Fort Delaware near Delaware City, and Fort Mott in New Jersey were thought to be too far up the river to be a viable defense. The observation towers along Delaware's coast were part of the overall defense of the coast. They were the spotters for two 16-inch guns, two 12-inch guns and four 6-inch guns at Fort Miles. An underwater minefield was also set up from Cape Henlopen to Cape May. Each mine could be turned off electronically to allow friendly ships to pass.

Tower locations

Thirteen observation towers were built to protect the entrance to Delaware Bay. Eleven are along Delaware beaches from Fenwick Island to Cape Henlopen. Two towers, numbers 9 and 11, are located near Cape May, New Jersey. Tower 7 in Cape Henlopen State Park has been renovated.

Tower 7
The observatory
This 75-foot tower was repaired and is open to the public. A spiral staircase in its interior replaced the ladder.

Tower 4
Dewey Beach
Two towers still stand off Tower Road in Delaware Seashore State Park south of Dewey Beach.

Tower 1
Below the inlet
Two smaller, 40-foot towers, one near the Cotton Patch Hills development and the other in Fenwick Island State Park.

Gordons Pond
The two towers near Gordons Pond are being hit by waves at high tide.

Observation deck
The steel railings are still intact on most of the towers. Wooden railings on some have since collapsed or been taken down.

The reader and observer plot coordinates.

The number of observation slits varies from tower to tower, from one opening on the smallest structures to three on the tallest ones. They provide a 270° view of the beach and ocean around the tower.

The walls
Foot-thick concrete walls were held together with wire mesh and steel reinforcing bars.

Steel reinforcing bar supports

Windows were in place during the war.

Spotting

Observer with azimuth range finder

Observation

Towers were equipped with various optical intruments for acquiring and observing targets. The most common was the azimuth sighting range finder. The range finder were mounted on concrete columns inside the towers positioned to see through the tower's slits. These scopes were used to determine the position of a target. An azimuth is a measure along the horizon of the angle between an object and a reference point. An observer and a reader worked together to determine the azimuth of a target. The coordinates obtained with the scope were sent to a base station bunker or a gun battery (see "Triangulation" below).

Inside

Soldiers climbed a ladder through the center of the tower that reached all the way to the top. At the time, the towers were equipped with wooden floors and glass windows. After 60 years, only the concrete remains. The towers were heated in winter. Each floor was large enough to hold four to six men comfortably.

Dimensions

- Height: Ranges from 39-75 feet
- Diameter: 16 feet
- Walls: 1 foot thick
- Built: Continuous-flow concrete structure
- Heat: 440-volt electric heaters
- Cost: Tower 12 cost $29,500 to build

The towers range in height from about 39 feet near Fenwick Island to the 75-foot observation tower open to the public at Cape Henlopen State Park.

Construction

The foundation is a series of 14 creosote-coated pilings that were hammered into the sand. A concrete base was laid on top and then the tower was built. They are constructed from reinforced concrete. Wire mesh and steel reinforcing bars were used for strengthening. Concrete was poured into a form in a continuous stream, which took about 24 hours to complete. Although built to last only 20 years, the towers still stand after 60.

Triangulation: Targeting the enemy

Contrary to popular belief, the towers were not built to shoot German ships and submarines but to sight enemy warships off the coast. They were not equipped with weapons. The towers were built at specific sites and the distances between them determined. Once a ship was sighted, observers took azimuth readings every 30 seconds and relied on a simple math triangulation method.

1. Once a ship was sighted, in this case by **Tower A** and **Tower B**, the coordinates of their sightlines were telephoned to the battery commander station.
2. The battery commander station plotted the coordinates along with the known base-line distance between the two towers.
3. Together, the three lines created a triangle, which could then be used to determine the angle and direction of artillery fire. The guns at Fort Miles on Cape Henlopen were never called upon to fire at an enemy ship.

Sources: National Archives, Delaware State Archives, Delaware Division of Parks and Recreation. News Journal research by Dan Garrow and Molly Murray. Graphics by Dan Garrow

Delaware State Parks
The News Journal

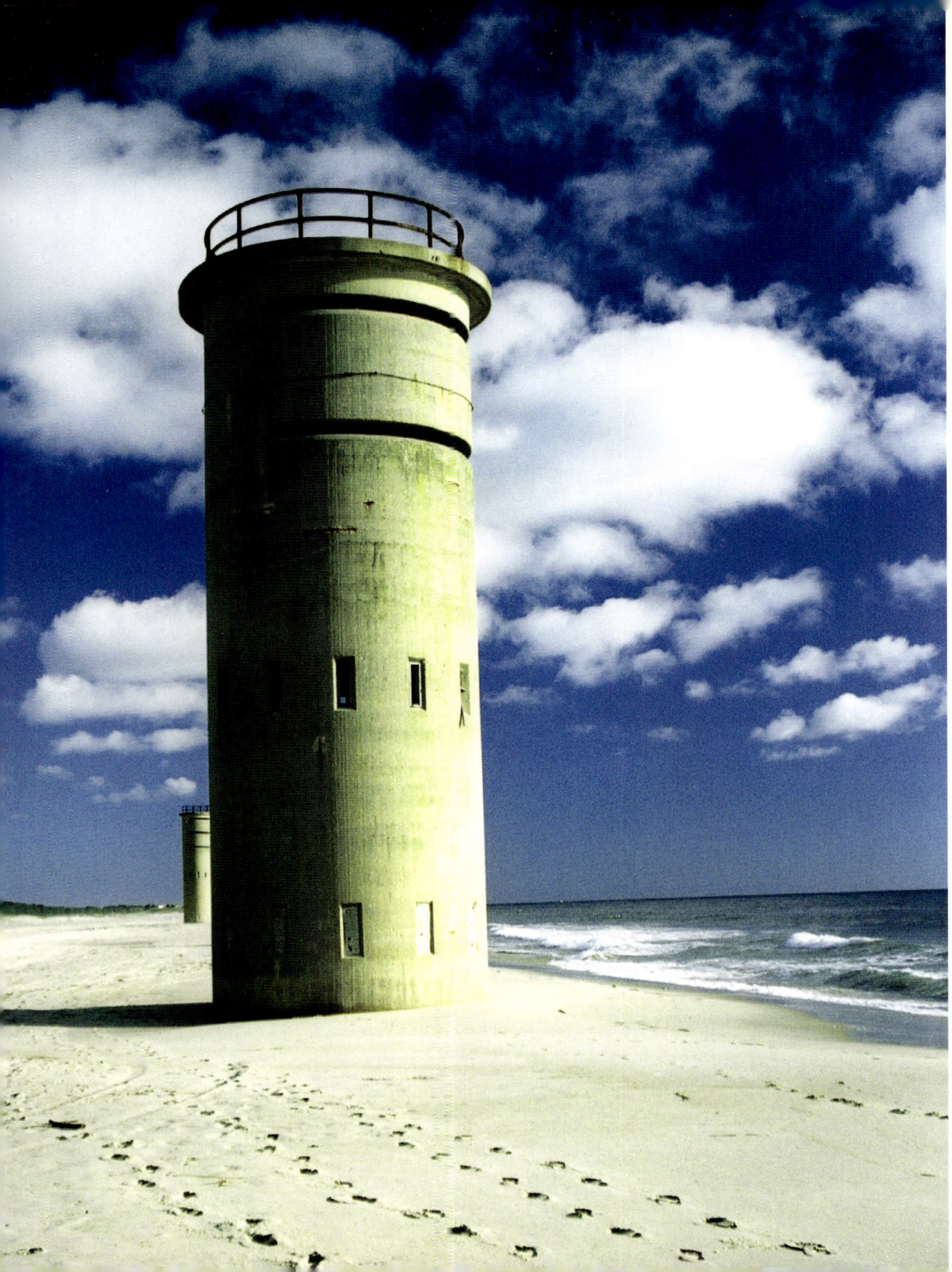

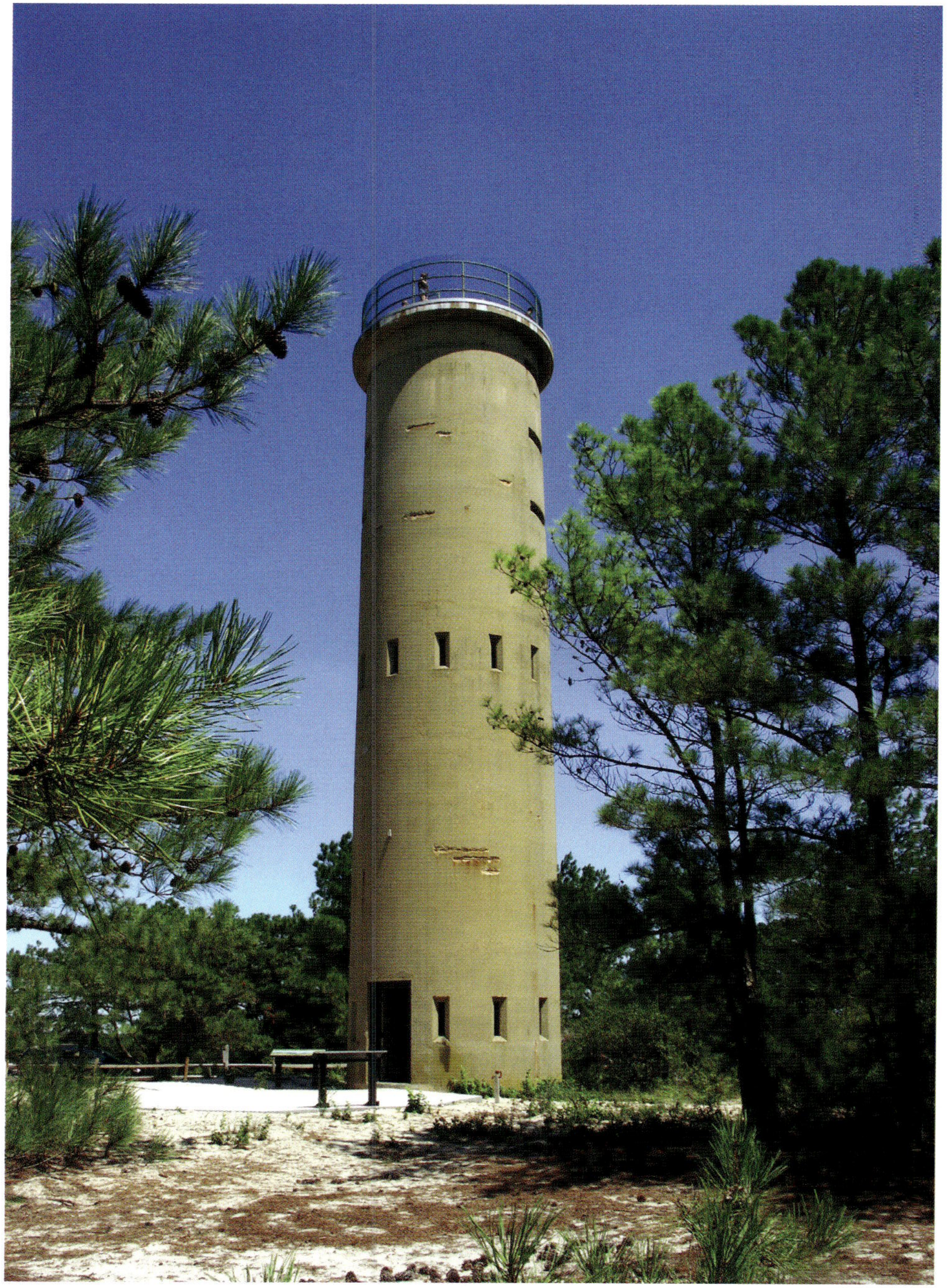

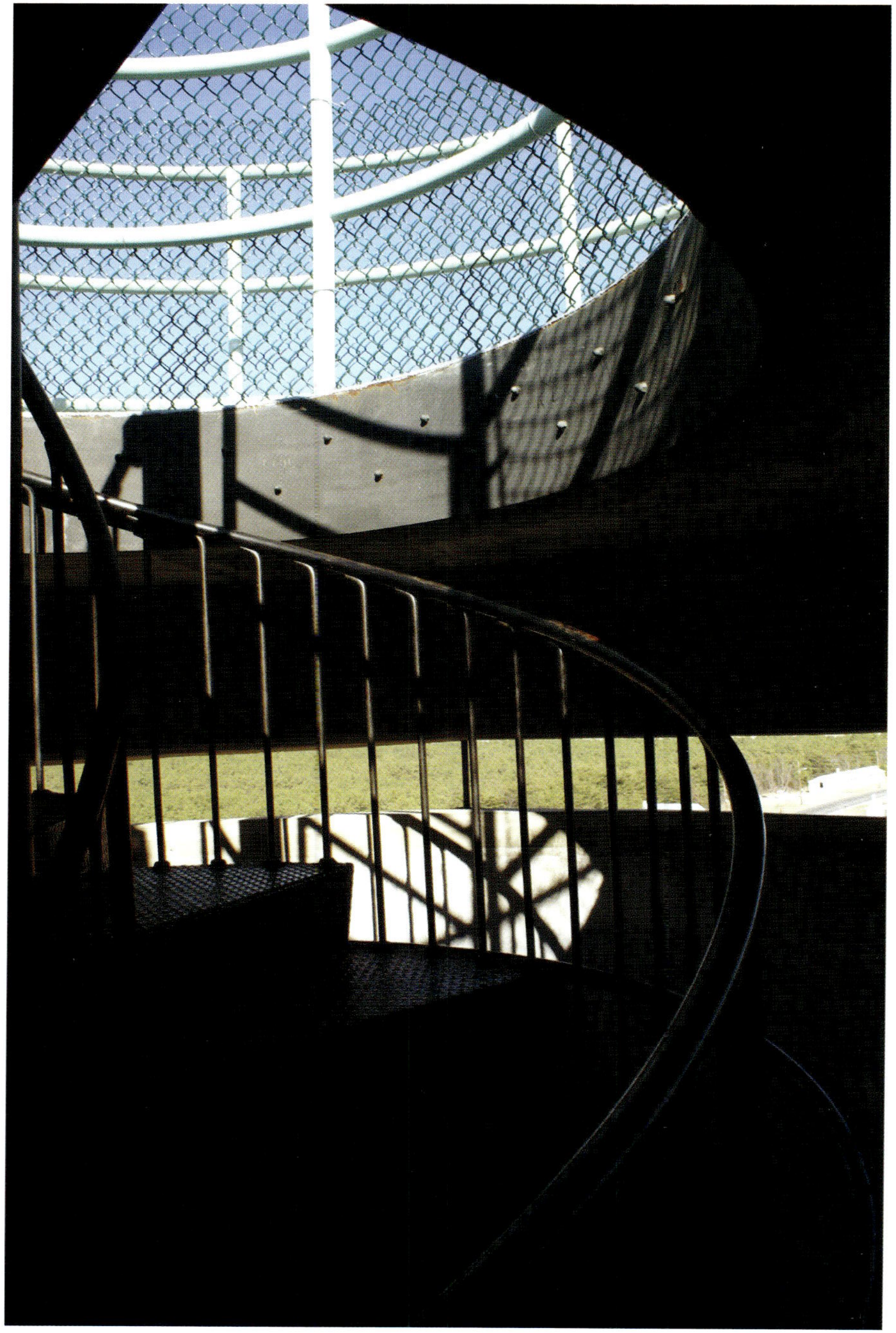

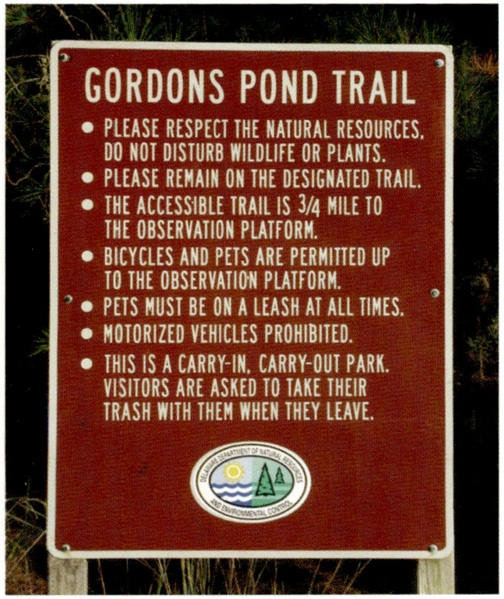

Gordon's Pond Wildlife Area includes a saltwater impoundment, walking trail, and viewing deck, making it a popular stop for nature lovers and birdwatchers.

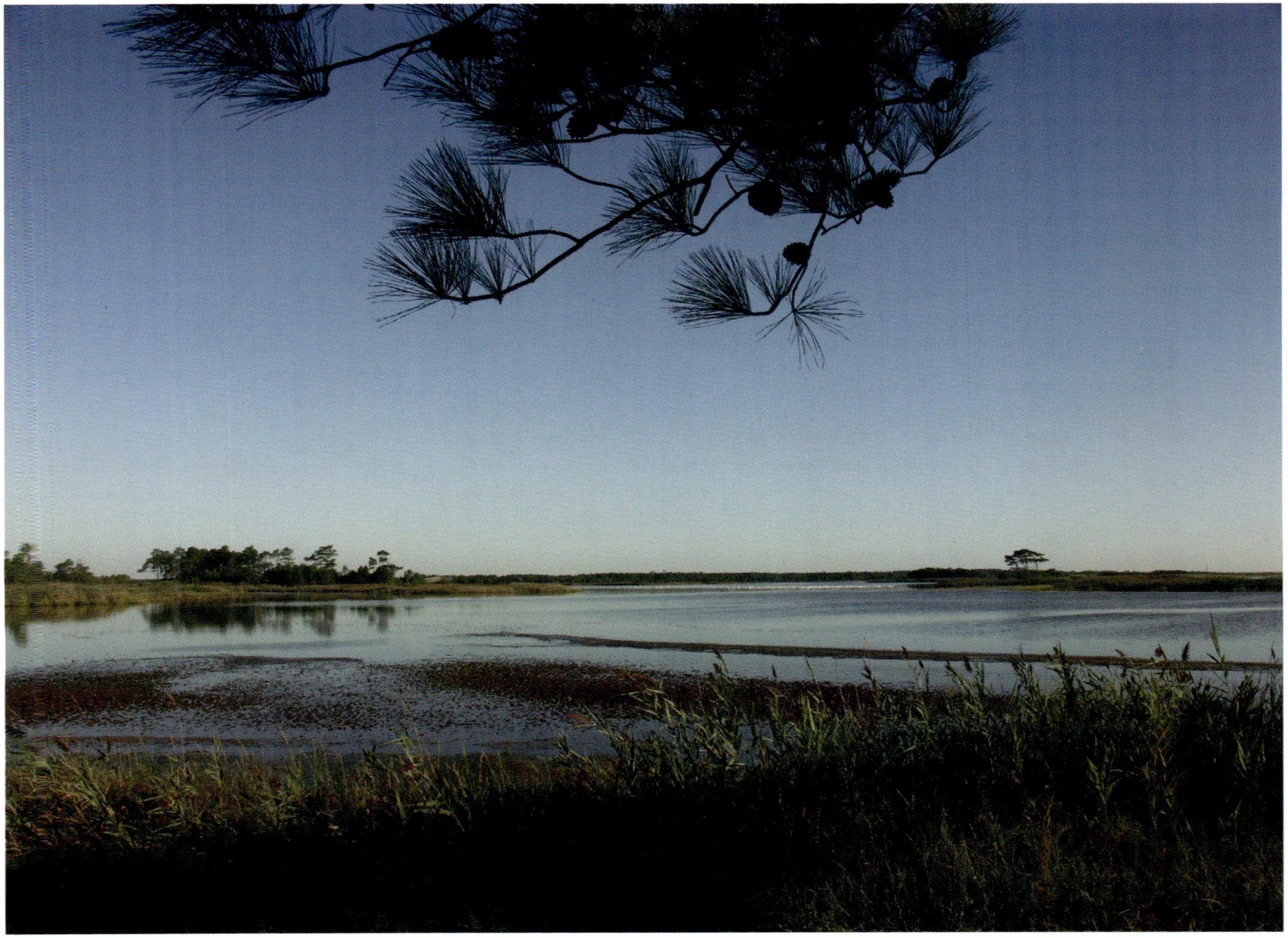

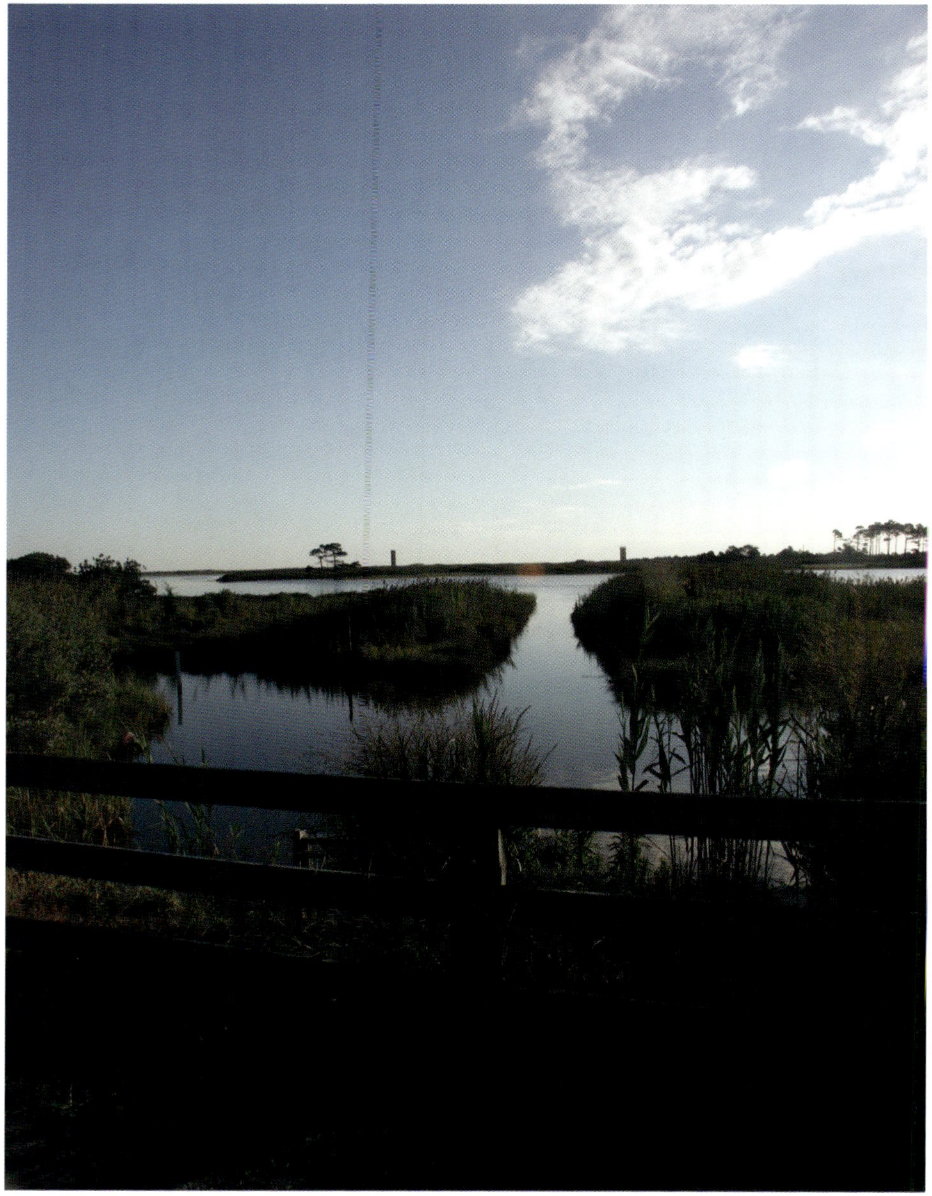

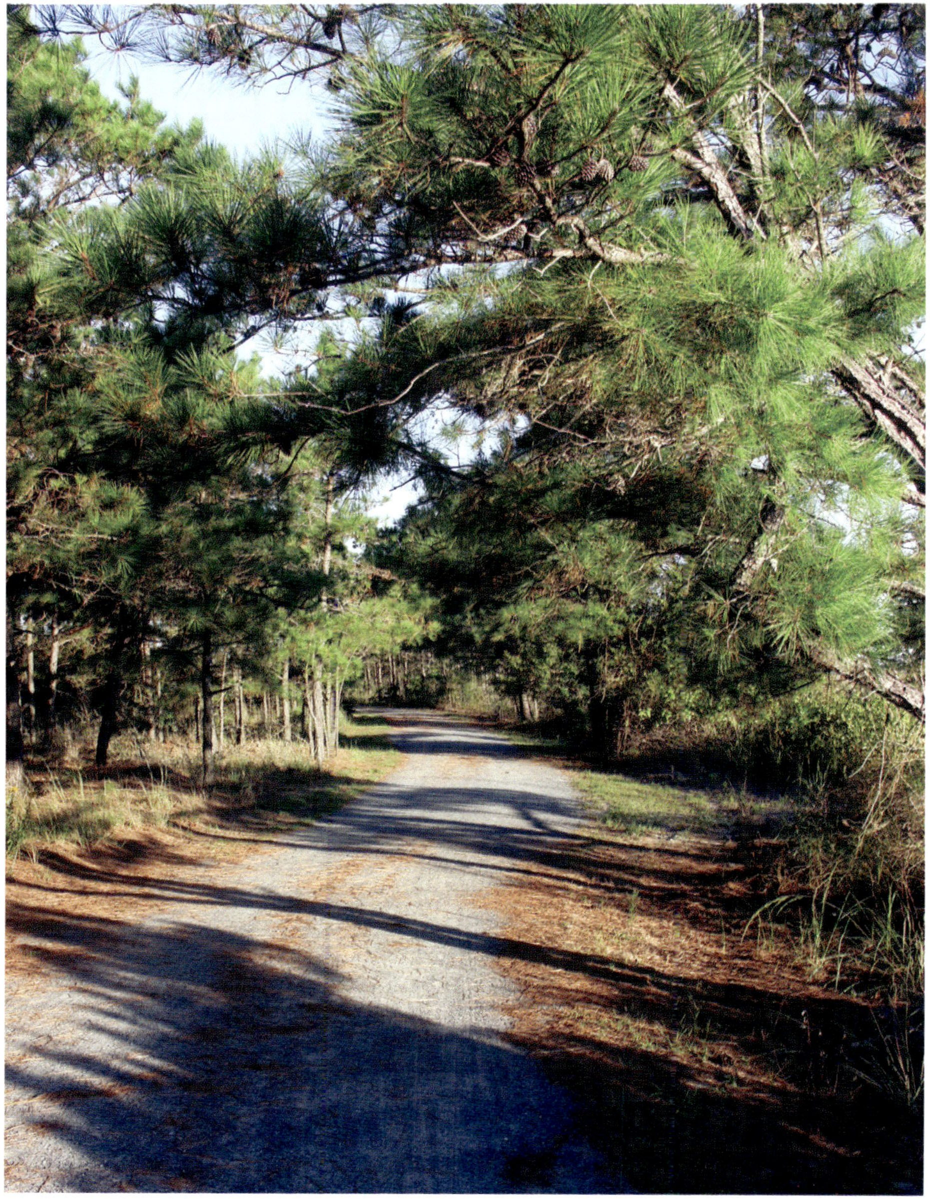

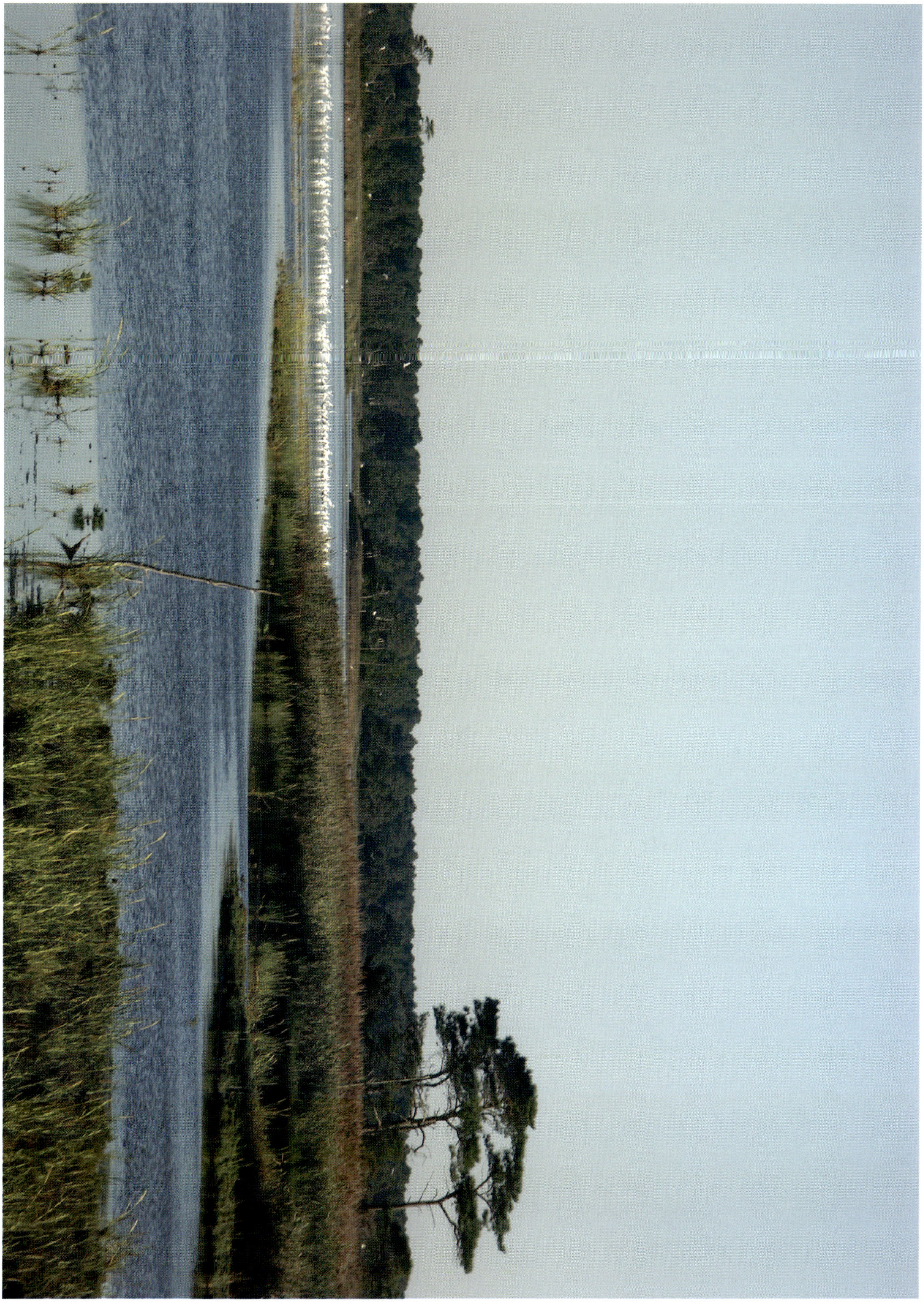

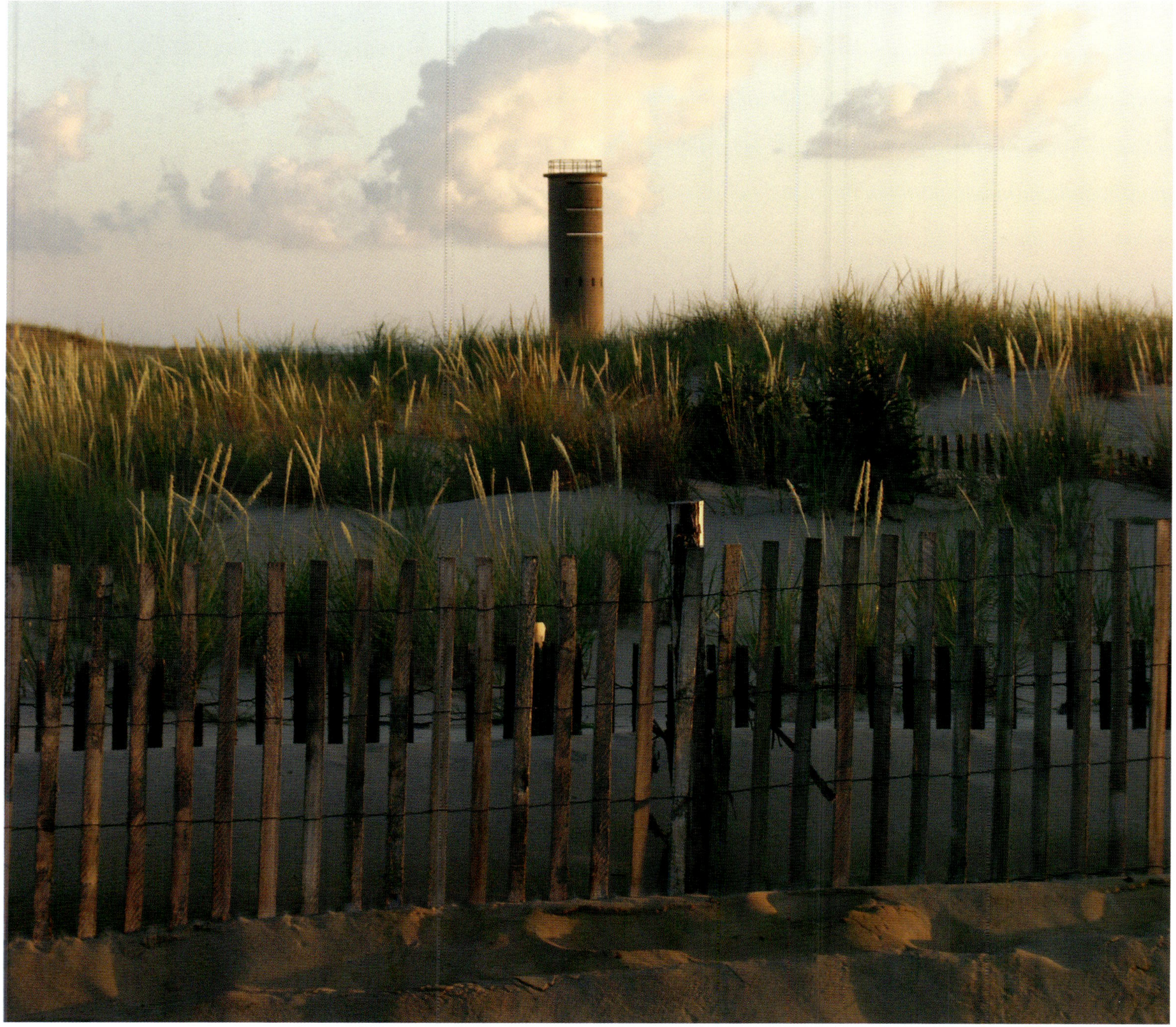

Cape Henlopen State Park features both ocean and bay beaches, towers and dunes, jetties and decks, and panoramic views.

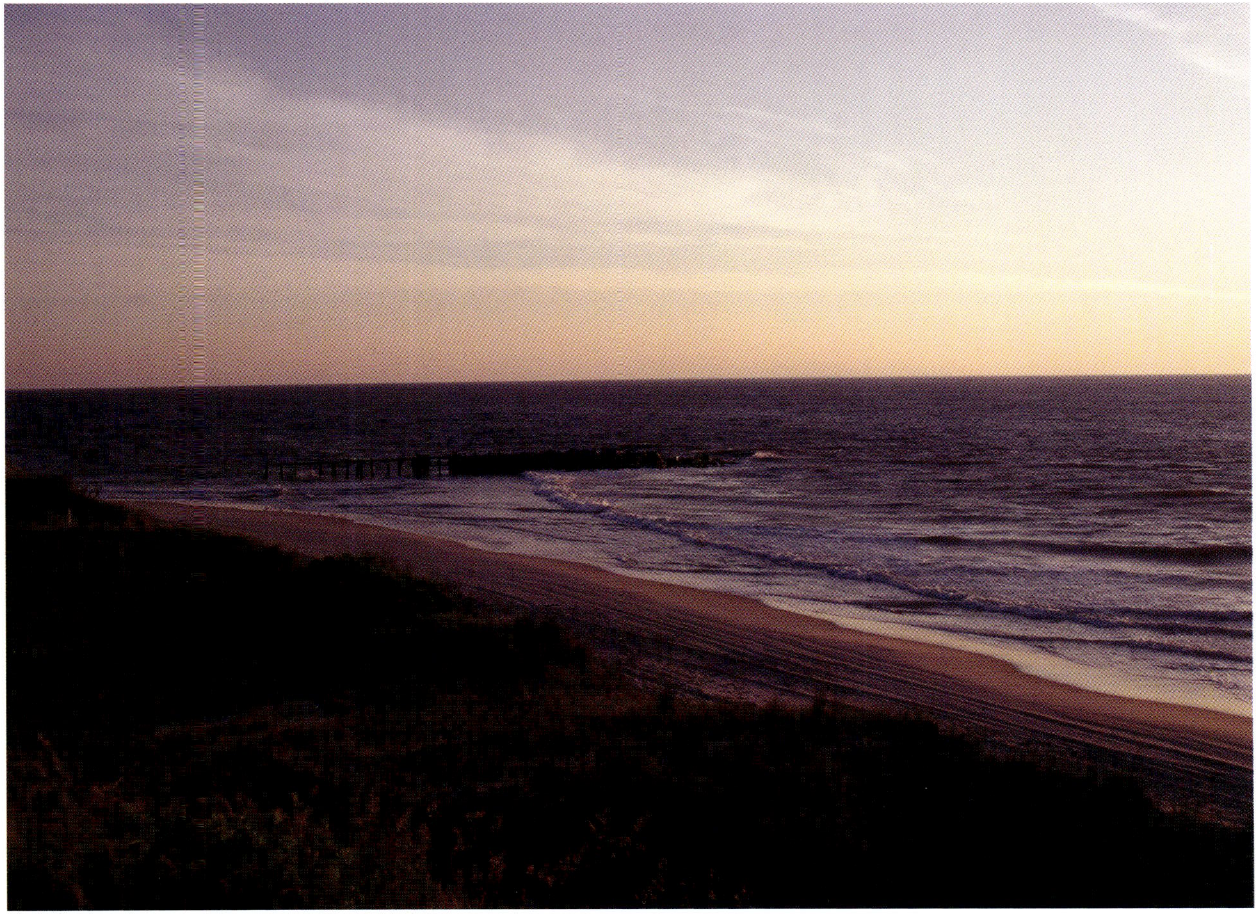

In 1941, the 261st Coastal Artillery was mobilized to defend against German sea vessels; shortly thereafter the Department of Defense constructed Fort Miles. Bunkers and casements were built, as were thirteen artillery control towers along the coast. The base was also used for training and served as headquarters for German and Italian prisoners of war.

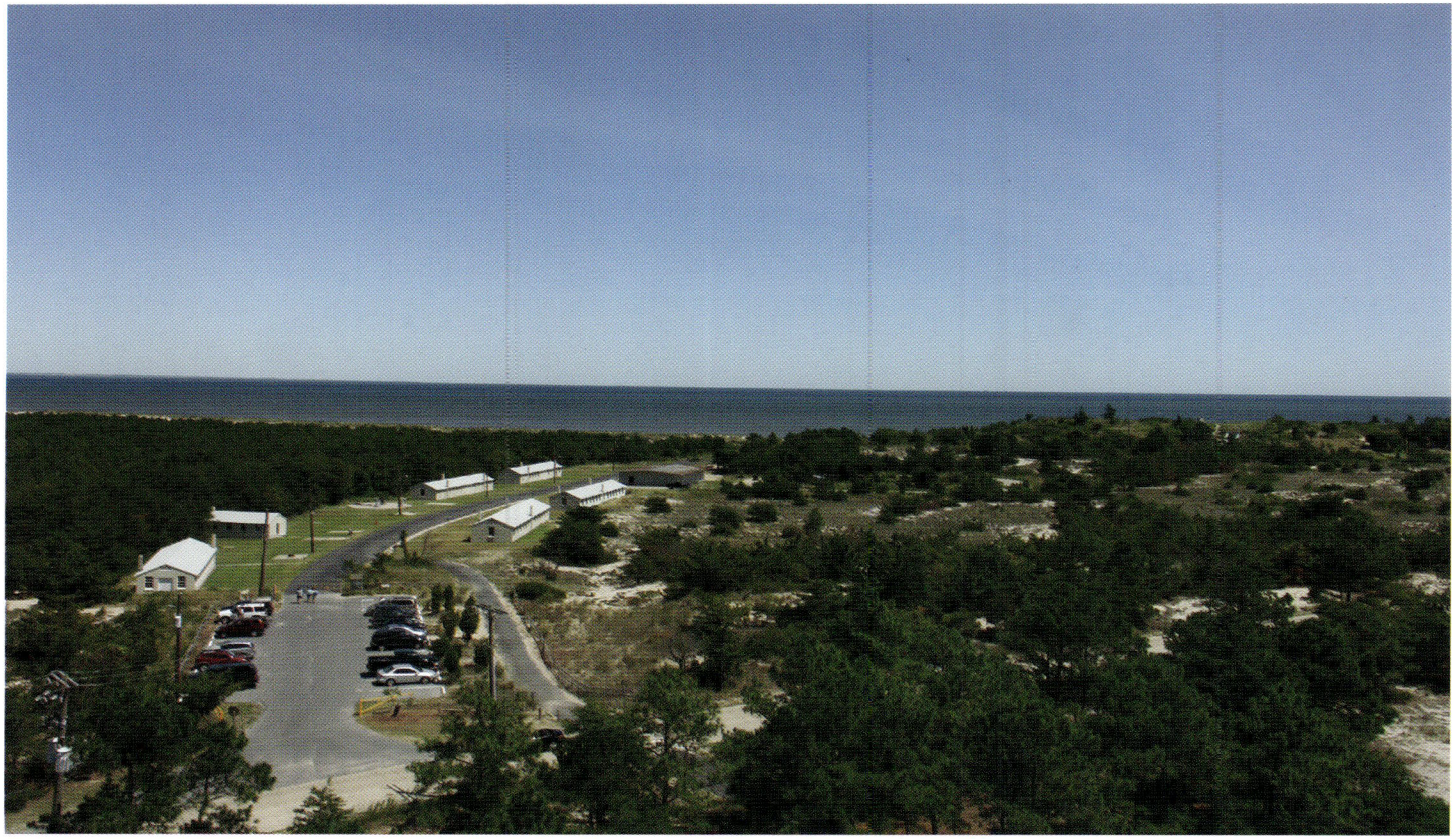

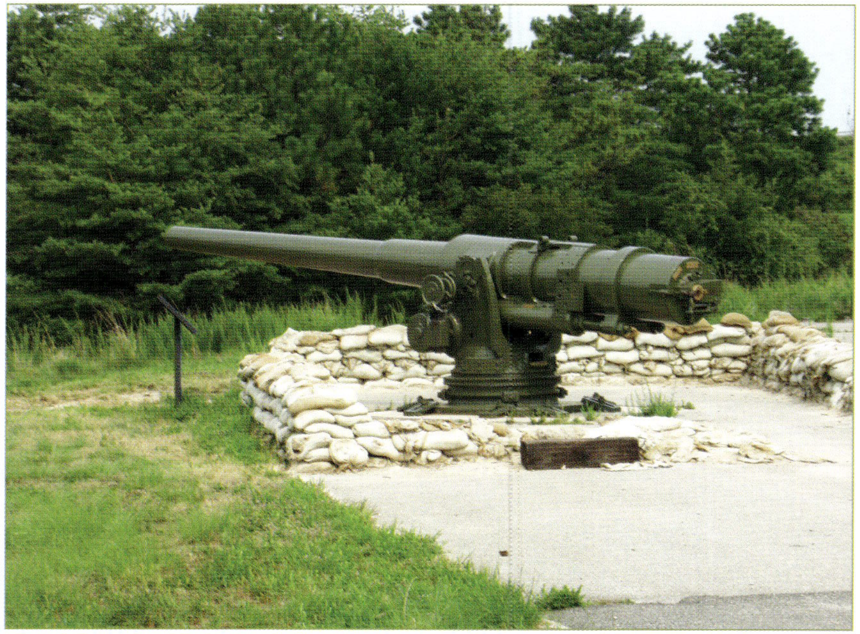

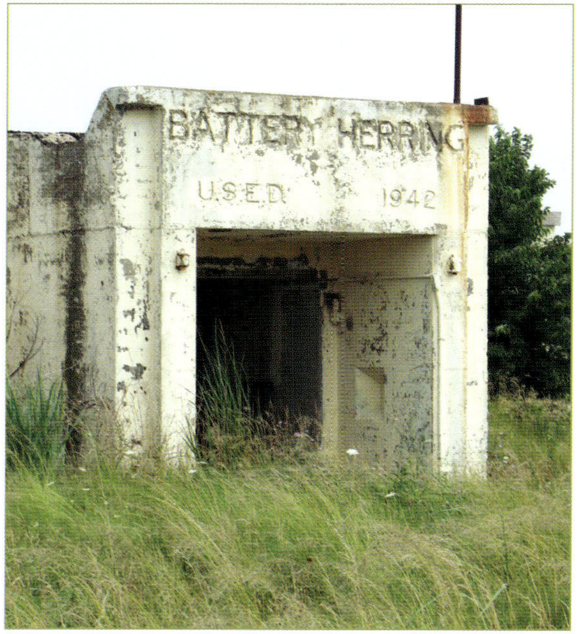

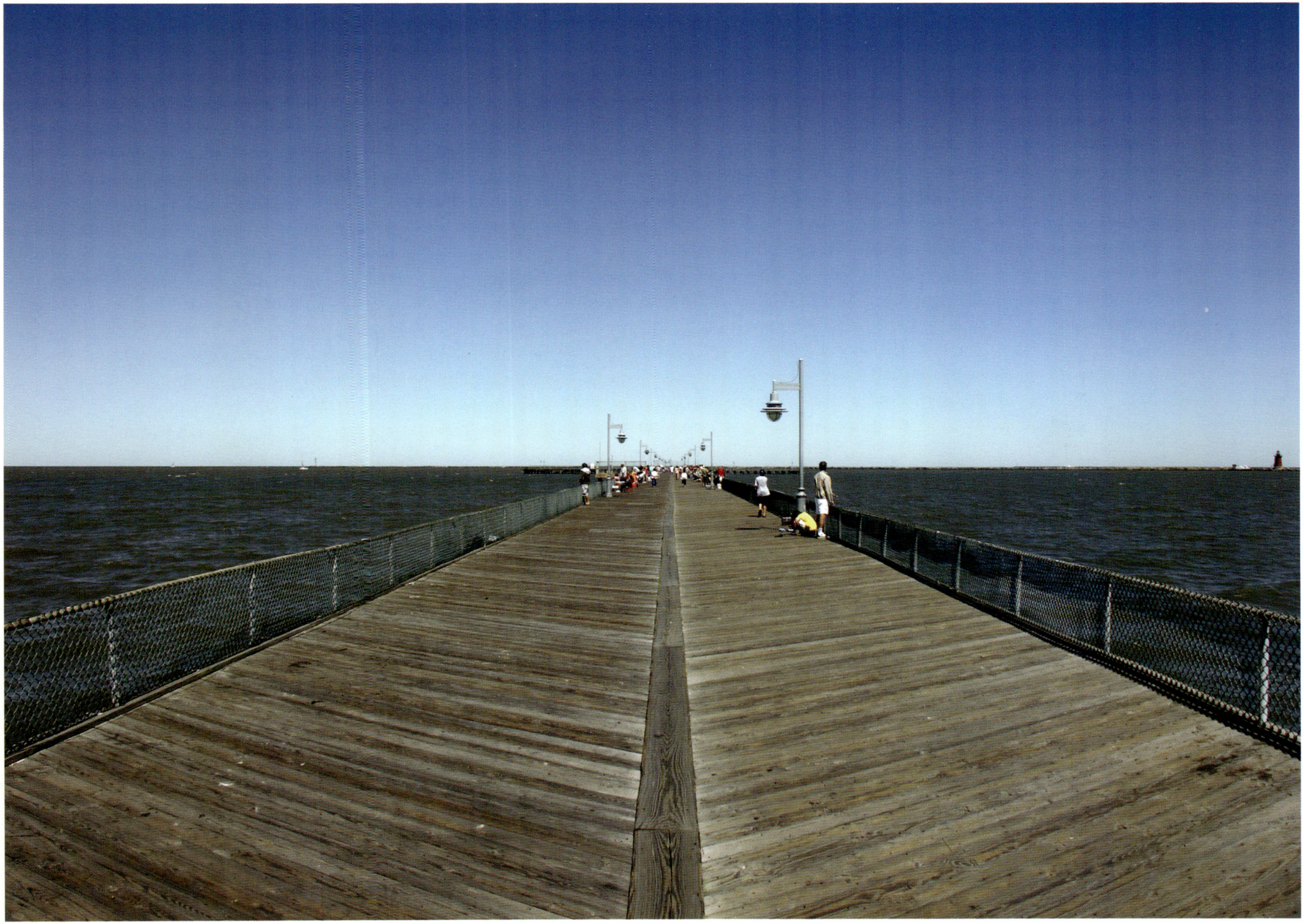

The Cape Henlopen Fishing Pier was constructed during World War II to help with the laying of mines in the Delaware Bay.

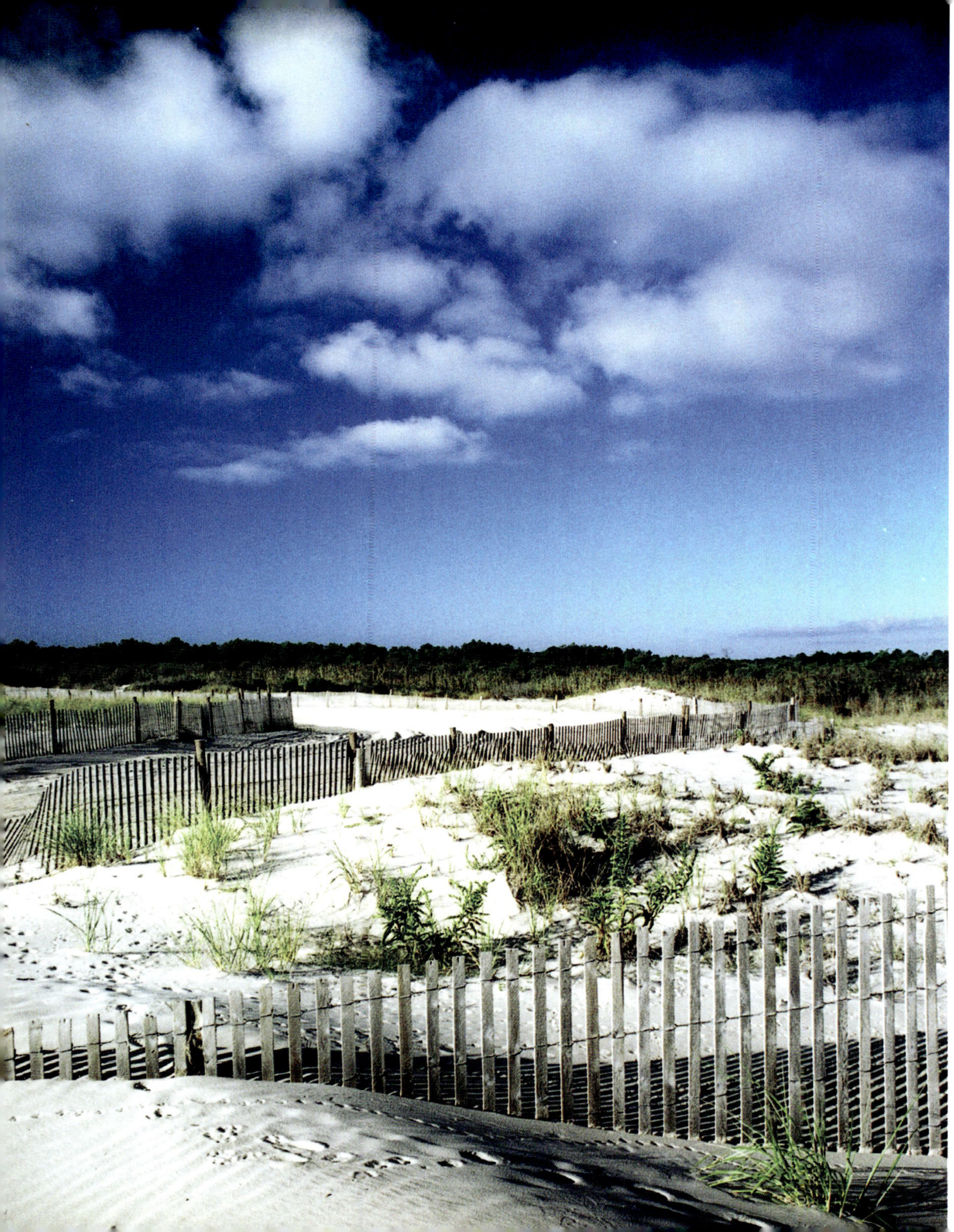

Cape Henlopen is famous for its dunes, including the Great Dune, which at 80-feet is the tallest dune between Cape Cod and Cape Hatteras. The park is also known for its "walking dunes," which shift with time.

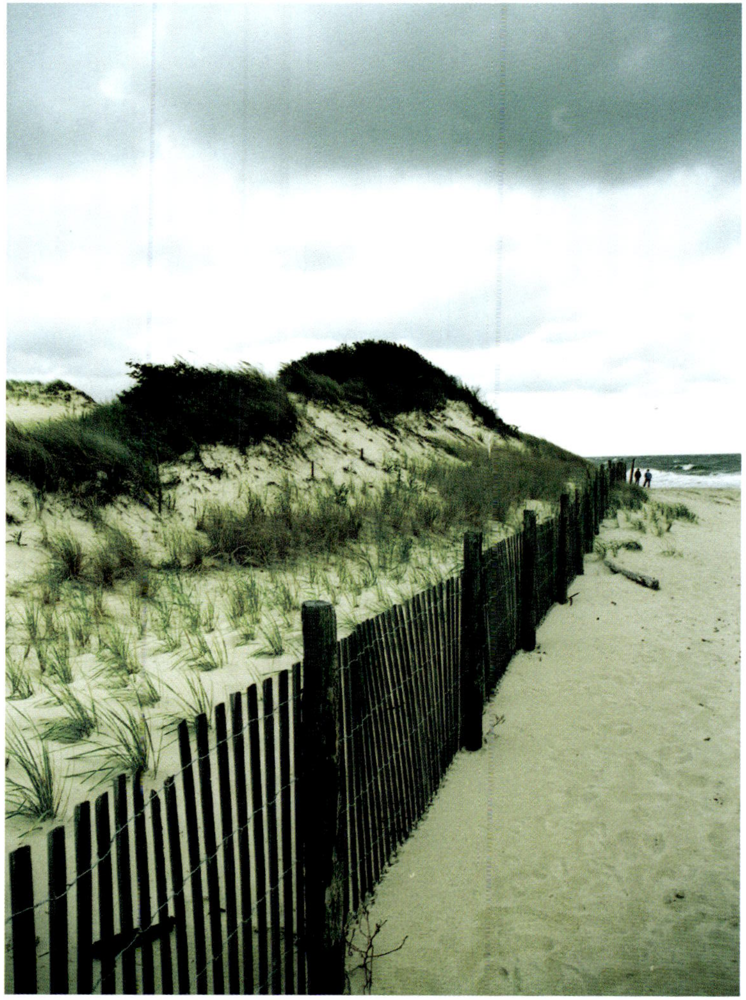

The Harbor of Refuge breakwater was constructed from 1897 to 1901, and temporary lights as well as a fog bell were placed upon it. In 1908, a lighthouse and keeper's house were built. Unfortunately, a severe 1920 storm damaged the lighthouse and washed away the keeper's house. The cast-iron Harbor of Refuge Lighthouse was placed in 1926 and automated in 1973. Today, the 76-foot tower is open for tours on special occasions.

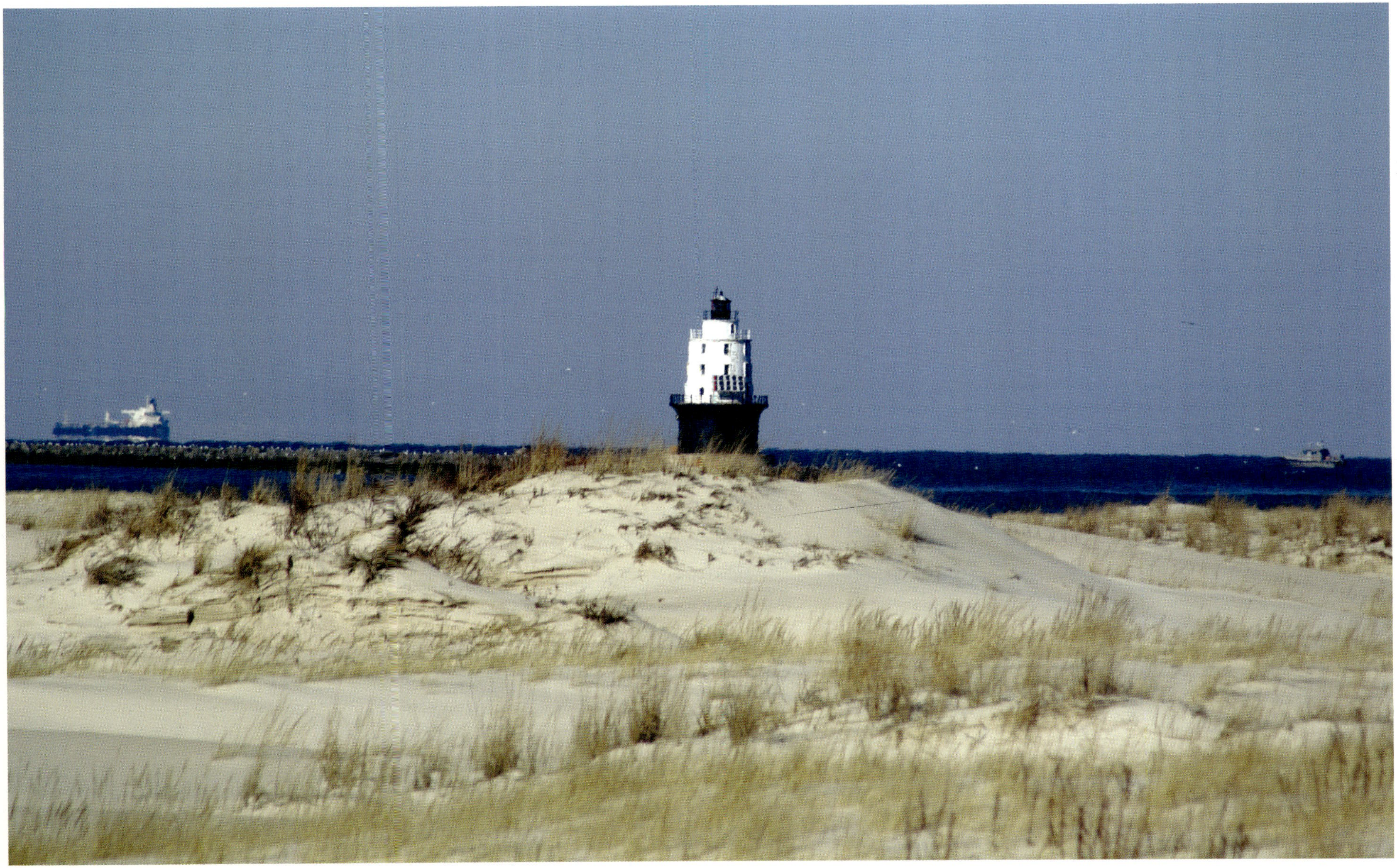

On July 1, 1964, the Cape May – Lewes Ferry made its inaugural voyage. The ferry was one of several Chesapeake Bay ferries purchased and refurbished for use on the Delaware Bay. Since that time, over 34 million passengers and 11 million vehicles have made the 17 mile, 80 minute trek. The ferries today are capable of holding up to 100 cars and 1,000 passengers. In 2001, new facilities were constructed at Lewes and Cape May, NJ.

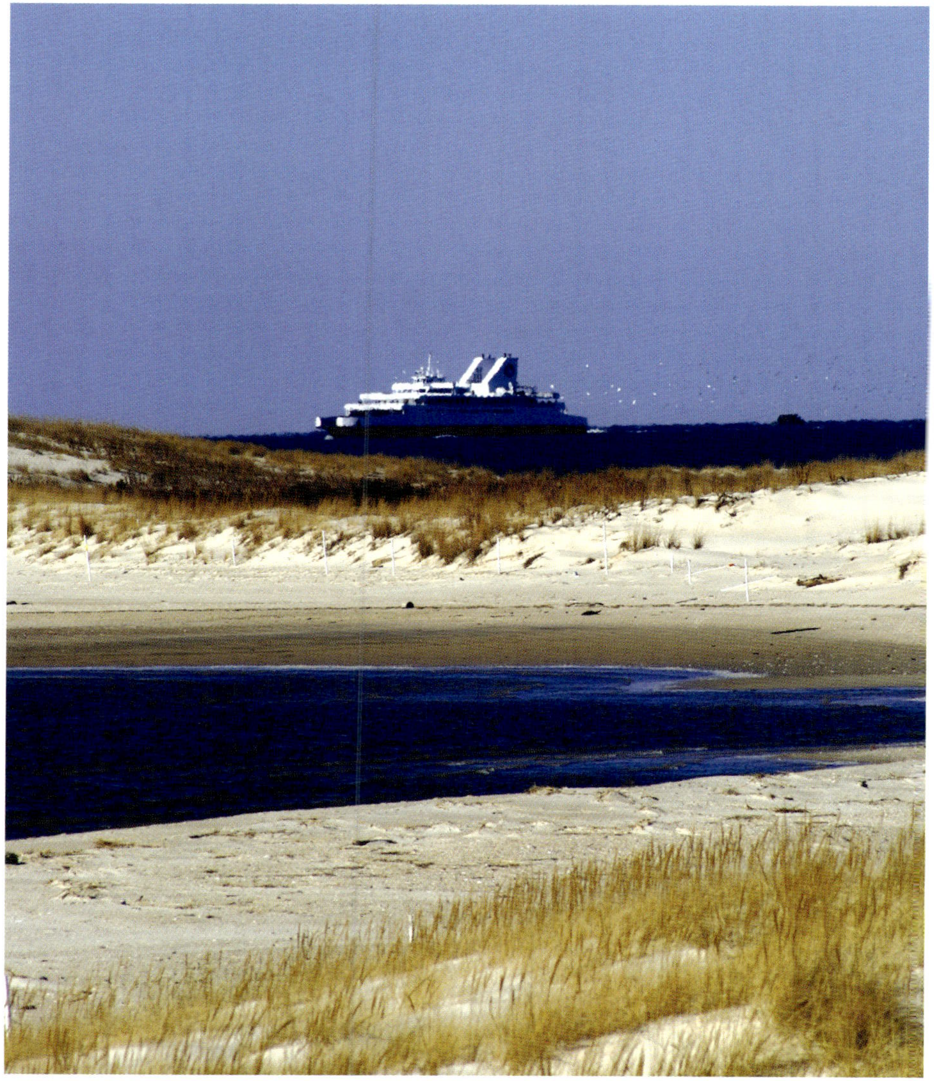

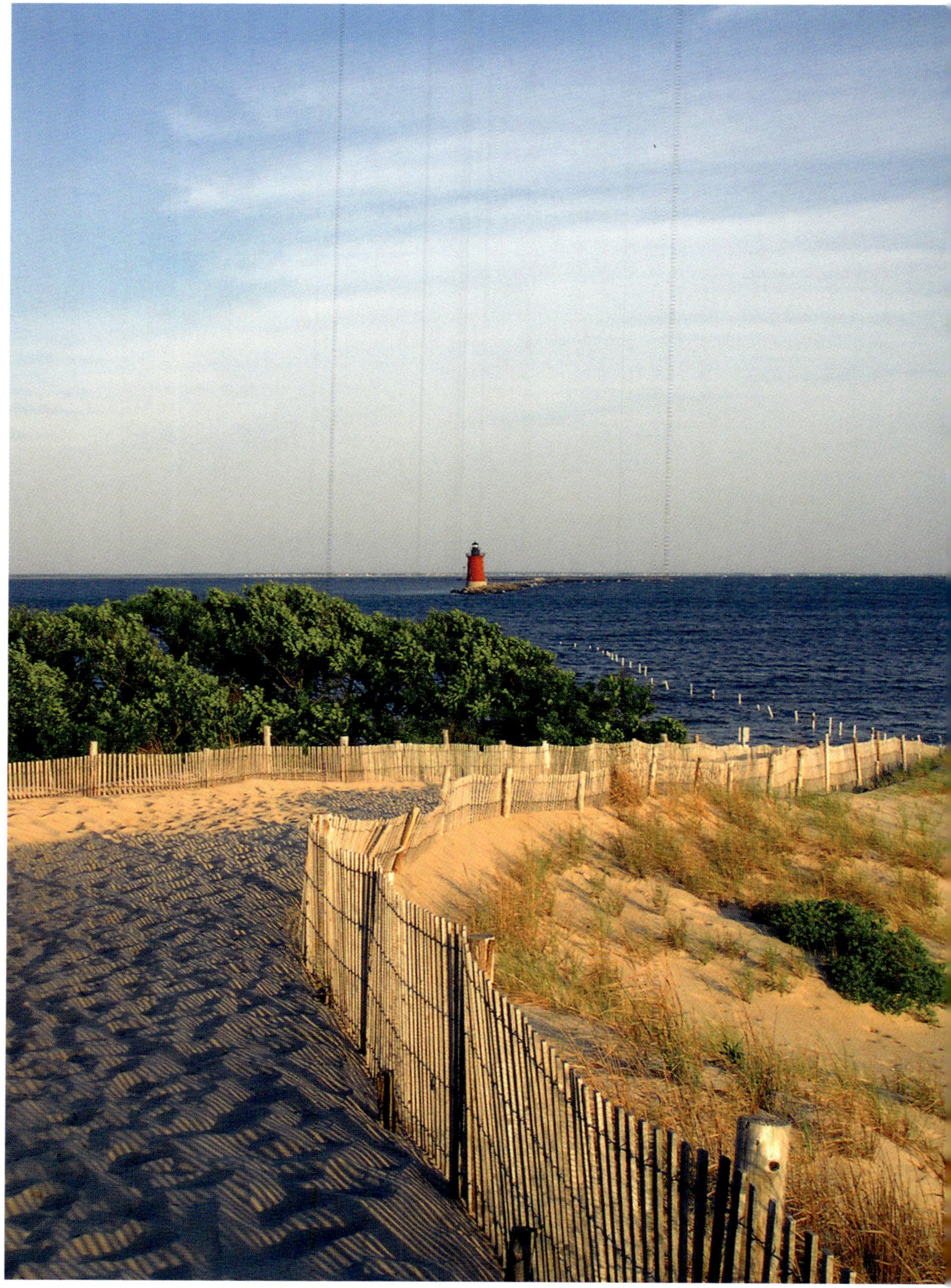

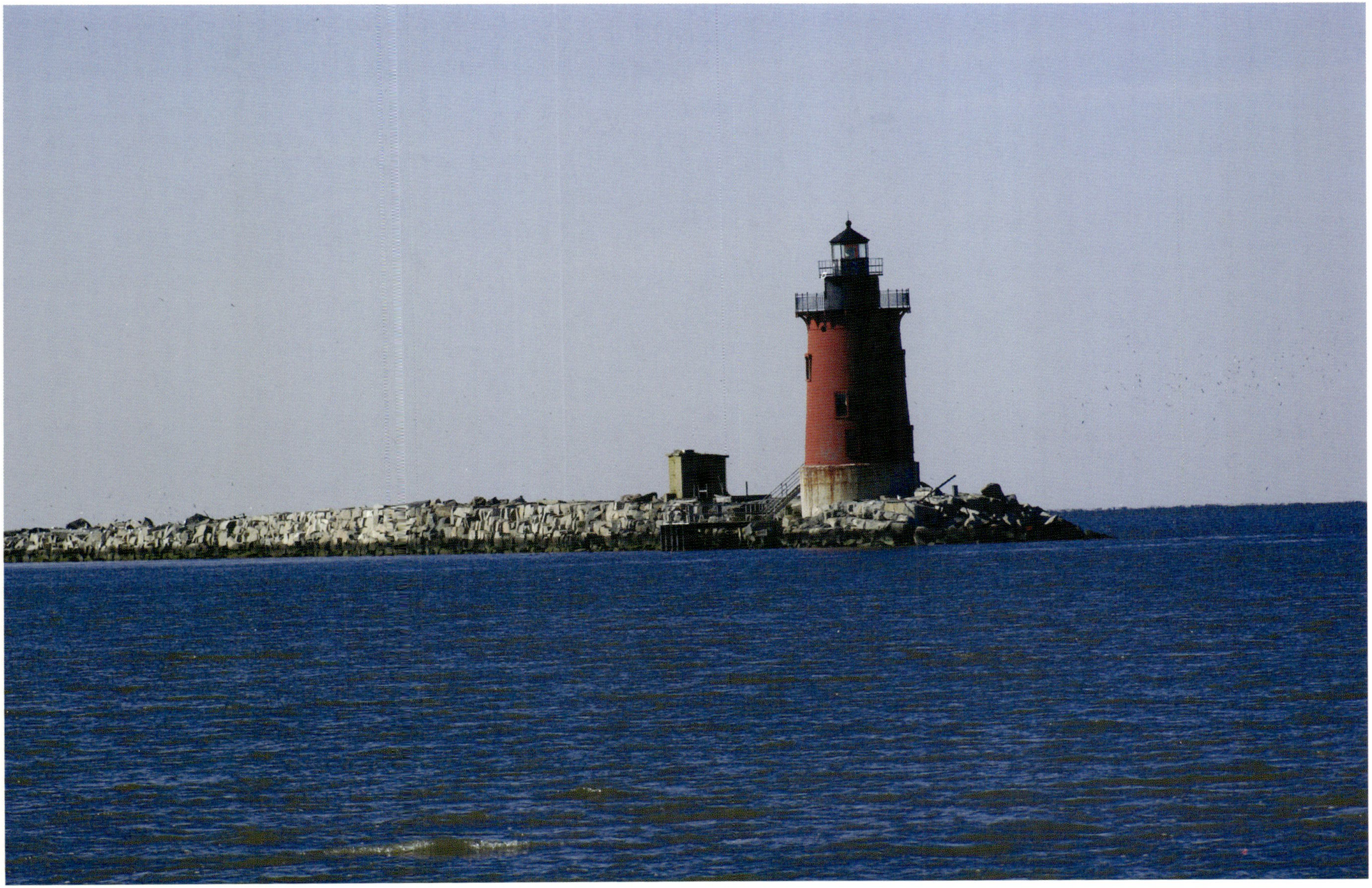

The 2,586-foot Delaware Breakwater was completed in 1869 and was one of the longest breakwaters in the world. Construction on the breakwater actually began in the late 1820s, and in 1849 a lighthouse was built on the western end. It was extinguished in 1903. The Delaware Breakwater East Lighthouse was constructed of brick in 1885. A wharf and oil house were built the following year. The Delaware River & Bay Lighthouse Foundation operates tours of the lighthouse and nearby Harbor of Refuge Lighthouse.

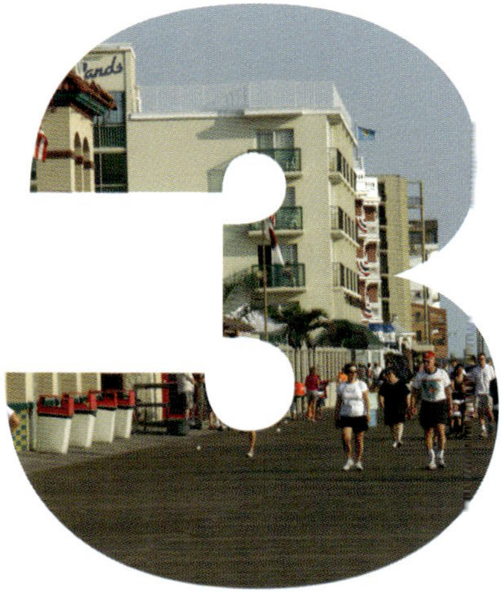

Rehoboth Beach: *The Nation's Summer Capital*

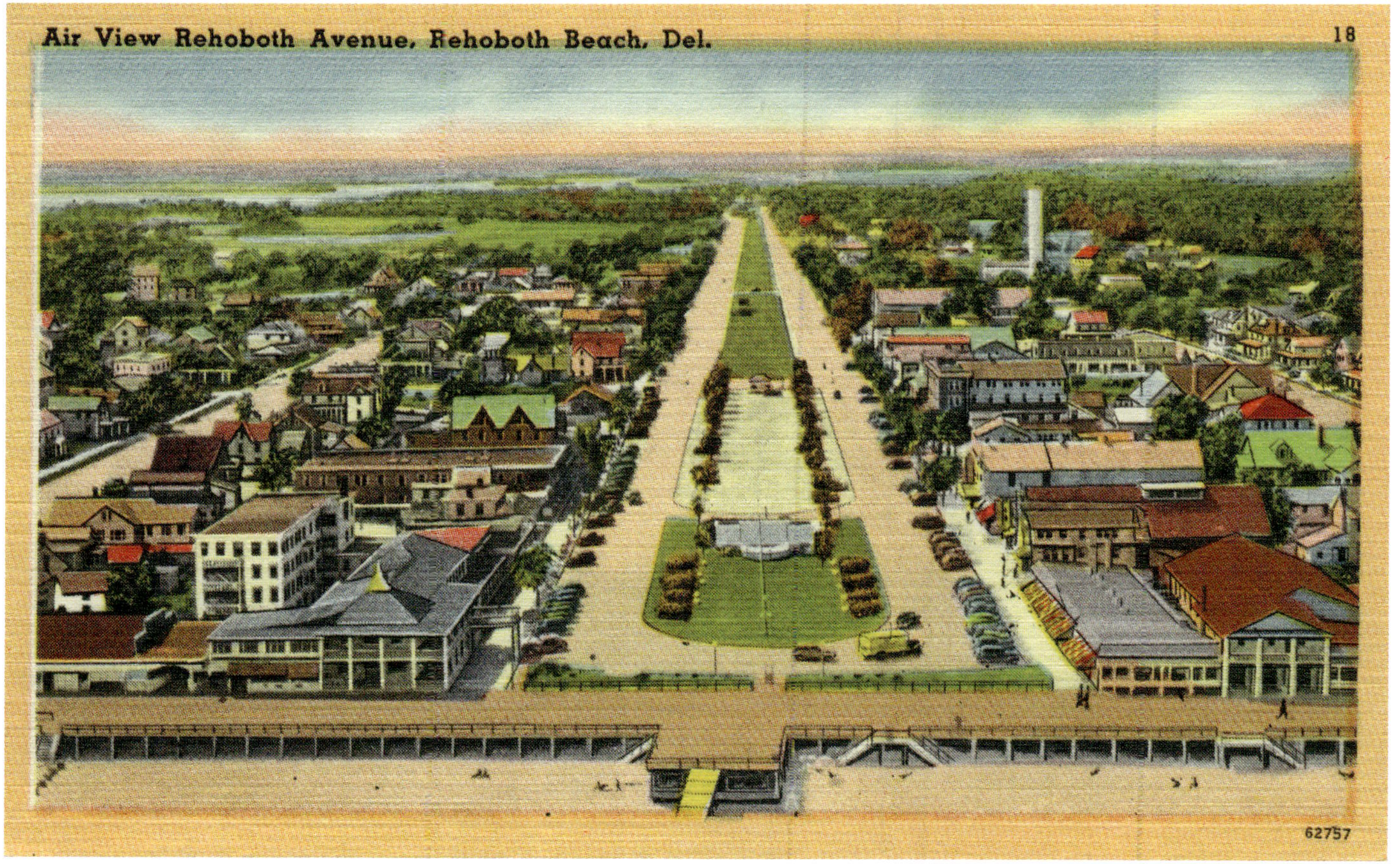

Today known as "The Nation's Summer Capital," Rehoboth Beach is rooted in humble beginnings. Rev. Robert Todd of the Wilmington, Delaware St. Paul's Methodist Episcopal Church, worked to establish the Rehoboth Beach Camp Meeting Association. Small, single-room wooden structures known as tents were built, as was a short wooden boardwalk – the first of many to occupy this stretch of the Delaware coast. The inspiration for this new retreat was a similar one in Ocean Grove, New Jersey.

In 1878, the railroad arrived from Lewes, allowing the fledging retreat camp to expand. By 1891 the community had grown enough to be incorporated. It was named Cape Henlopen City. Two years later the name was changed to Rehoboth.

It was also in 1893 that work on a canal began. By 1916, the Lewes & Rehoboth Canal was open, connecting the young town with Delaware's oldest town. A pier was constructed in 1903, reaching 150-feet into the ocean. Its days were numbered, however; a severe storm in 1914 destroyed both the pier and the boardwalk. The latter was soon rebuilt.

A drawbridge was built over the Lewes & Rehoboth Canal in 1925, and twelve years later the town of Rehoboth became the City of Rehoboth Beach. As a popular vacation spot, the community prospered. Mother Nature showed two sides to the town. Her sun baked the beaches in copper hues, proving irresistible to city residents looking for a summer escape; however, her winds occasionally churned up an angry ocean, totally destroying the boardwalk in 1962 and causing extensive damage again in 1992.

But the wooden boards have been replaced, again and again. And though the beaches may slowly seep to the sea floor, they are continually replenished as the ocean gives then takes away then gives again.

Today, Rehoboth Beach has the reputation of an arts community filled with creative residents and visitors. In May 2006, *Reader's Digest* named the Rehoboth boardwalk "Best of America" for seaside strolls with "views of bright blue water and shops galore." The AARP also recognized the community's charms, selecting it as one of the "Best Places to Retire."

The heart of Rehoboth Beach is its mile-long boardwalk that parallels the Atlantic coast. Hotels of all shapes and sizes line the boardwalk, and a large bandstand marks the intersection of the boardwalk and Rehoboth Avenue, the retail district of Rehoboth Beach.

The name Rehoboth translates as "room for all," something for which the town prides itself. So in Rehoboth, you'll find lots of "all" – all types of lodging, from large resorts to quaint bed and breakfast inns; all types of shopping, from local chains to distinctive stores and galleries; and all types of dining, from traditional crabhouses to four-star restaurants.

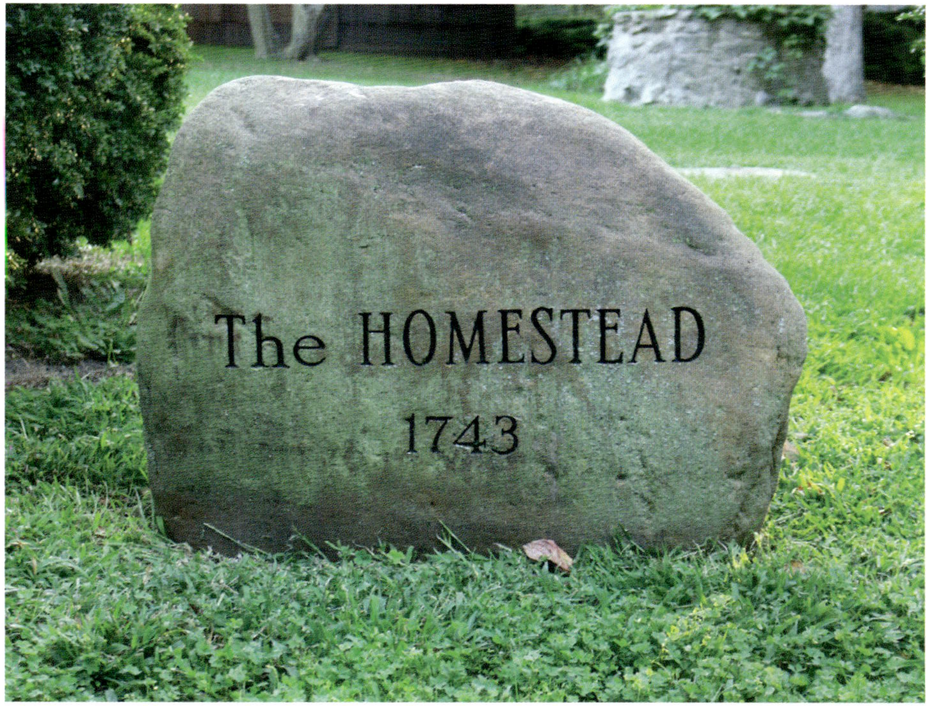

The Rehoboth Art League was founded in 1938 and acquired the Homestead property in 1978. The Homestead was constructed in 1743 by Peter Marsh, making it one of the oldest buildings in the Rehoboth Beach area.

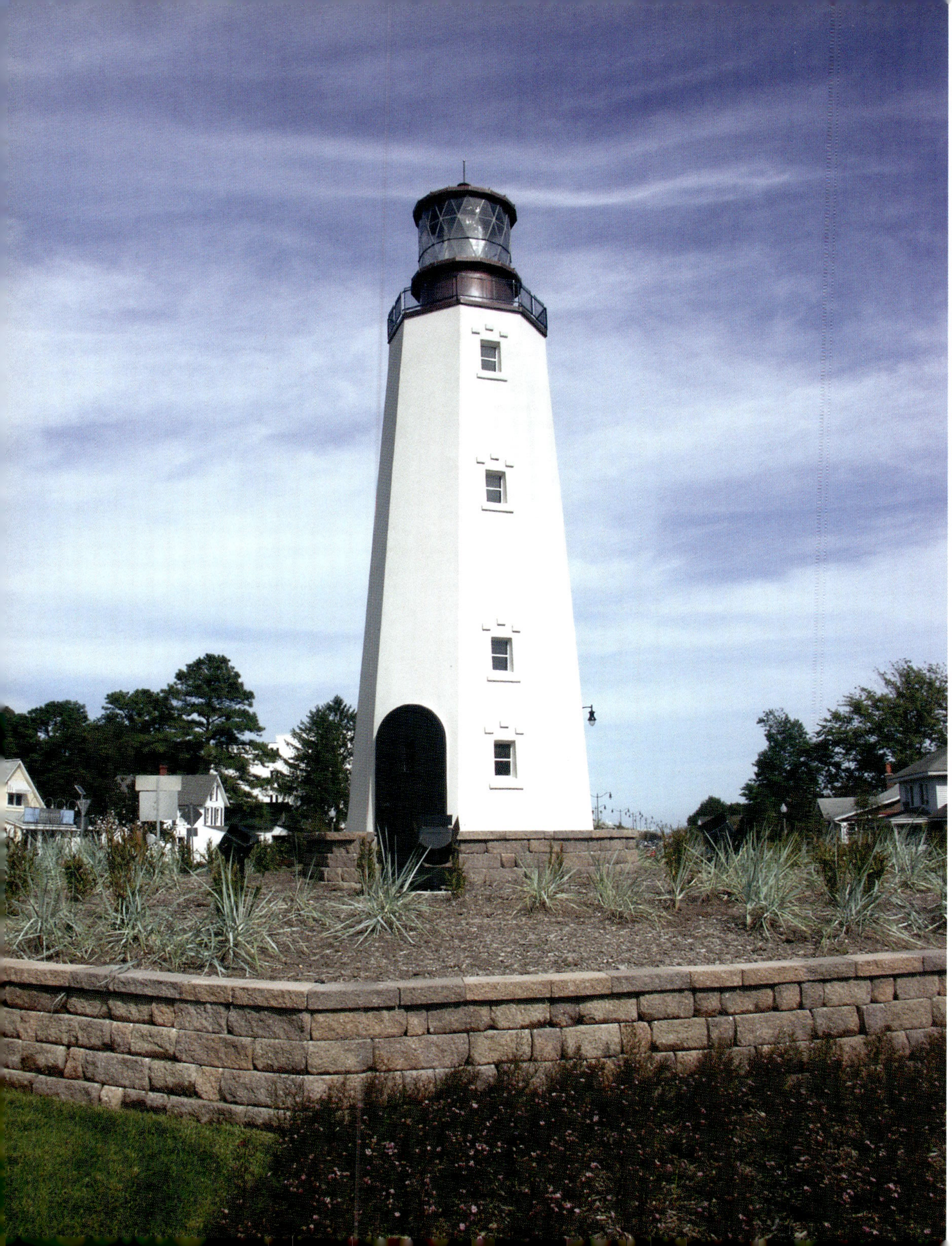

This reduced-size replica of the Cape Henlopen Lighthouse stands in a traffic roundabout that was completed in 2004 as part of a major streetscape enhancement project. Today the lighthouse serves as a gateway into Rehoboth Beach.

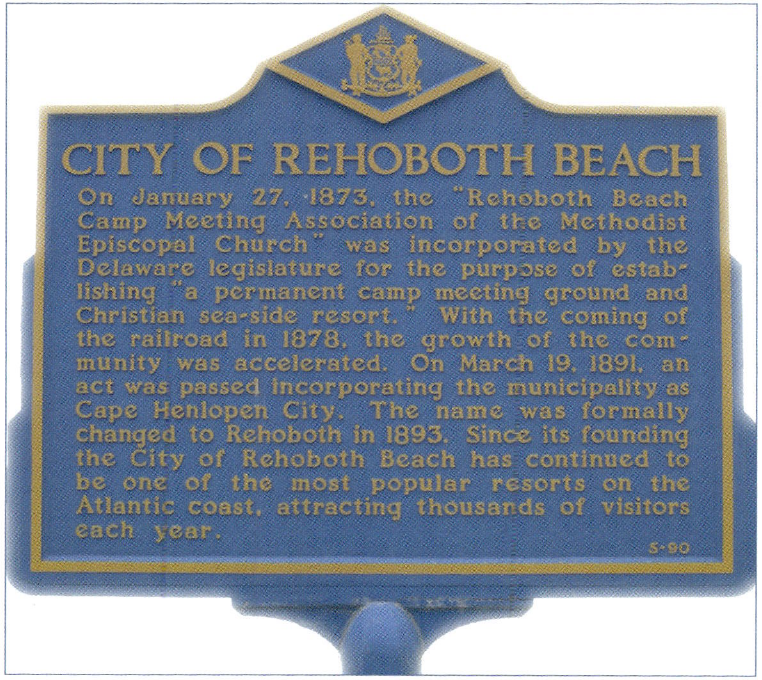

Rehoboth Beach dates to 1873 when the Rehoboth Beach Camp Meeting Association was chartered. In 1891 the town was chartered as Cape Henlopen City, though the name was changed to Rehoboth two years later.

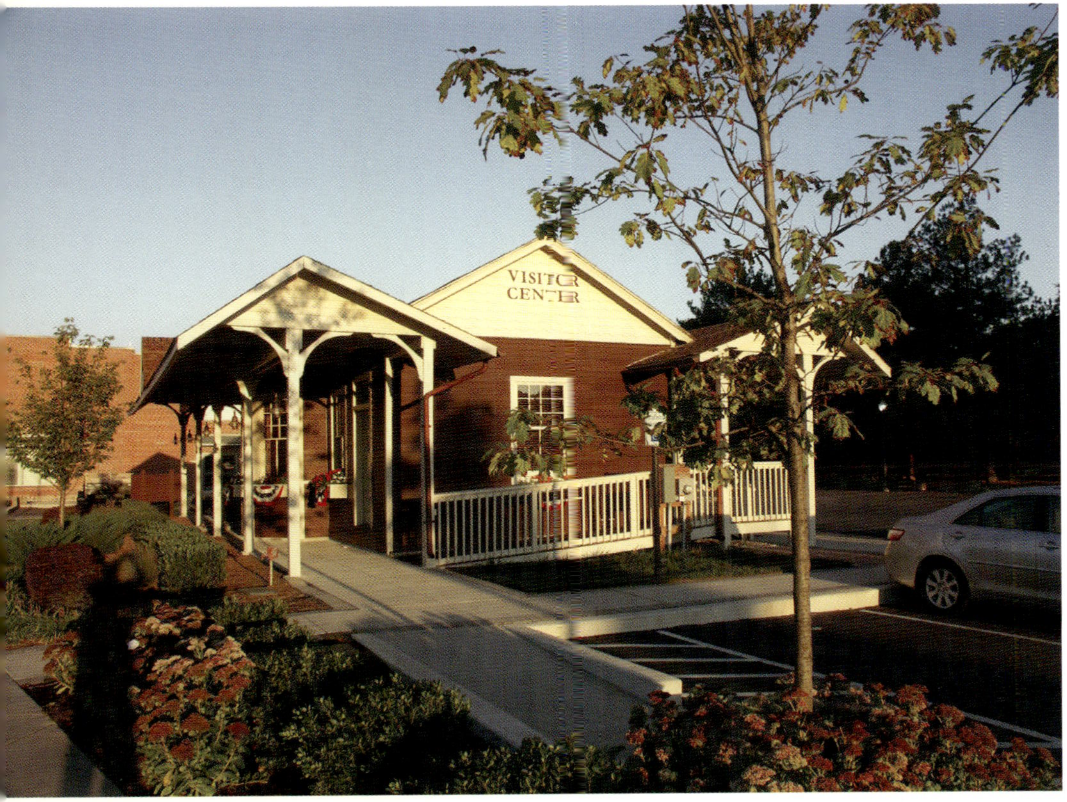

This attractive railroad station was built in 1879 and has been relocated several times over the years. Passenger and freight railroad service first arrived in Rehoboth in 1878. Today, the railroad station is home to the Rehoboth Beach-Dewey Beach Chamber of Commerce and a visitors center.

The Anna Hazzard Museum is located in one of the original "tent" houses constructed for the Rehoboth Beach Camp Meeting Association. A tent house was a one-room, wood-framed building. Ten tent houses were originally constructed. Anna Hazzard, a civic leader, once owned this property.

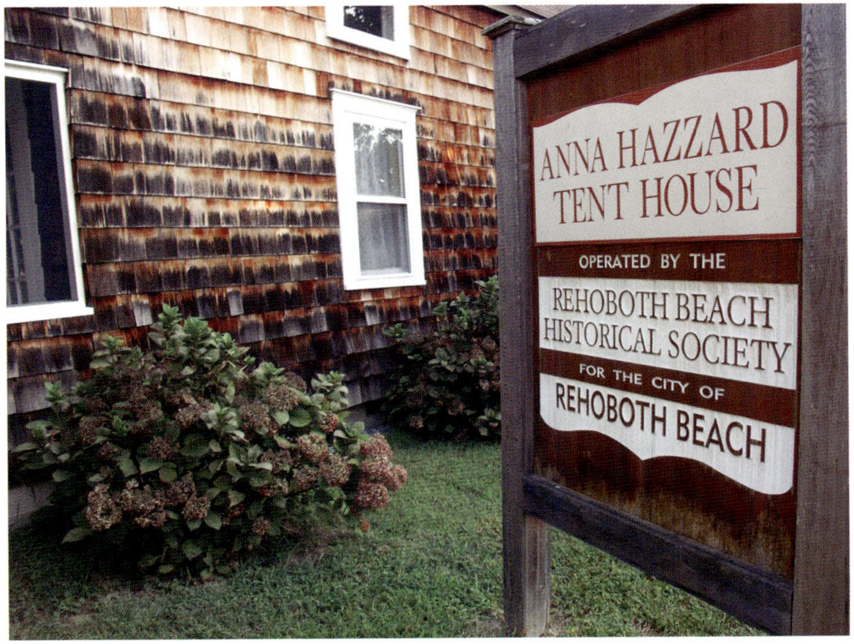

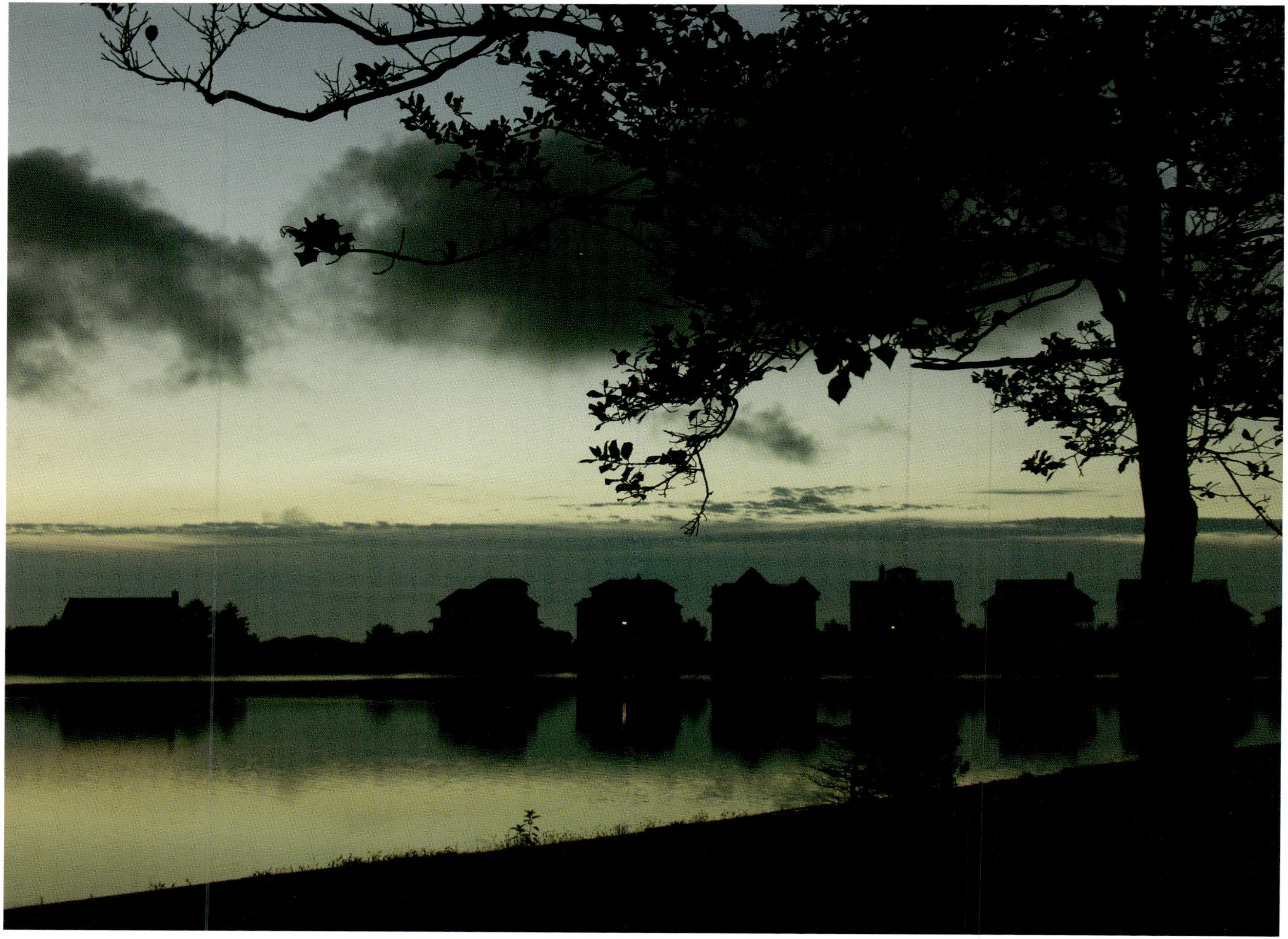

Silver Lake shimmers in the pre-dawn light, silhouetting the beachfront homes.

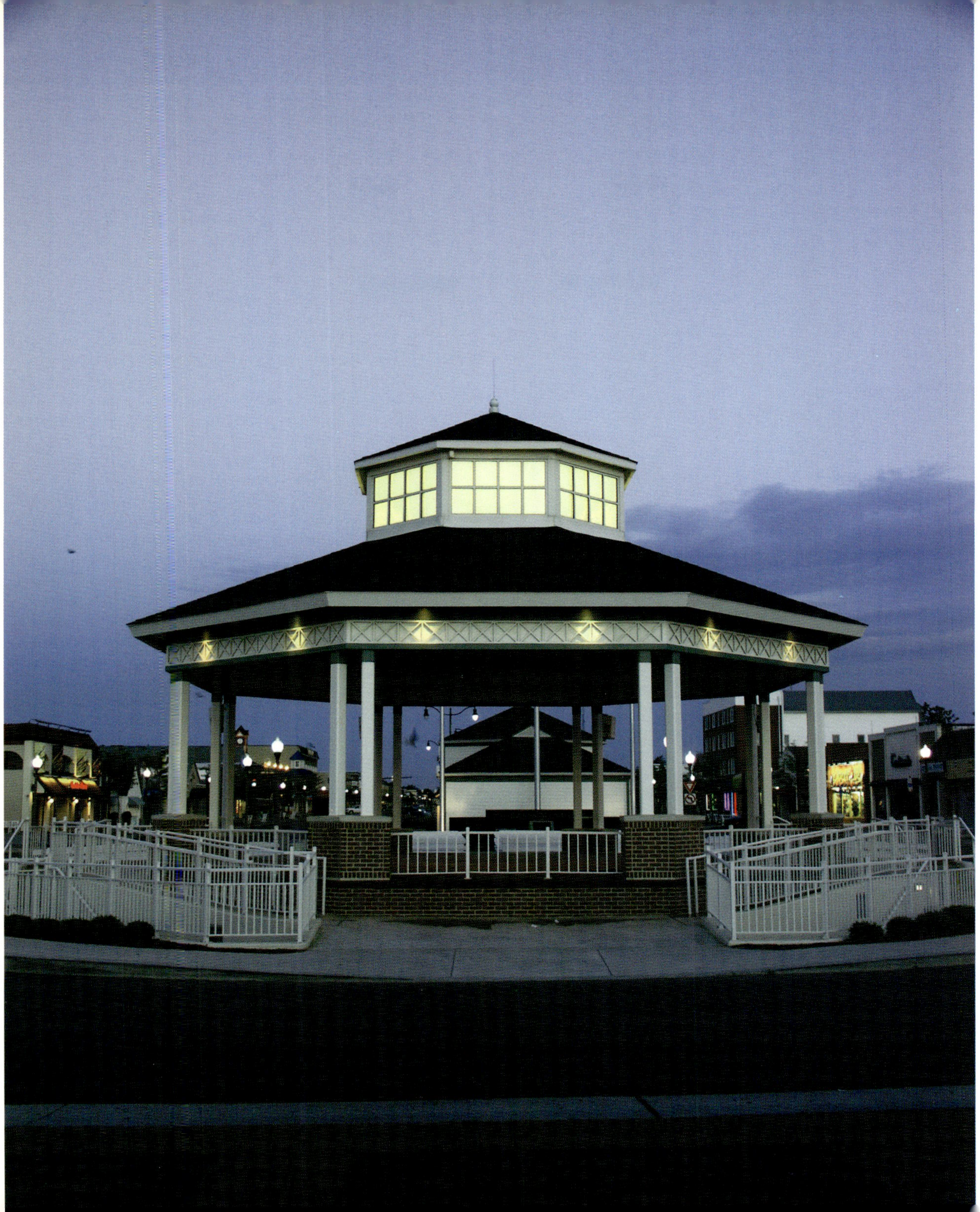

The "Pavilion" was constructed in 2005-2006 as part of a major $34 million streetscape enhancement project along Rehoboth Avenue. Replacing an earlier bandstand, the structure is still known as the Rehoboth Beach Bandstand.

Dawn arrives at Rehoboth Beach. Every minute offers a different color, a different cloud formation, or a different reflection in the ocean as the dawn gives way to an effervescent sunrise.

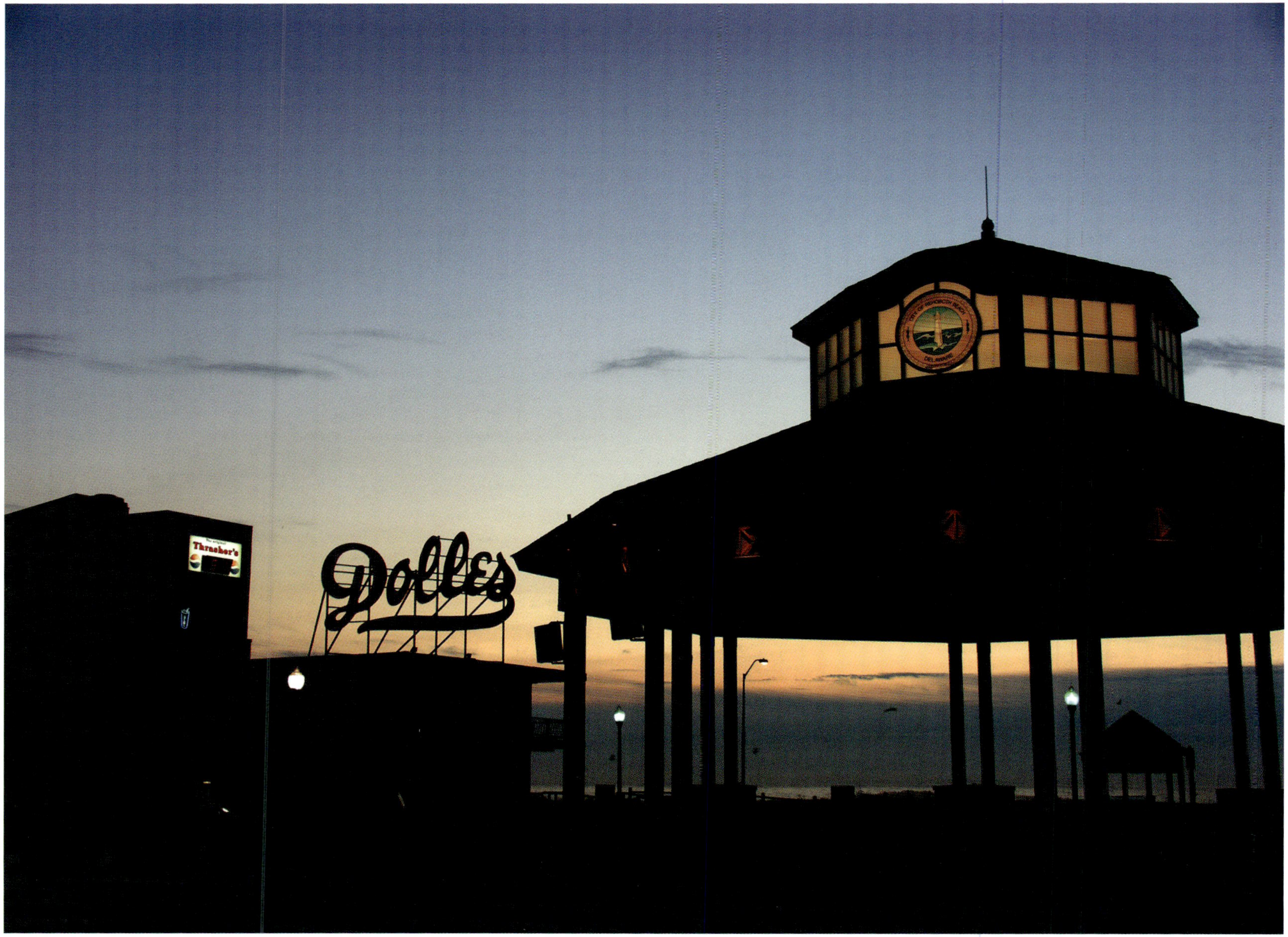

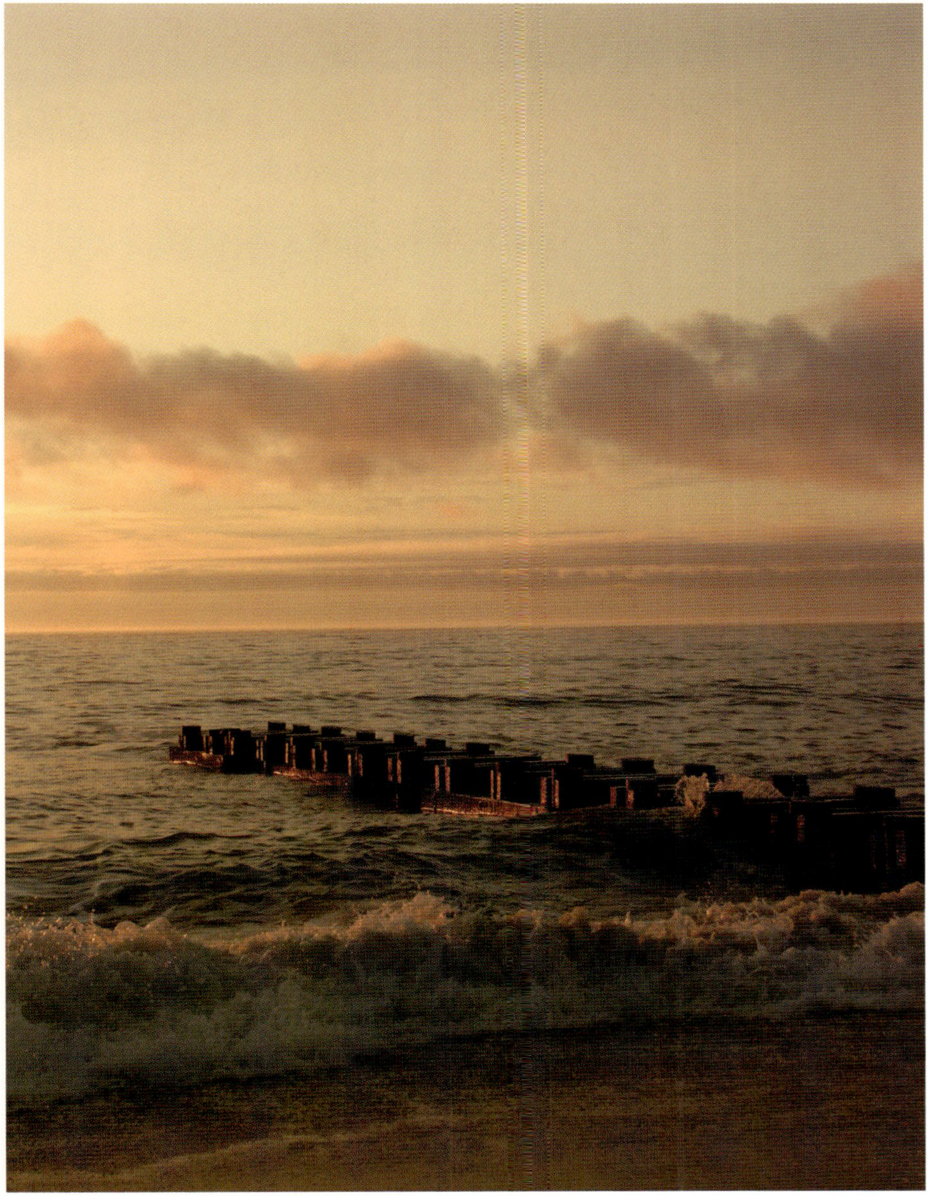

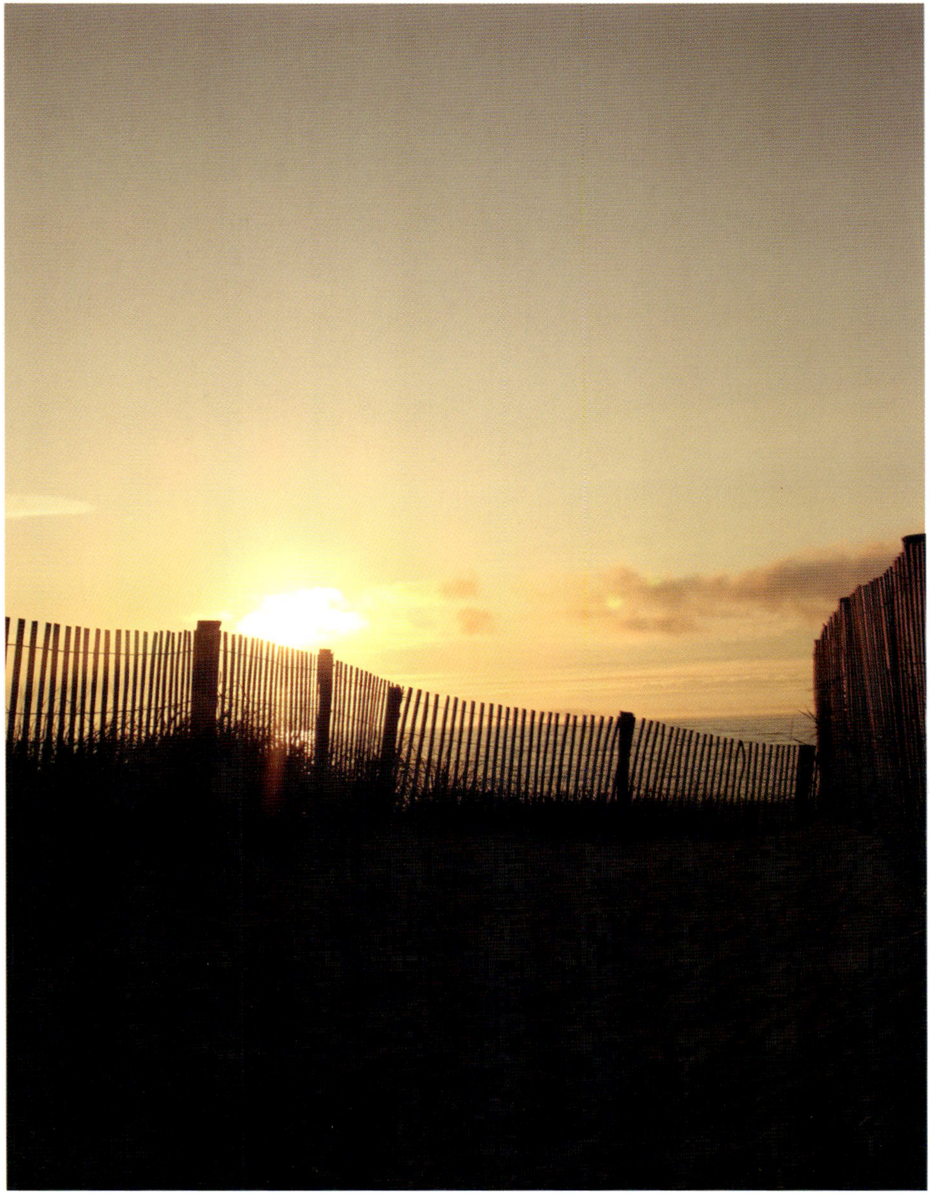

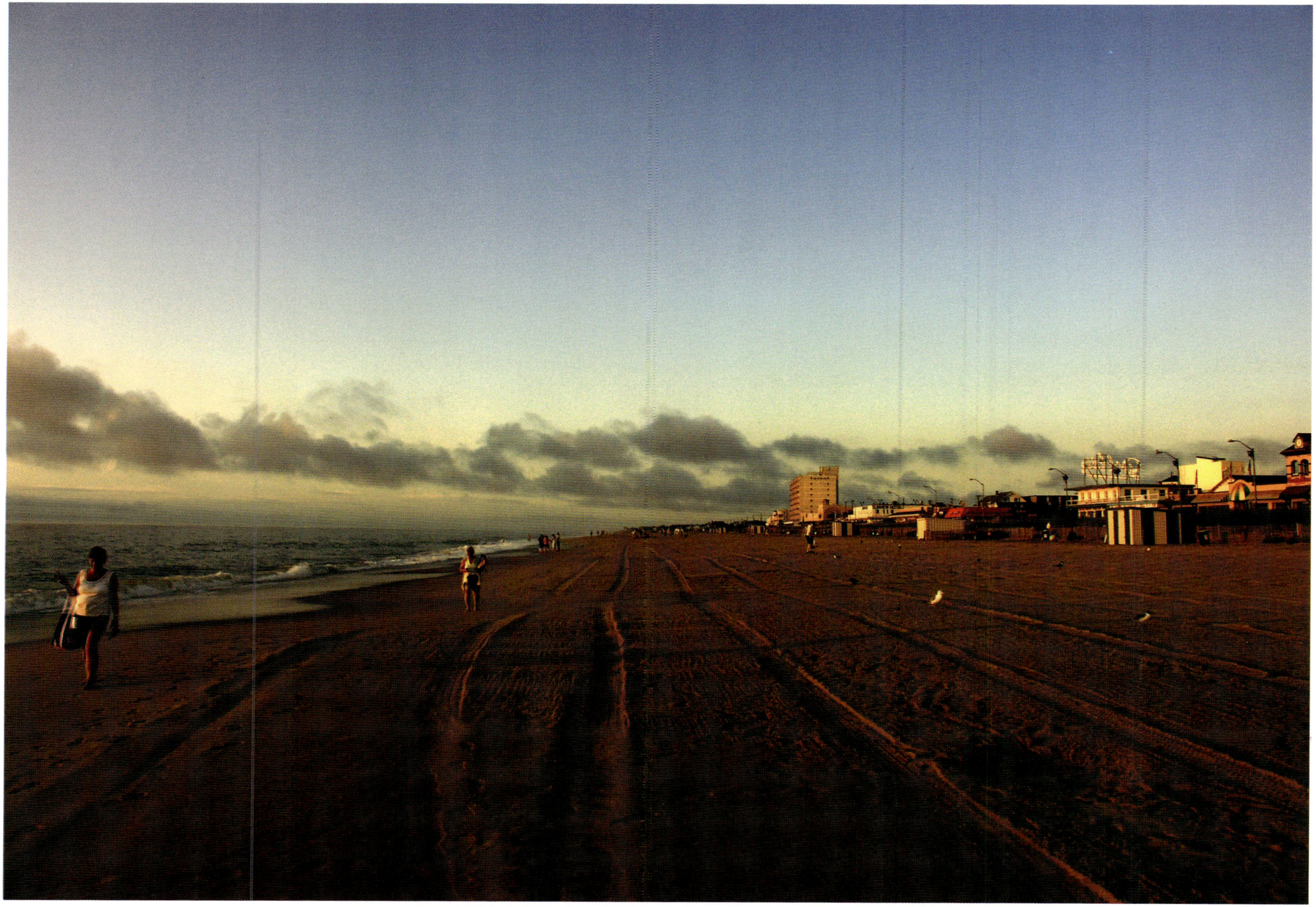

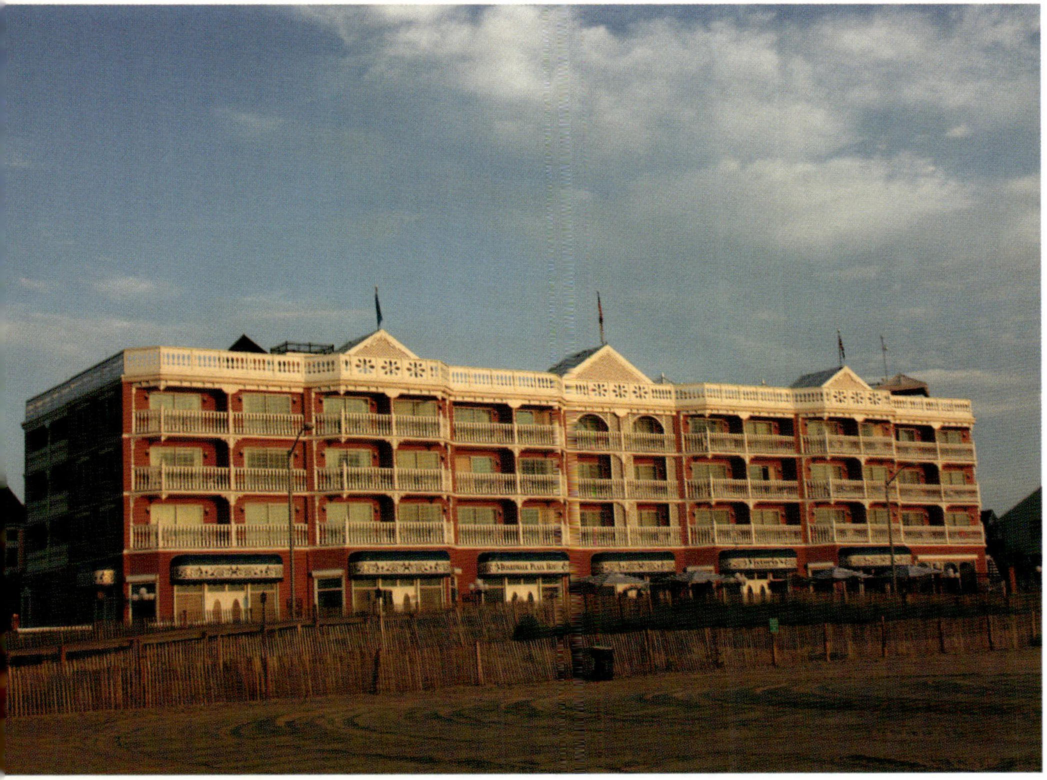

The Boardwalk Plaza Hotel offers a touch of Victorian Charm with spectacular seaside views.

The Rehoboth Beach Boardwalk has a long and storied history, dating to 1873 when the first boardwalk was constructed. It was built of 8-ft. wide wood planks and was 1,000 yards in length. Today, the boardwalk is "The Best of America" according to *Reader's Digest* magazine.

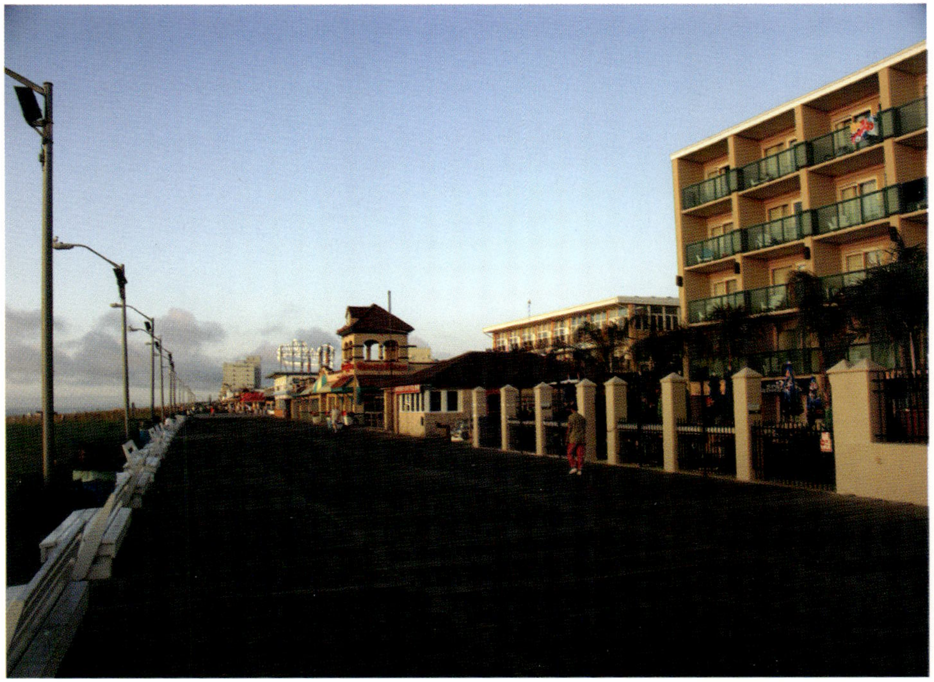

Sunrise over Rehoboth Beach. Pastel reds and oranges blend with golden rays and chalk blue skies, creating a kaleidoscope of color.

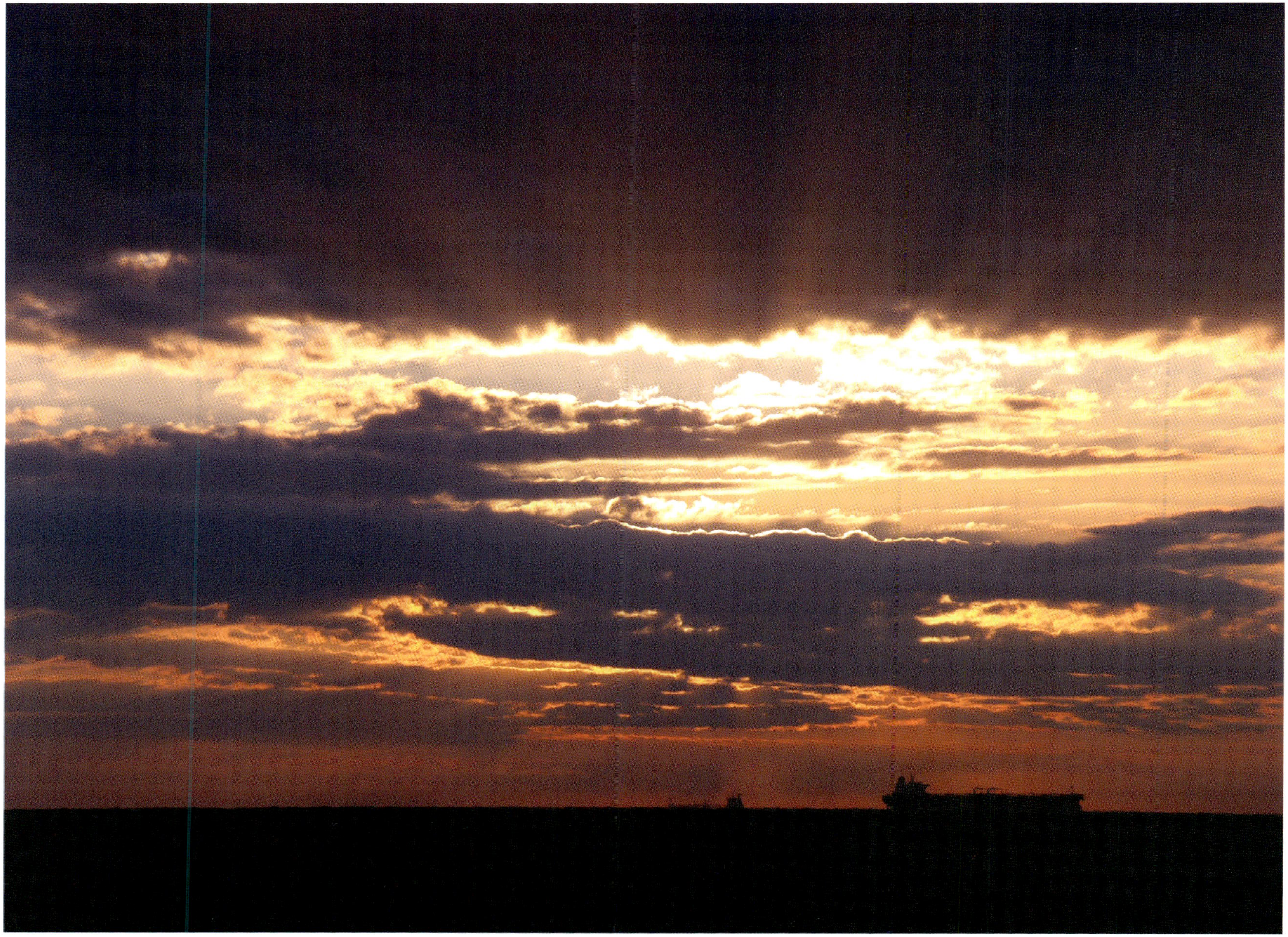

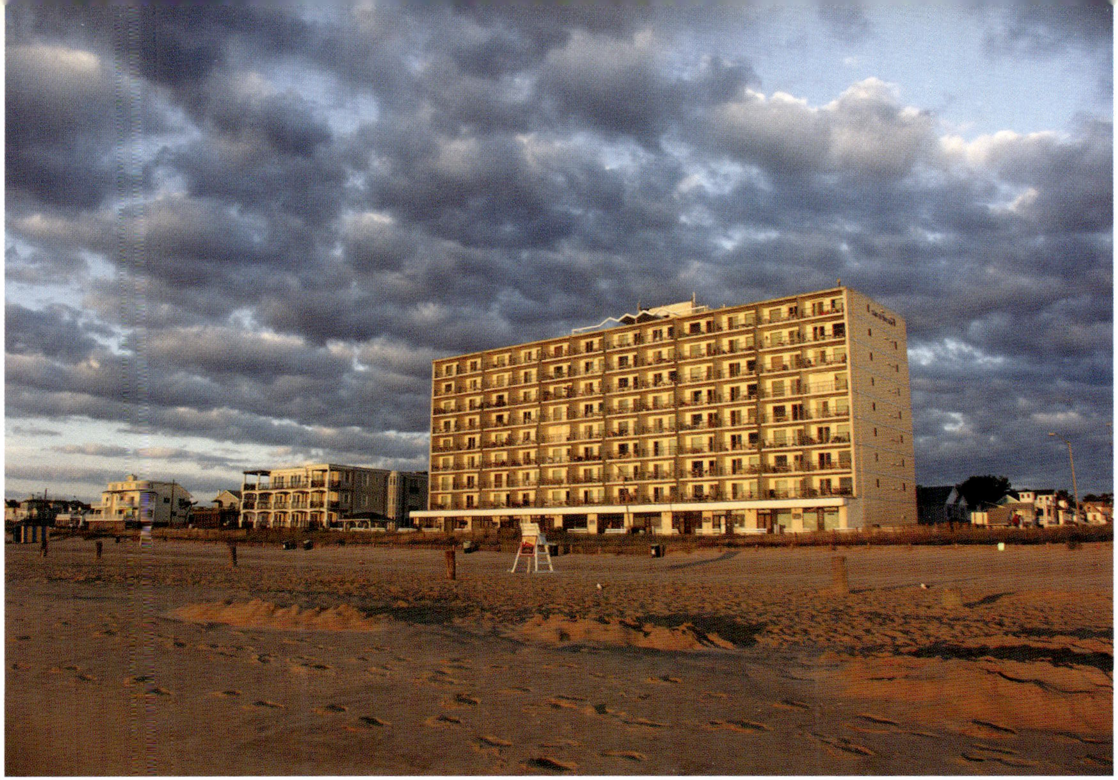

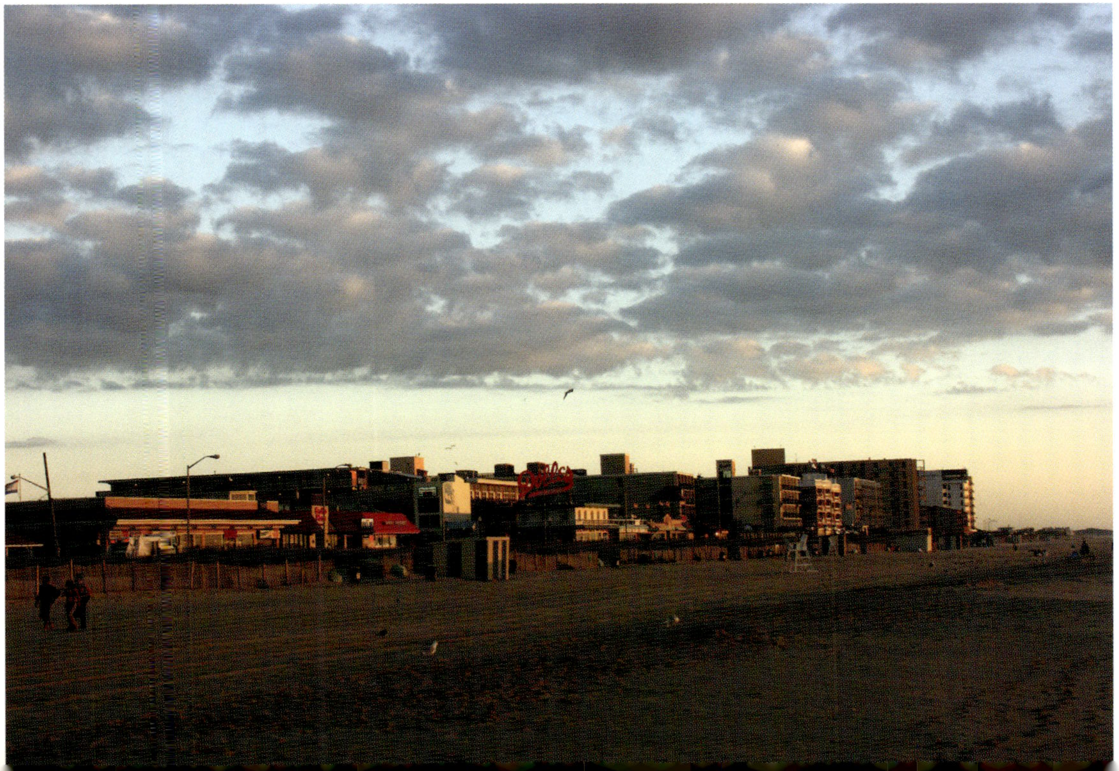

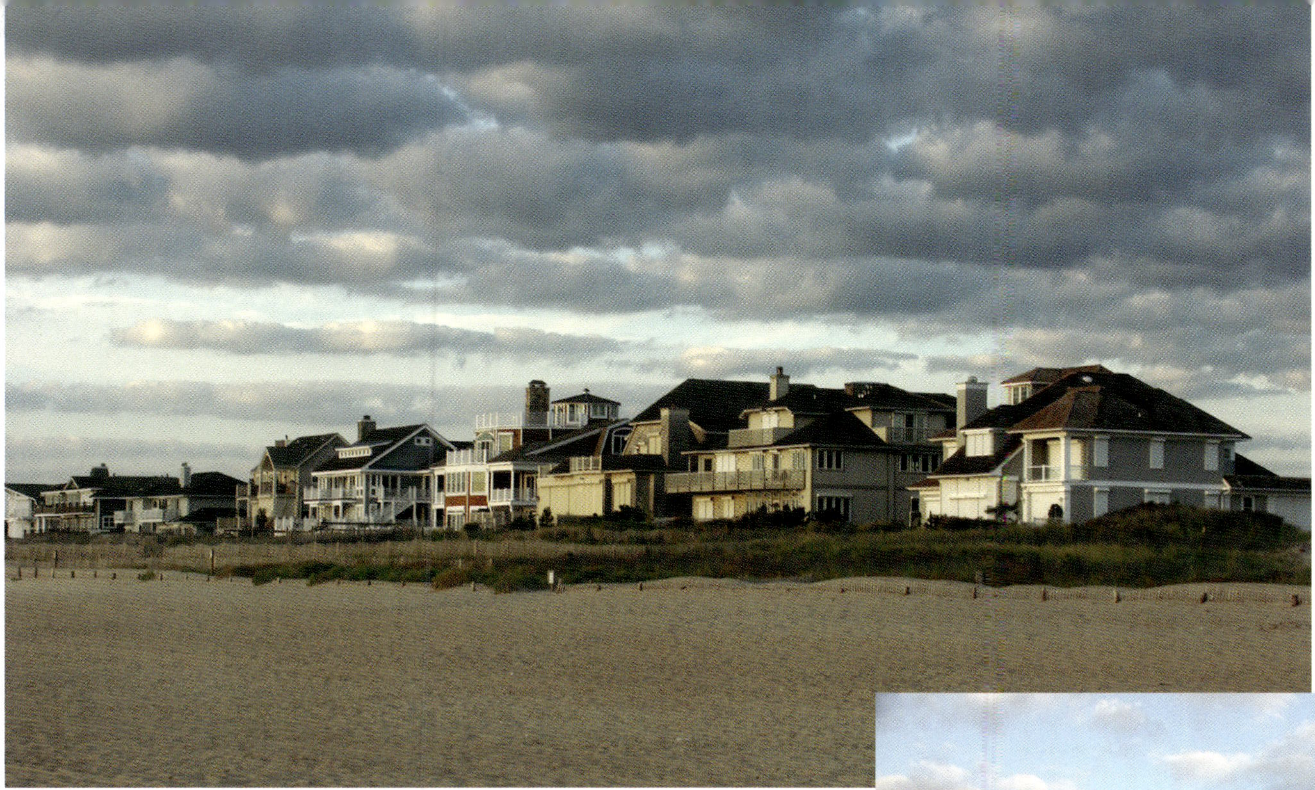

Beautiful beachfront houses located south of the boardwalk combine seaside architecture of the past and the present with stunning ocean views.

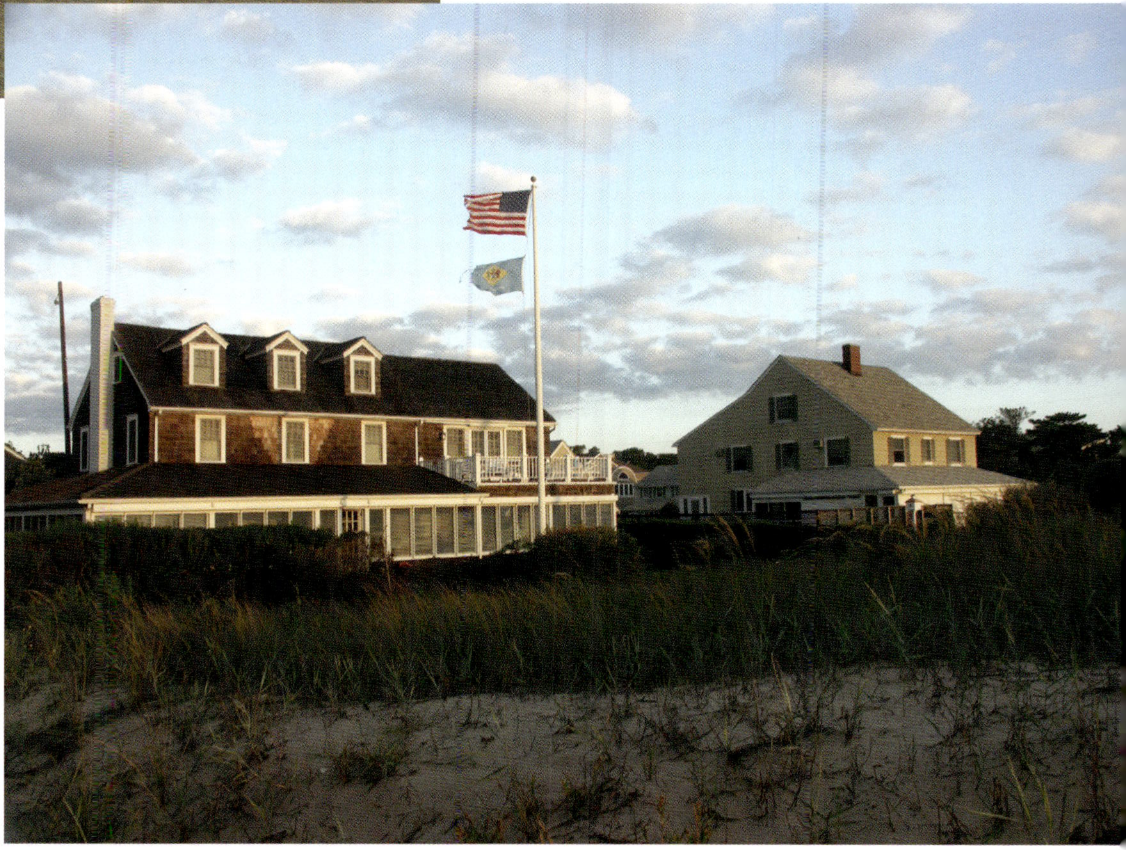

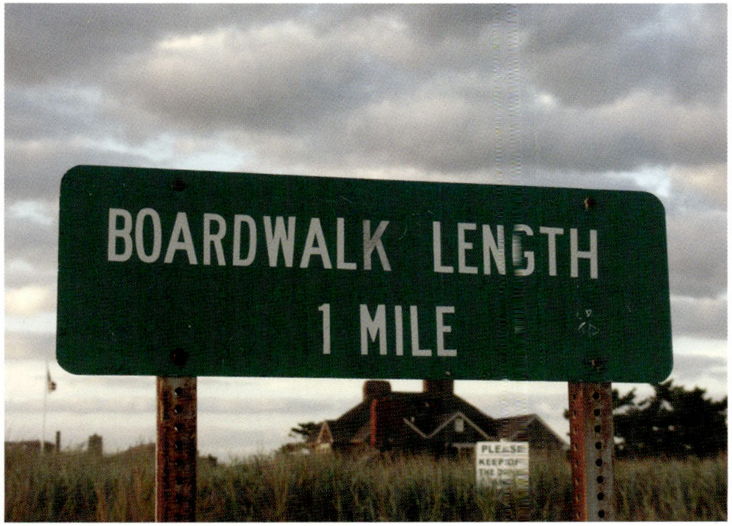

The Rehoboth Beach Boardwalk of today is one mile in length, quite a bit longer than the original 1,000 yard boardwalk. The first boardwalk was later expanded, and an amusement pier was constructed. Both were destroyed in a 1914 hurricane. But the boardwalk was rebuilt, only to be destroyed again in a 1962 storm. Hurricane Gloria damaged the boardwalk again in 1984, as did a nor'easter storm in 1992.

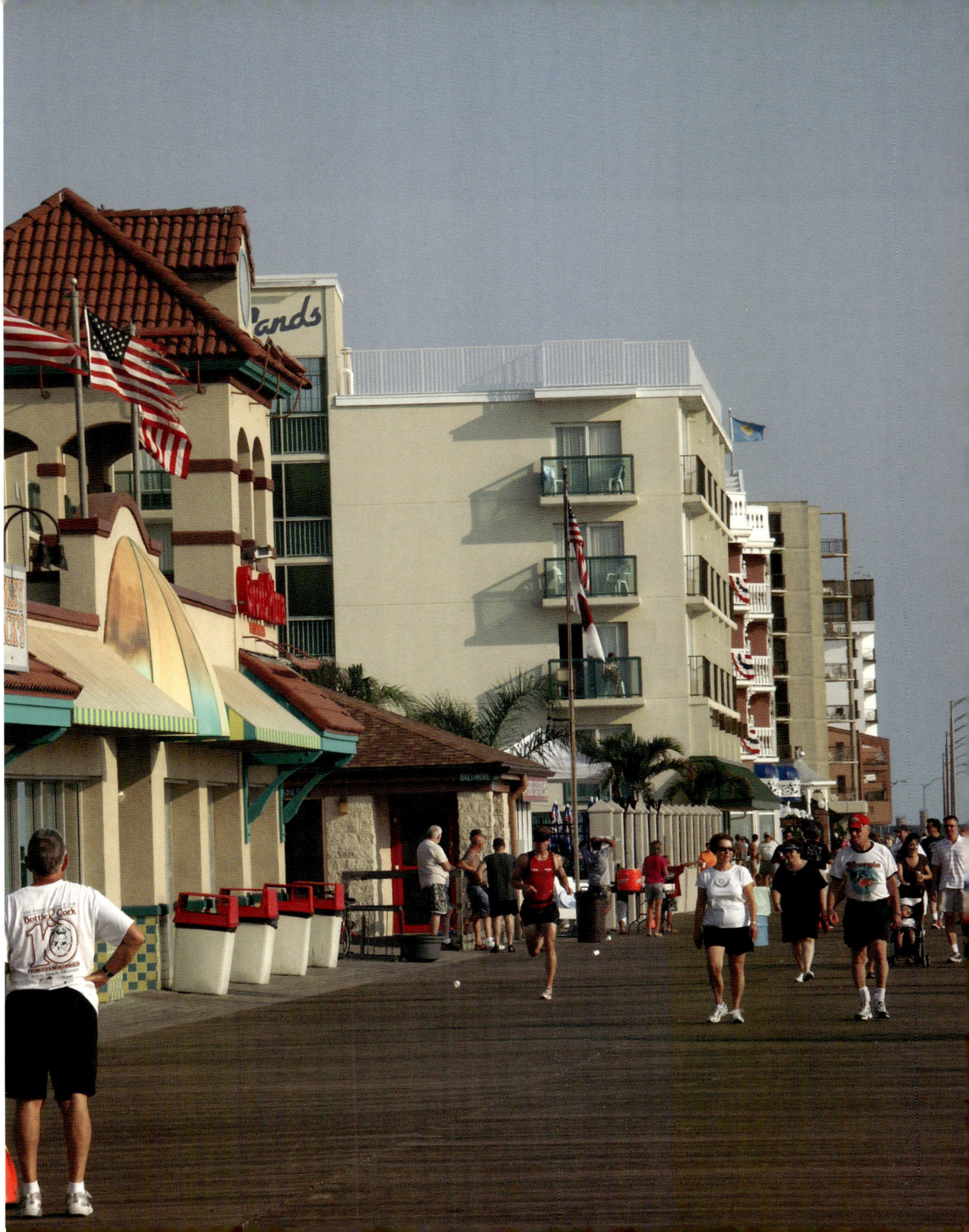

Dolle's Candyland on the Rehoboth Boardwalk is an institution that has delighted generations of visitors with its famous caramel popcorn and salt water taffy.

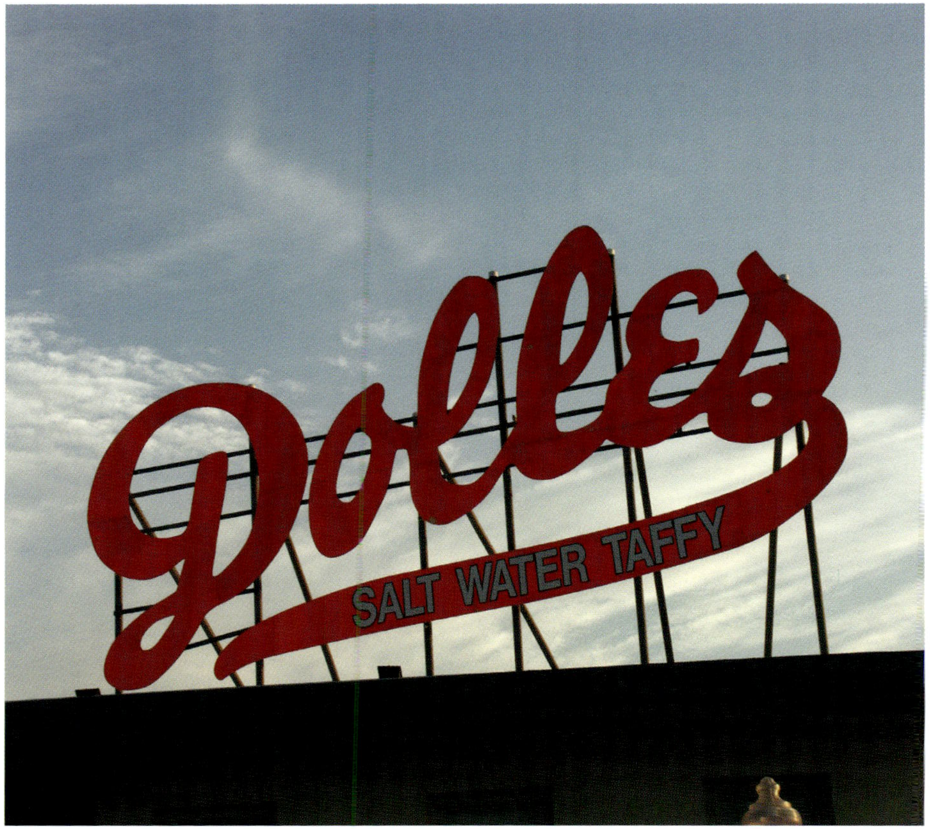

No visit to the Delaware coast is complete without a stop at Grotto Pizza, "The Legendary Taste of Delaware." The chain was founded in 1960 as a Rehoboth Beach restaurant. The first weeks were difficult for the fledging business, as no one knew what pizza was. Today, Grotto Pizza is found throughout the coastal resorts as well as locations in northern Delaware and beyond.

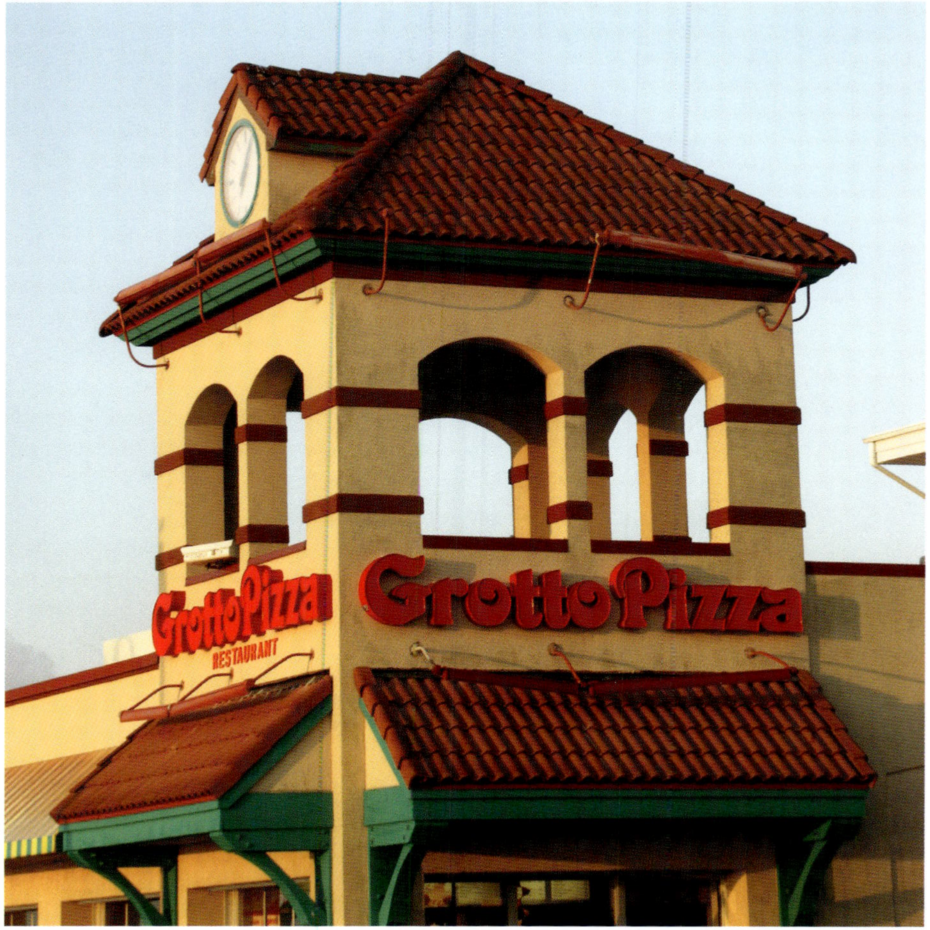

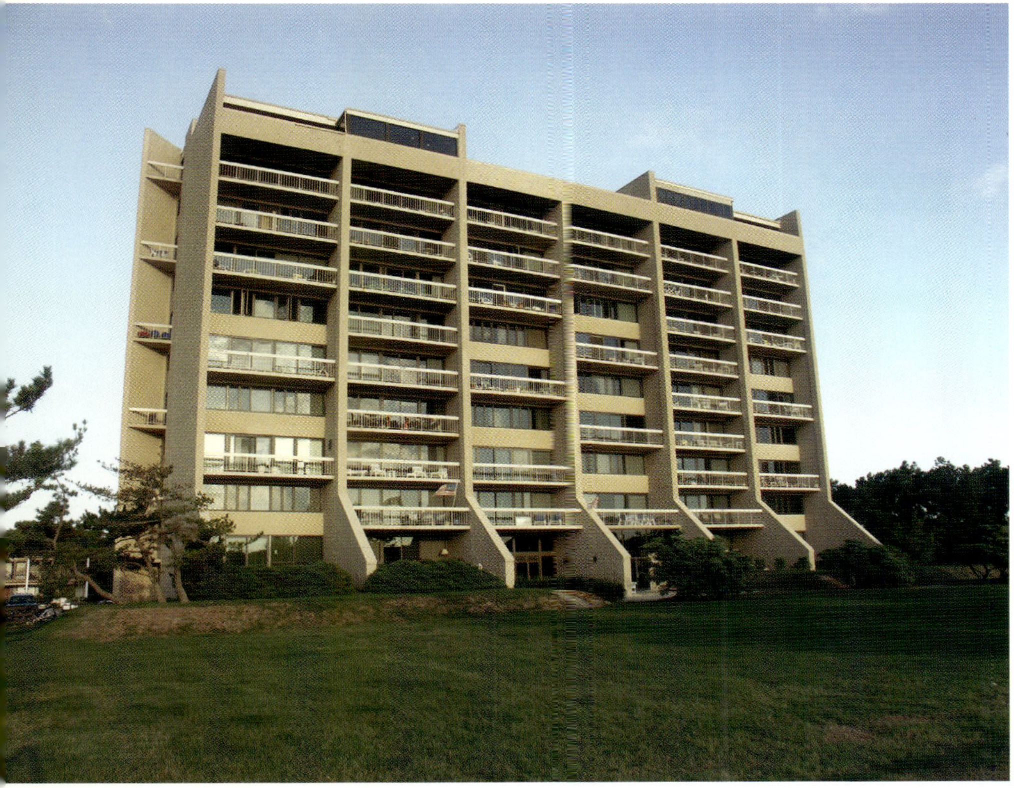

The condos at 21 Ocean Drive in North Shores provide picturesque views and convenient access to Cape Henlopen State Park and Rehoboth Beach.

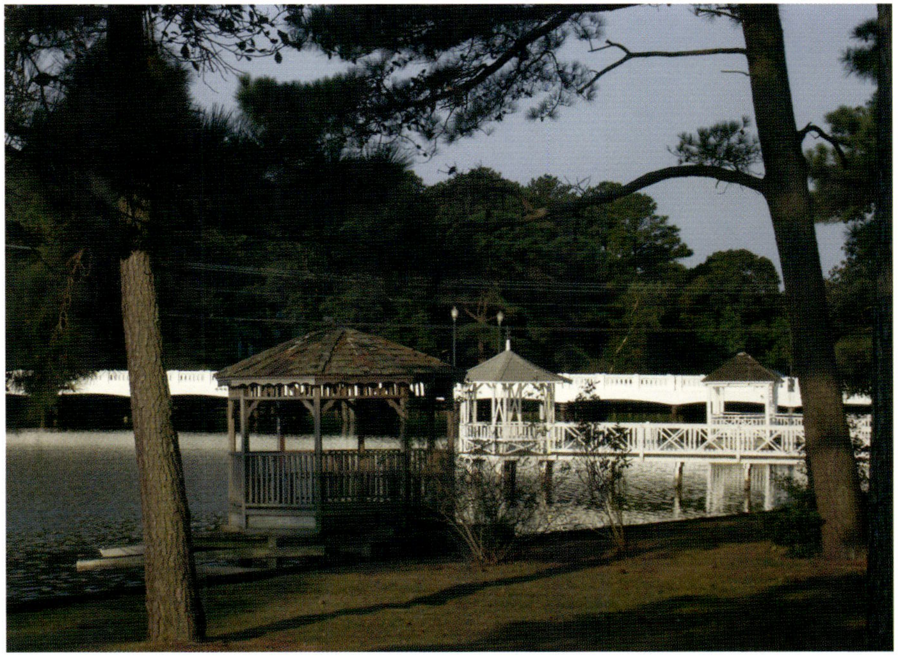

Silver Lake is nestled among the cottages and large homes of Rehoboth Beach. The placid pond is a popular destination for birdwatchers.

Rehoboth Avenue offers an abundance of retail and dining options for every taste and budget.

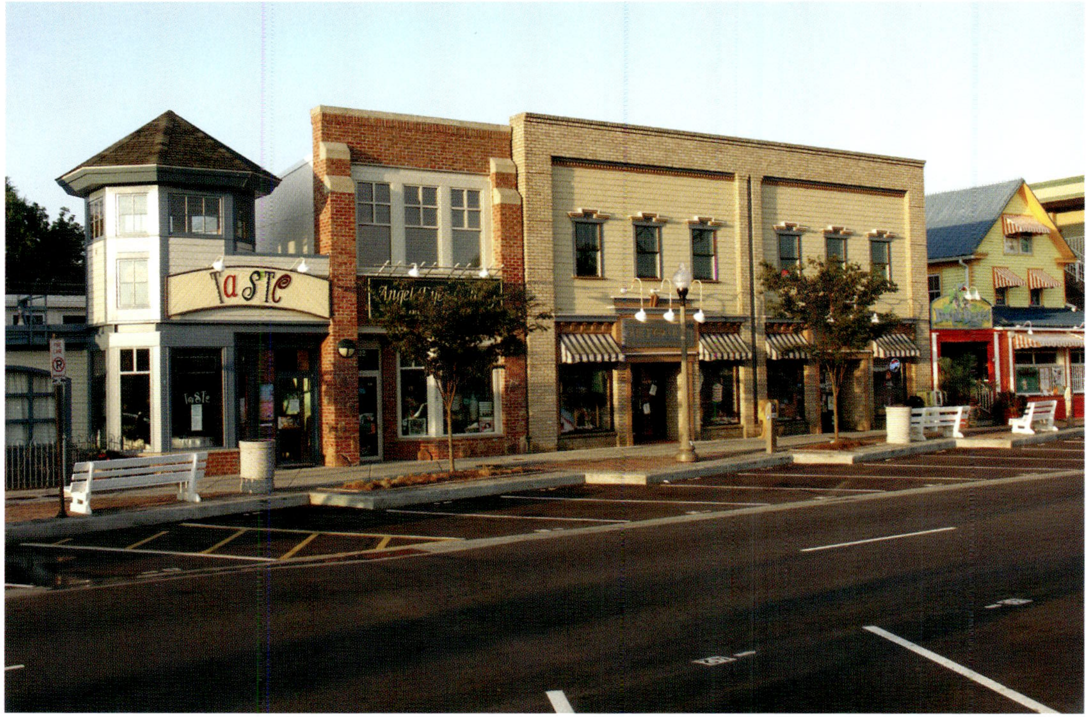

The Rehoboth Beach Bandstand was first conceptualized in 1963 by William Hayes. As no bandstand yet existed, Hayes created a musical venue in a grassy area adjacent to the boardwalk. Musicians performed "on the green." Later, a bandstand was constructed, and it stood for over 40 years before being replaced by this public Pavilion.

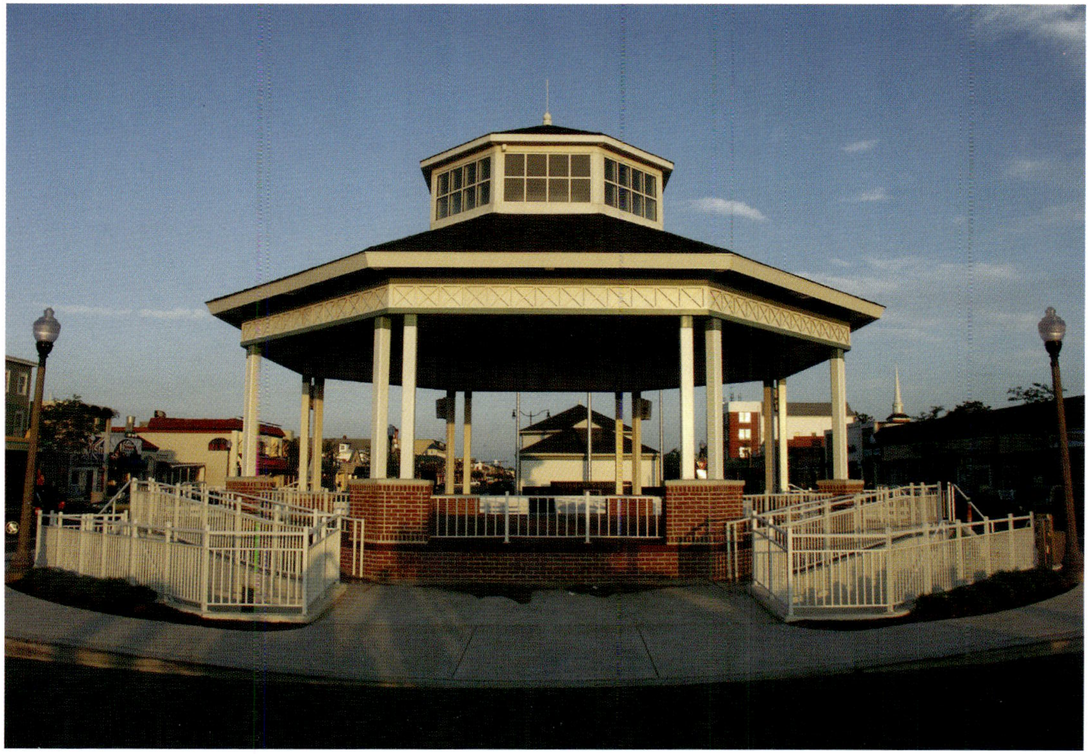

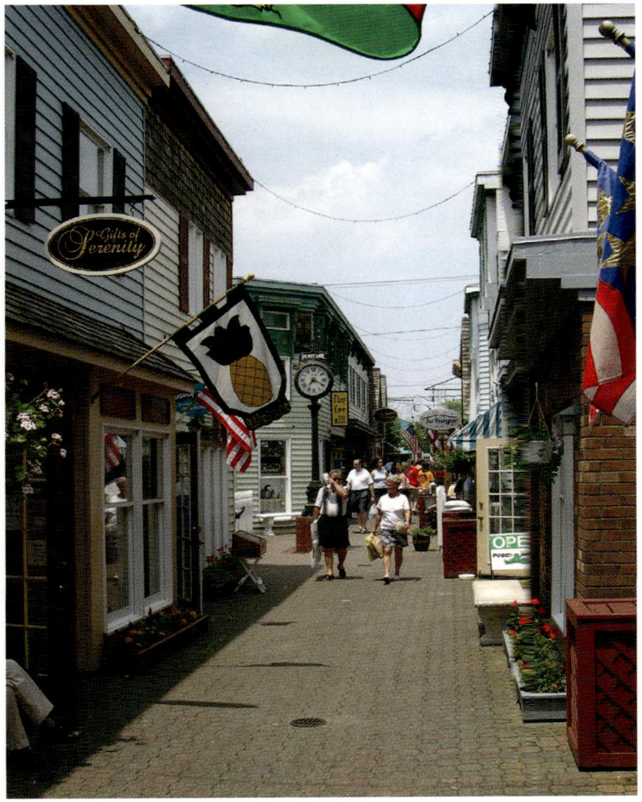

Penny Lane is located perpendicular to Rehoboth Avenue and is home to several of the more unique stores in town as well as a popular French café.

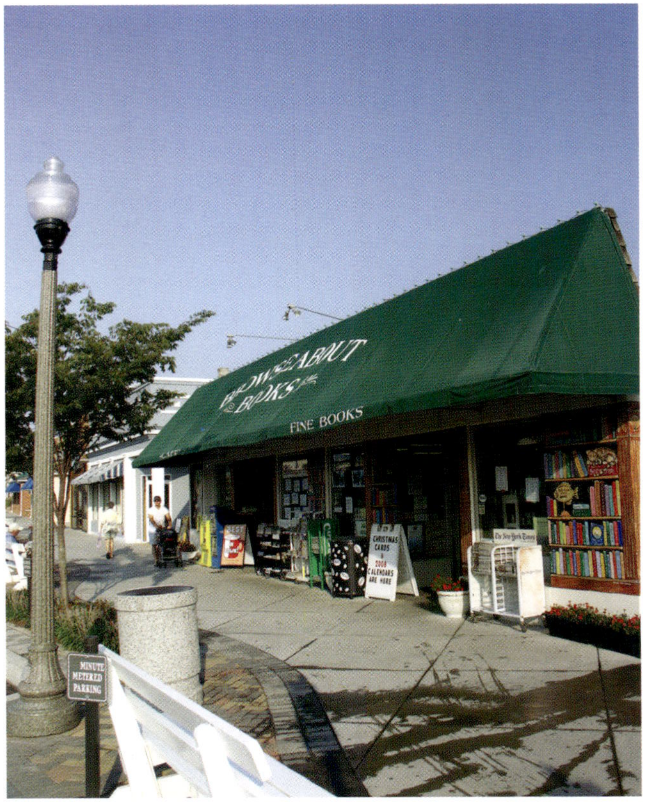

Browseabout Books has been named "Best Bookstore" on several occasions by *Delaware Today*. One of the largest independent bookstores in the country, Browseabout Books also has a popular café.

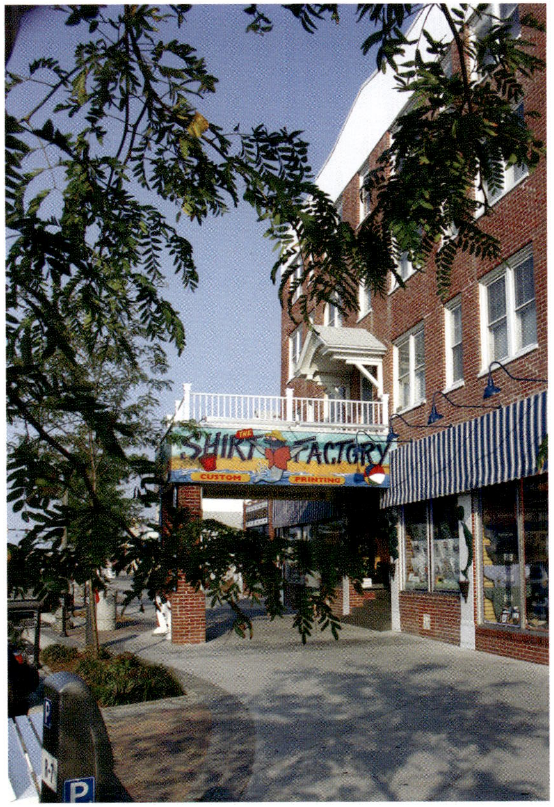

The Shirt Factory is a popular stop for custom made t-shirts.

If the Atlantic Ocean is a sea of aqua and turquoise, then Rehoboth Beach is a sea of yellows, reds, greens, and blues.

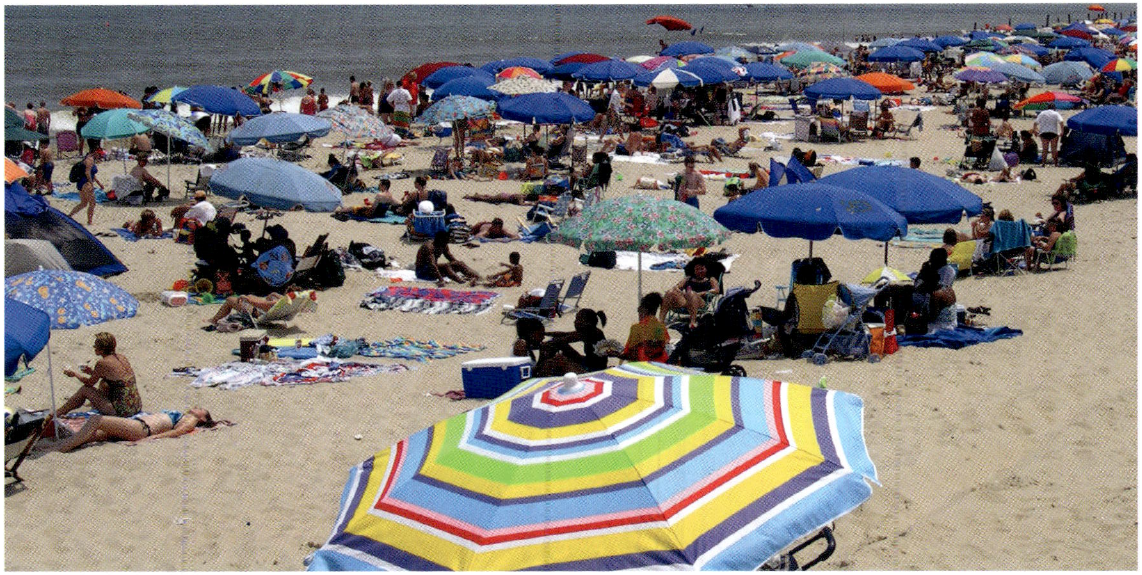

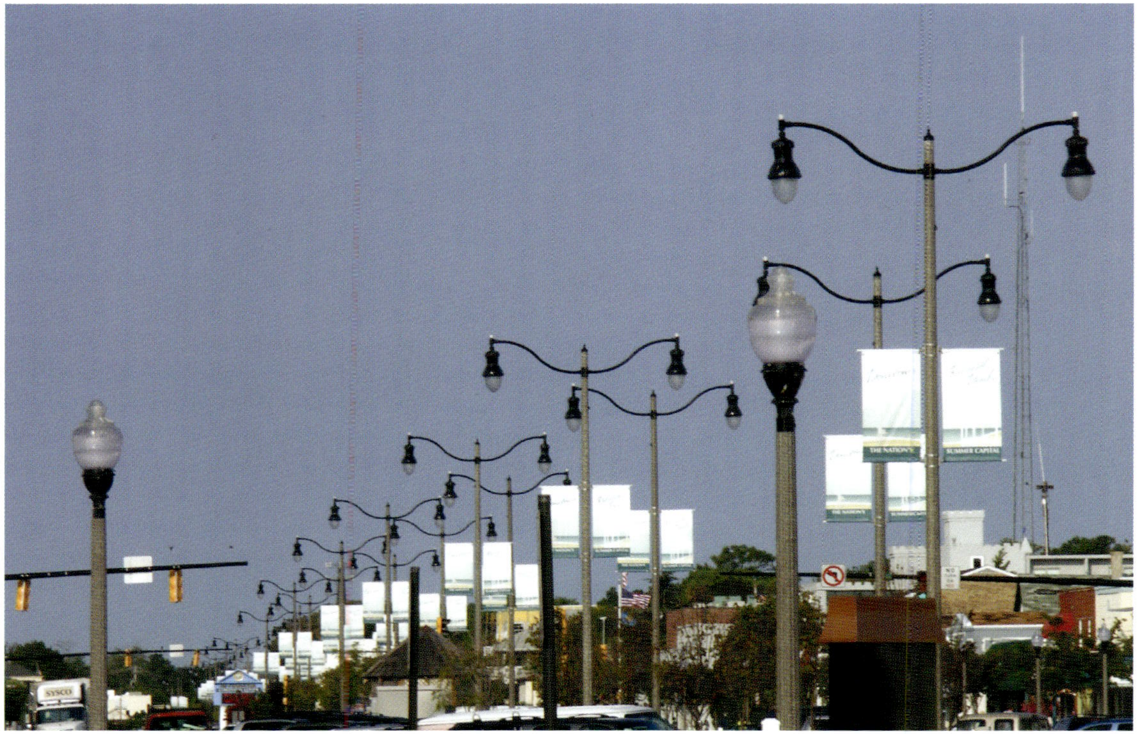

From 2002 to 2006, Rehoboth Avenue underwent a major transition as part of a streetscape enhancement project that involved new lighting, wider sidewalks, a traffic roundabout with lighthouse, new public pavilion, and more.

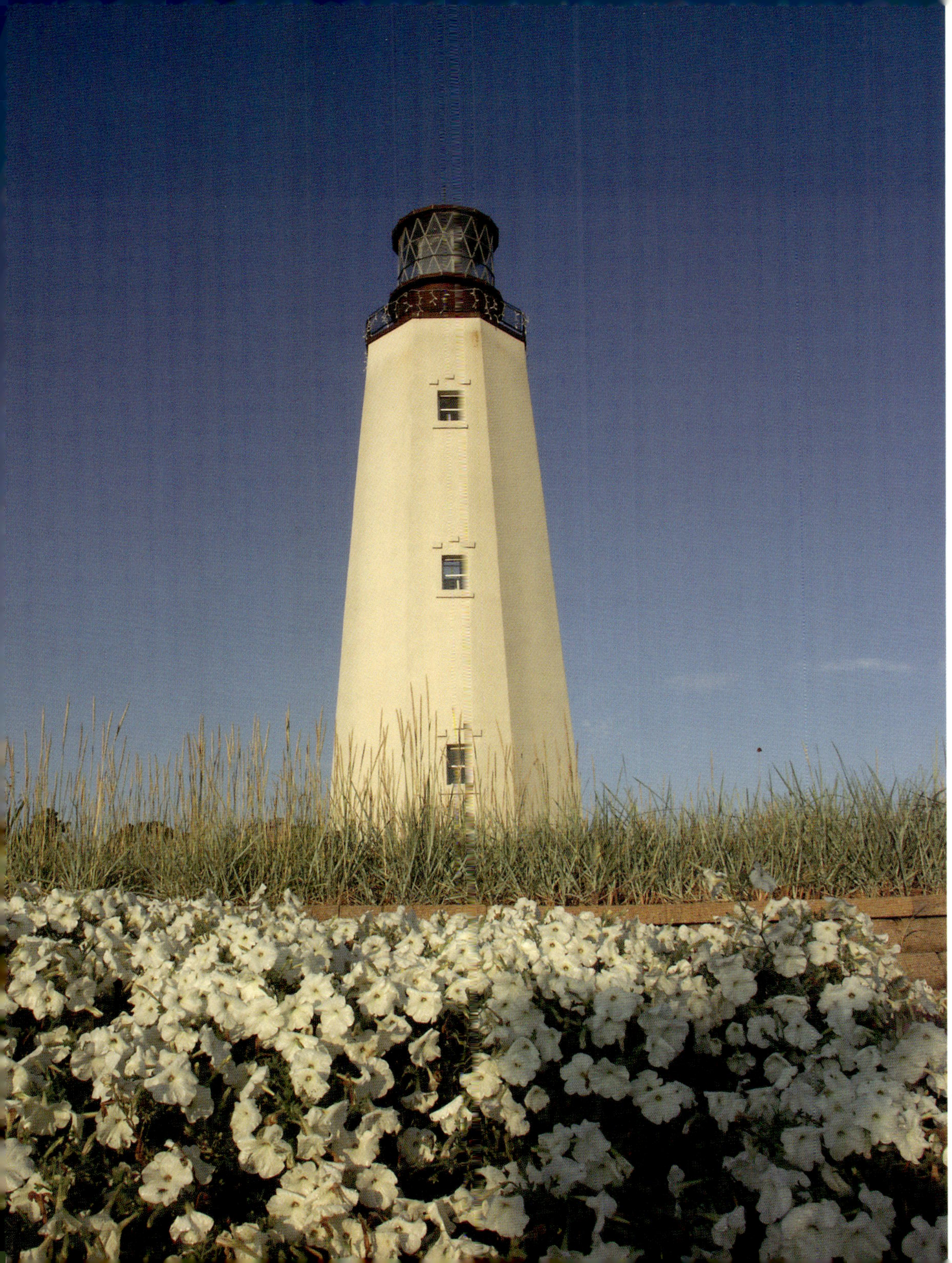

The original Cape Henlopen Lighthouse was constructed in 1765, making it the sixth lighthouse in the American colonies. It was gutted by fire in 1777, possibly by the British Army, and repaired several years later. In 1926, it fell into the sea. This replica pays homage to an important piece of Delaware maritime history.

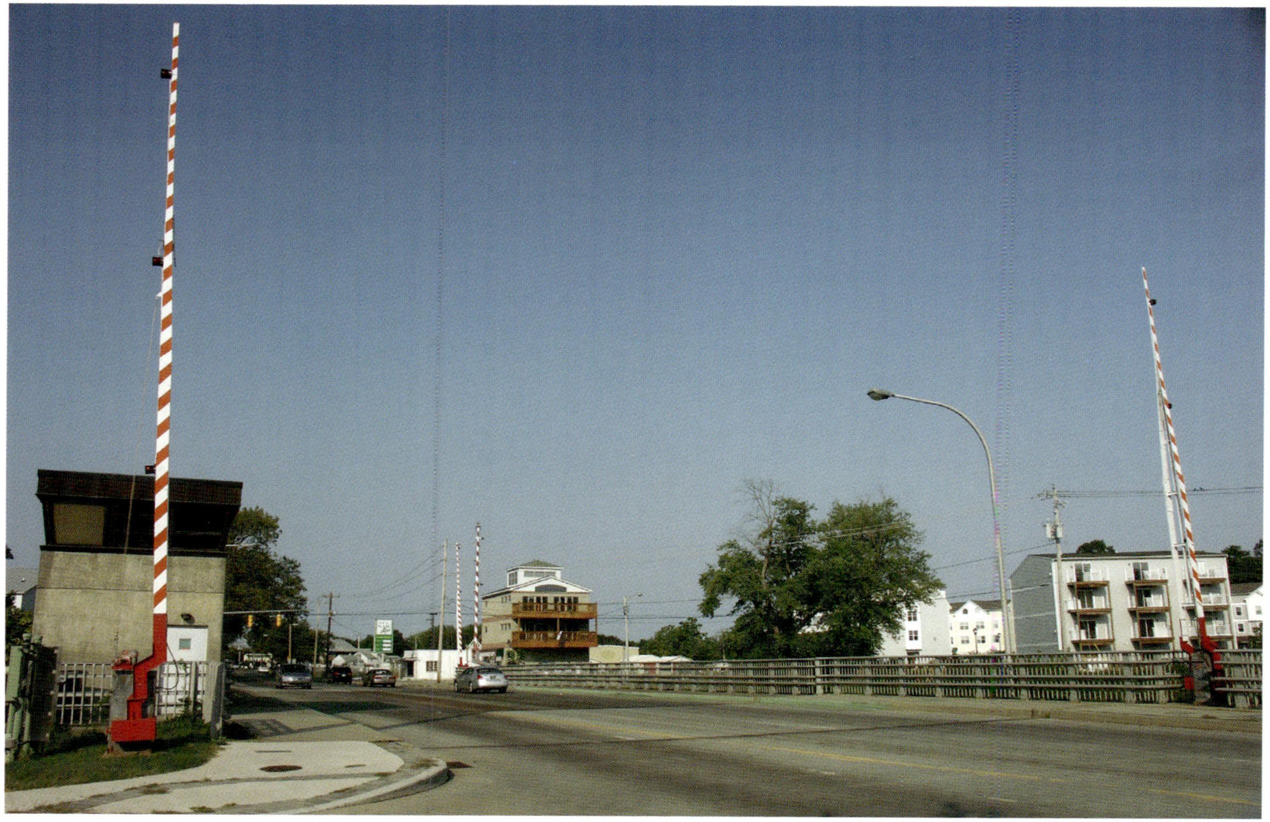

The drawbridge over the Lewes & Rehoboth Canal visually announces arrival in "The Nation's Summer Capital."

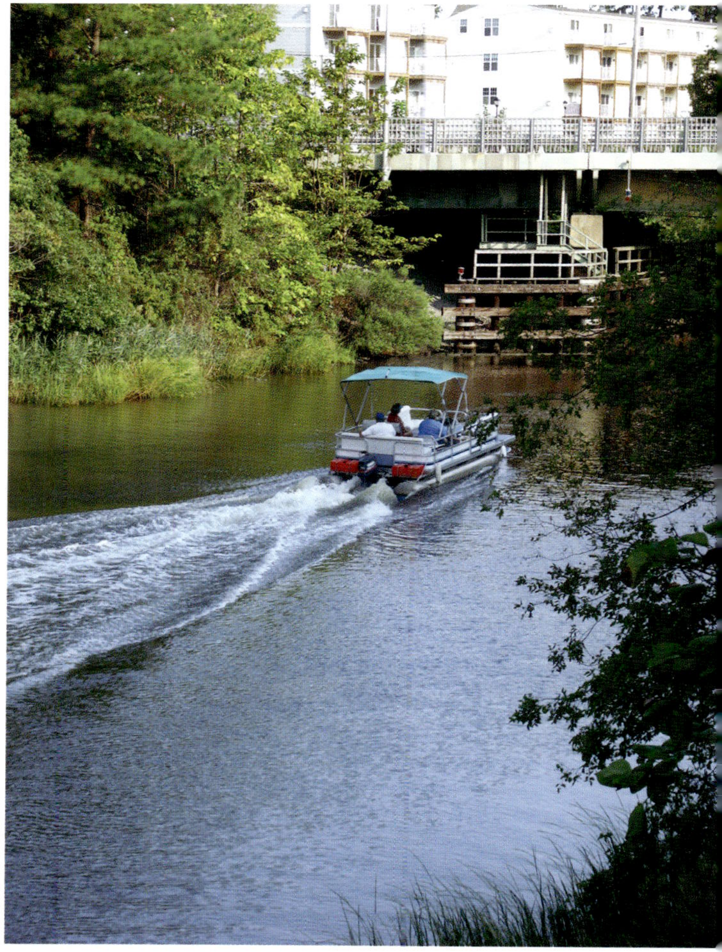

The Lewes & Rehoboth Canal was completed in 1916, and has provided convenient boat access between the two towns ever since.

Nighttime in Rehoboth Beach – the daytime colors transition into bright colored lights and neon, creating an energy and excitement as illuminated as the early morning sun.

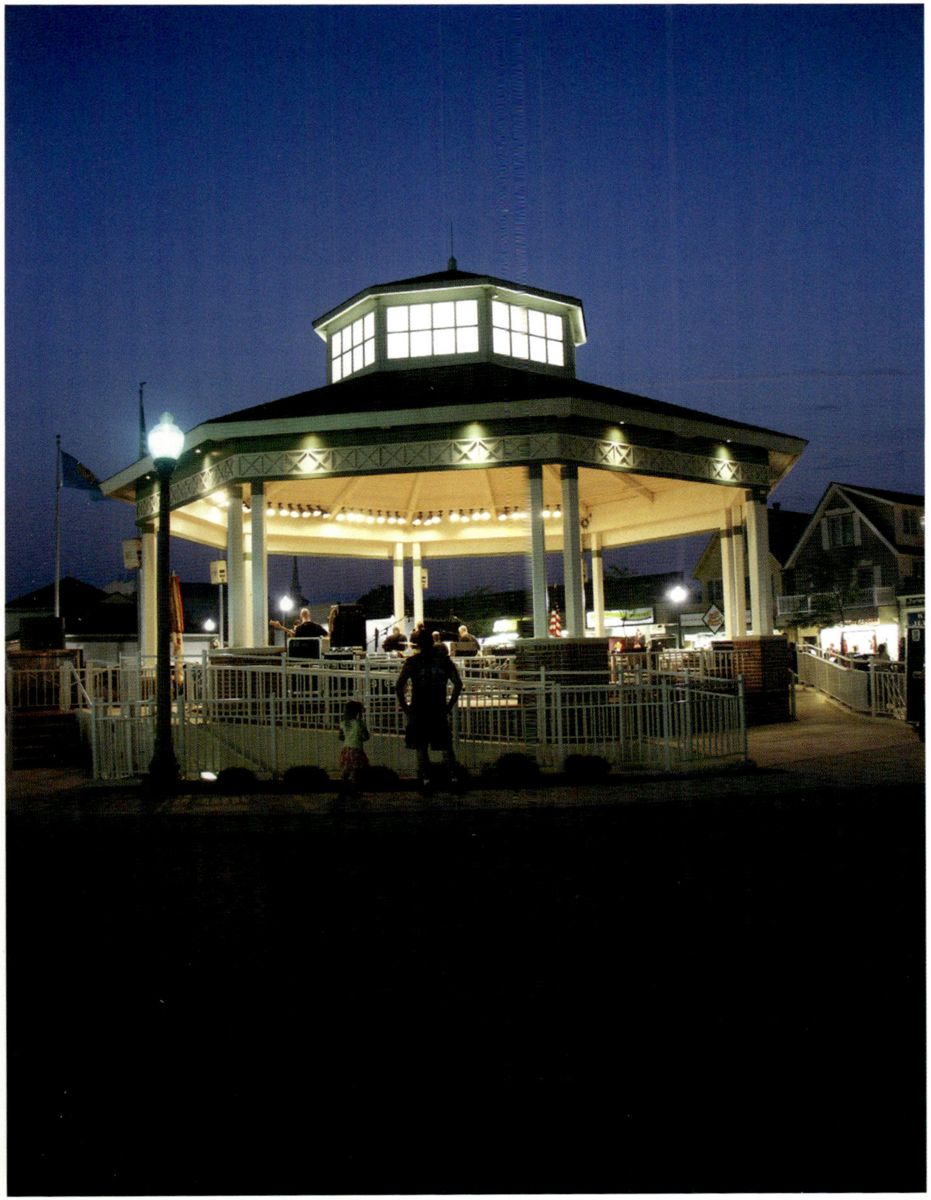

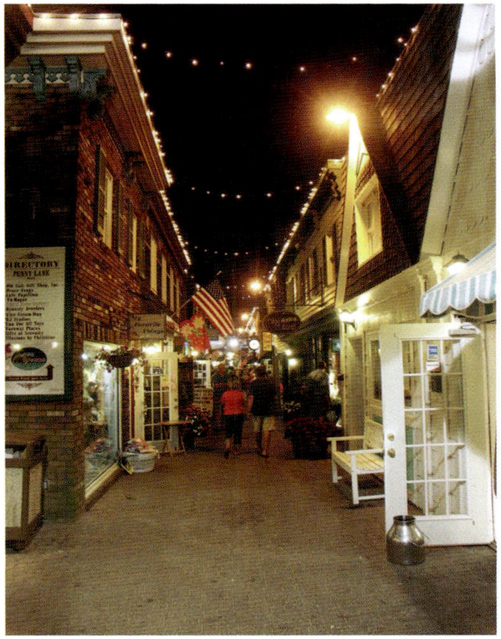

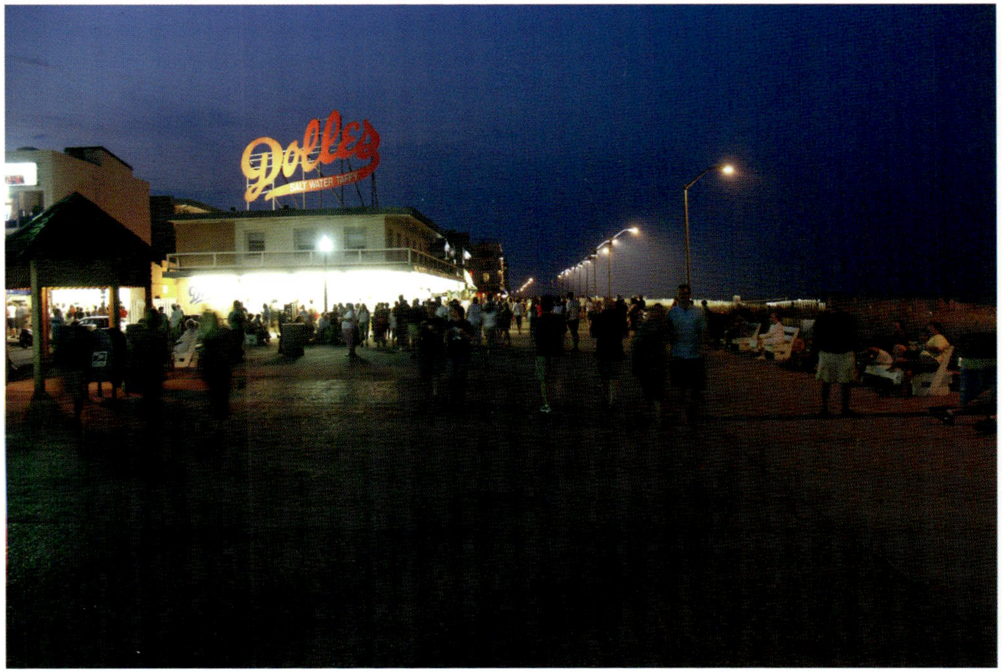

A visit to Thrasher's for a bucket of french fries is another tradition for Rehoboth Beach visitors. To the south, Thrasher's has been operating in Ocean City, MD since 1929.

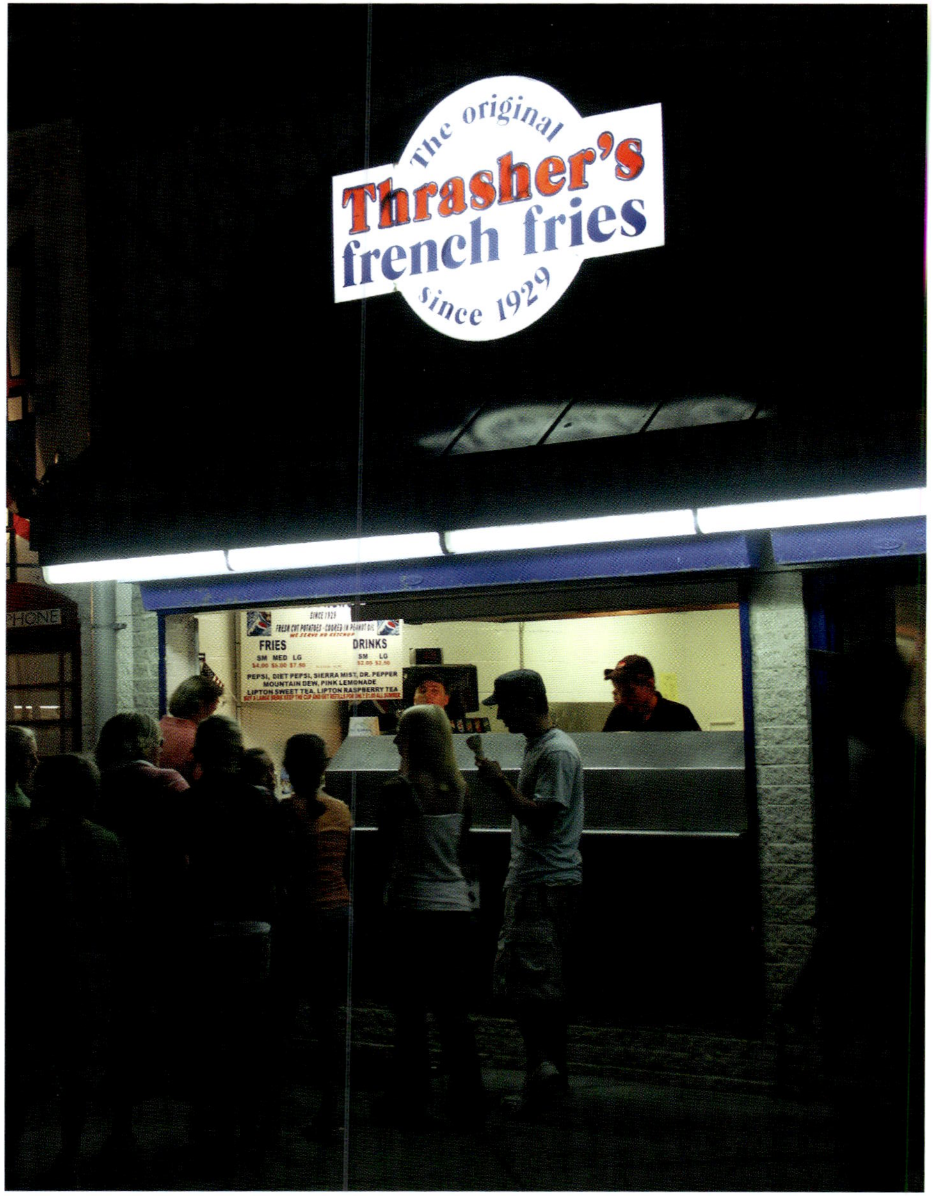

Kohr Bros. and Fisher's Popcorn are popular stops along Rehoboth Avenue for frozen custard and caramel popcorn, respectively.

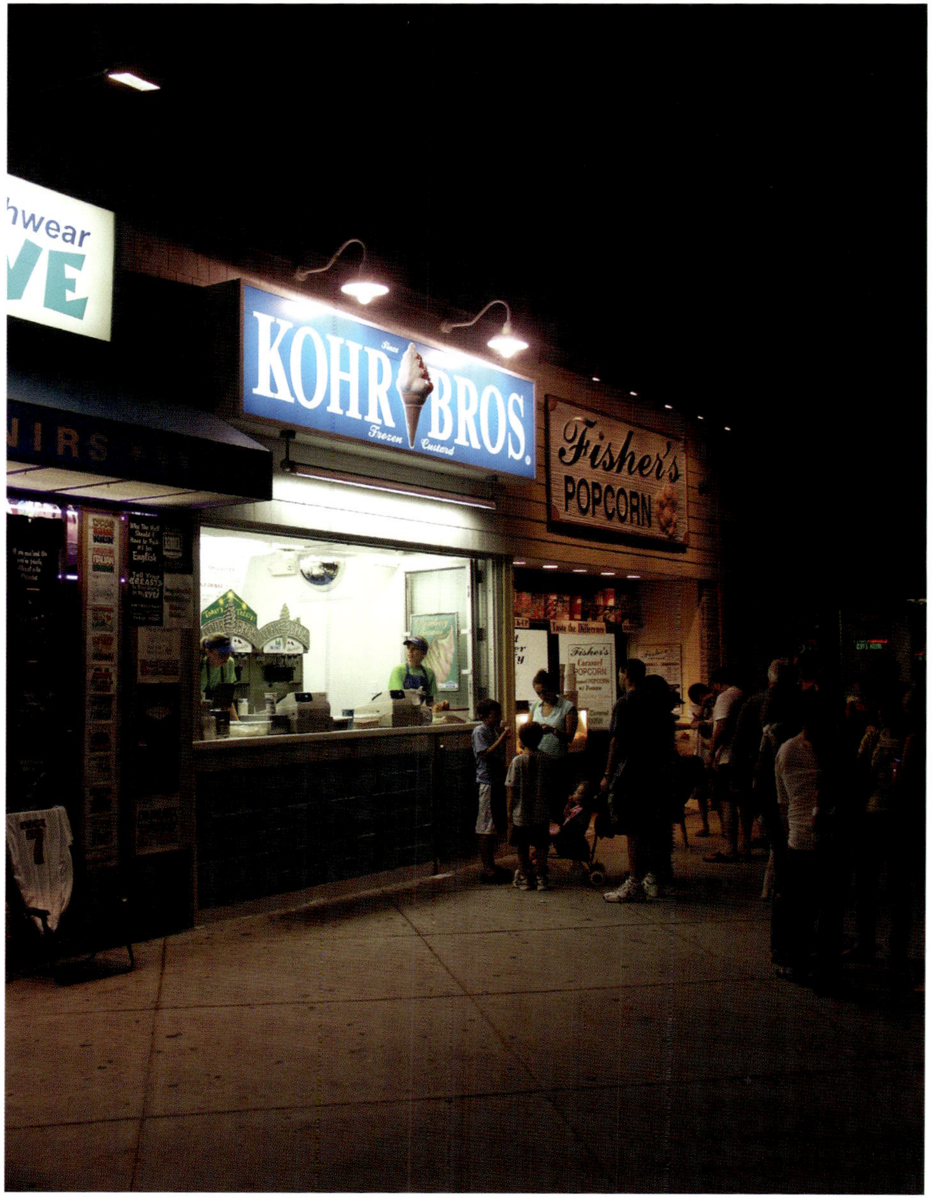

Since 1937 Candy Kitchen has been serving up mouth-watering homemade saltwater taffy, creamy fudge, and delectable chocolates. A Delaware tradition, over 20 shops can be found from Rehoboth Beach to Ocean City, MD.

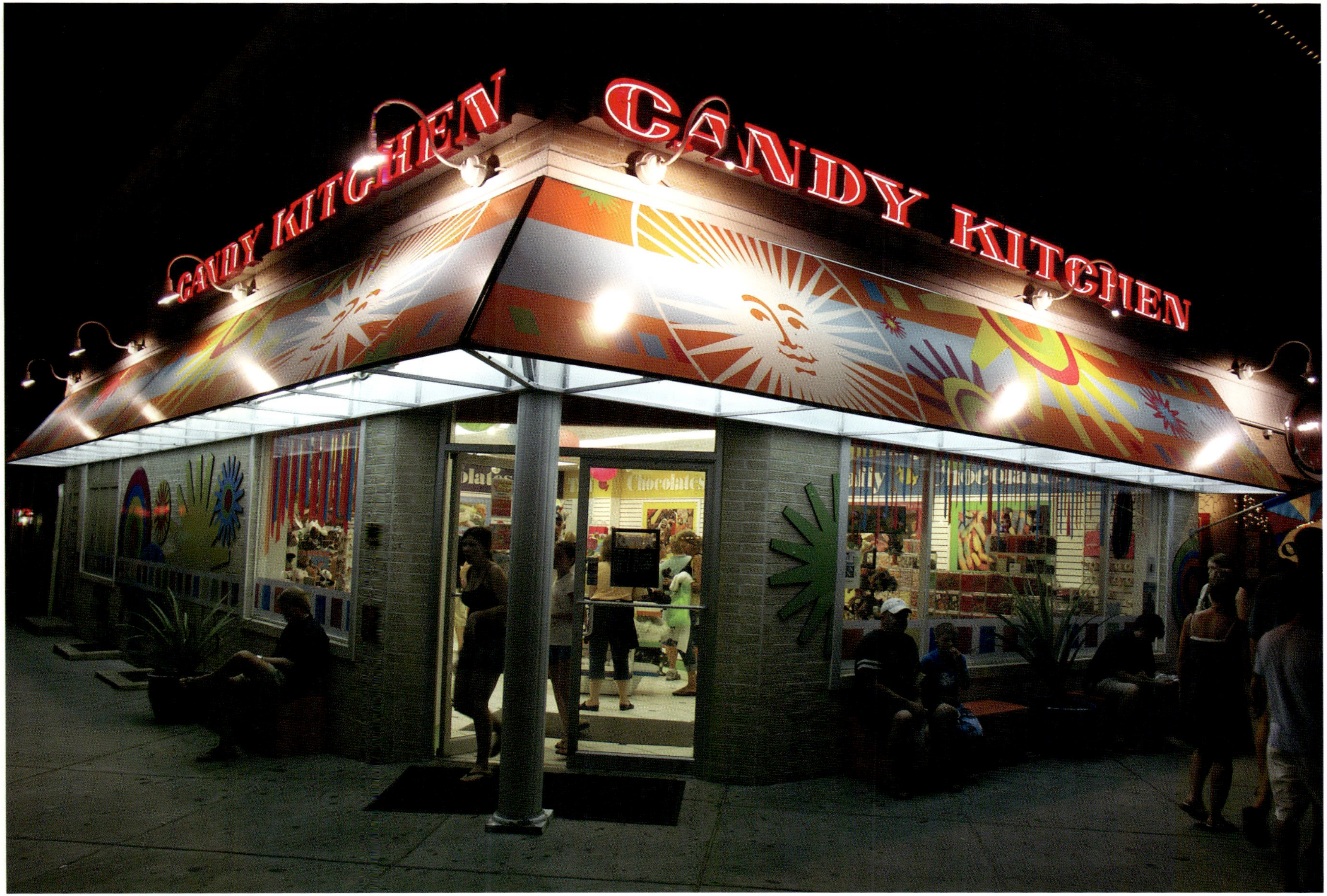

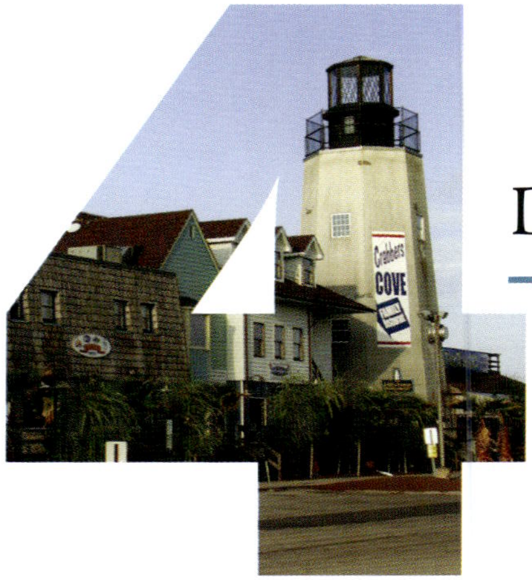

Dewey Beach: 22 *Blocks of Summer Fun*

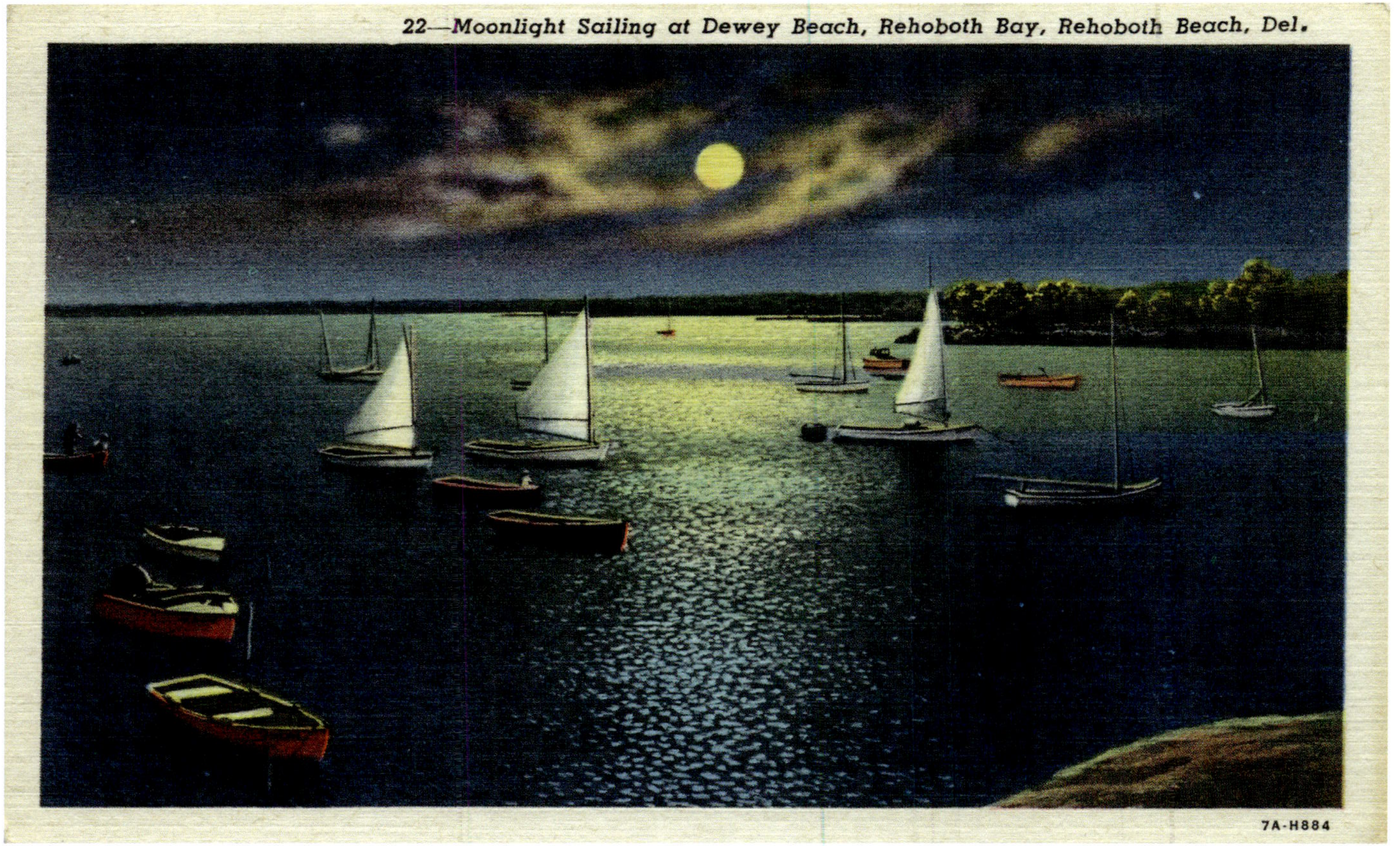

Dewey Beach is not old, nor is it as historic as its neighbors. The town was incorporated in 1981. And it is not large. In fact, only a few hundred people call Dewey Beach home year-round.

But Dewey Beach is something unique to itself. It is a way of life – at least according to the welcome signs along Coastal Highway. So what, exactly, is the Dewey Beach "way of life"?

To understand that, you have to understand the town. It is approximately one mile long – about the length of the Rehoboth Boardwalk – and two blocks wide. It is ocean to the east, and bay to the west. It is Rehoboth Beach to the north, and Delaware Seashore State Park to the south.

And yet it has a personality all its own.

Like its neighboring communities, Dewey Beach is a summer resort, attracting visitors from Washington to Philadelphia. Dewey Beach is also one *happening* town, defined as much by the silvery bay as by the wide beaches and ocean. It is a place to party, a place to let loose, and a place to see live music. That is the "way of life."

During the day, Dewey Beach offers the appearance of a typical seaside resort – sun worshippers with bronze tans heading toward the oceanfront beaches, adventurous water lovers sailing and parasailing in the bay. But after the fiery sun retreats below the horizon, the lights come on, the amplifiers hum to life, and a vibrant nightlife emerges from an otherwise tranquil community. In fact, the seaside community can even boast its own reality show: "Surf & Rescue: Dewey Beach" is a TRUE TV series.

Touring national acts can be found in Dewey Beach at places like the Bottle and Cork – which bills itself as "The Greatest Rock and Roll Bar in the World." Music festivals abound, including the Delaware Music Festival, Dewey Beach Popfest, Dewey Beach Music Conference, and Dewey Beach Americana Music Festival. There's even an Elvis Festival, thank you very much.

Dewey Beach was incorporated in 1981, making it the youngest of Delaware's coastal towns. The town is known for its vibrant nightlife and music festivals that help define "A Way of Life," which happens to be the town motto.

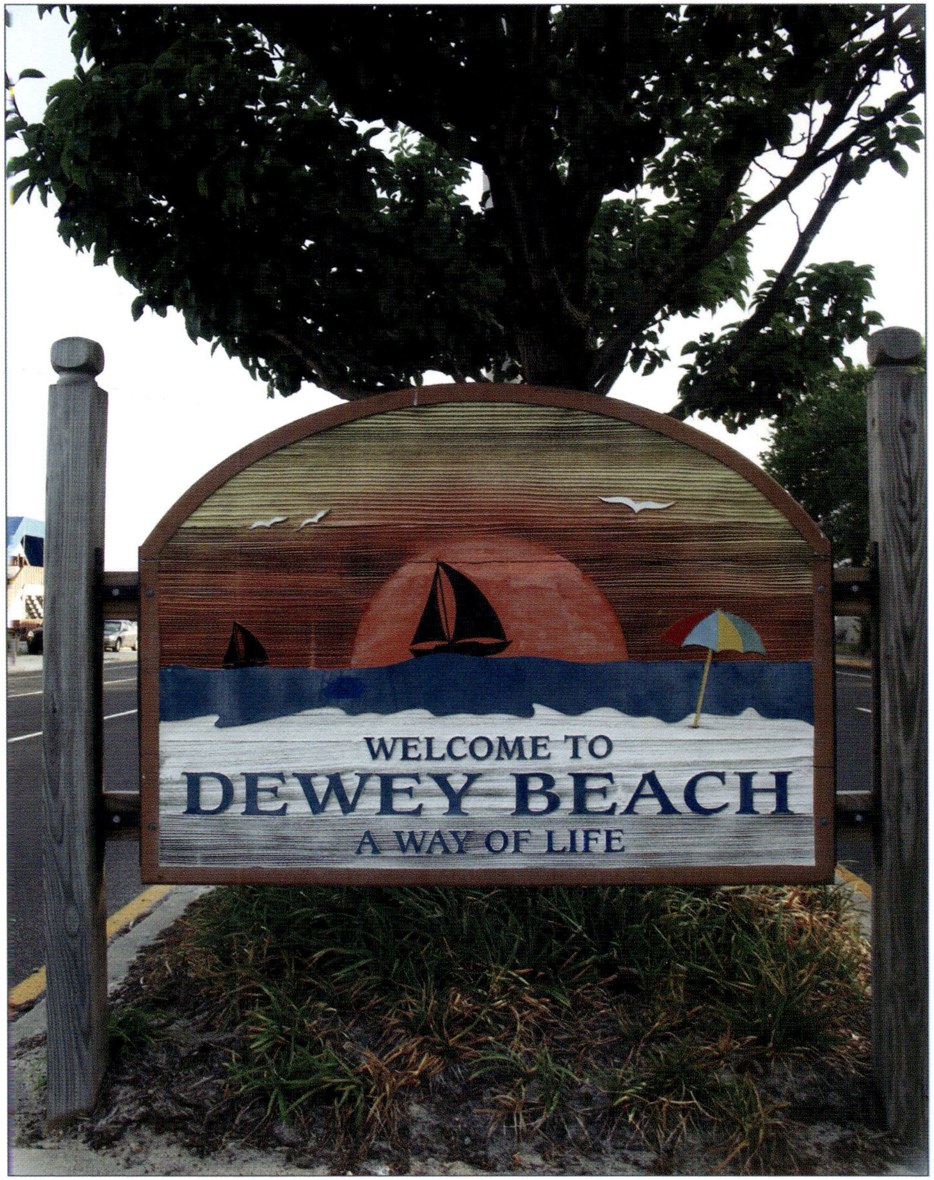

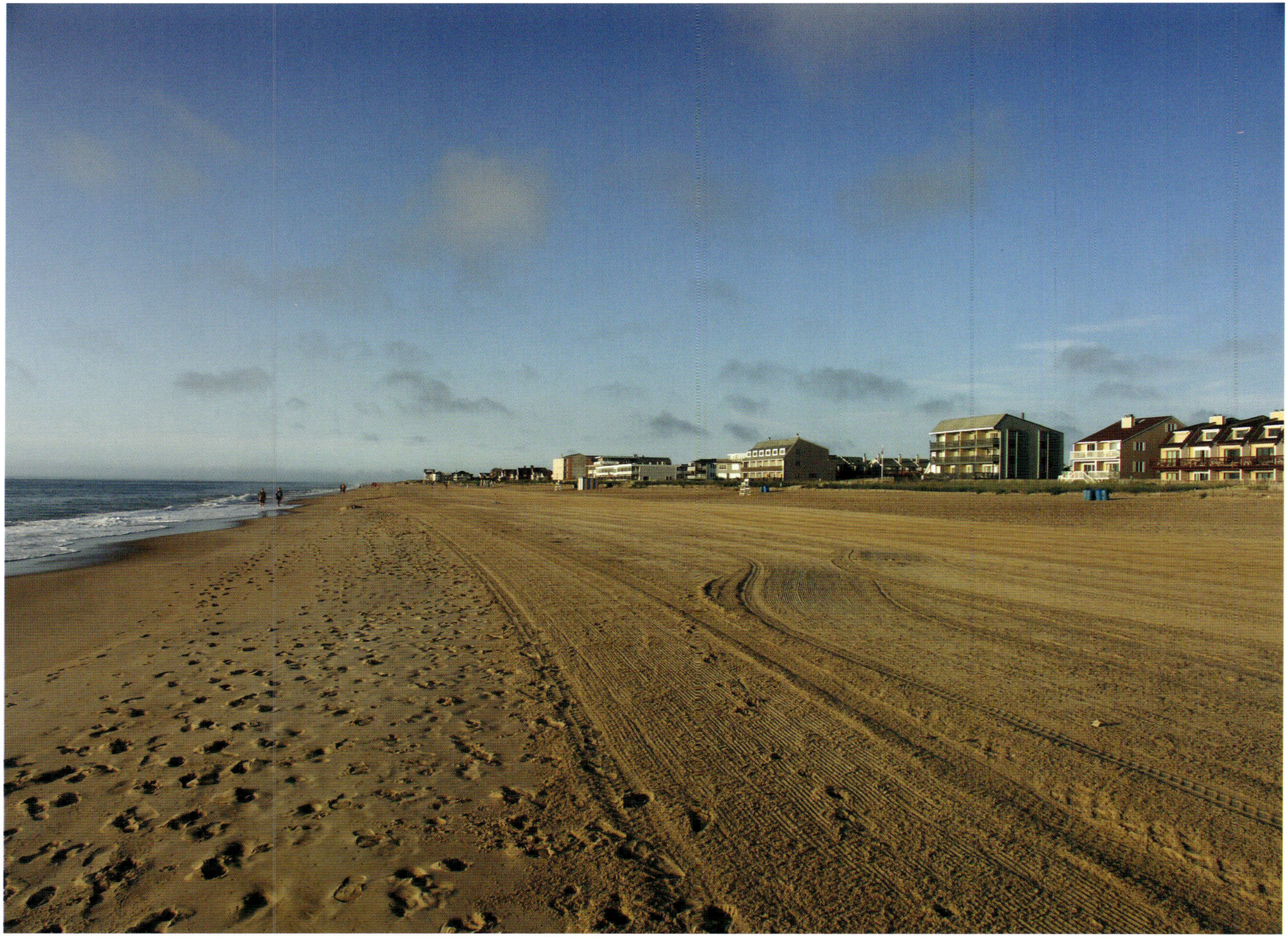

A 2005 beach replenishment project created a 150-ft. wide beach with 25-ft. wide dune crest.

The Rehoboth Bay Marina offers both full and half-day boat rentals including fishing skiffs and pontoon boats.

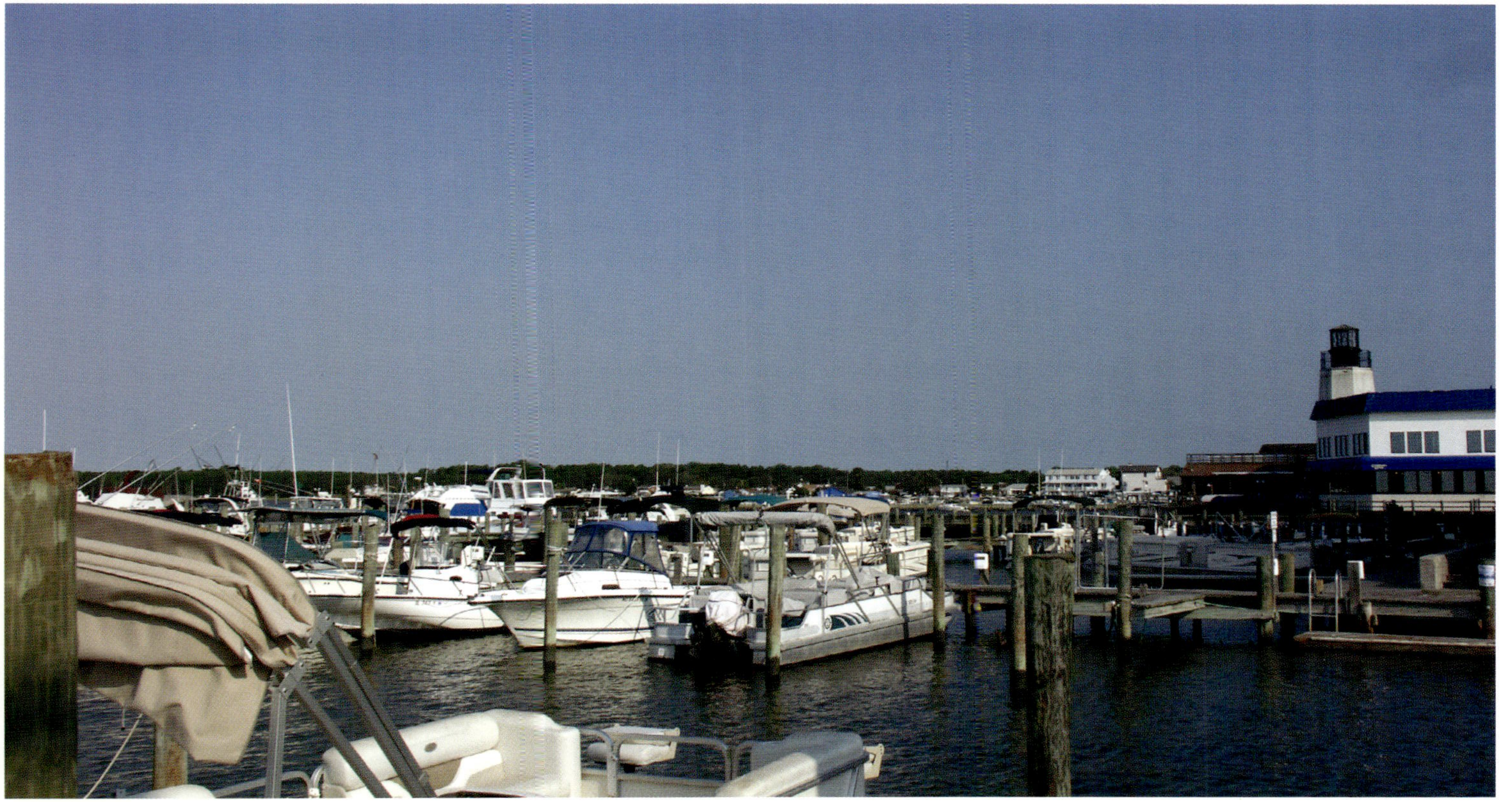

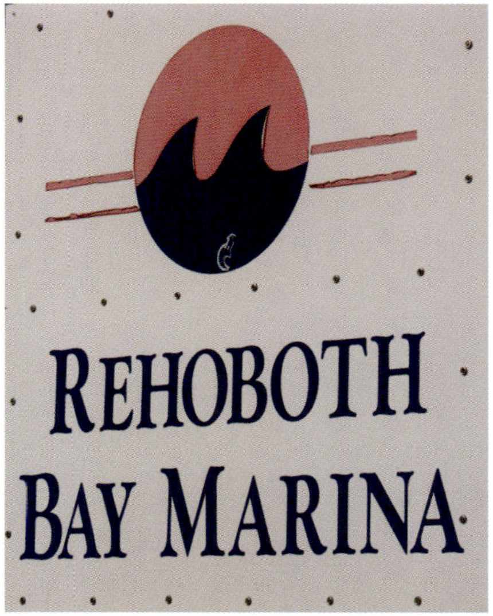

The Dewey Beach Club caters to year-round and summer residents.

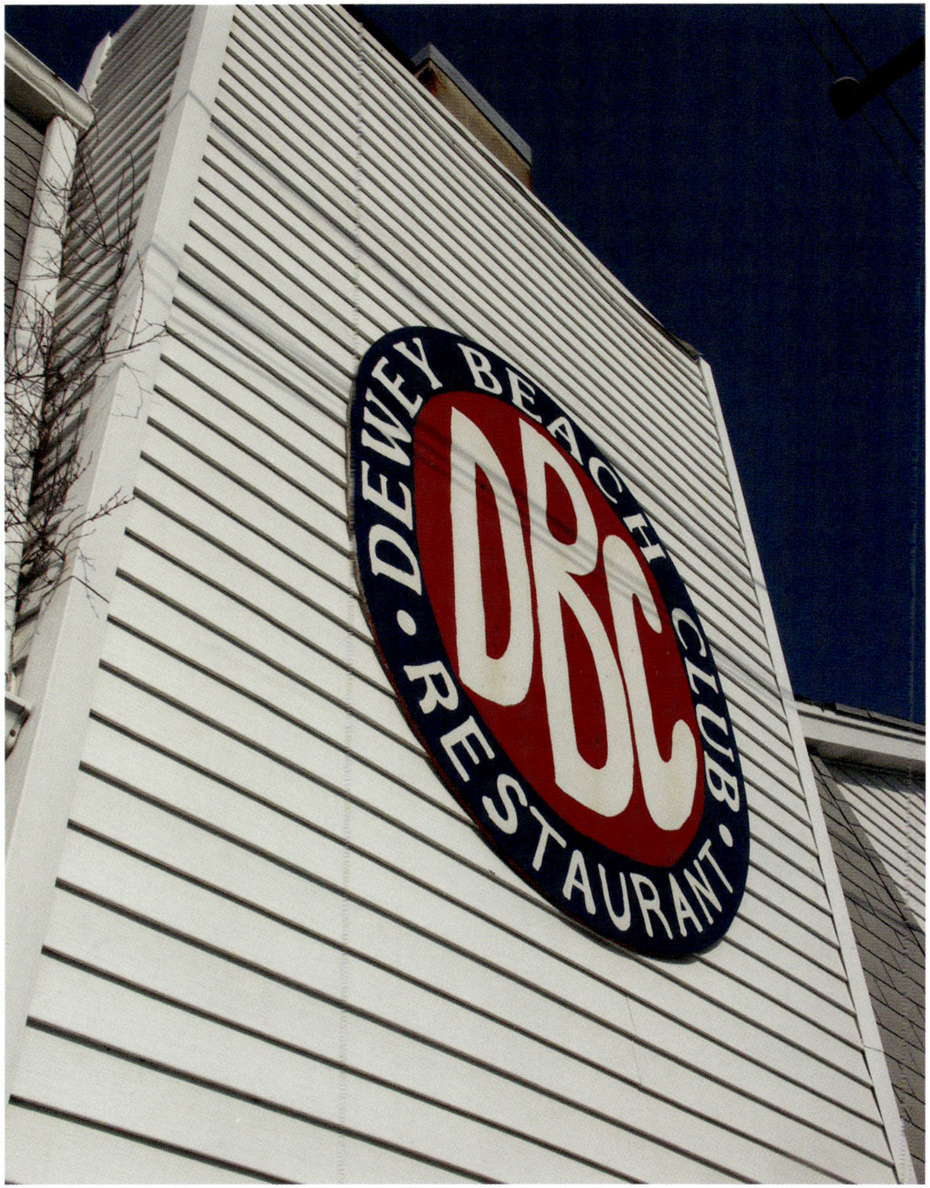

Rehoboth Bay Sailing Association was created in 1963 by three students looking to earn extra income. Today, the sailing and tennis club has a membership of 150 families.

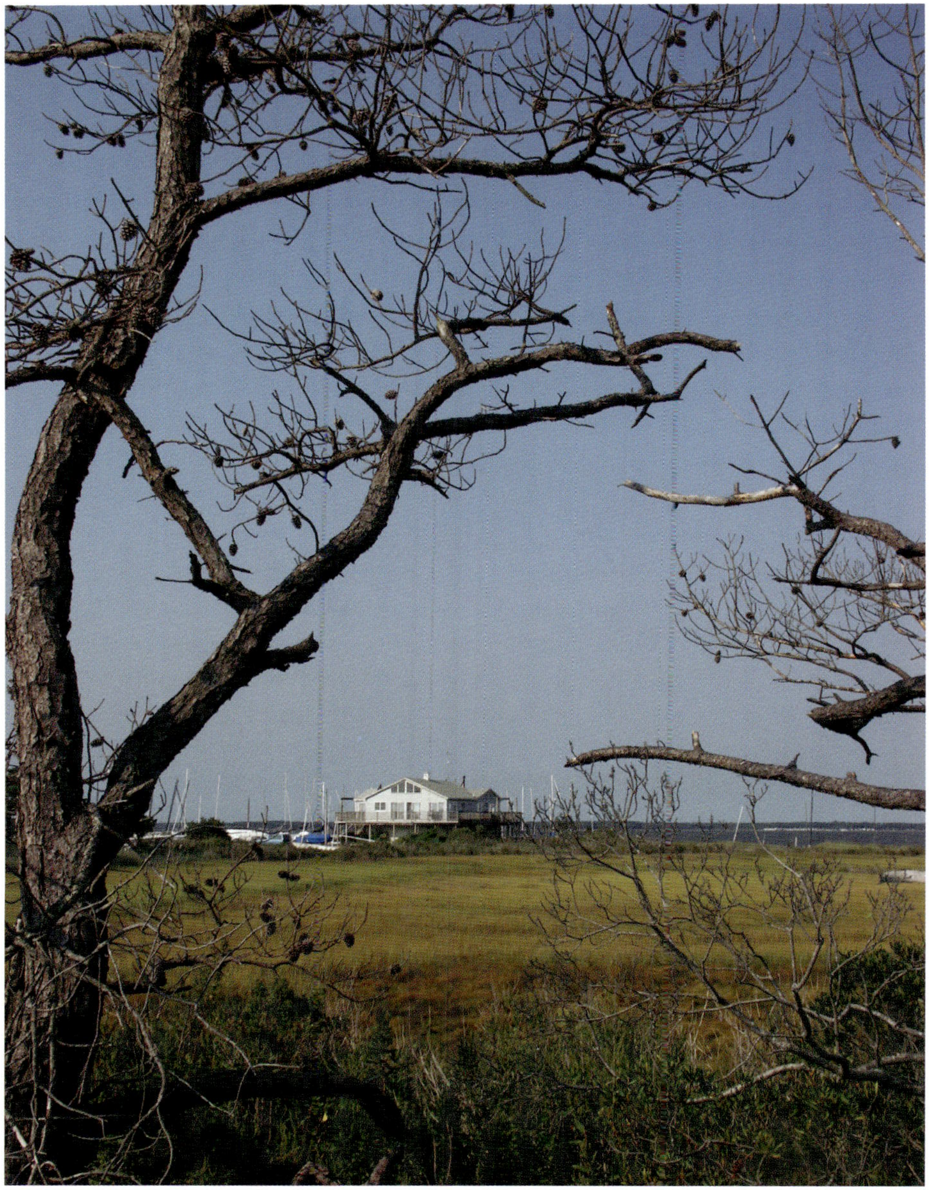

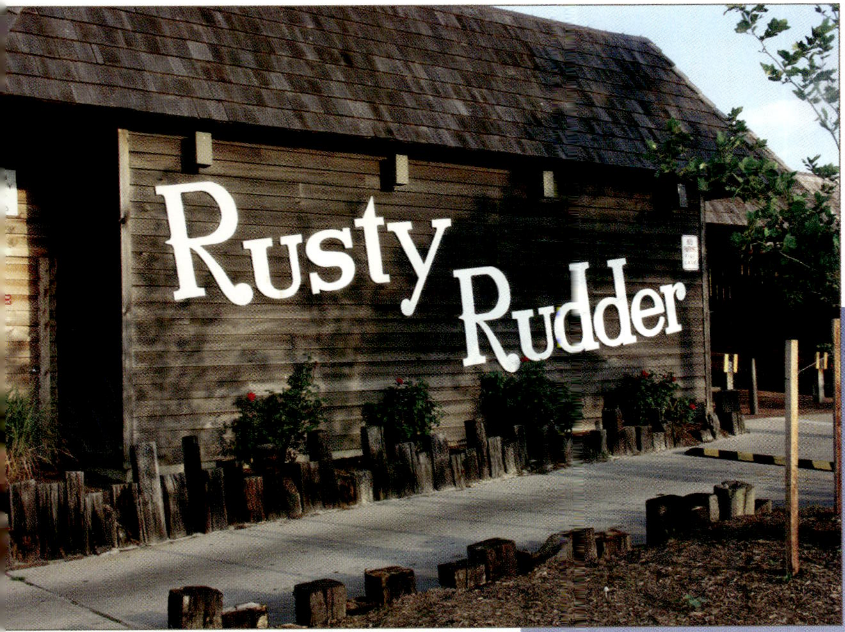

Ruddertowne has been an anchor of the Dewey Beach community since 1981. The adjacent Rusty Rudder is a popular restaurant and night spot, while Ruddertowne boasts popular restaurants and attractions including The Lighthouse, Crabbers Cove, Booksandcoffee, Qué Pasa, and the Bay Center for the Performing Arts.

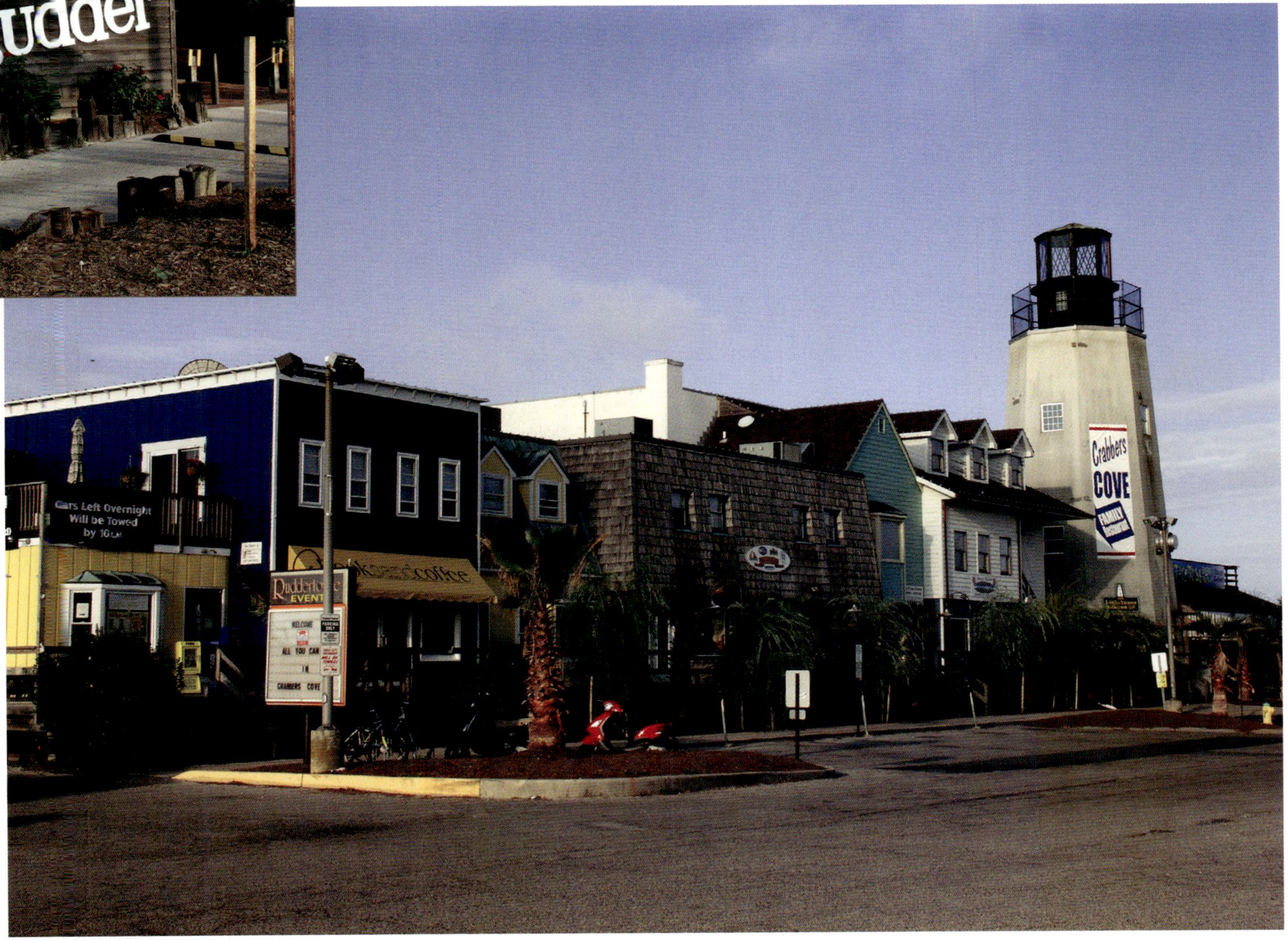

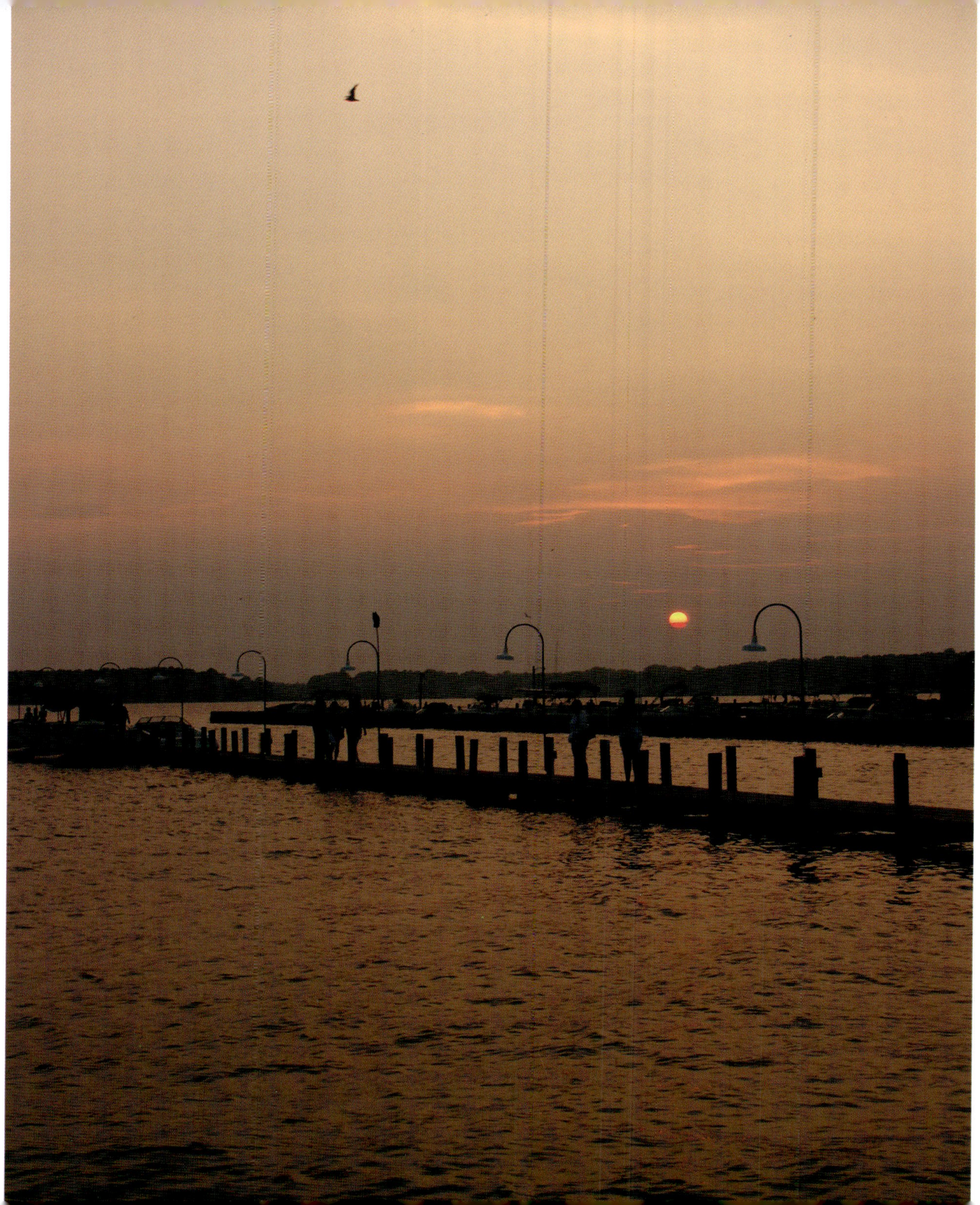

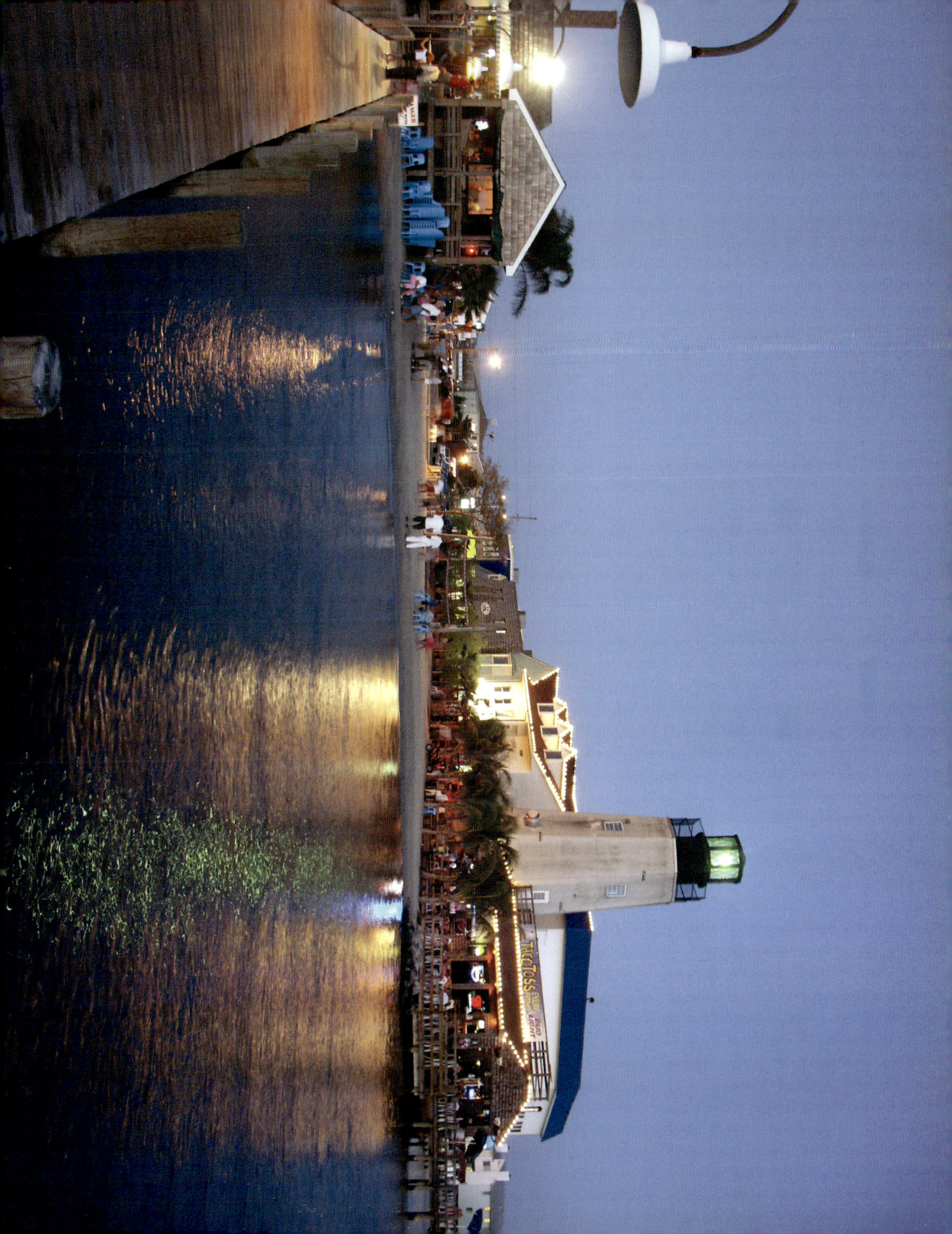

When the suns sets over Dewey Beach, the lights come on and the nightlife scene thrives until the early morning hours.

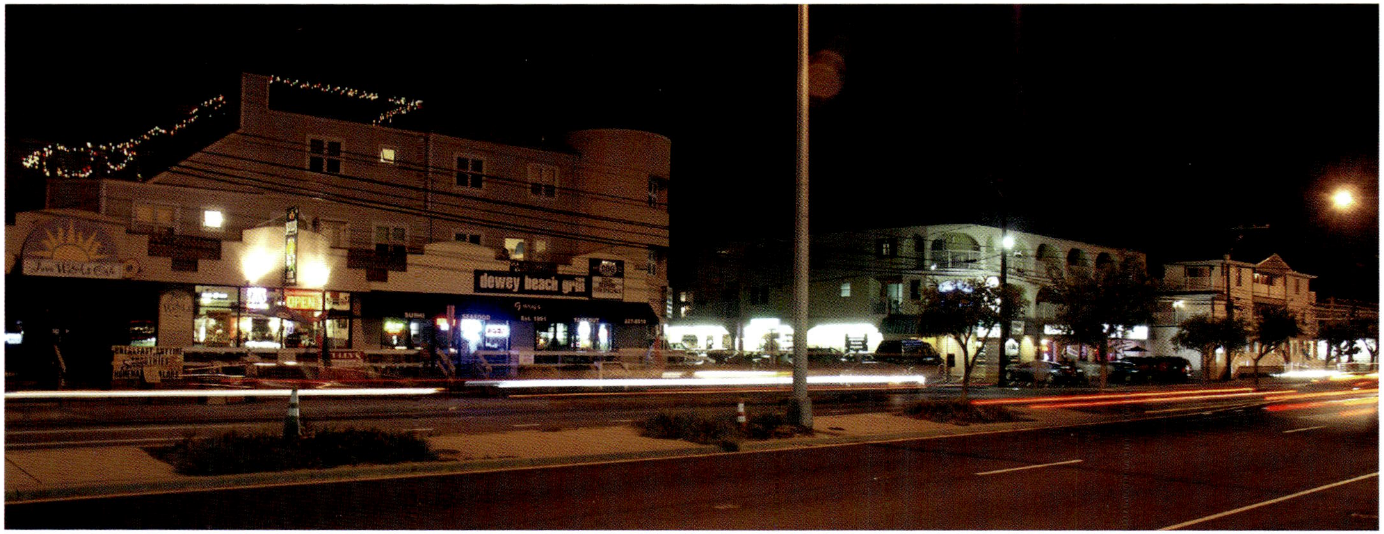

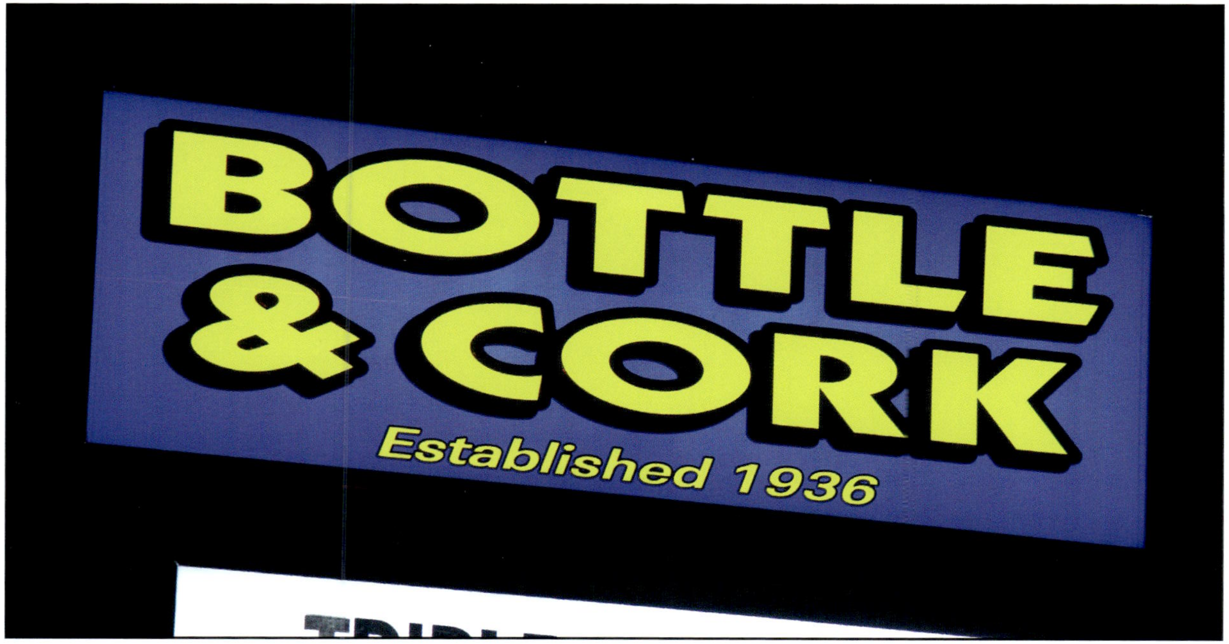

Bottle & Cork, known as "The Greatest Rock and Roll Bar in the World," has hosted many national musical acts including the Dave Matthews Band, Goo Goo Dolls, Cyndi Lauper, Robert Palmer, and Live, to name a few.

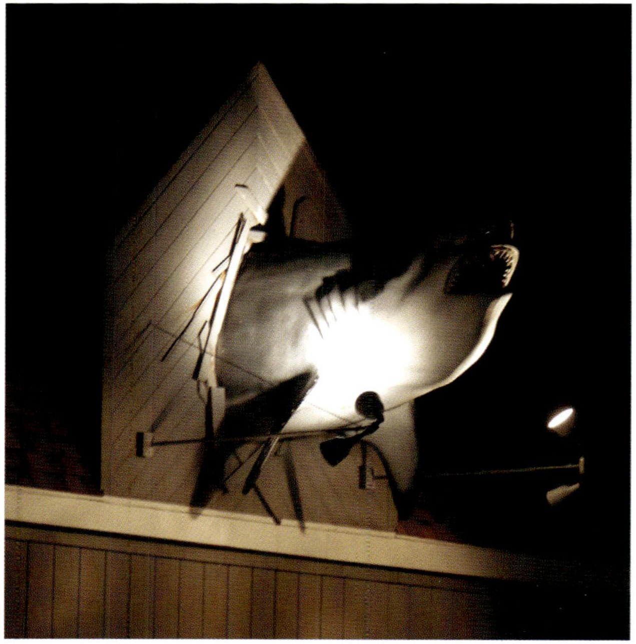

Another popular nightspot along Coastal Highway is the Starboard, which opens early and stays open late. The bar is known both for the large shark jutting out of its façade as well as its "World Famous Bloody Mary Smorgasbord."

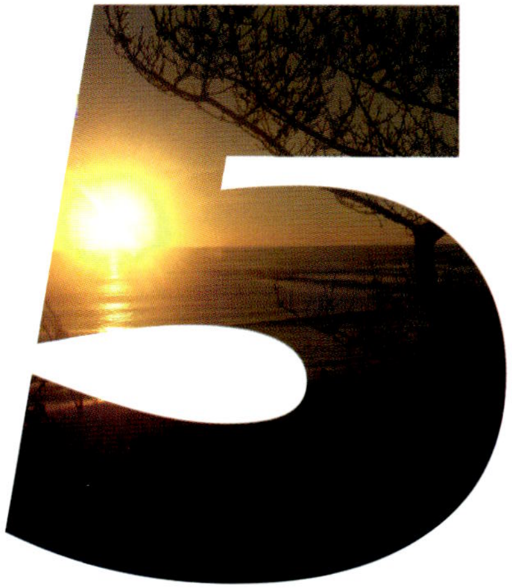

5

Delaware Seashore State Park & Indian River Bay

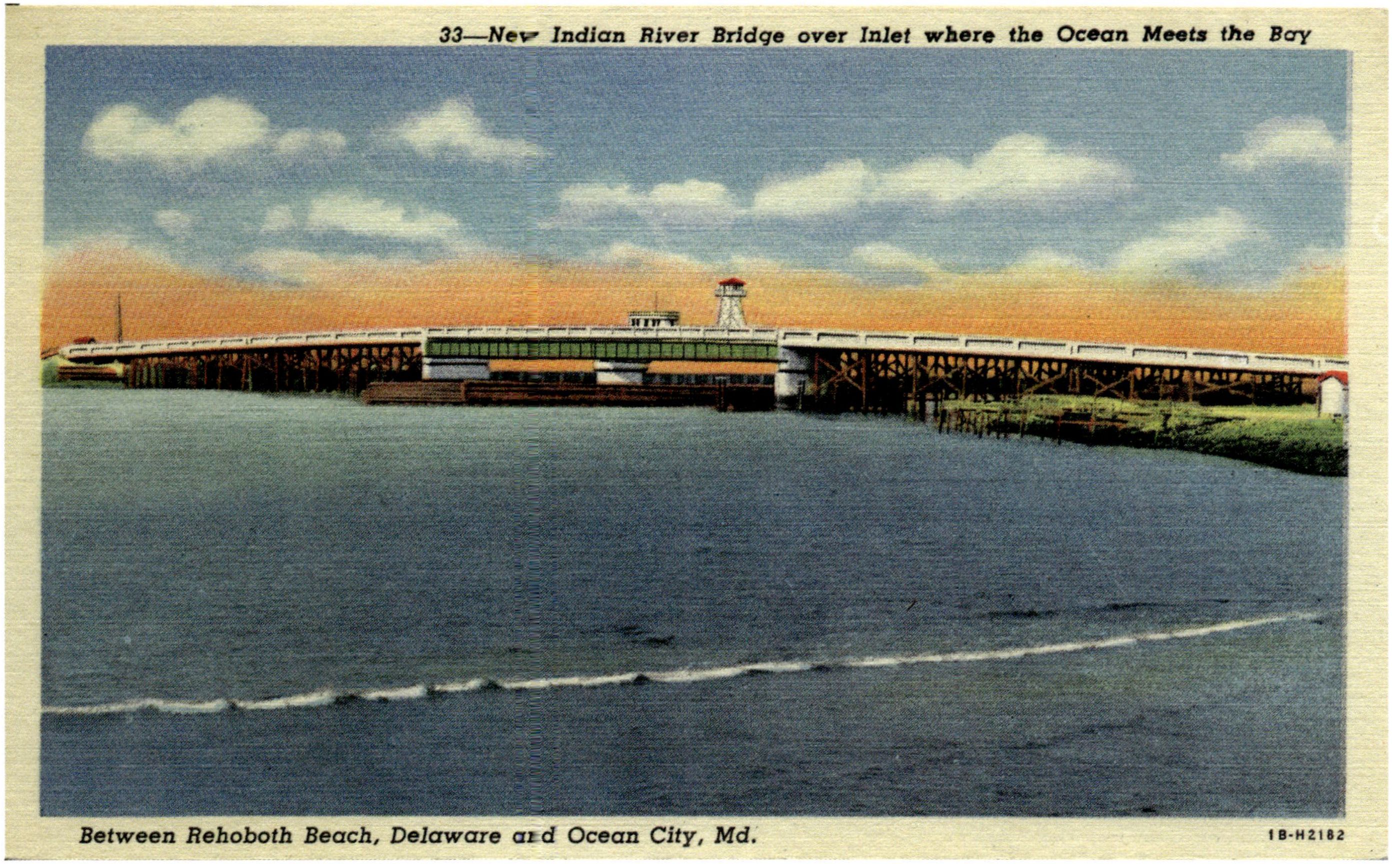

Dewey Beach to the north and Bethany Beach to the south are the bookends of Delaware Seashore State Park. Whereas Dewey is known as a lively town, and Bethany as a quiet resort, Delaware Seashore State Park is a six mile stretch of ocean, bay, and shoreline – and not much else. On the northern end of the park stand two observation towers built in conjunction with Fort Miles at Cape Henlopen. Toward the southern end of the park is the Indian River Inlet and Marina.

Delaware Seashore State Park is on a barrier island that changed frequently throughout the years as the inlet's location moved up and down the coast due to shifting sediment caused by storms and tides. The first inlet bridge was constructed in 1934; five years later, two stone and steel jetties were built, creating a permanent Indian River Inlet that was 500-ft. wide. The first bridge was damaged by storms in 1940, and replaced later that year. Ice flows caused the second bridge to collapse in 1948 – it was repaired and reopened four years later. In 1962 the bridge was severely damaged in a storm, resulting in bridge closure. A new bridge was constructed in 1965, with a second span opening in 1976. Continued erosion has resulted in damage to the inlet bridge, necessitating plans for a new bridge after the turn of the 21st century.

The park dates from 1965 when it was opened by the Delaware State Park Commission. The park has changed over the years, and recently expanded to include Thompson Island, creating a park of 2,825 acres. With the Atlantic Ocean, Rehoboth Bay, and Indian River Bay bordering the park, it has attracted millions of visitors who have flocked there for water-related activities like swimming, sunbathing, surfing, sailboarding, fishing, and boating.

A campground and waterfront cottages allow for overnight stays. The Indian River Marina provides access to the bays and to the ocean. It is also a place to find head boats and charter boats – or just to walk around and enjoy the beautiful boats and watch the fishermen arriving with their day's catch.

The historic Indian River Lifesaving Station is also located in the park, just east of Route 1. The Victorian station was constructed in 1873 for use by the U.S. Lifesaving Service. The Lifesaving Station today showcases its 1905 appearance. Originally, the building was located several hundred feet closer to the ocean; however, a sand dune soon began to form around it, so it was relocated in 1877.

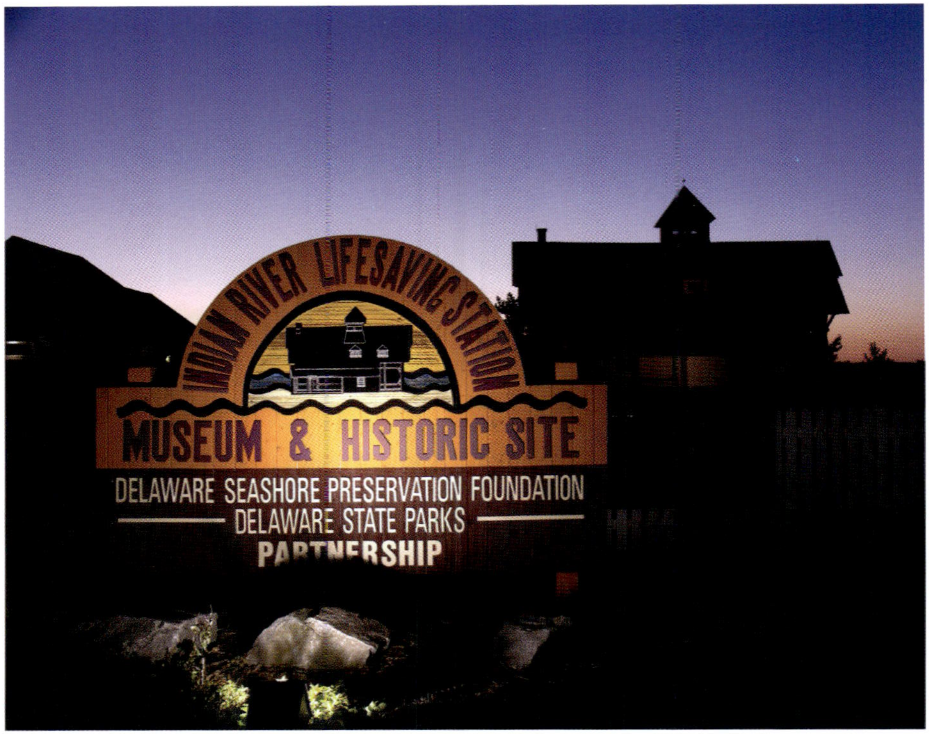

The Indian River Lifesaving Station was constructed in 1876 by the U.S. Lifesaving Service. The attractive Victorian structure is located one mile north of the Indian River Inlet and was constructed to help survivors of coastal shipwrecks.

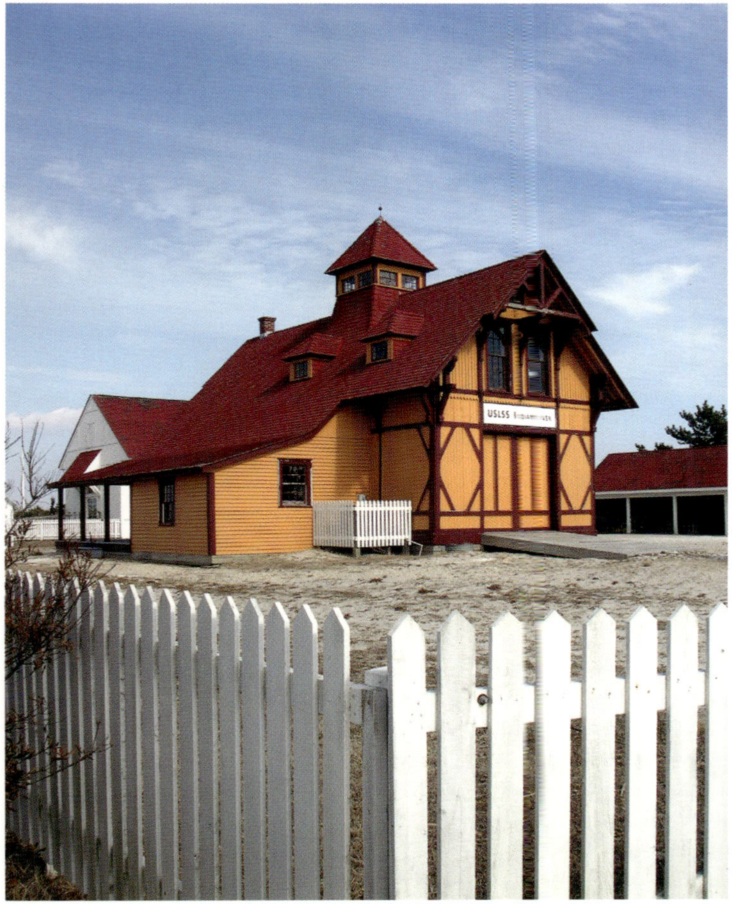

Delaware Seashore State Park contains two swimming areas with modern bath facilities, guarded beaches, and World War II era artillery control towers.

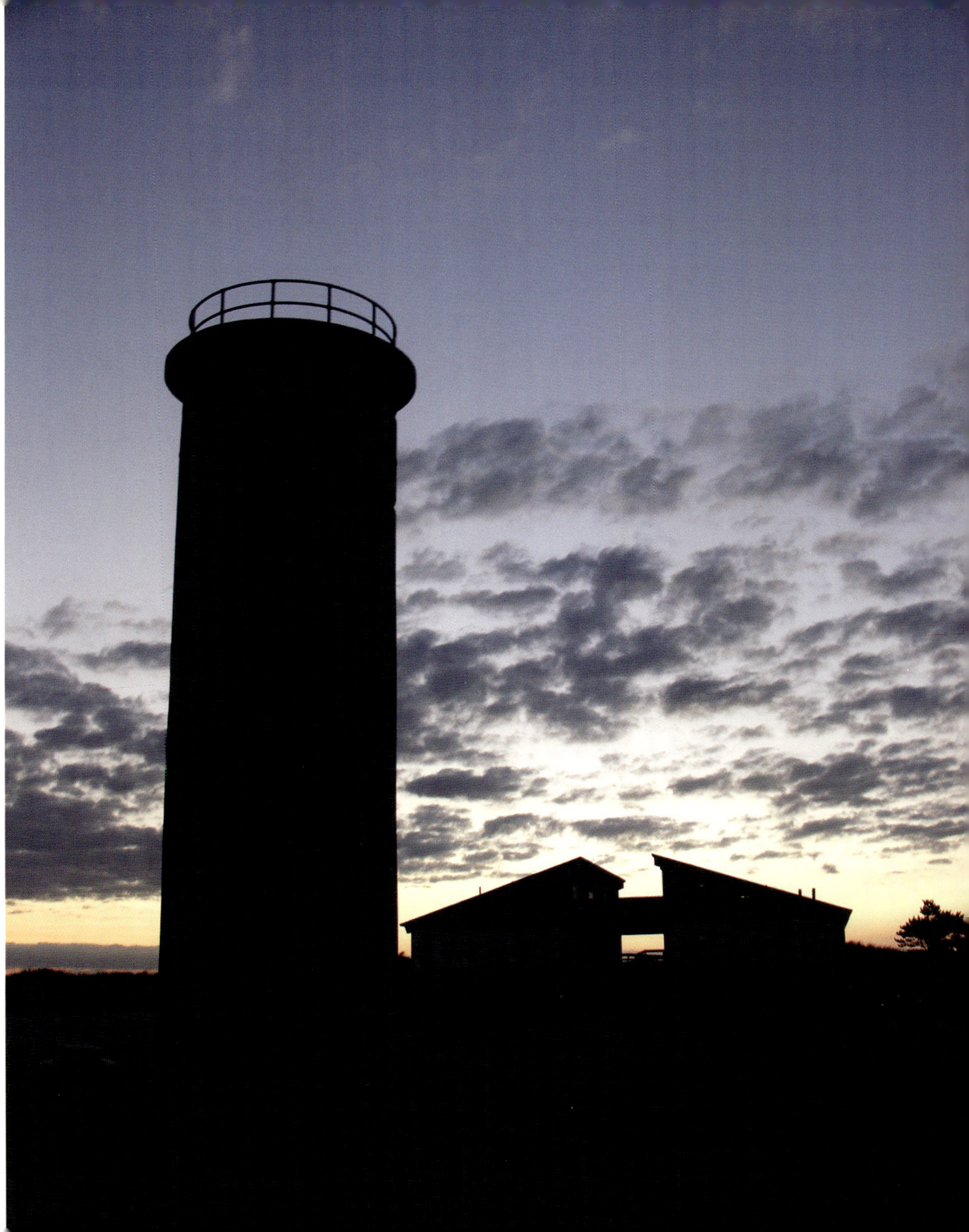

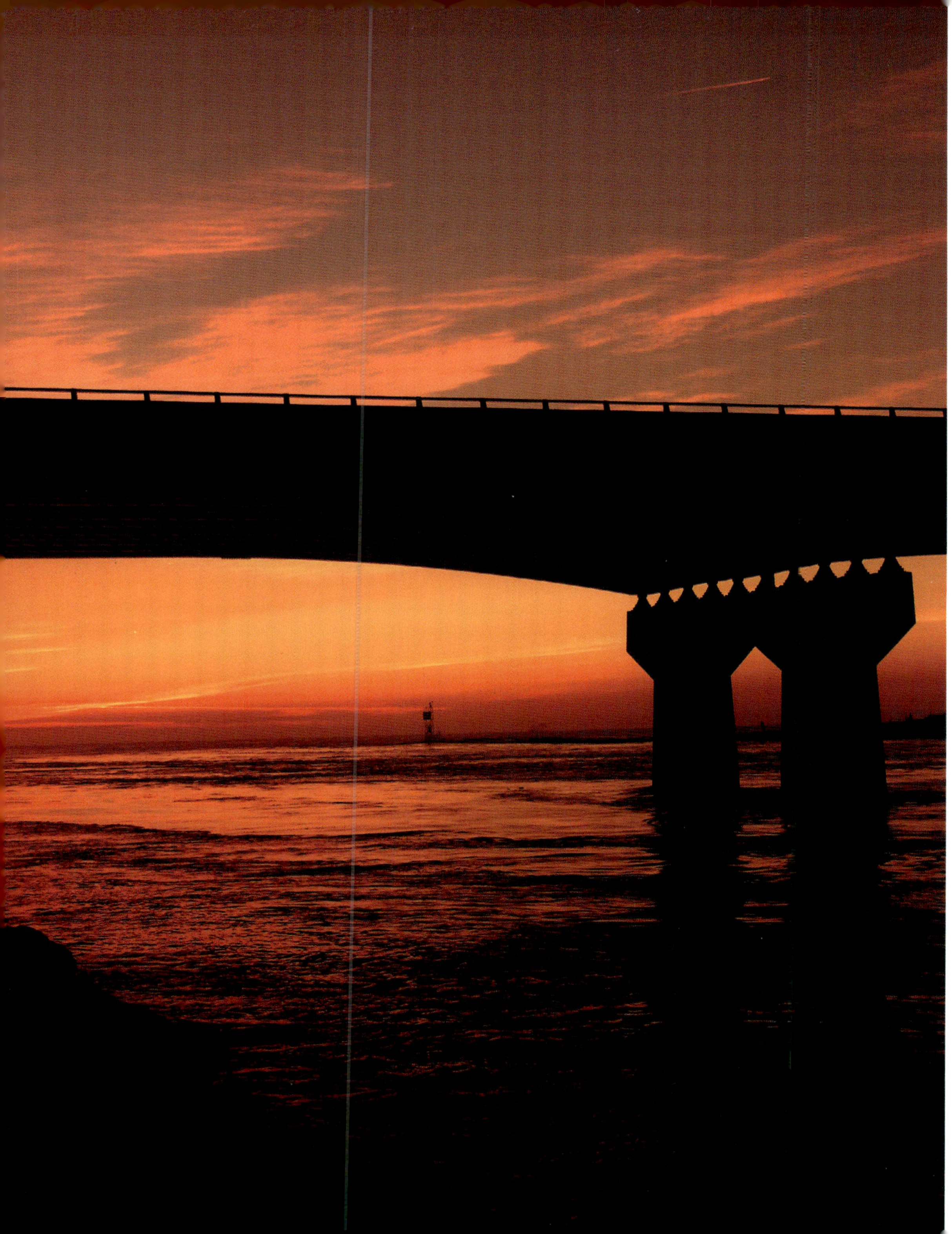

Prior to 1938, the Indian River Inlet was transient. Coastal tides, storms, and winds kept the inlet from maintaining permanence. That changed when new stone and steel jetties were constructed, creating a 500-ft. wide inlet. There have been several bridges over the inlet as storms, erosion, and ice jams have caused extensive damage and destruction.

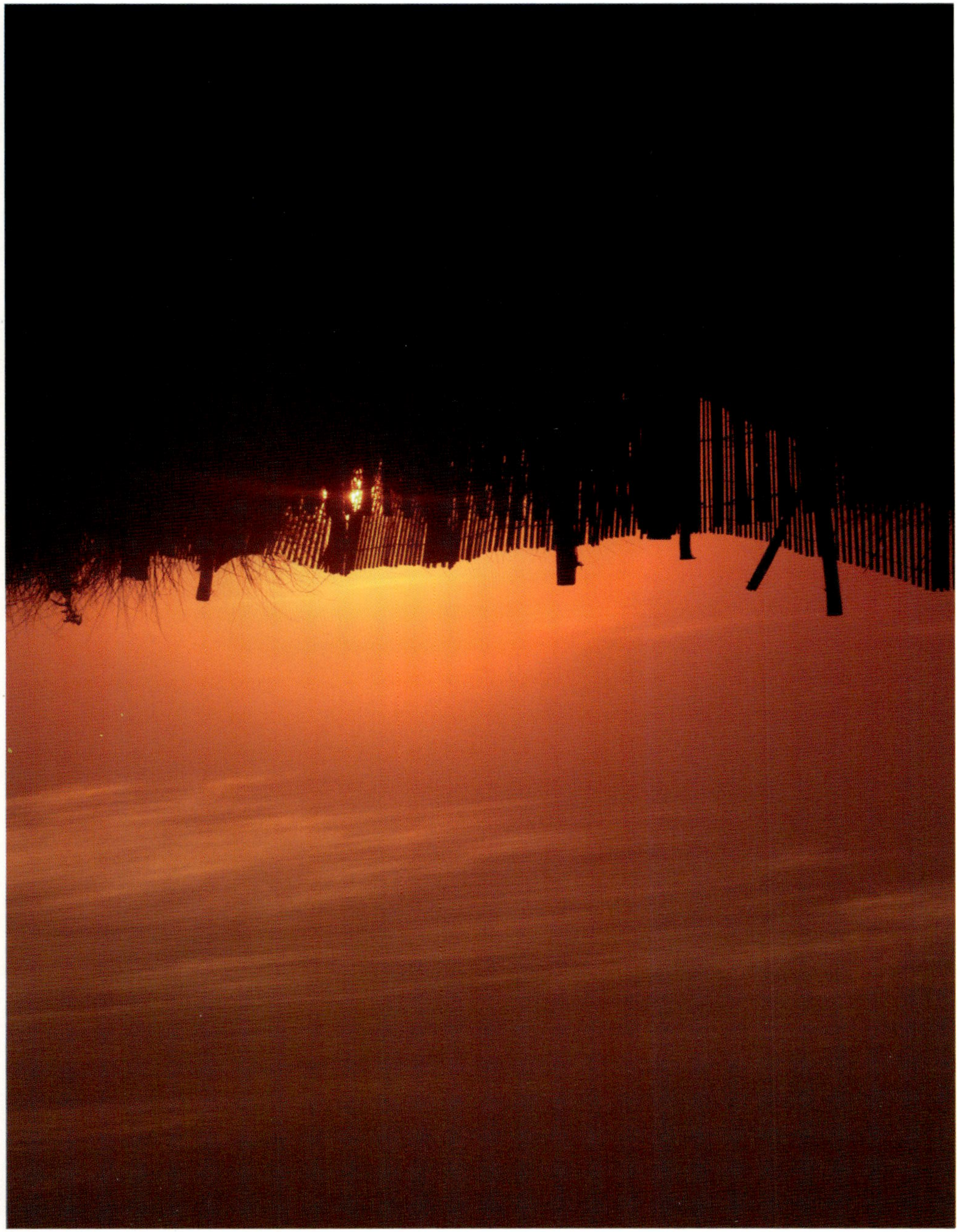

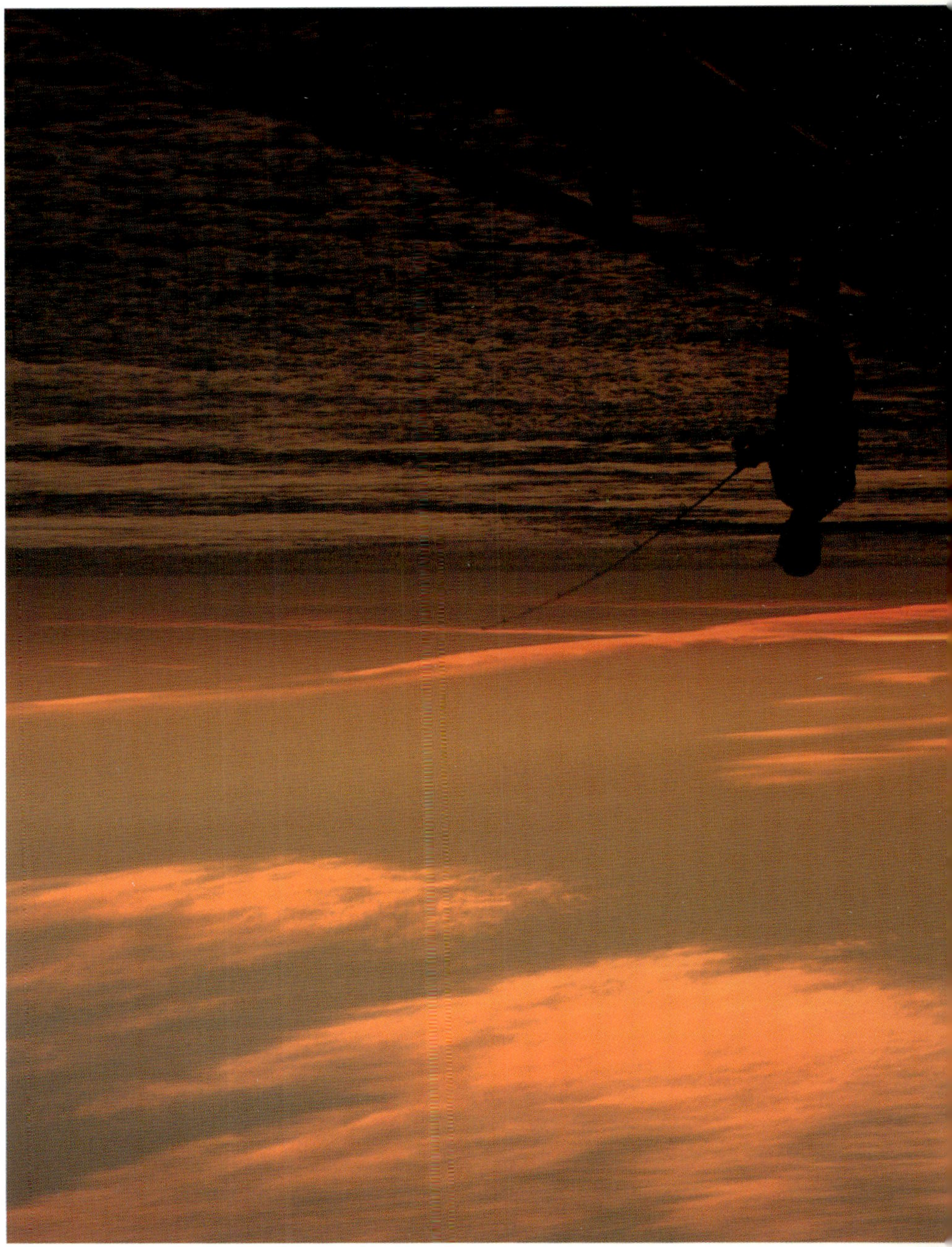

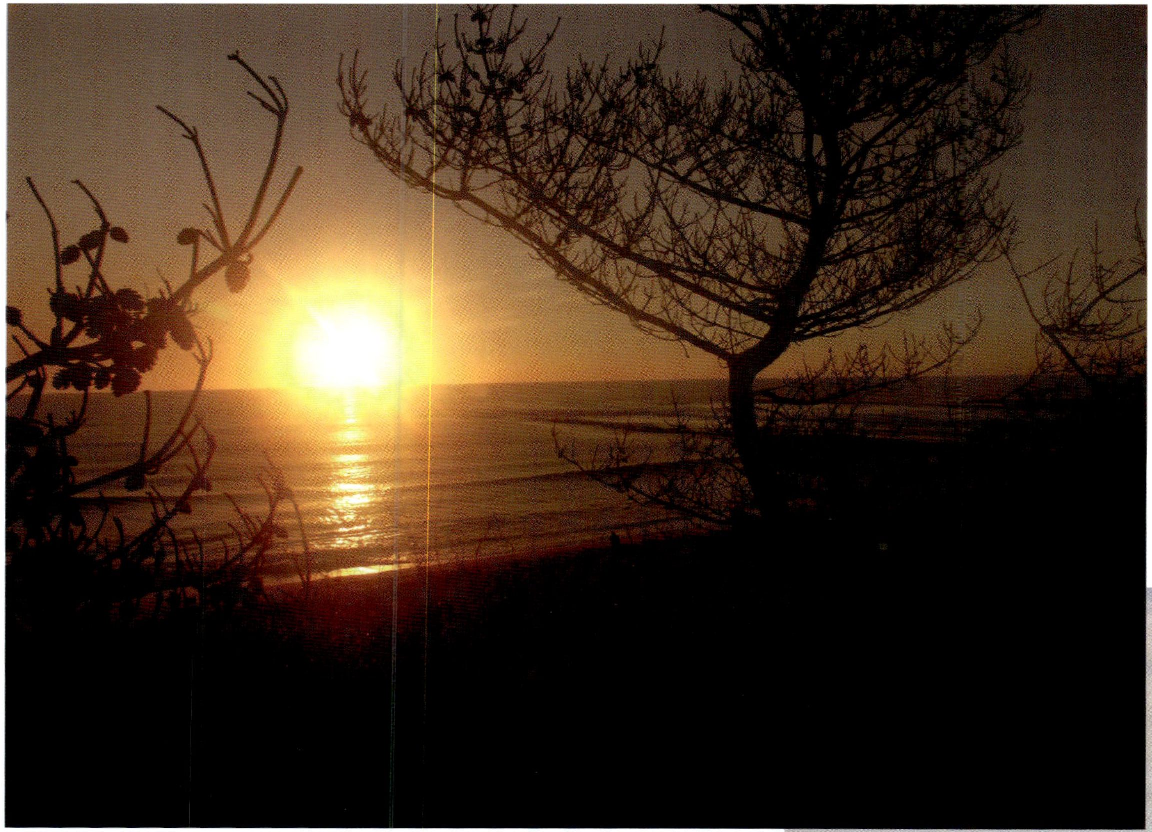

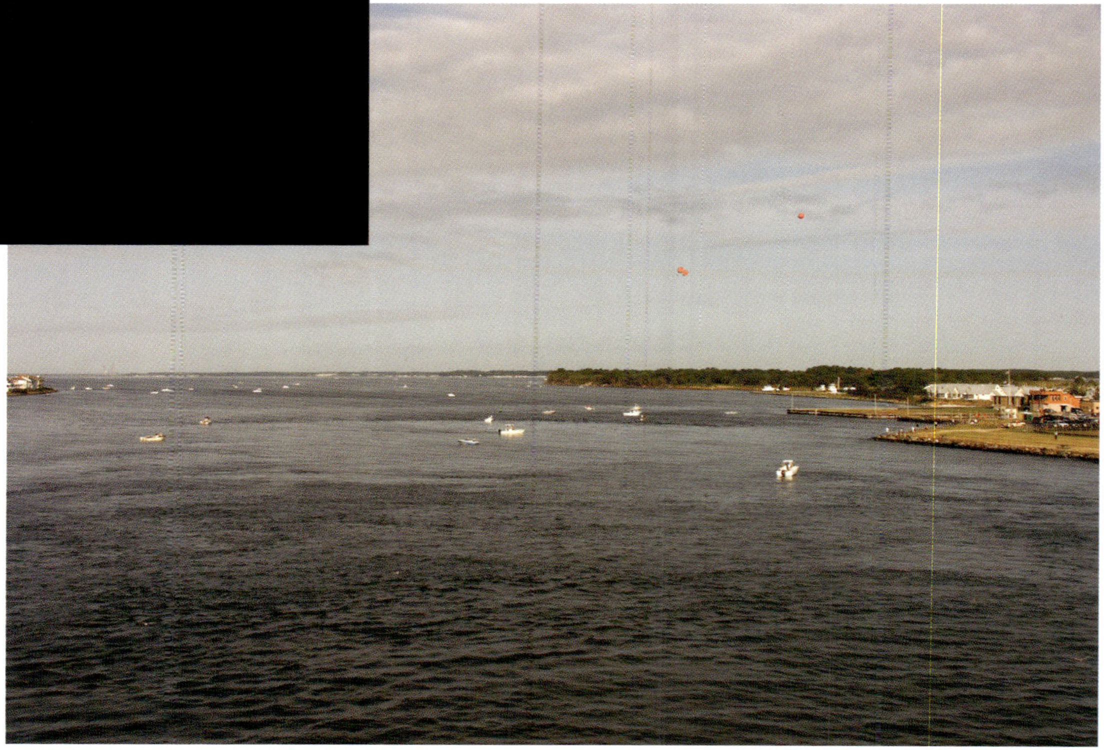

The 2825-acre Delaware Seashore State Park was established in 1965 to offer visitors sun, sand, swimming and surfing.

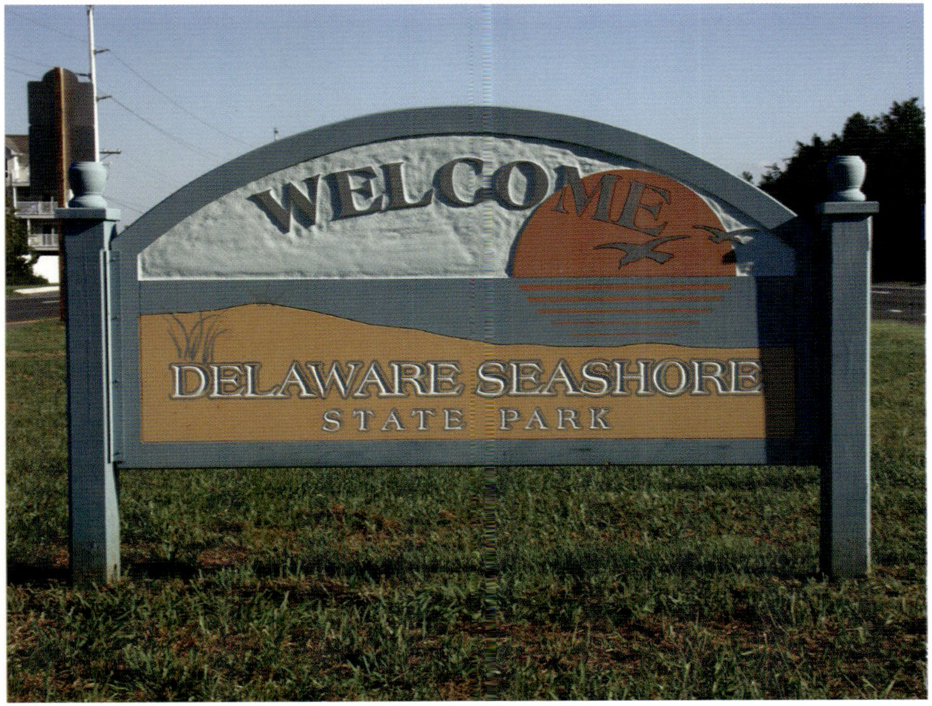

The Indian River Yacht Club is located near Oak Orchard, providing docks and easy access to the Indian River Bay.

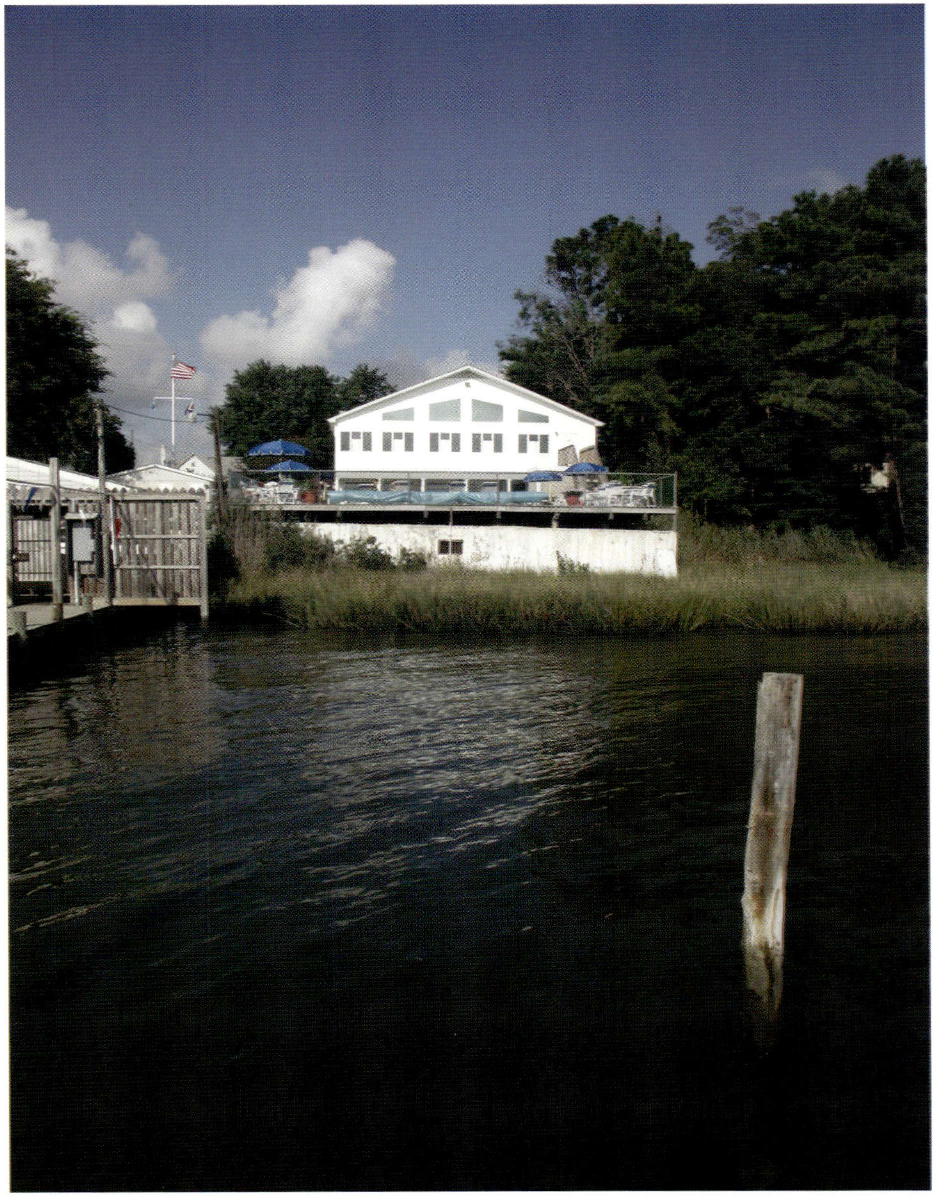

The Indian River Marina is located on the north side of the inlet. Here you'll find charter boats, head boats, storage areas, and docks.

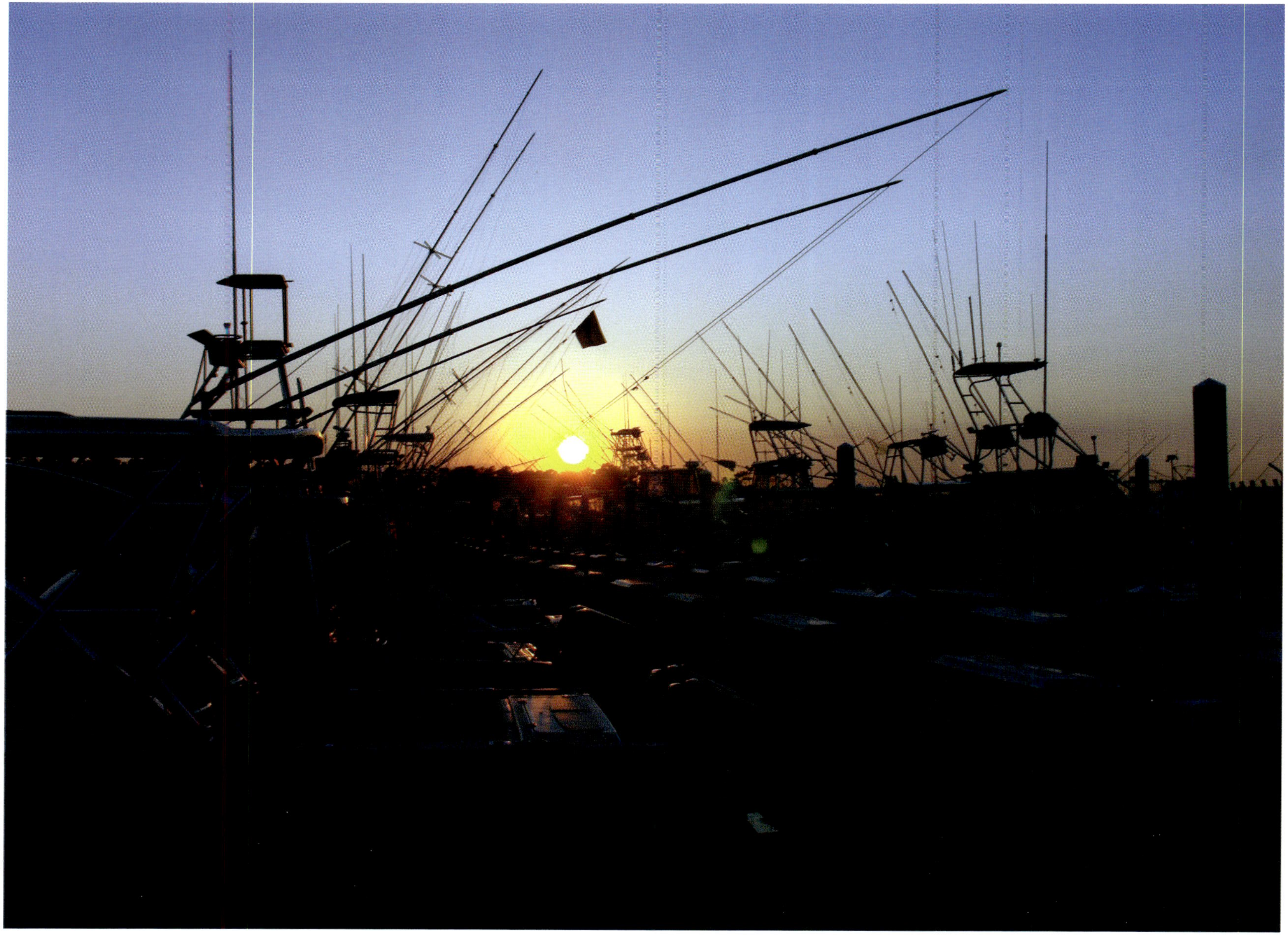

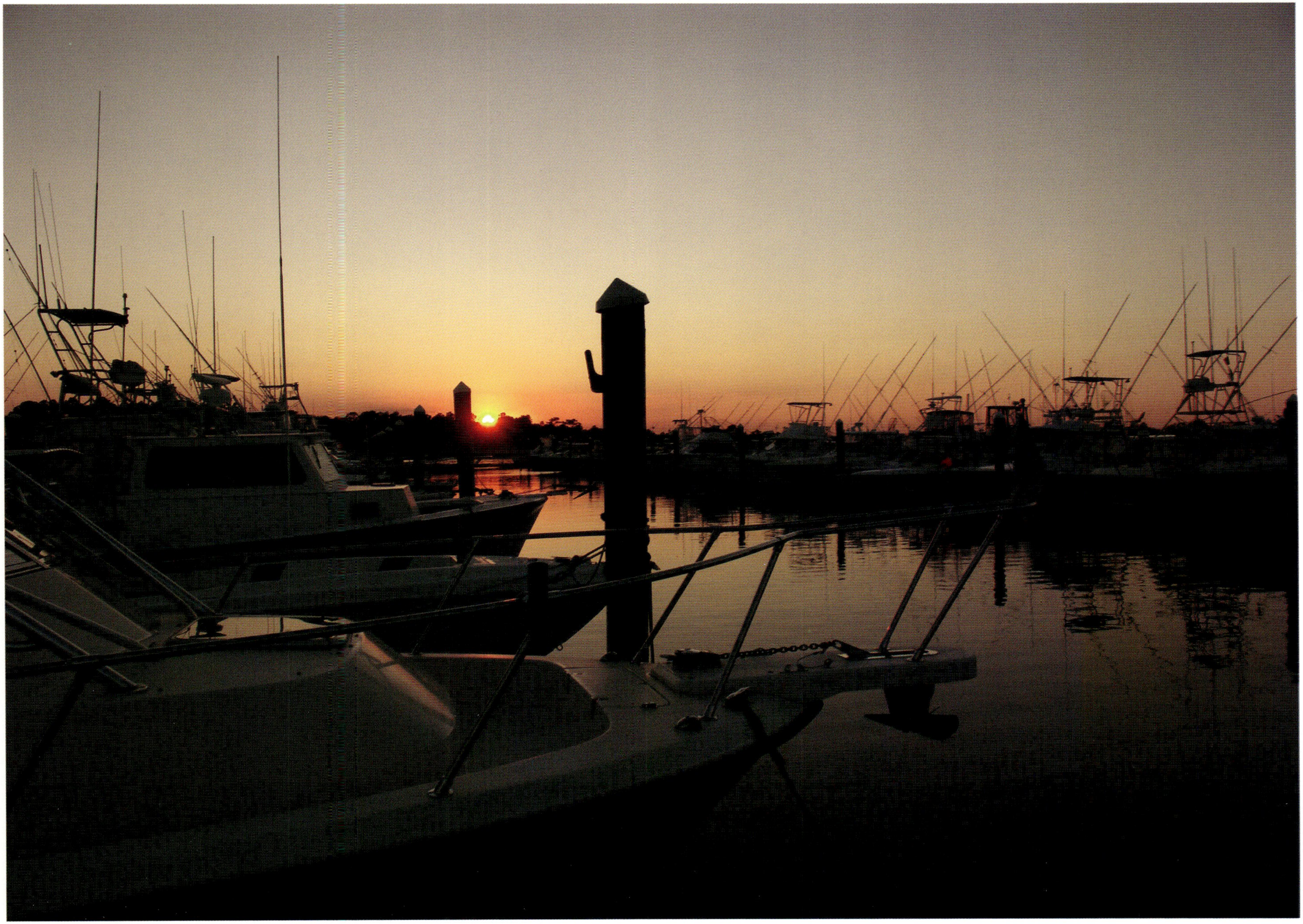

Picturesque Indian River Bay provides access to the Indian River, Assawcman Canal, Rehoboth Bay, and Atlantic Ocean.

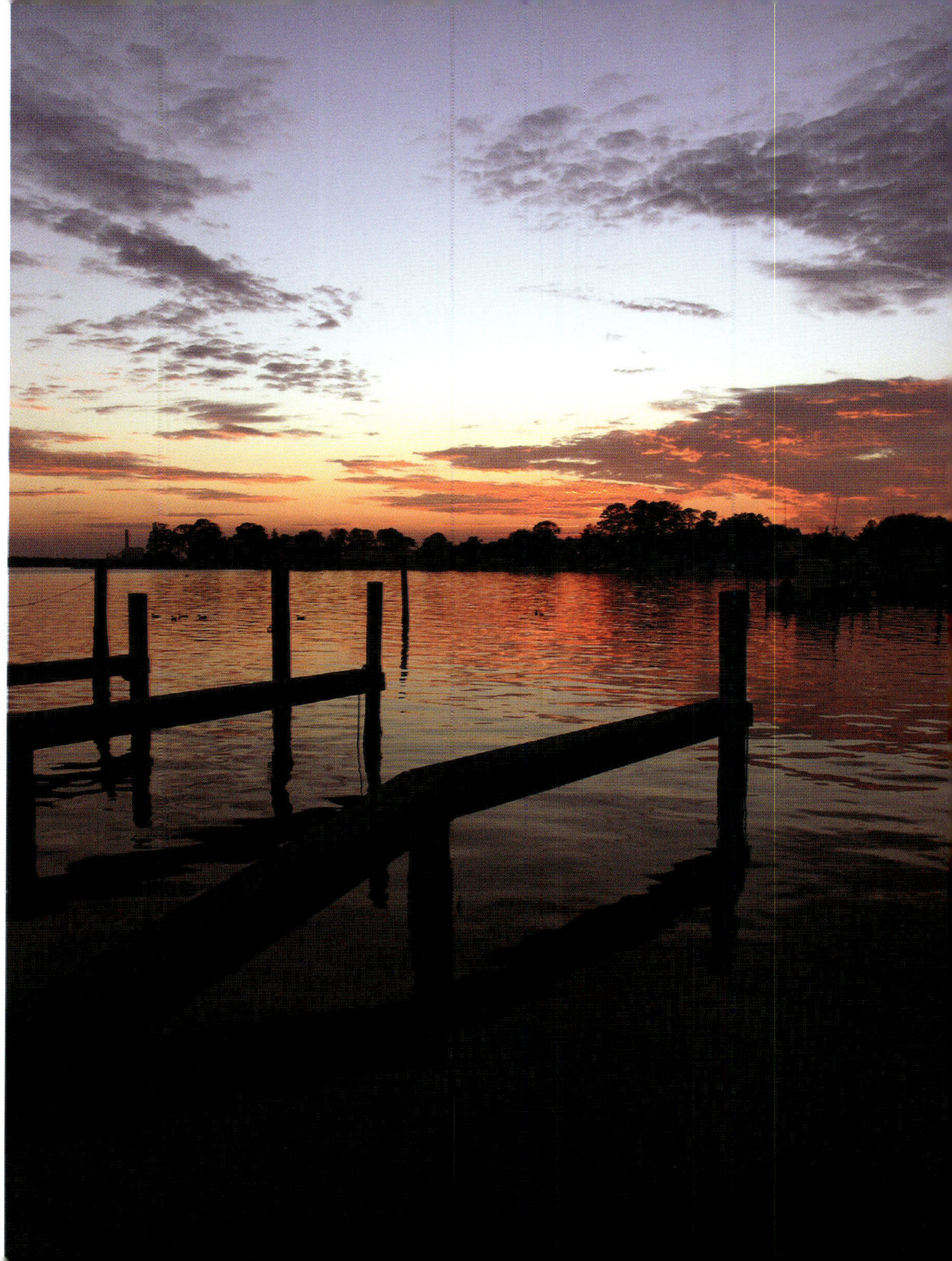

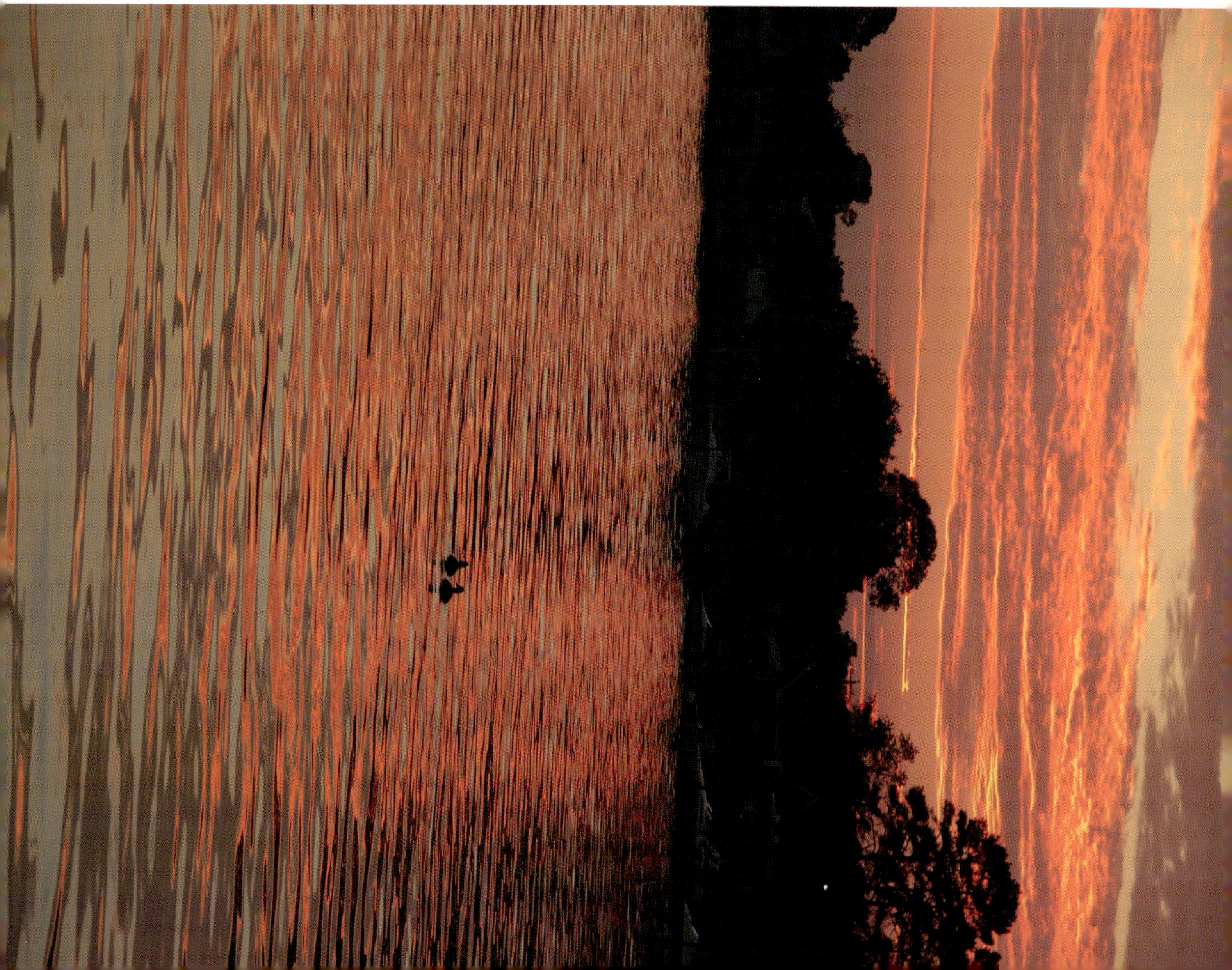

6

Bethany Beach: *The Quiet Resort*

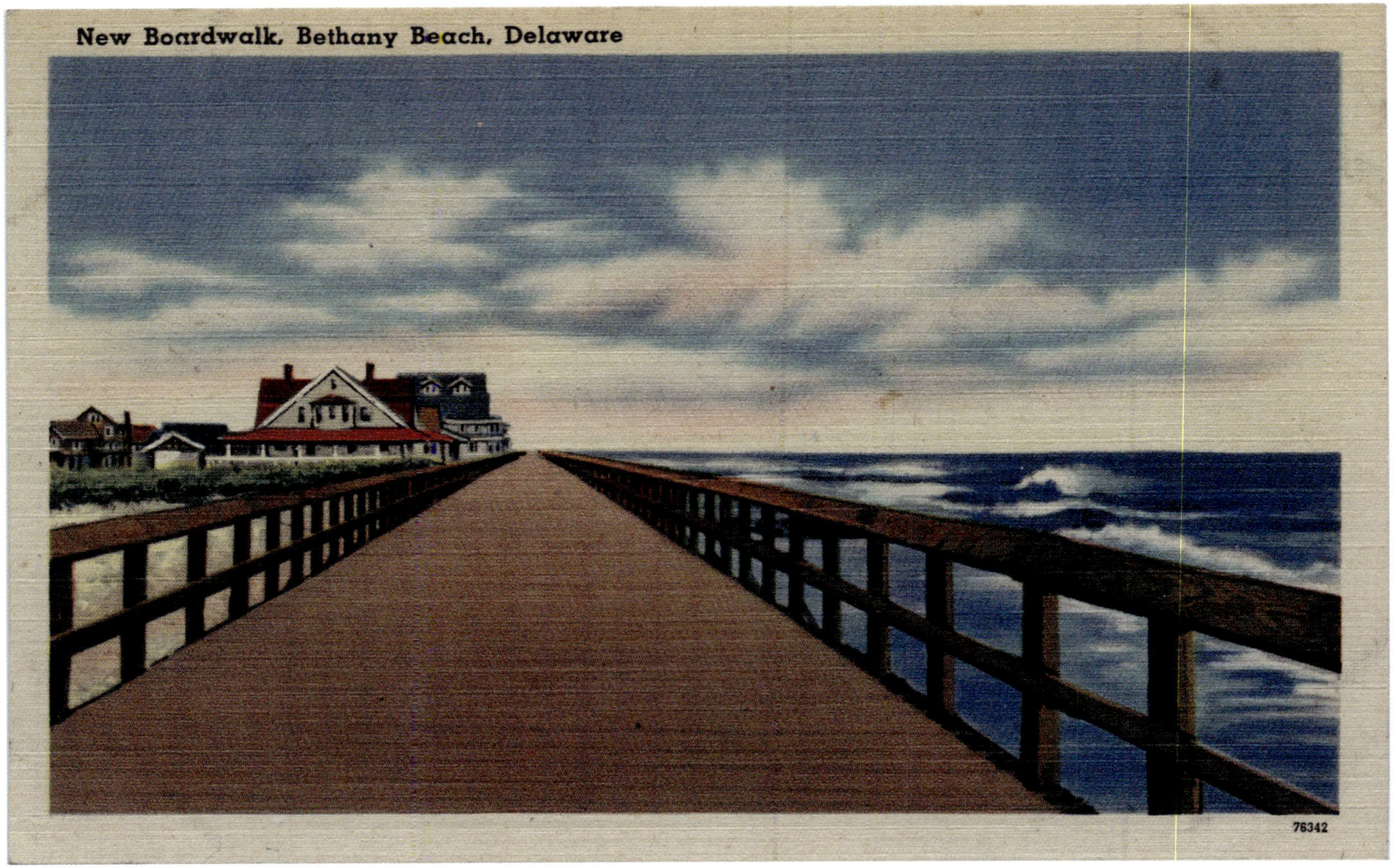

University of Delaware Library Postcard Collection, University of Delaware, Newark, Delaware

Like nearby Rehoboth Beach, Bethany Beach traces its origins to a religious retreat. In 1901, the Disciplines of Christ founded a seaside assembly and summer camp. H. L. Atkinson named the community, doing so in a nationwide contest that offered an oceanfront lot as prize.

Bethany Beach's first building was, appropriately, an octagonal tabernacle constructed on the grounds of the Christian Missionary Society. The Bethany Beach Improvement Company set out to develop a town, but struggled. A railroad had been planned, but it never materialized.

In 1902, six men from Pittsburgh took over the company and began development. Beachfront lots were sold for $200, with inland lots available for $75. The first boardwalk was constructed one year later, as were three roofed pavilions.

What Bethany Beach lacked in those early days was easy access. A 1907 project dredged a canal, allowing boats from Rehoboth to deliver passengers. A paved road from Rehoboth Beach was not completed, however, until 1934.

Perhaps Bethany Beach's most notable image is the sentinel that has watched over Coastal Highway in one form or another since 1977: Chief Little Owl. Originally a totem pole known as the "Whispering Giant," the sculpture was replaced in 1994 and again in 2002. The most recent incarnation was carved of Alaskan red cedar and based upon the likeness of a Nanticoke Indian Chief.

Today, Bethany Beach is known as one of the Quiet Resorts, along with Fenwick Island, South Bethany, Millville, Ocean View, and other nearby communities. While the town does have a half-mile boardwalk, it is nothing like the mega-summer resort to the south, Ocean City, Maryland. Bethany Beach promotes a family friendly atmosphere and a break from the hustle-and-bustle of other nearby resorts. Shopping and dining can be found on Garfield Plaza, and the overall design of the town is in some ways a mini-Rehoboth Beach: a street with retail offerings forming a "T" with the boardwalk, with a bandstand at the intersection of the two.

The boardwalk can be crowded on summer nights, particularly during free weekend concerts. A beach replenishment project has added large dunes; the once-elevated boardwalk is now protected from the ocean.

To the south of the boardwalk rises Sea Colony, a series of nine high-rise condominiums designed as towering sandcastles. With over 2200 oceanfront condominiums and nearby townhouses, Sea Colony also offers a half-mile of private beach, 34 tennis courts, and 12 swimming pools, earning it recognition as one of the top tennis communities in the nation from *Tennis Magazine*.

Further south, "The Best Little Beach in Delaware" – the community of South Bethany – is mostly residential, though commercial offerings can be found on the west side of Coastal Highway. The town was incorporated in 1968 and later expanded to include York Beach and Paradise Shores.

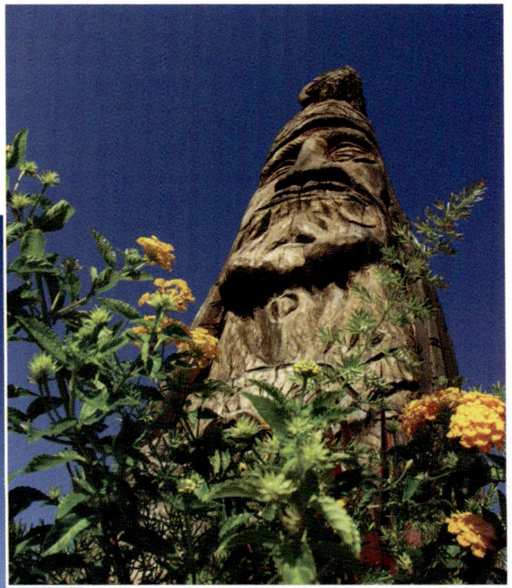

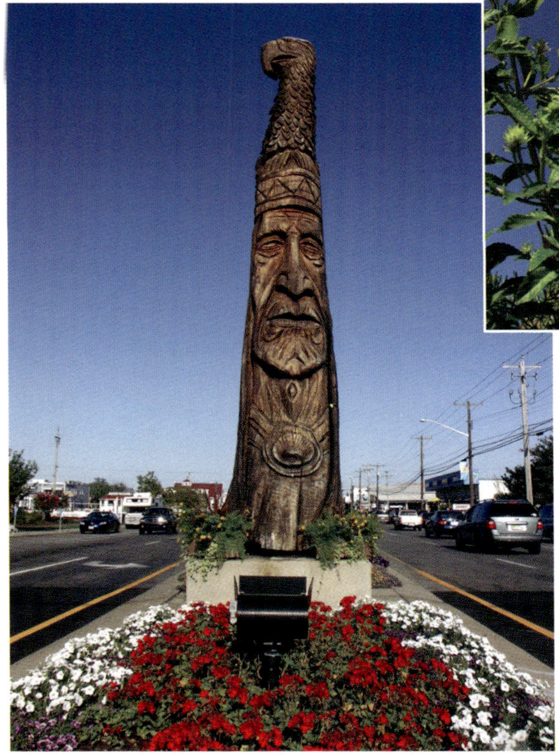

In 1976, a totem pole was erected in Bethany Beach as part of a project to place totem poles in all fifty states. Termites and storms have caused damage over the years, necessitating replacement. The current sculpture, "Chief Little Owl," was carved in 2002 from Alaskan red cedar by Peter Toth, who created the original structure.

Dawn and sunrise along the Atlantic Coast are like a painter's canvas – blank at first, but then becoming increasingly picturesque as layer after layer of color are added and blended, each minute revealing a different masterpiece painted by Mother Nature.

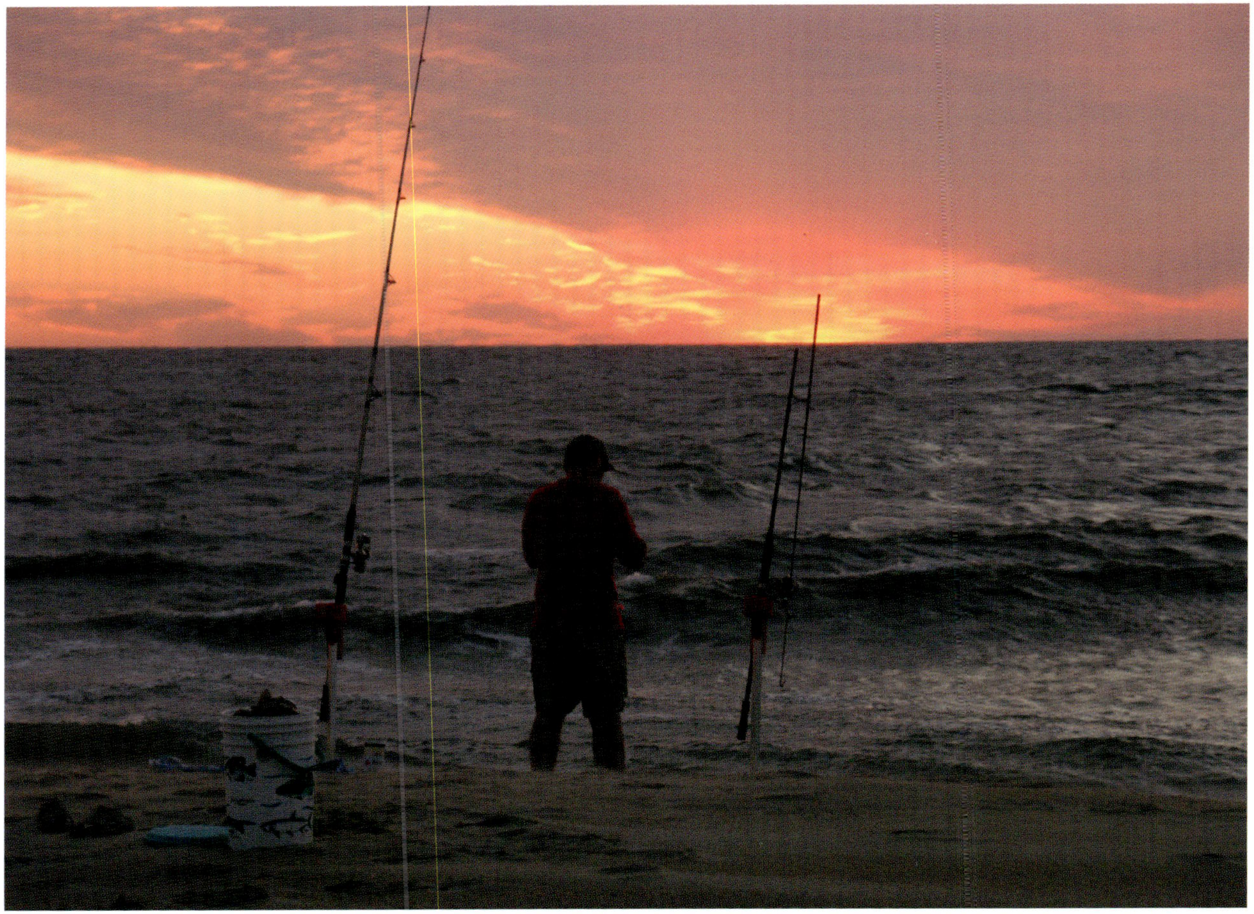

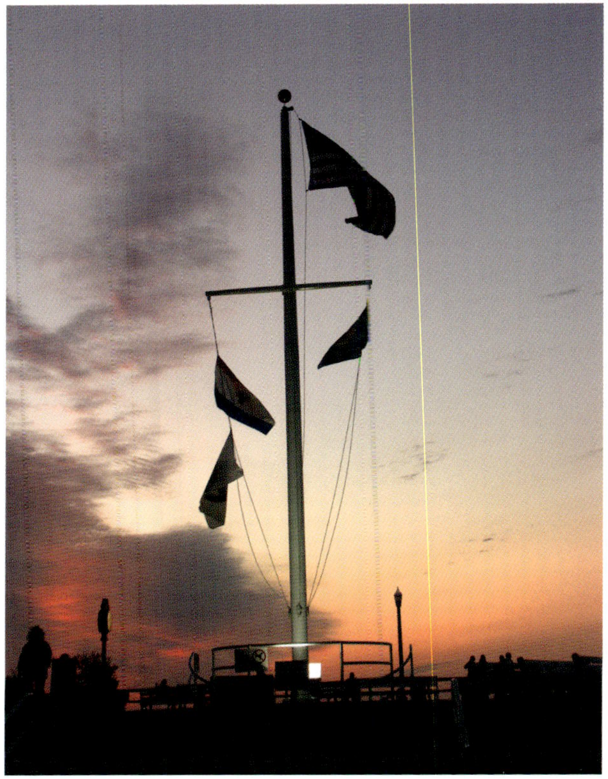

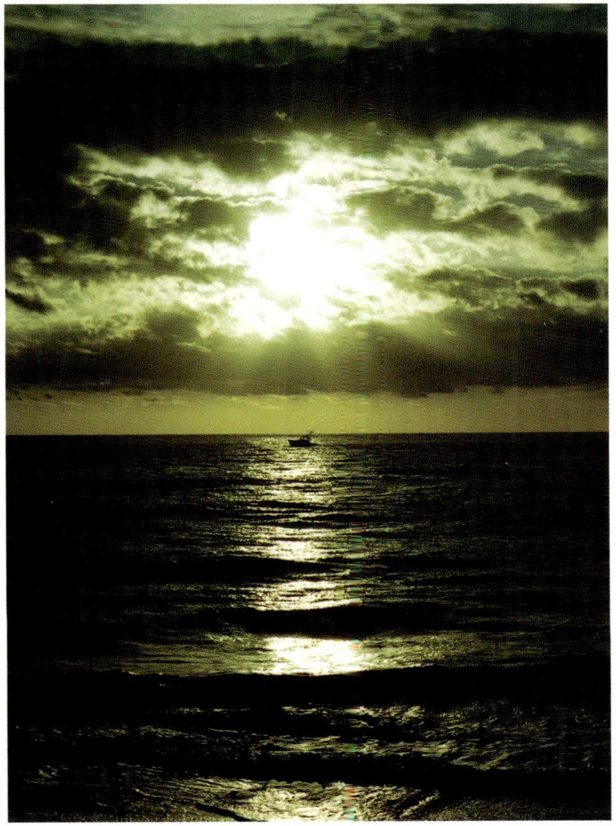

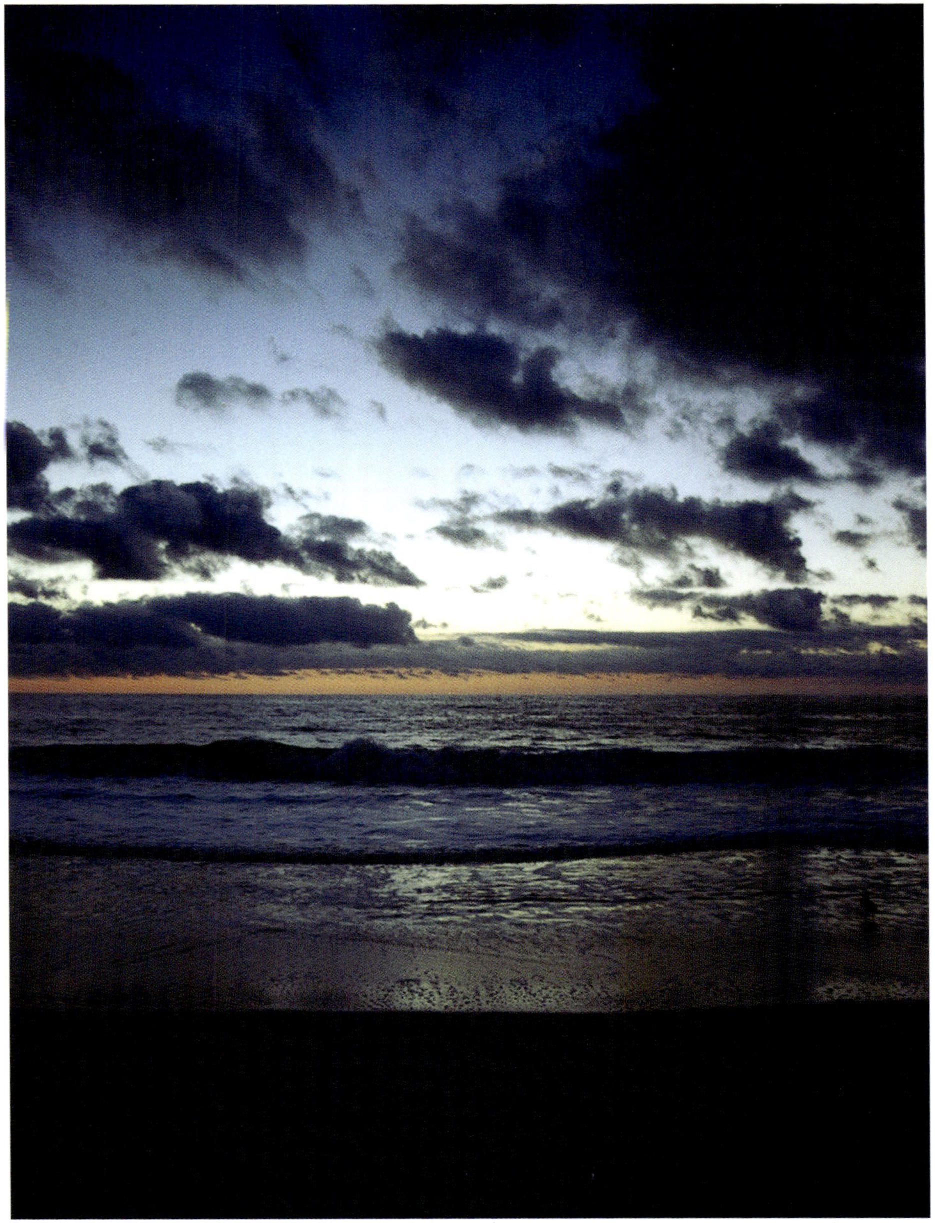

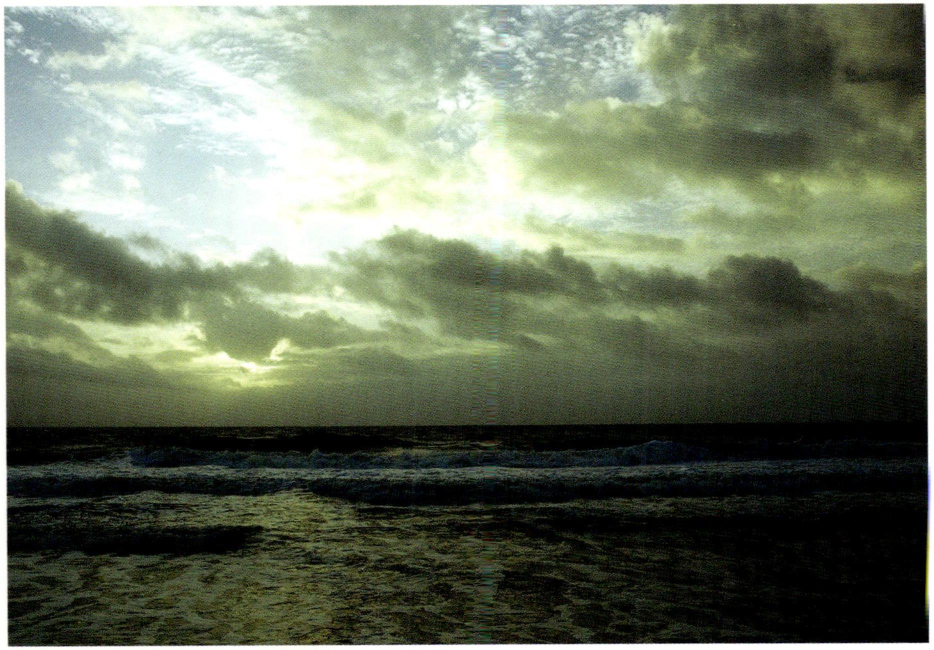

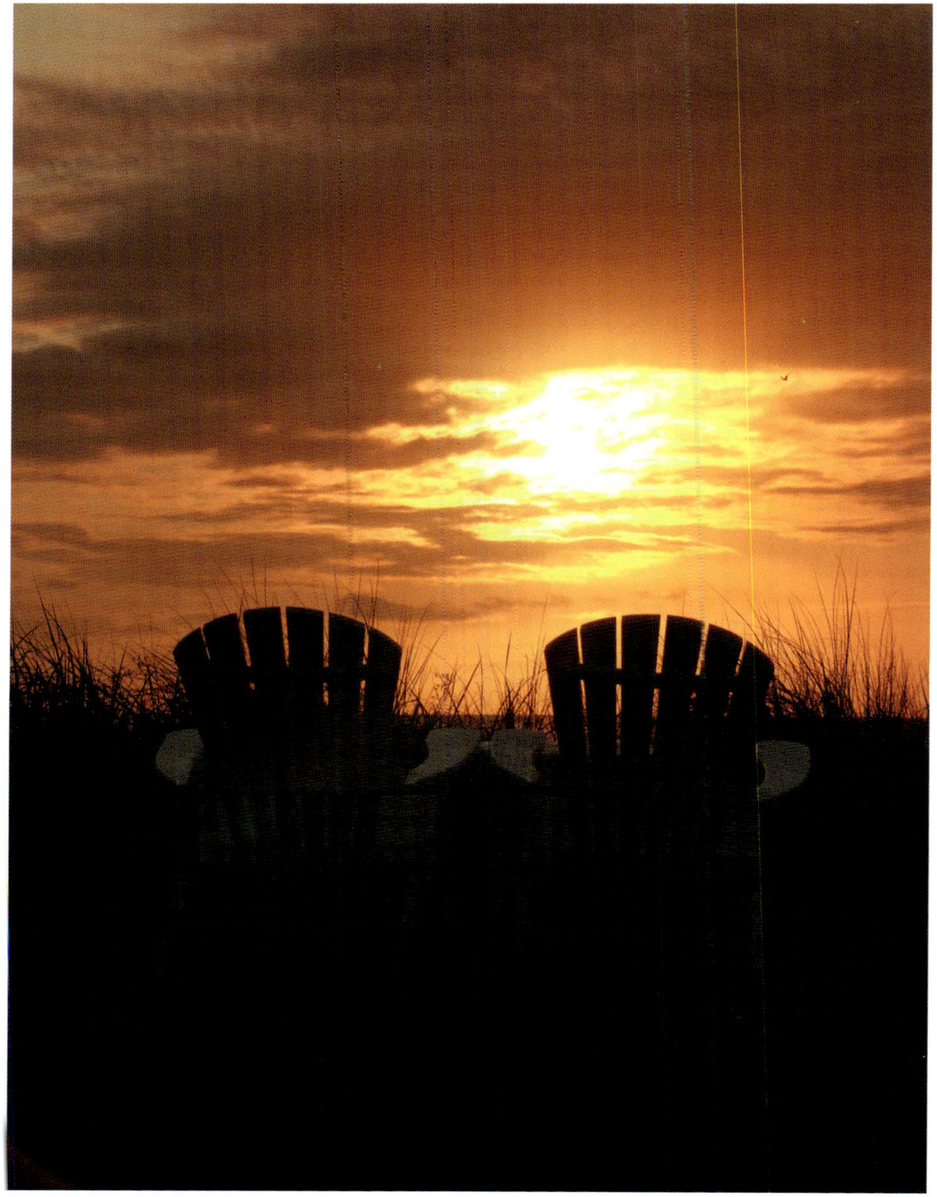

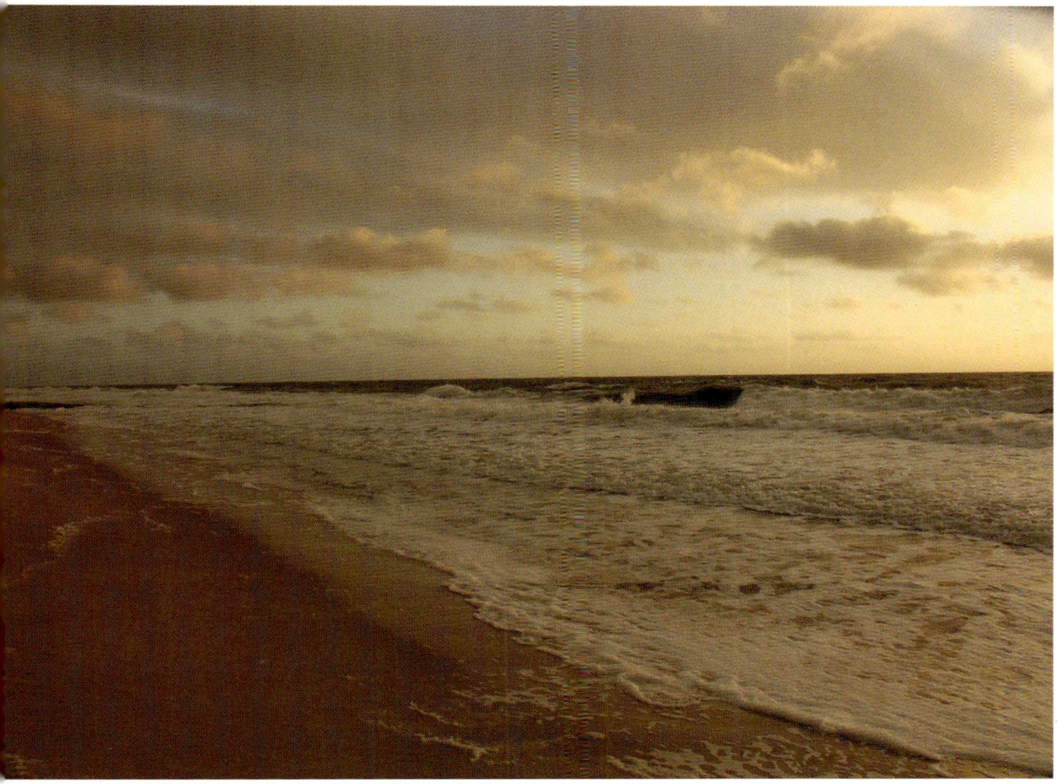

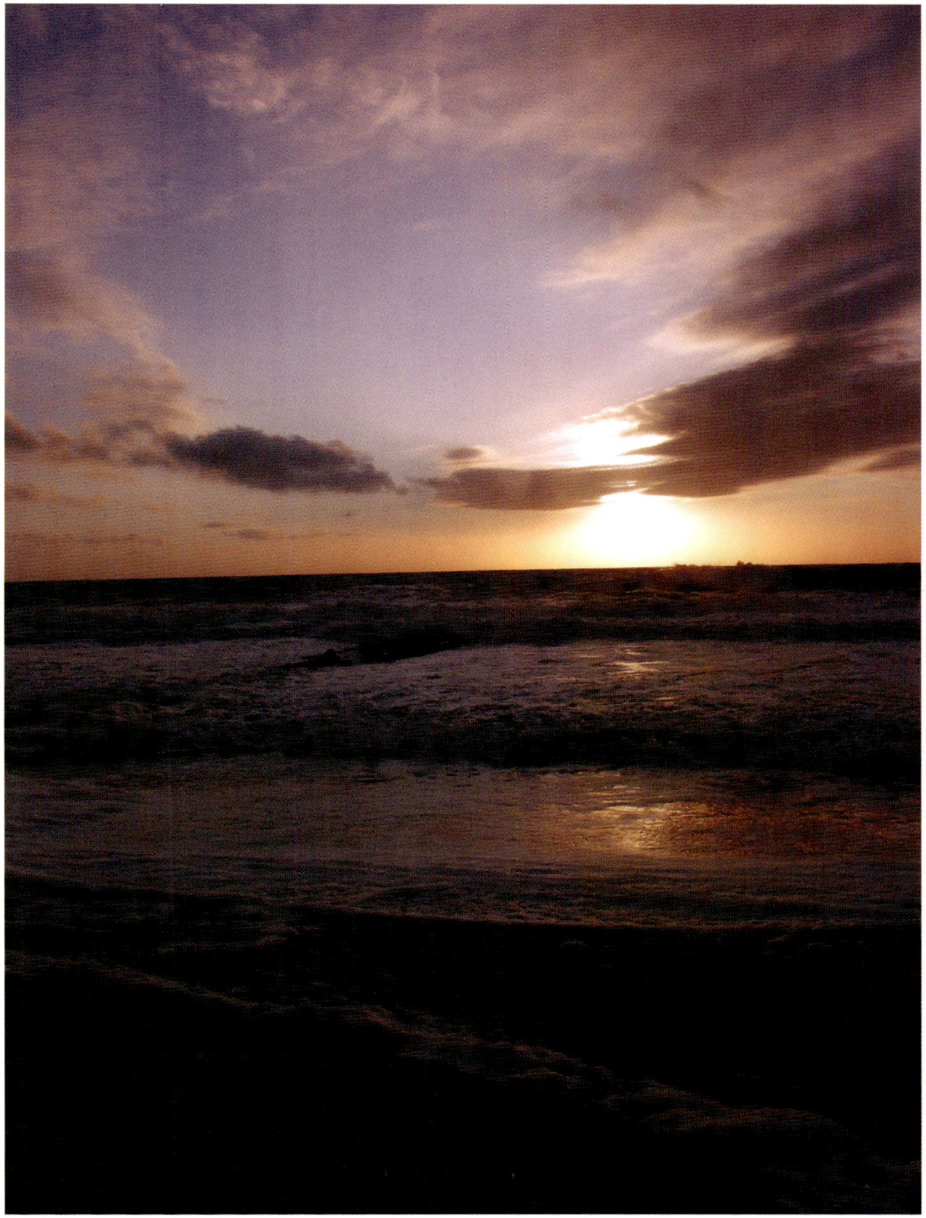

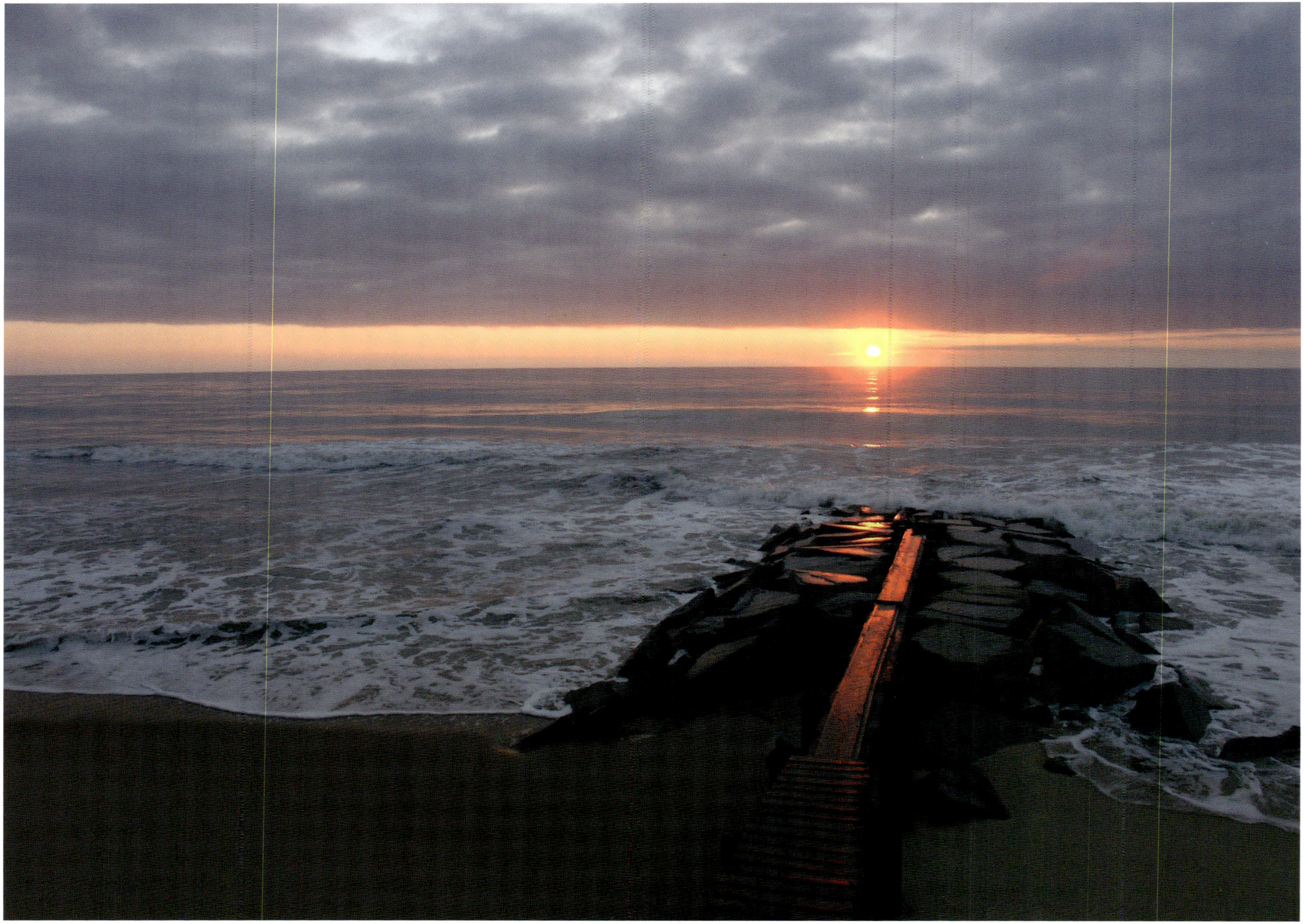

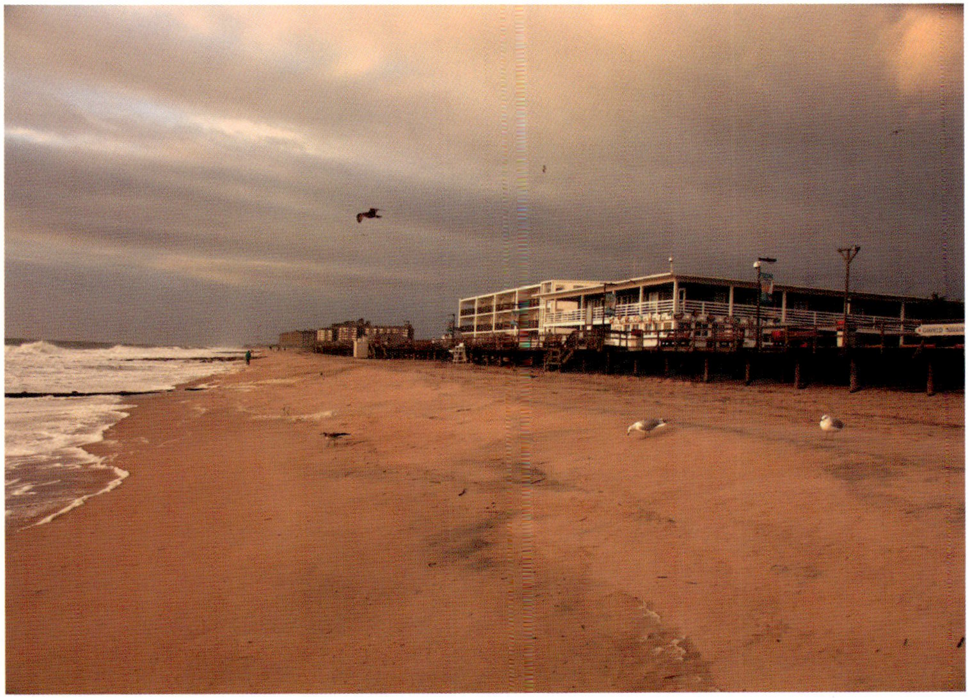

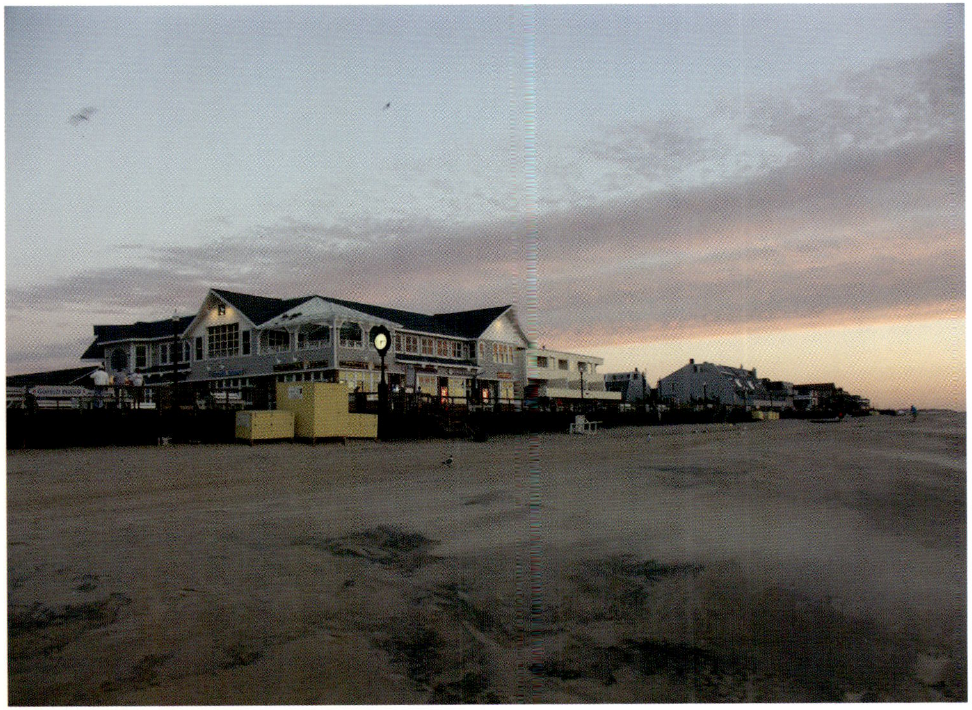

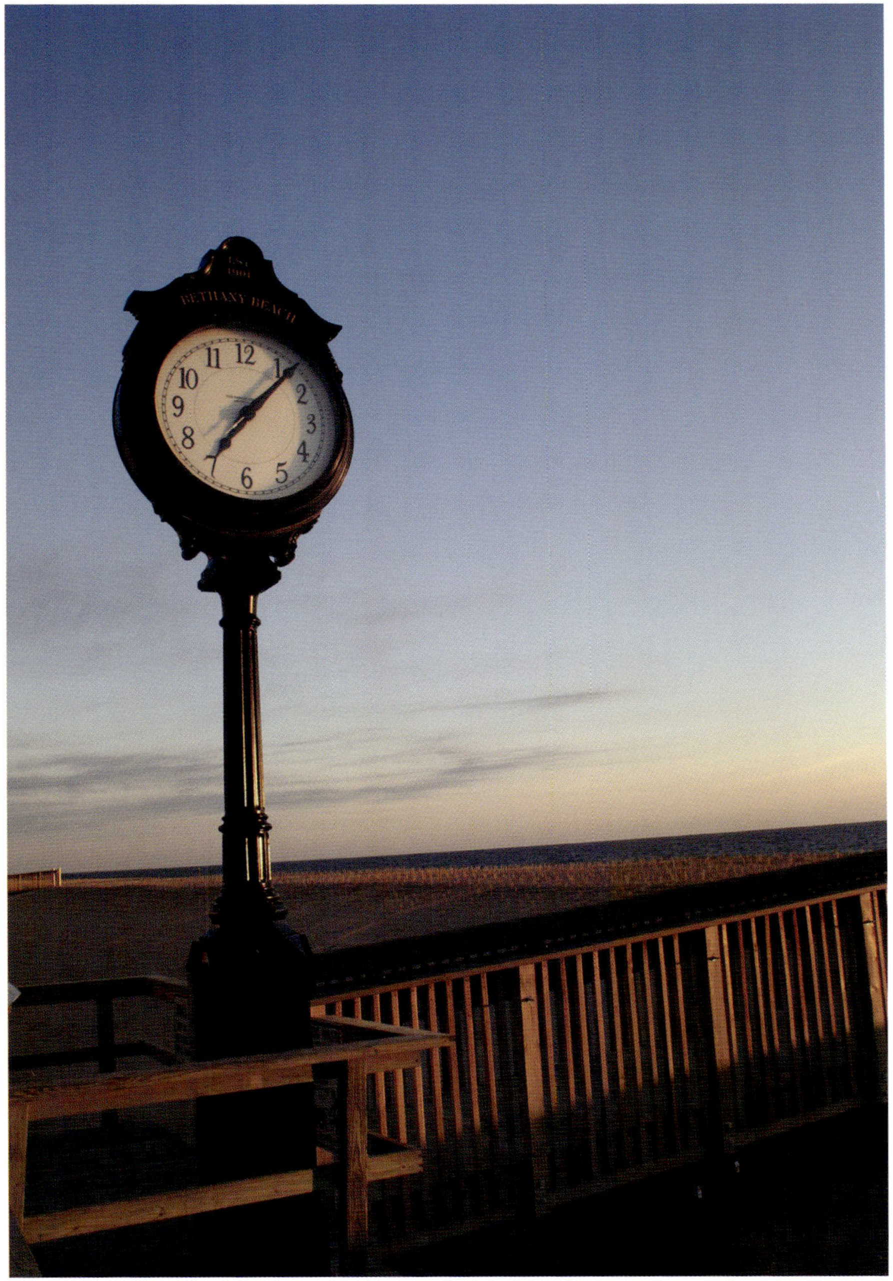
BETHANY BEACH

Today, the Holiday House is a building housing shops; however, many long-time residents and visitors remember the Holiday House as a restaurant which stood in the same location.

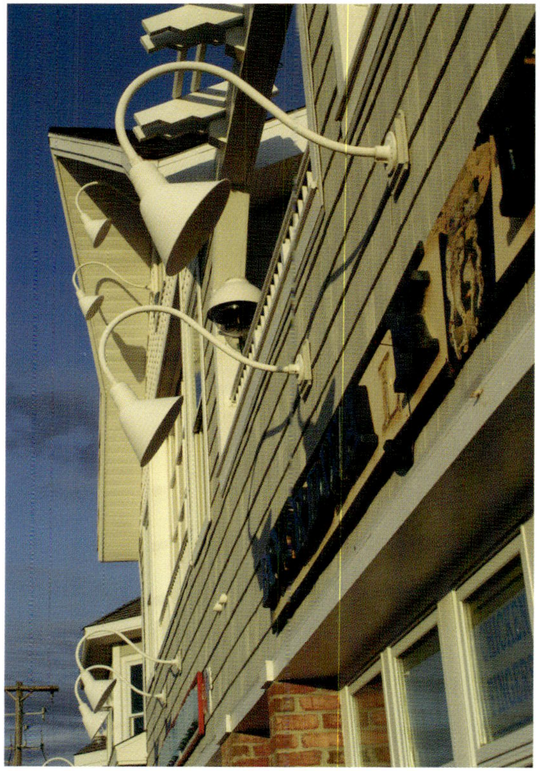

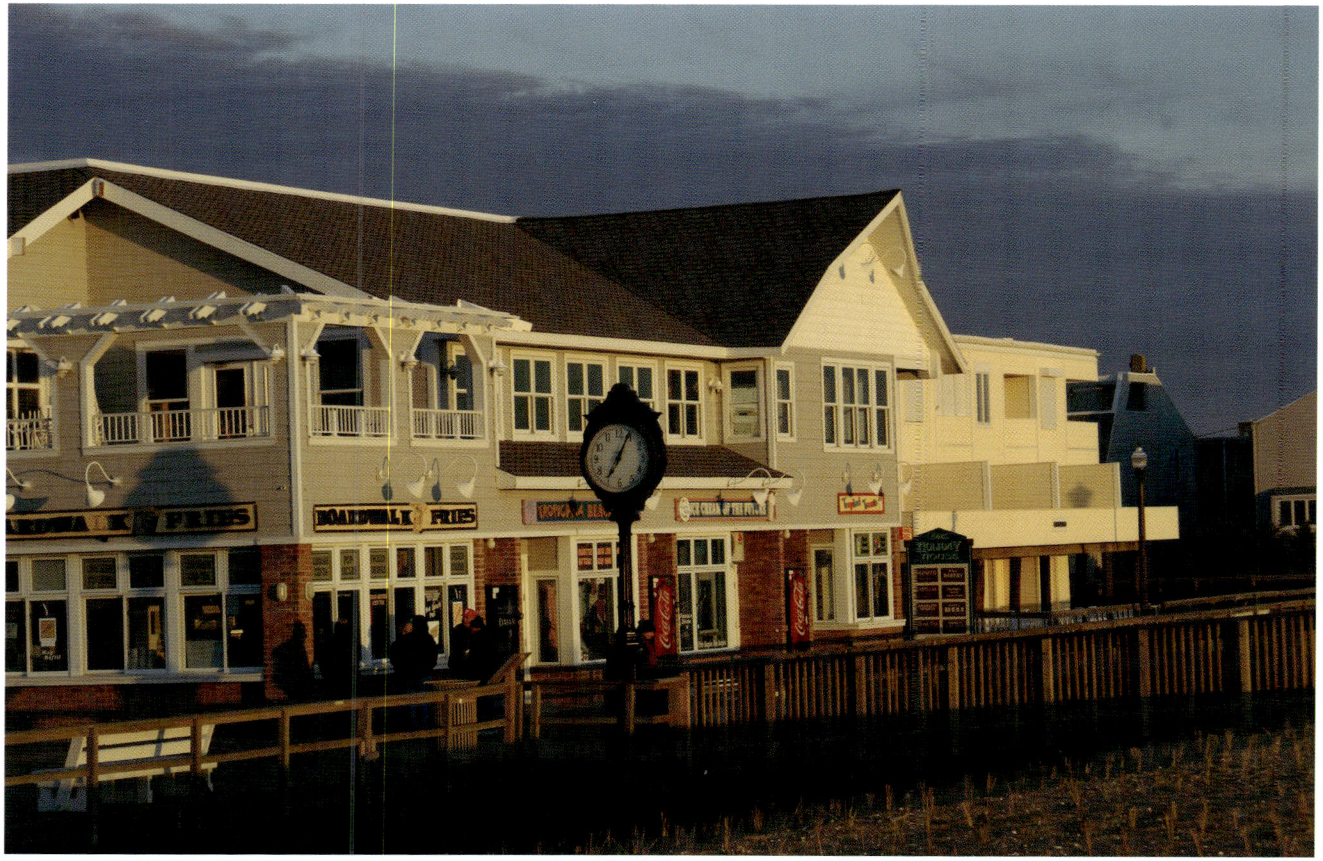

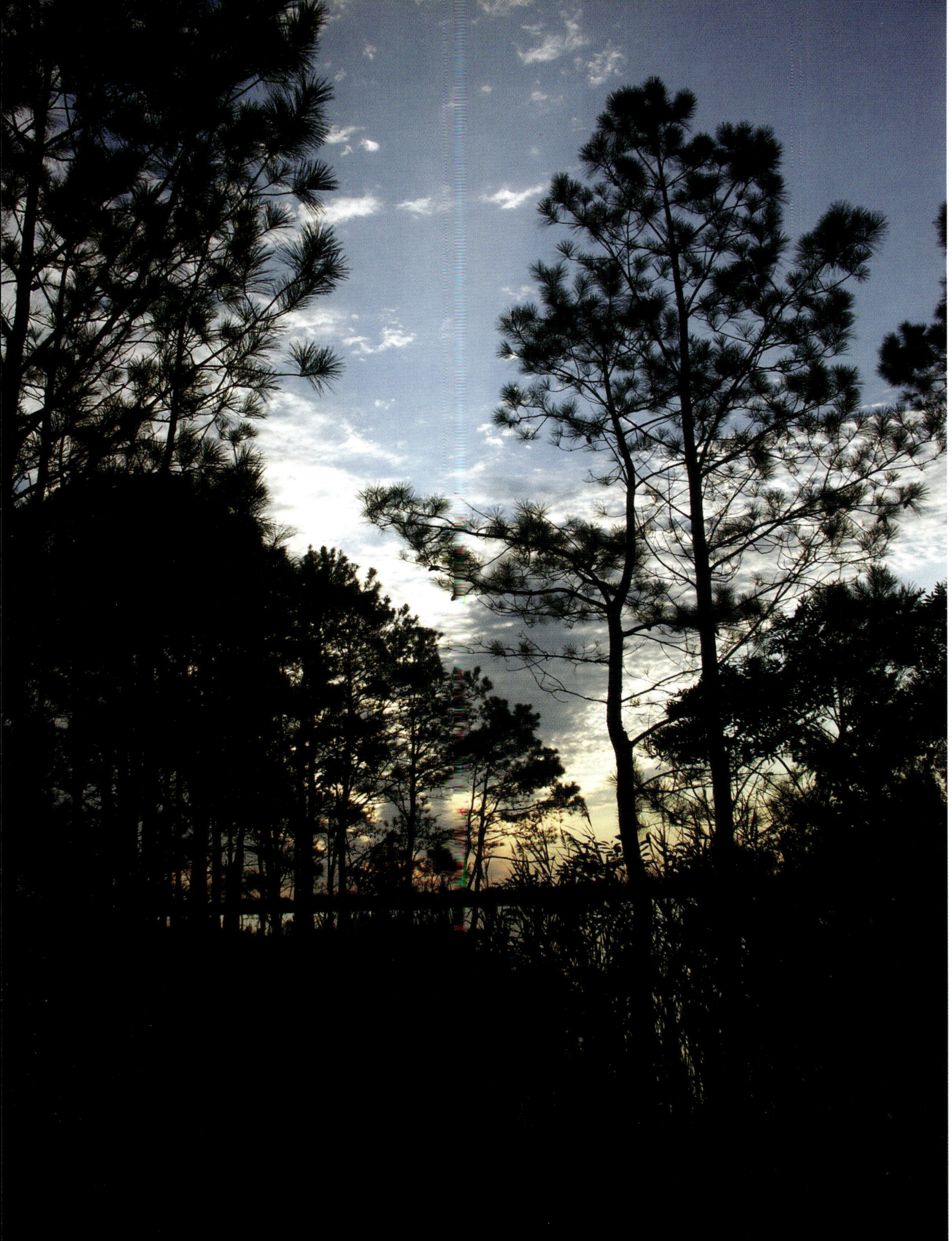

Early morning at the Salt Pond, north of Bethany Beach.

A 2007-2008 project replenished 2.8 miles of beach in Bethany Beach and South Bethany. The $19.8 million project created 150-ft. wide beaches with 25-ft. dune crests. Over 3.2 million cubic yards of sand were pumped in from the ocean floor.

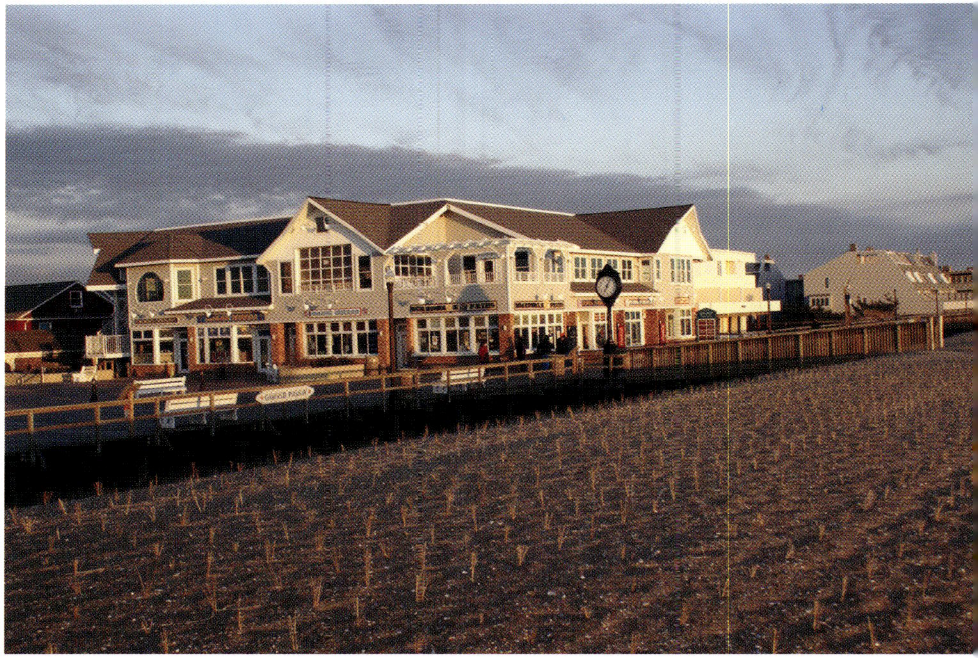

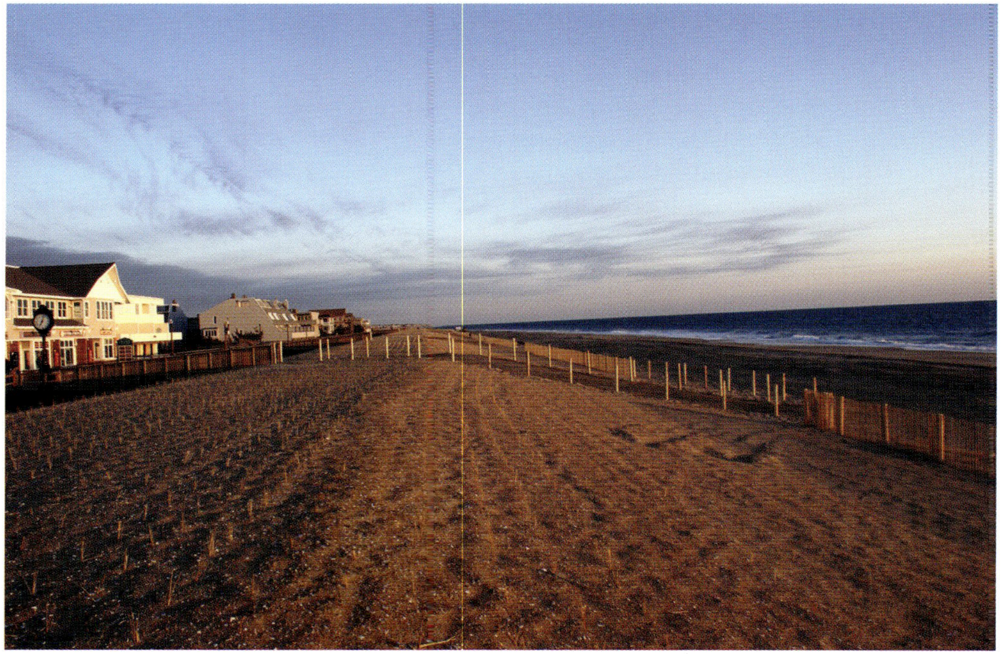

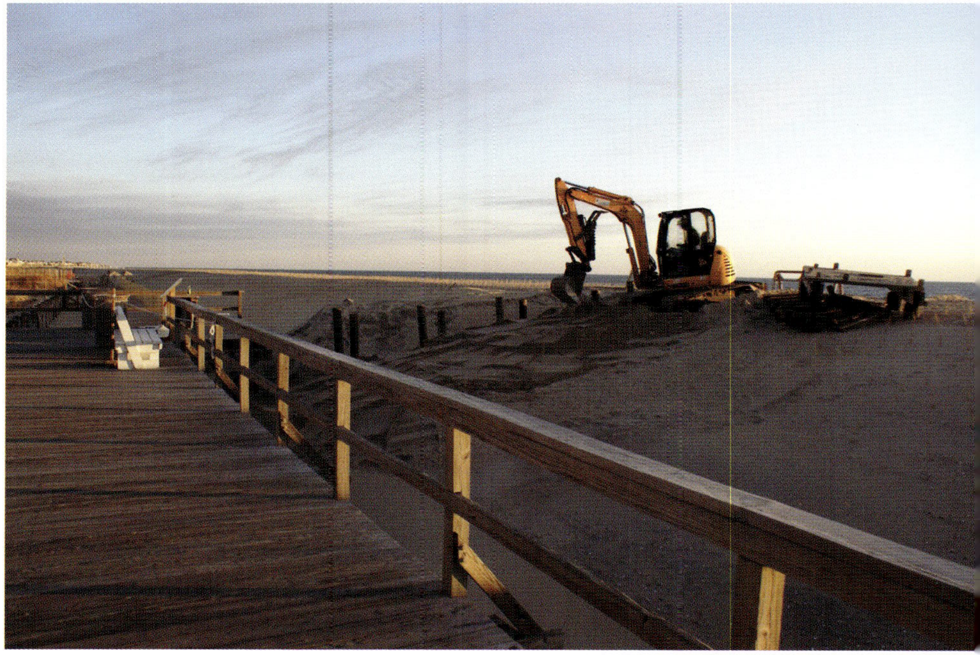

Garfield Parkway is Bethany Beach's version of Rehoboth Avenue, the retail district in its neighbor to the north.

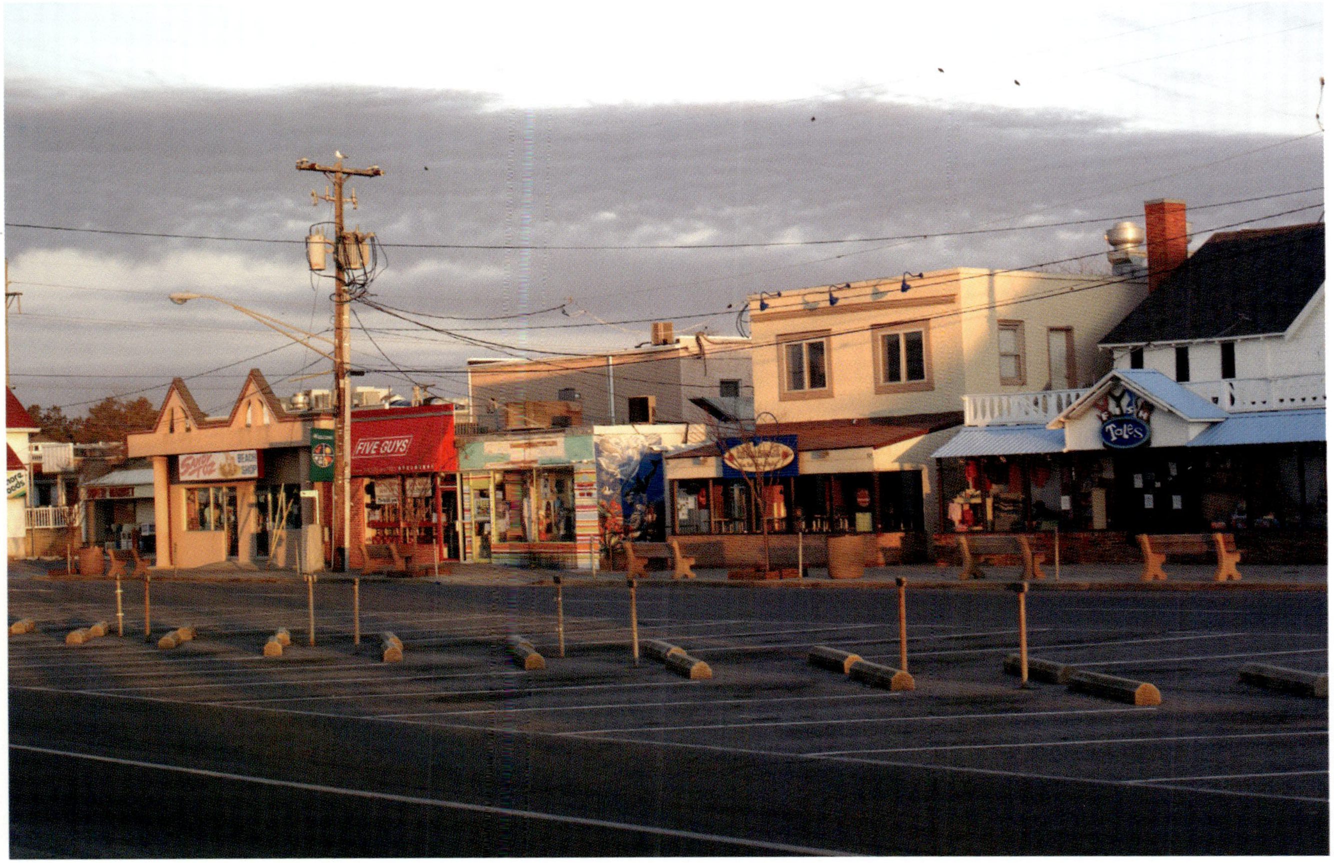

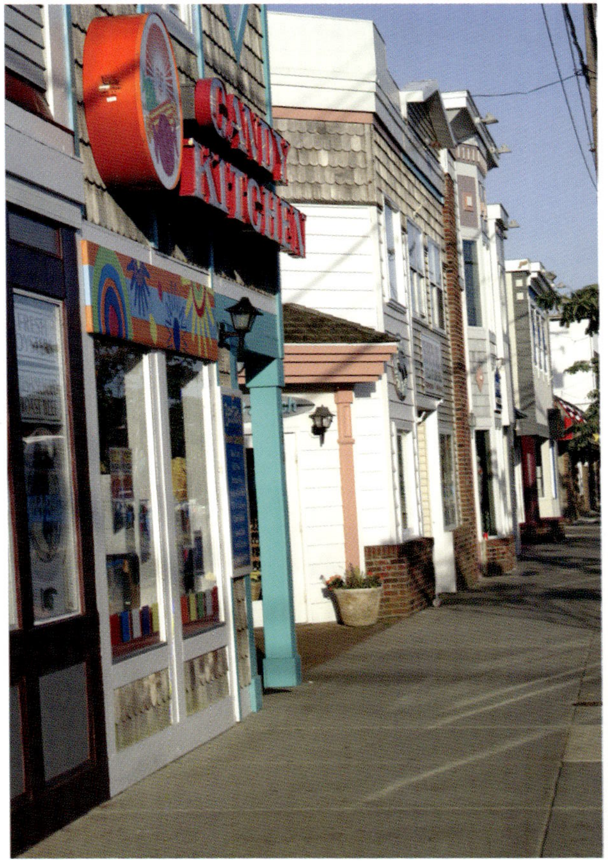

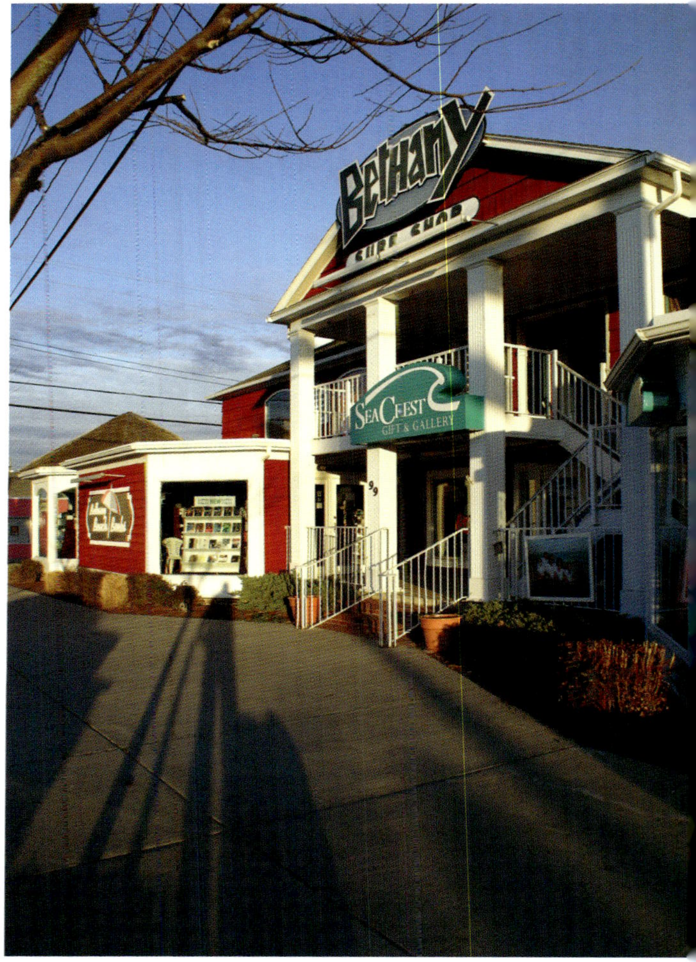

The Sea Crest Building was constructed in 1954 as a hotel – the first in Bethany Beach with private baths. Today, the building houses several prominent retailers, including Sea Crest Gift & Gallery. Other merchants include the popular, independently-owned Bethany Beach Books, which was established in 1991, and the Bethany Surf Shop, which dates from 1980.

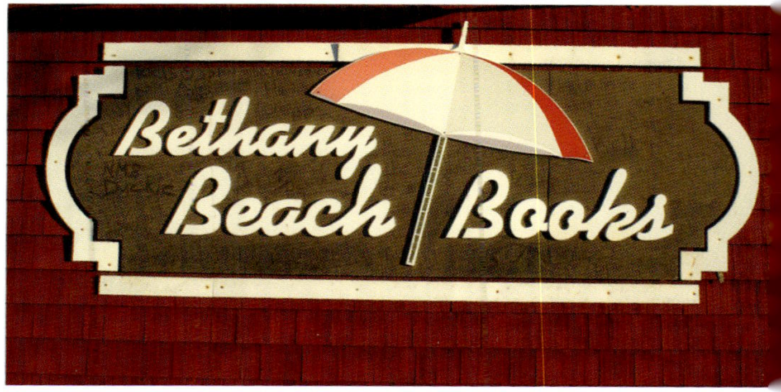

At Lighthouse Station on Garfield Parkway you'll find a cluster of distinctive shops.

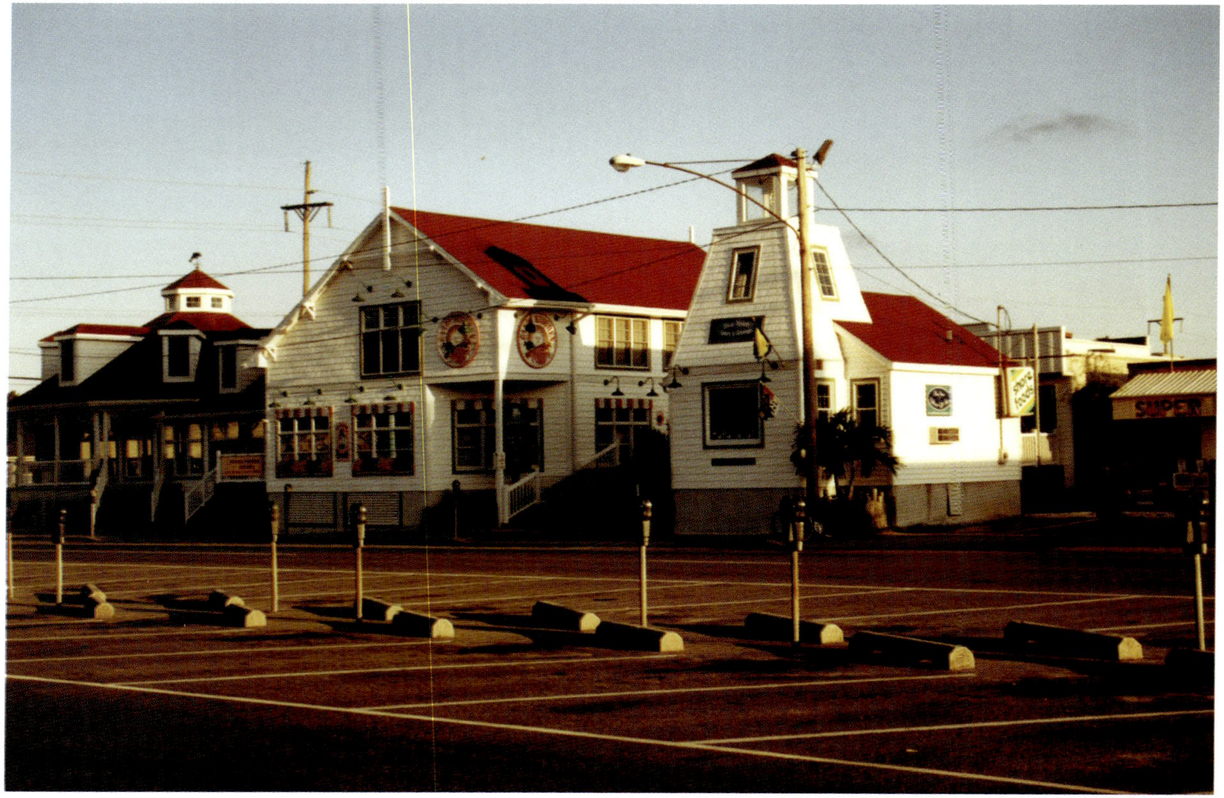

The Bethany Beach bandstand not only hosts musical acts on weekend evenings, but early-rising exercisers throughout the summer months.

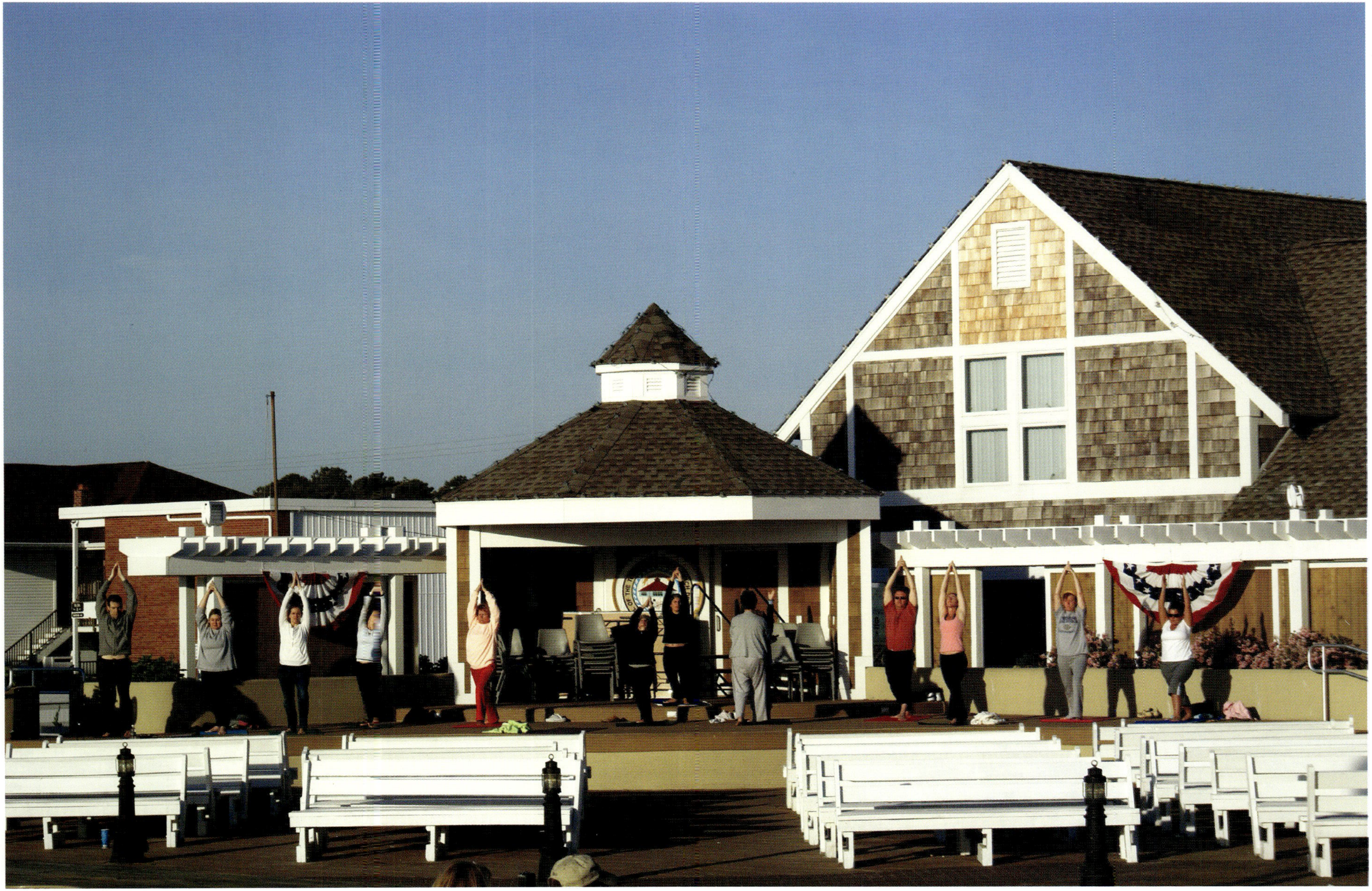

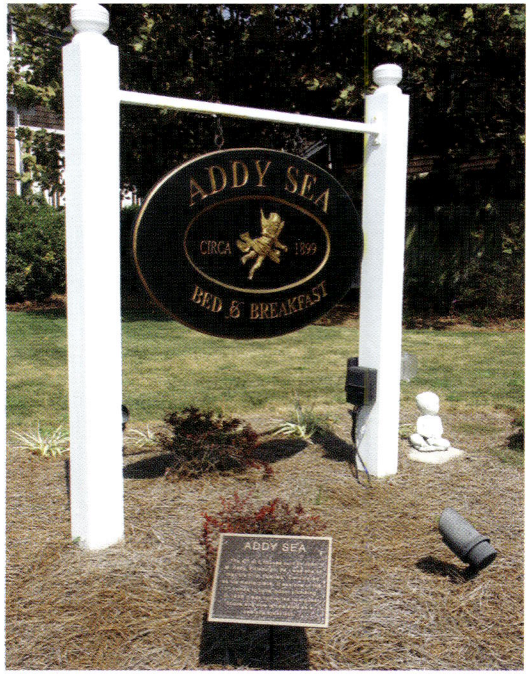

The Addy Sea was constructed in 1902 by a prominent early family in Bethany Beach. During the Great Depression, the facility was rented to church groups. More recently, the attractive Victorian home has operated as a bed & breakfast with thirteen well-appointed guest rooms.

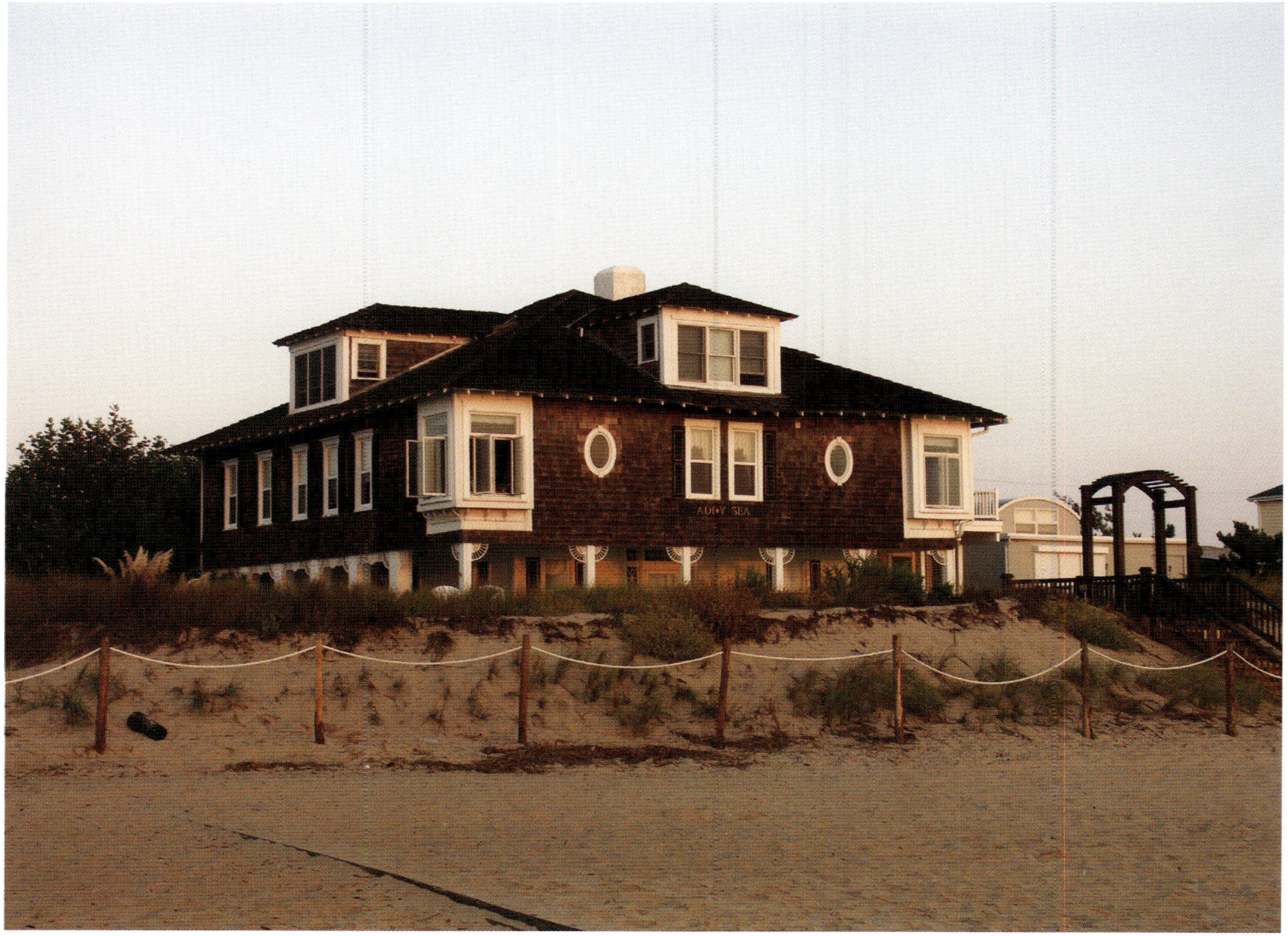

Bethany Town Center is a cluster of retail shops and eateries located at the intersection of Atlantic Avenue and Garfield Parkway.

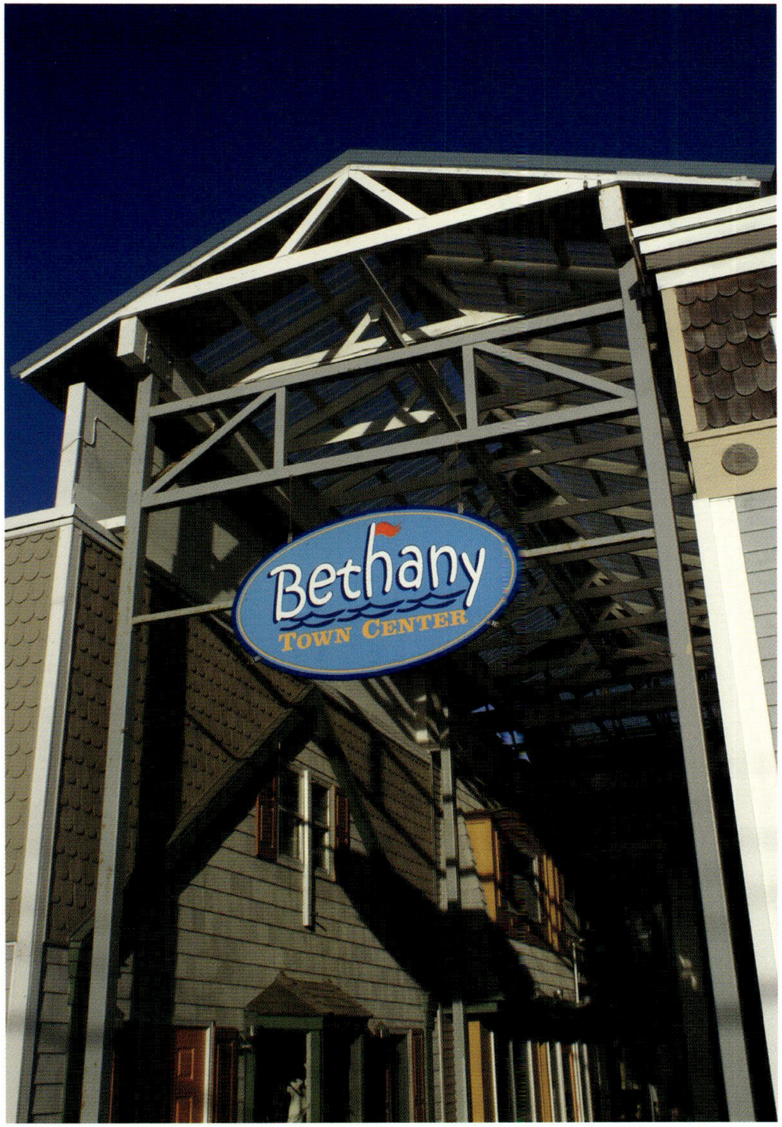

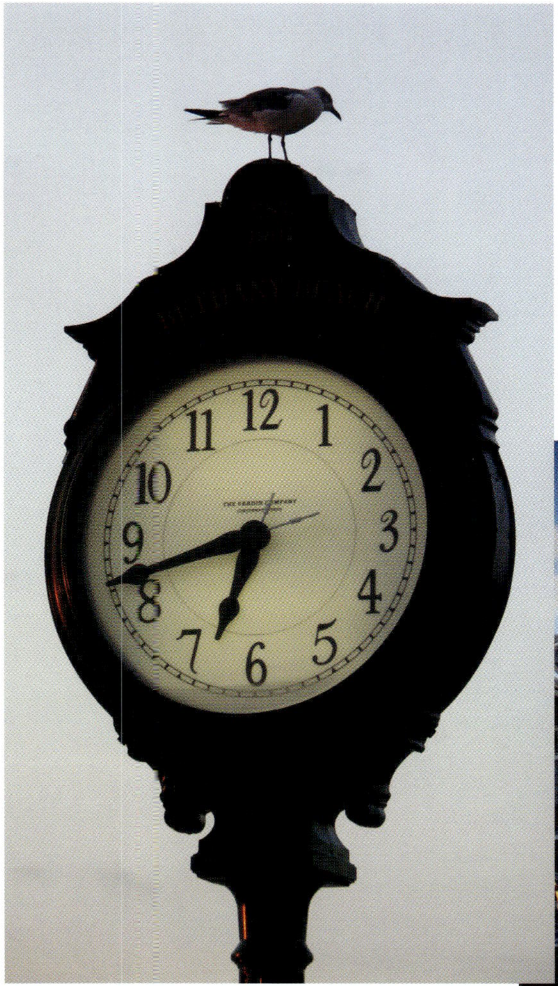

The "new" Bethany town clock was erected in 2005. Its Victorian character adds to the charm of the boardwalk, more so than the previous, modernistic town clock.

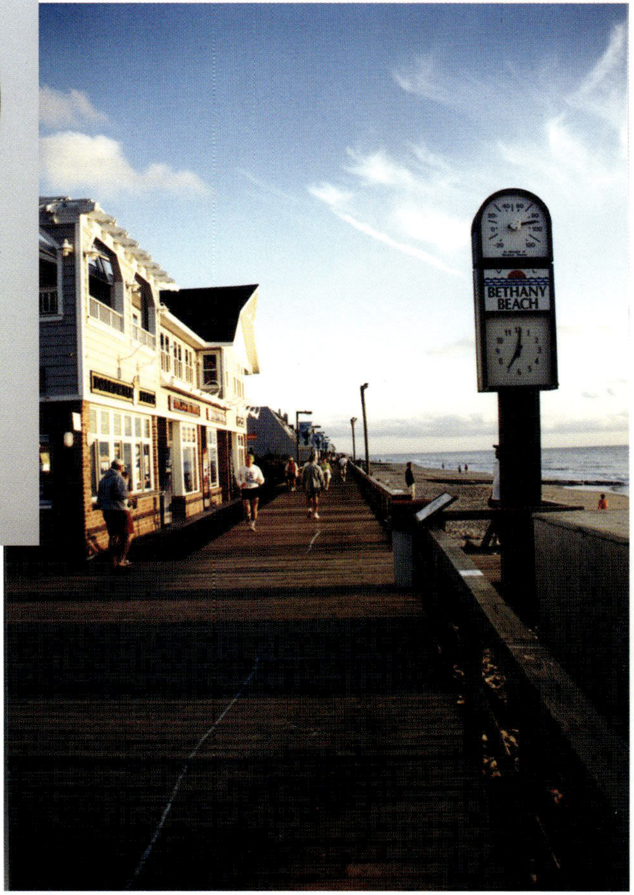

Constructed in 1970, Bethany Beach Town Hall is also the location of the Bethany Beach History Museum, which contains exhibits and memorabilia interpreting town history.

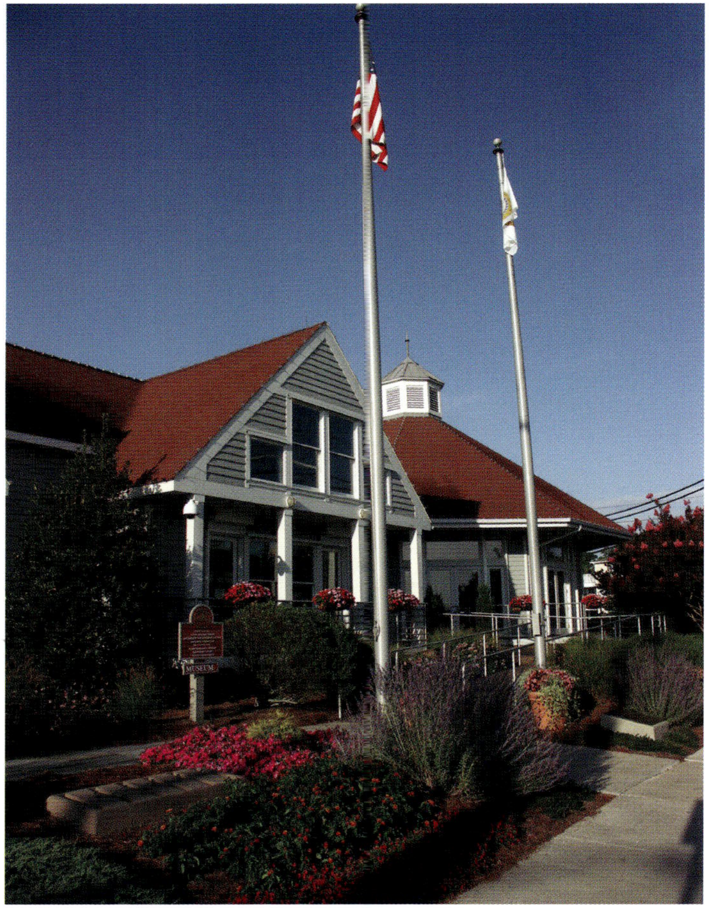

During the warm months of the year, Garfield Parkway becomes a sea of color.

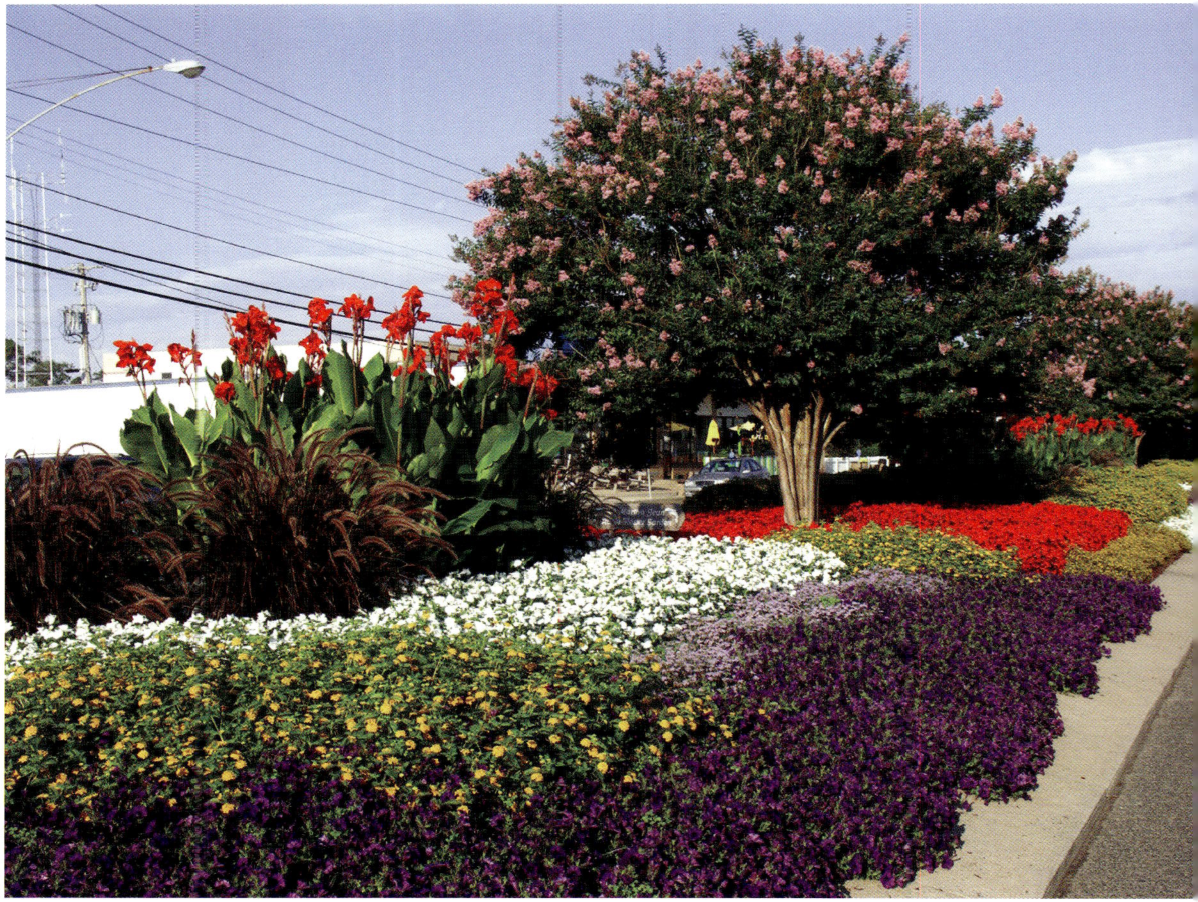

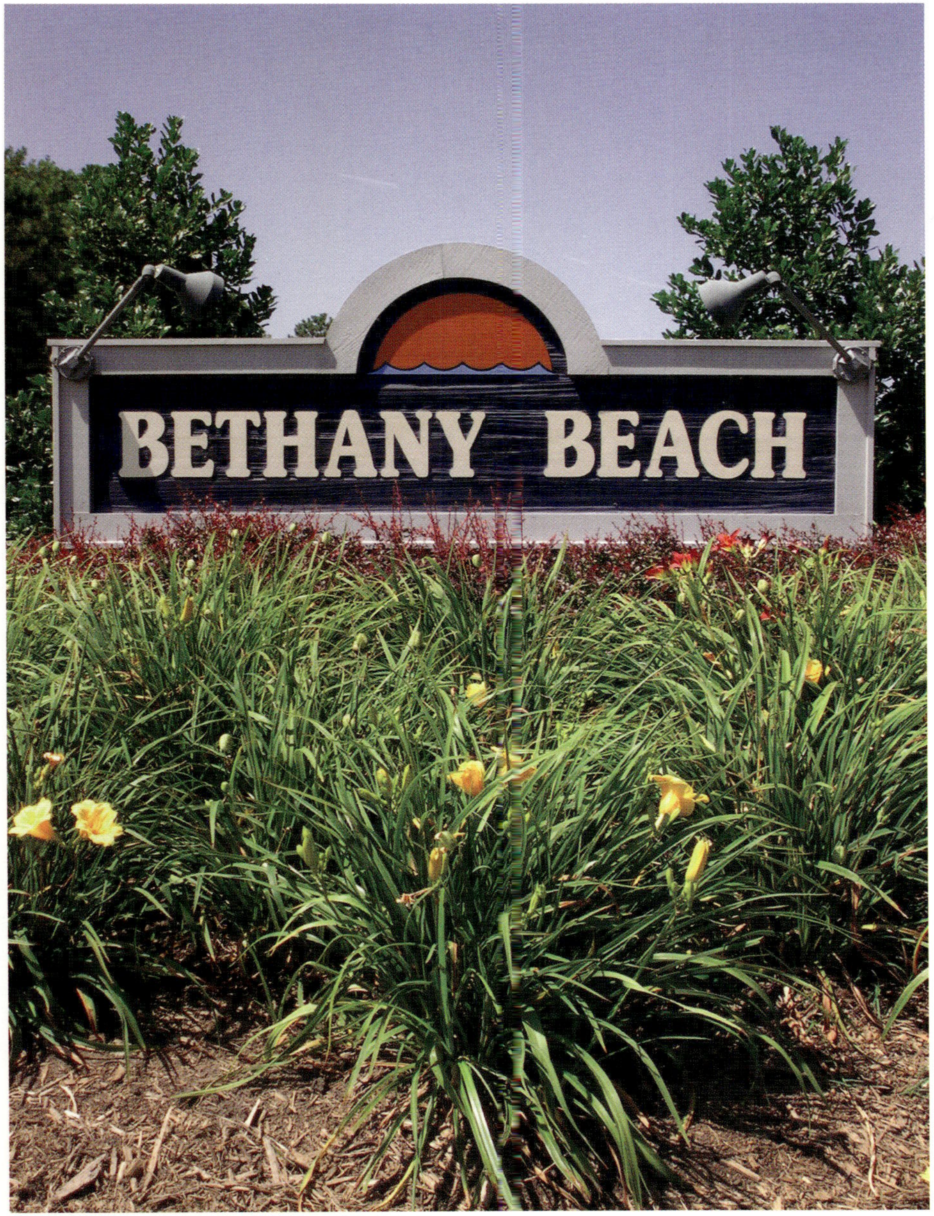

Since 1901, beachcombers have heard the call of the ocean at Bethany Beach, which is a town of about 1.2 square miles with less than 1,000 year-round residents.

South Bethany is a mostly residential community incorporated in 1969. Three years later, York Beach and Paradise Shores were annexed into the new town.

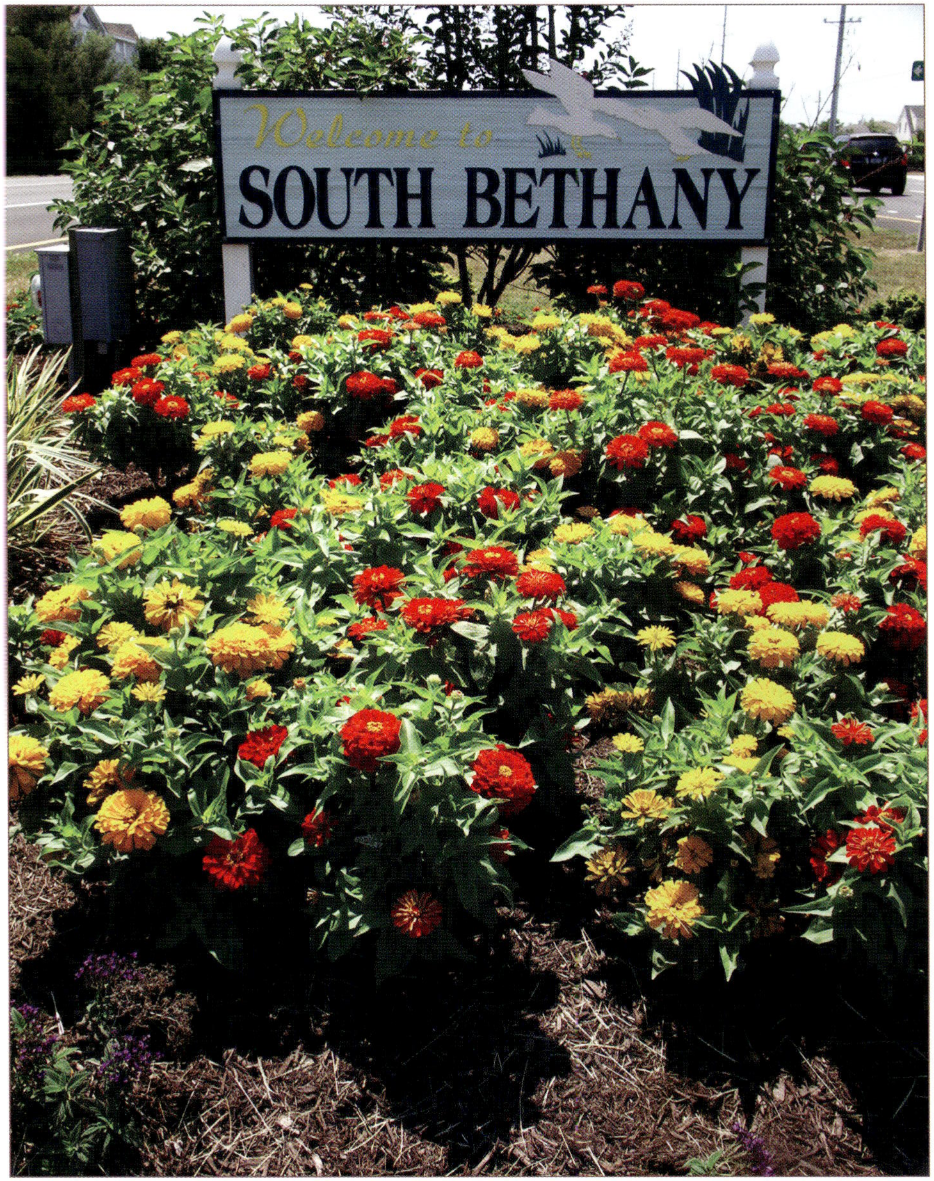

The first villa at Sea Colony was constructed in 1969. By 1972 Annapolis House was welcoming residents. Over the course of the next eight years massive sandcastles were built, with beachfront construction ending in 1980 with the opening of Island House. Beyond the beach, construction continued until 2004, when the last of approximately 2200 units was completed.

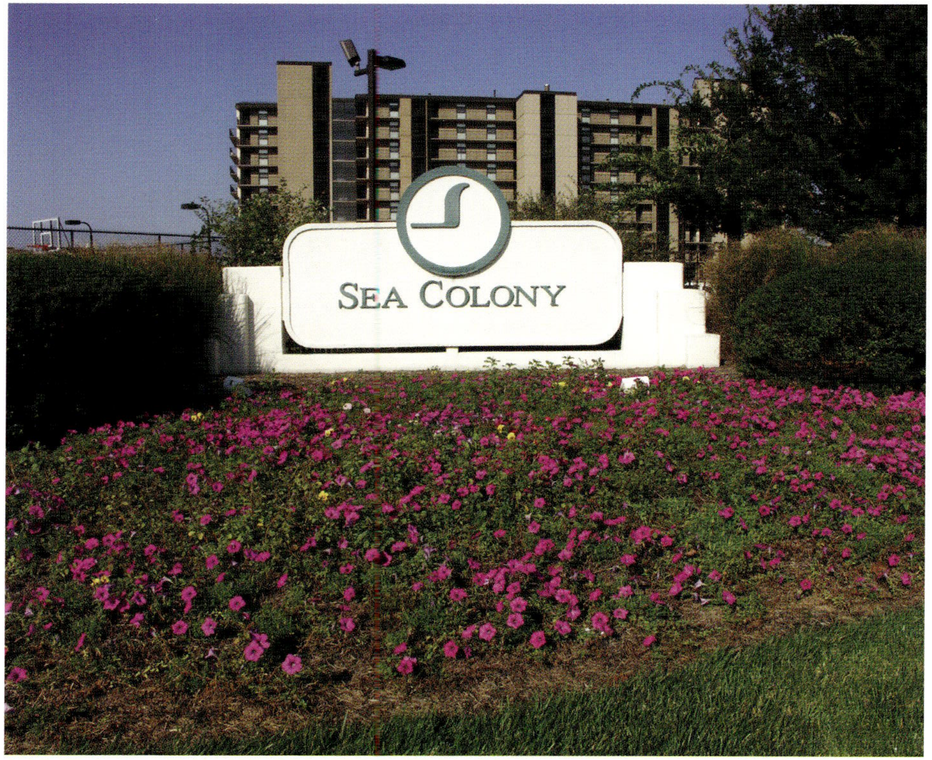

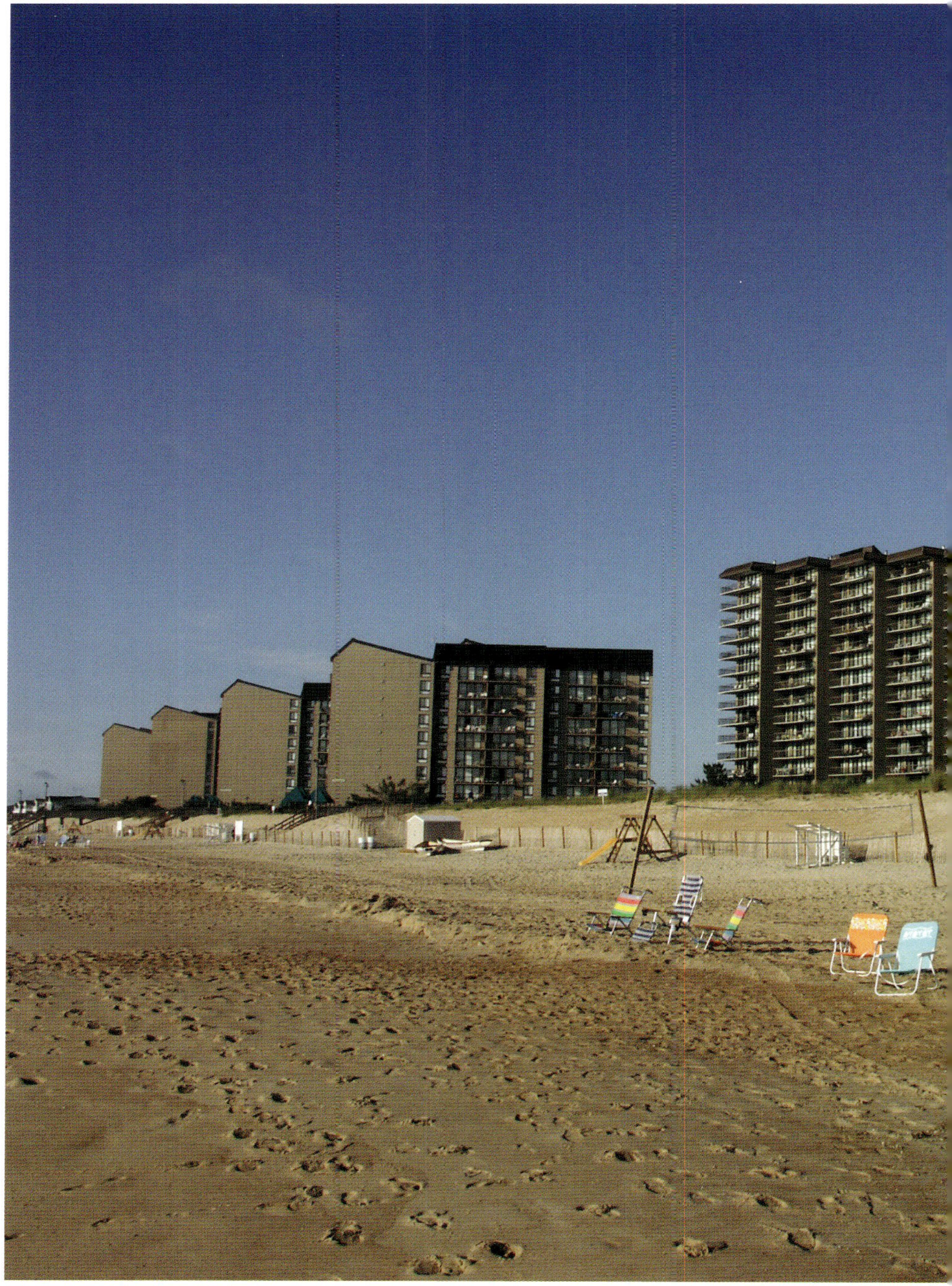

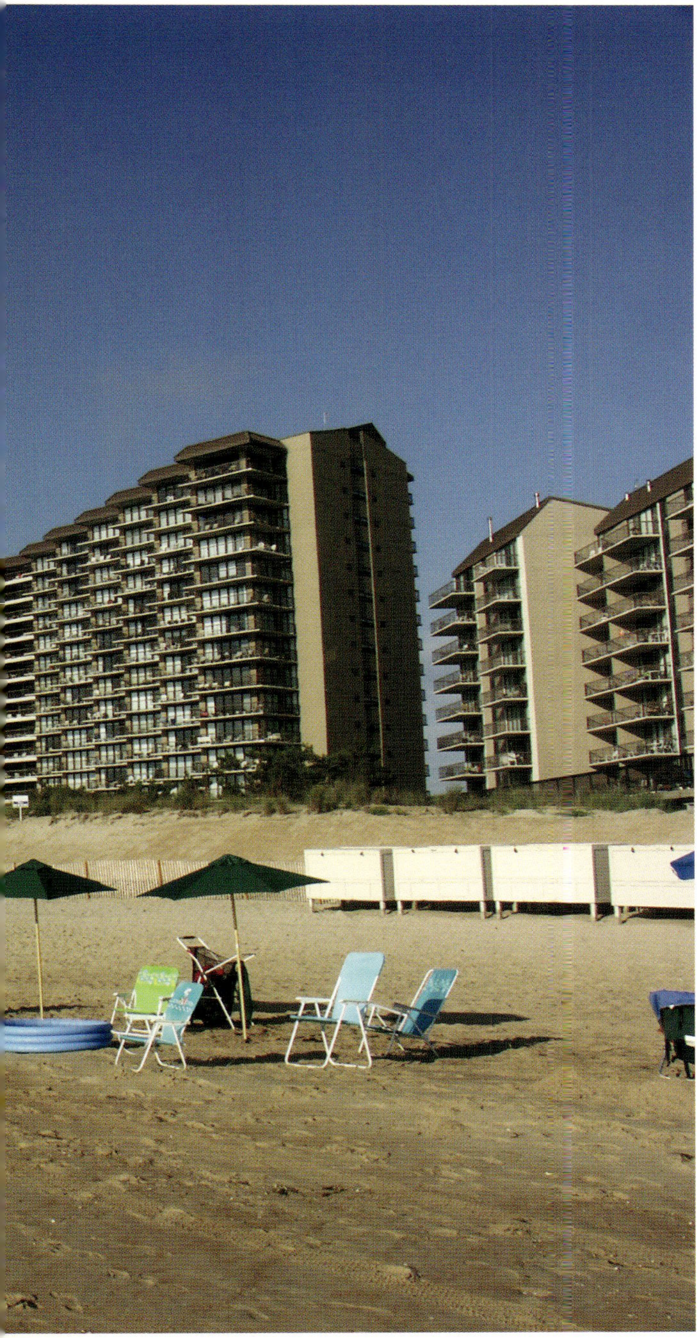

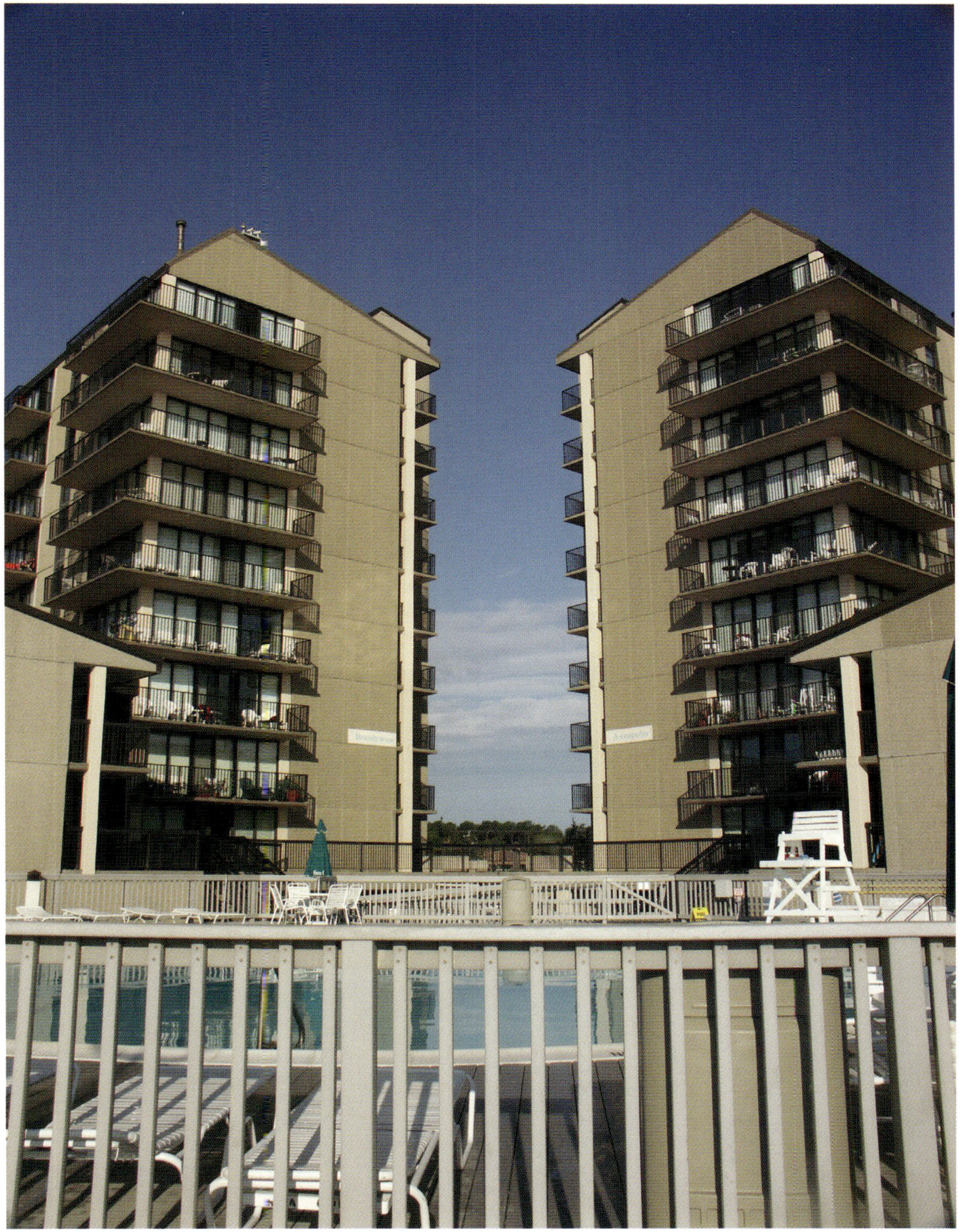

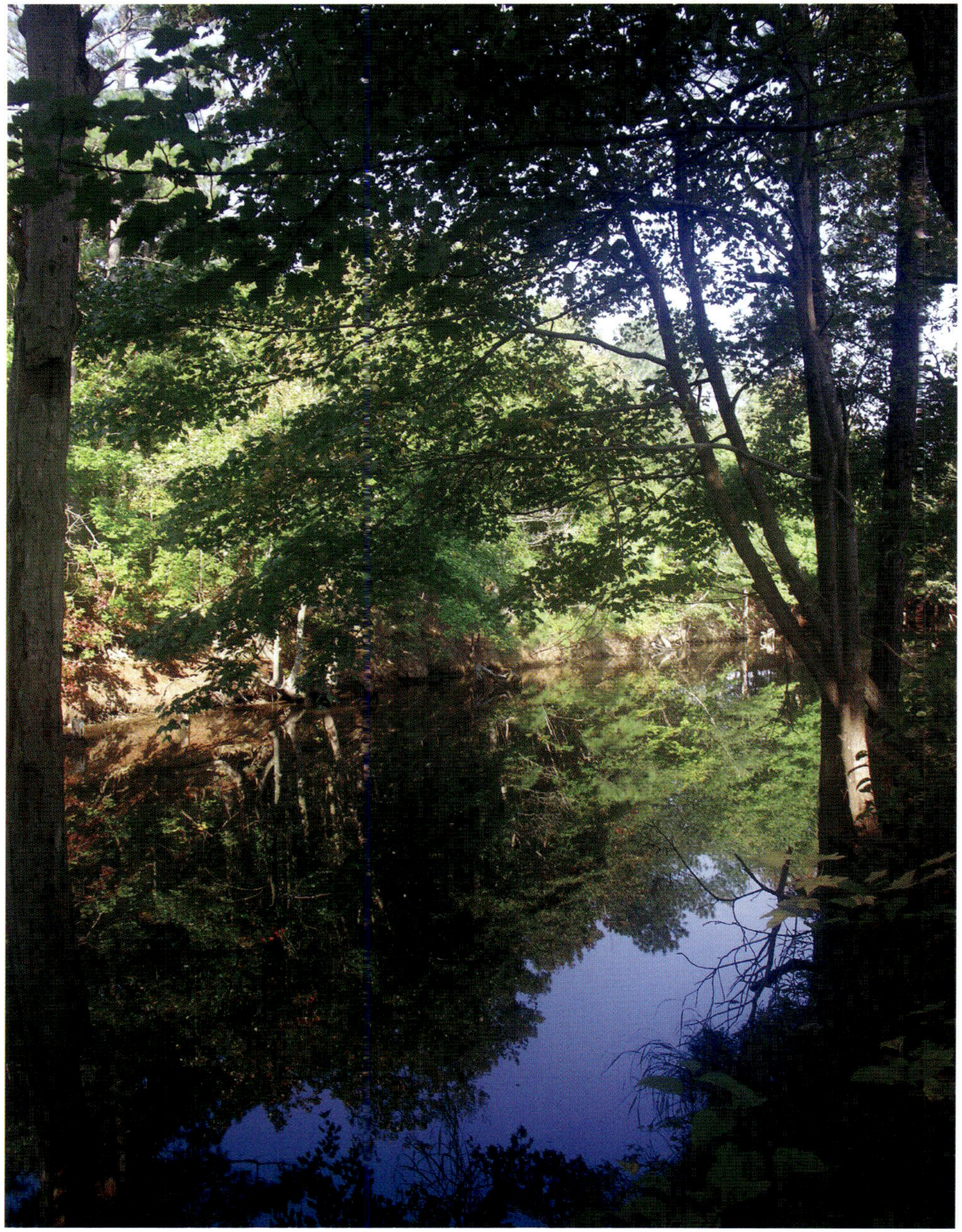

The Assawoman Canal was originated in 1886 to allow for a waterway connection between Chincoteague Bay, VA and the Delaware Bay, near Lewes. The primary purpose was to help farmers transport produce to market. The entire waterway project was not completed, but the narrow Assawoman Canal was connected in 1910 to the new Bethany Beach Loop Canal, which was constructed by the Bethany Beach Improvement Company to enable visitors from Rehoboth to make the trip in a single boat ride.

There are a variety of waterfowl to be found along the Delaware coast, including great blue herons, ospreys, gulls, and mallards.

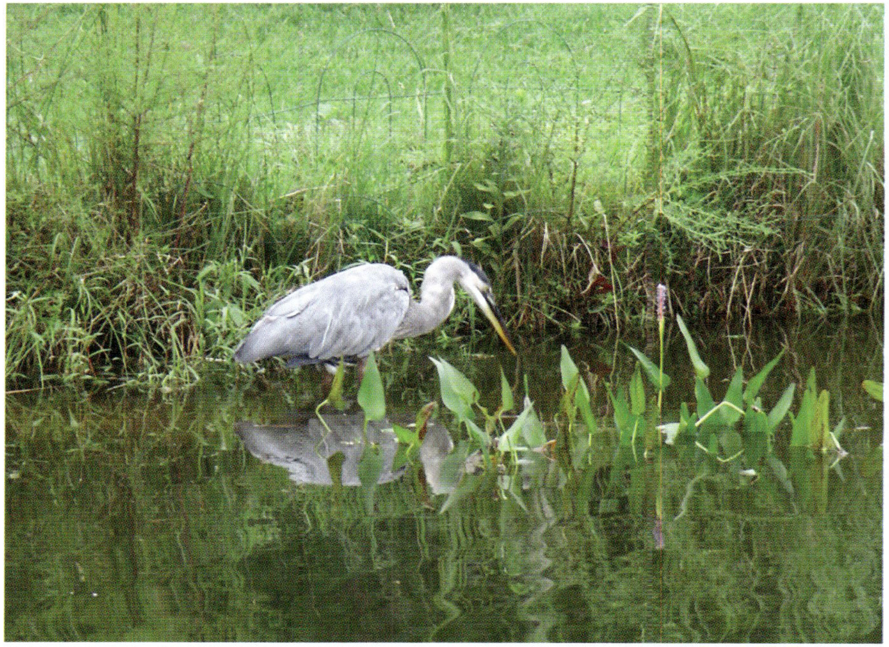

Fun in the sun, Bethany Beach sty e.

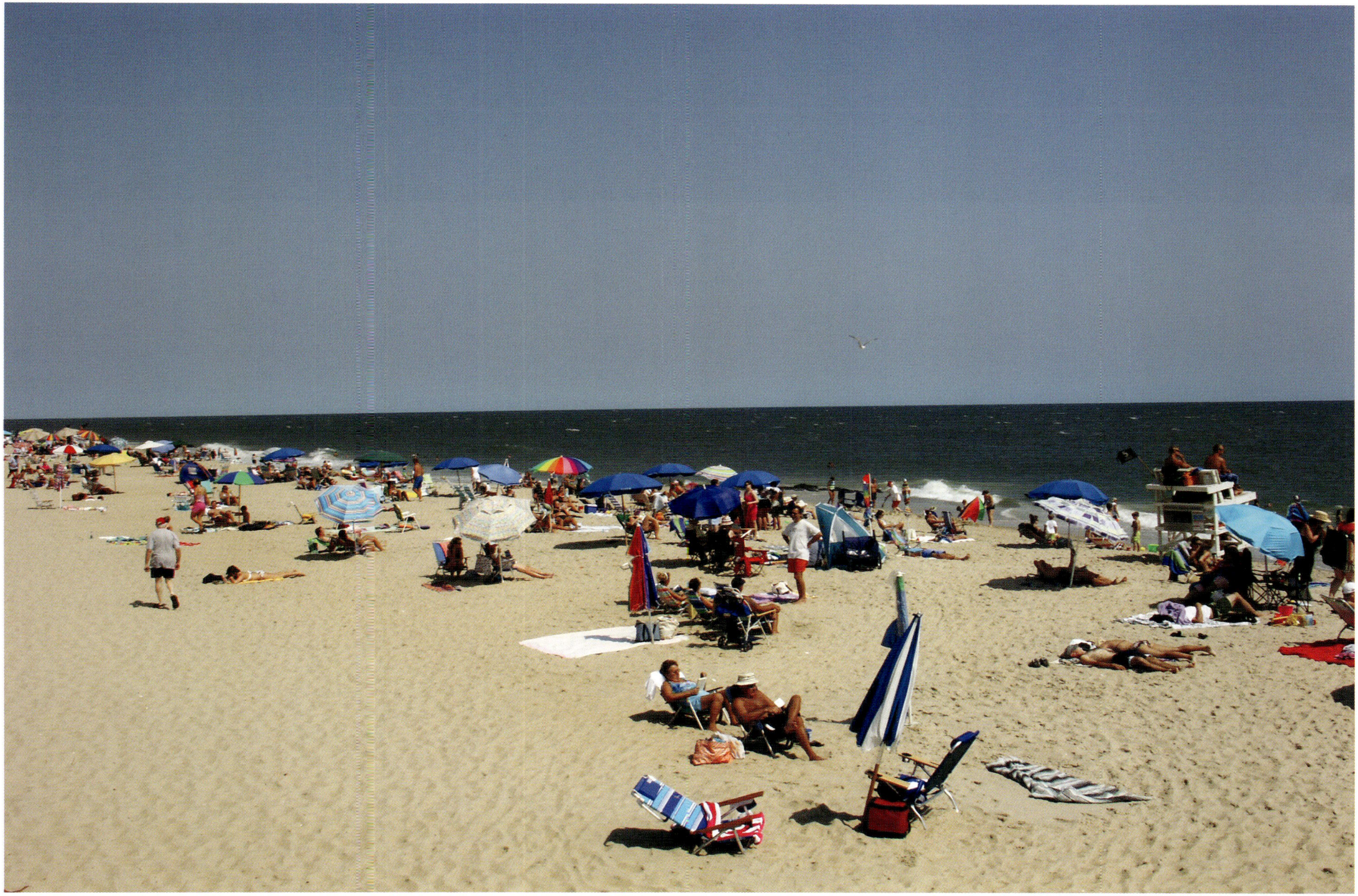

The Delaware National Guard Bethany Beach Training Site is home to the 193rd Regiment Regional Training Institute and Officer Candidate School.

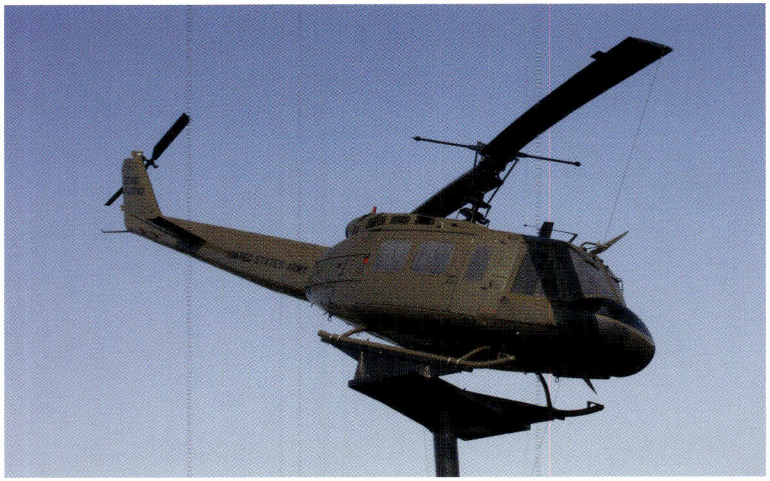

The first boardwalk was constructed in 1903. Though tropical storms and angry seas occasionally wreck havoc, the boardwalk has always been a defining feature of the community. Many a child has played under the elevated boardwalk over the years; however, that all changed in 2007 with a beach replenishment project that created dunes taller than the boardwalk.

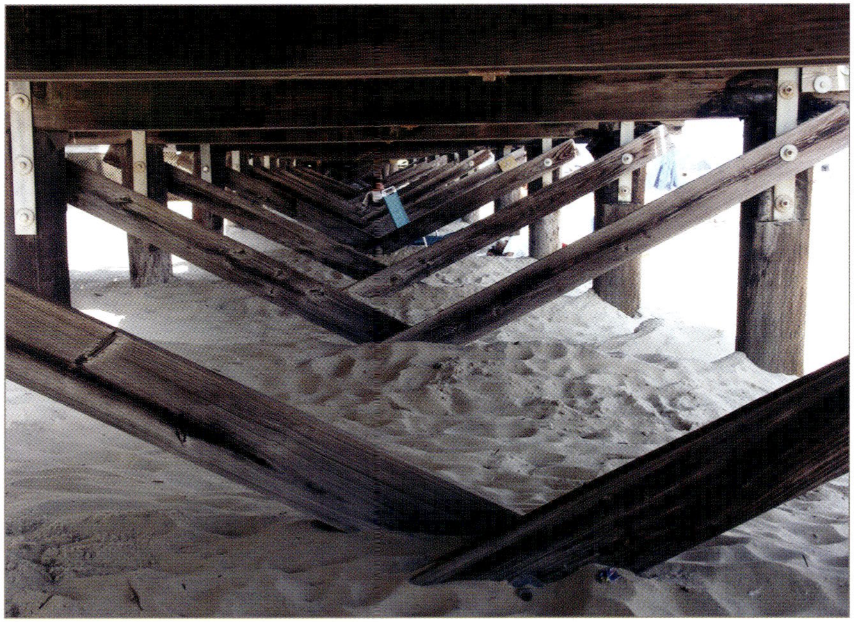

The Bethany Beach Boardwalk Arts Festival has been a popular annual event since the late 1970s. Artists far and wide apply to participate in the juried show, which is held on the Saturday after Labor Day. Every year 8,000 to 10,000 people attend the free event.

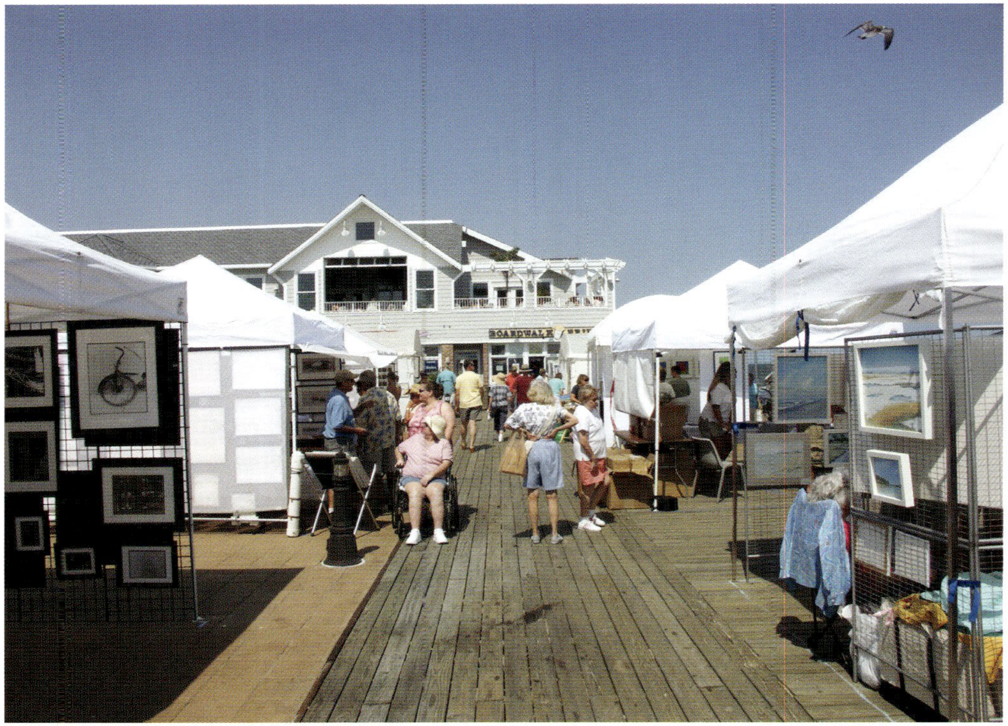

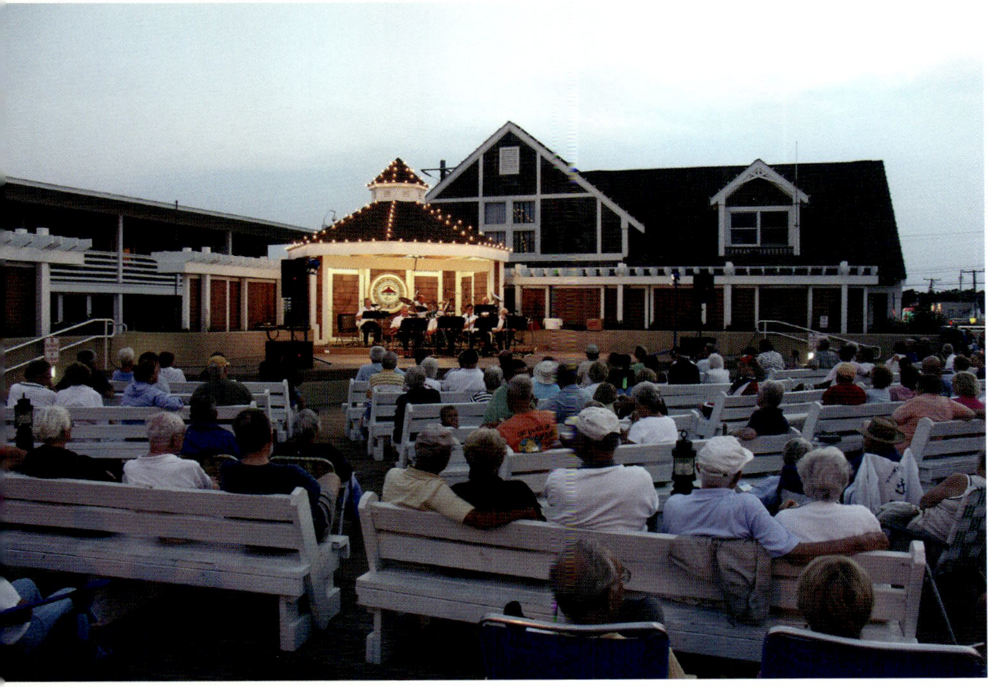

The Bethany Beach Bandstand hosts free weekend concerts throughout the summer months, providing an entertainment venue for military, brass, and tribute bands as well as an annual talent show. An earlier bandstand was demolished in late 2005 to make way for an open plaza and new bandstand.

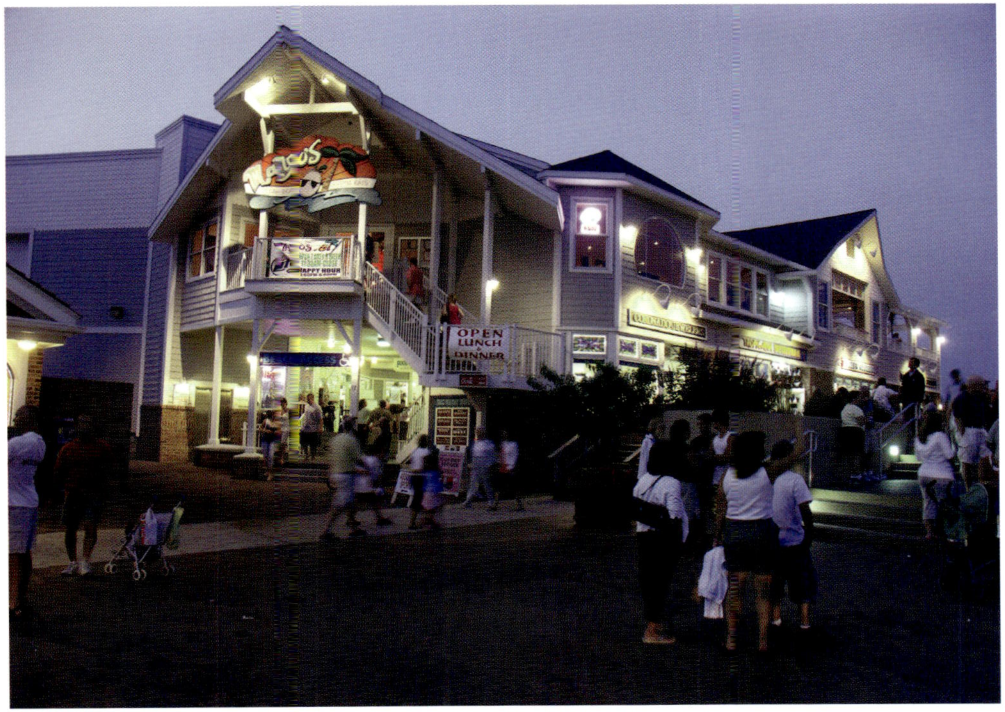

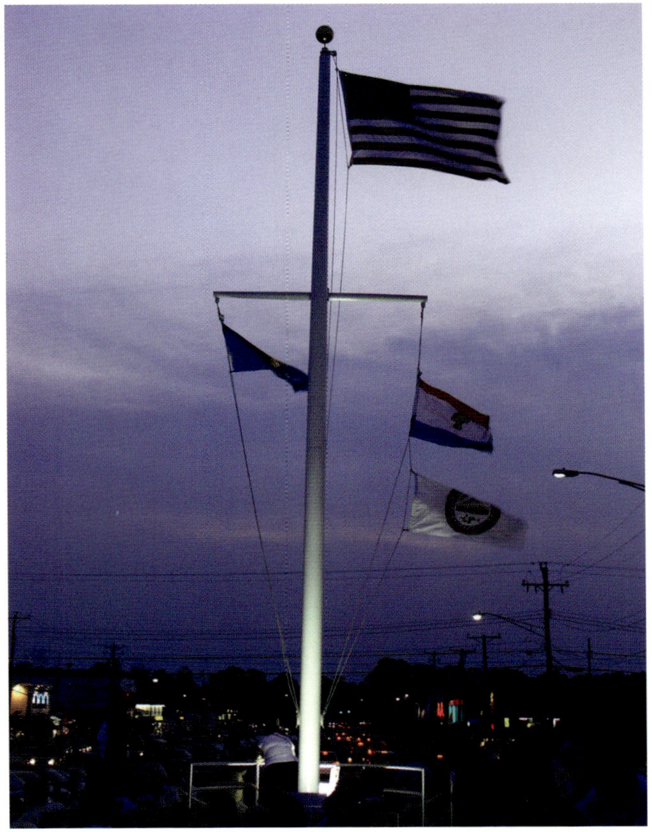

Summer nights in Bethany Beach buzz with a different atmosphere as the "Quiet Resort" transitions to a lively, though still very family-friendly, night spot.

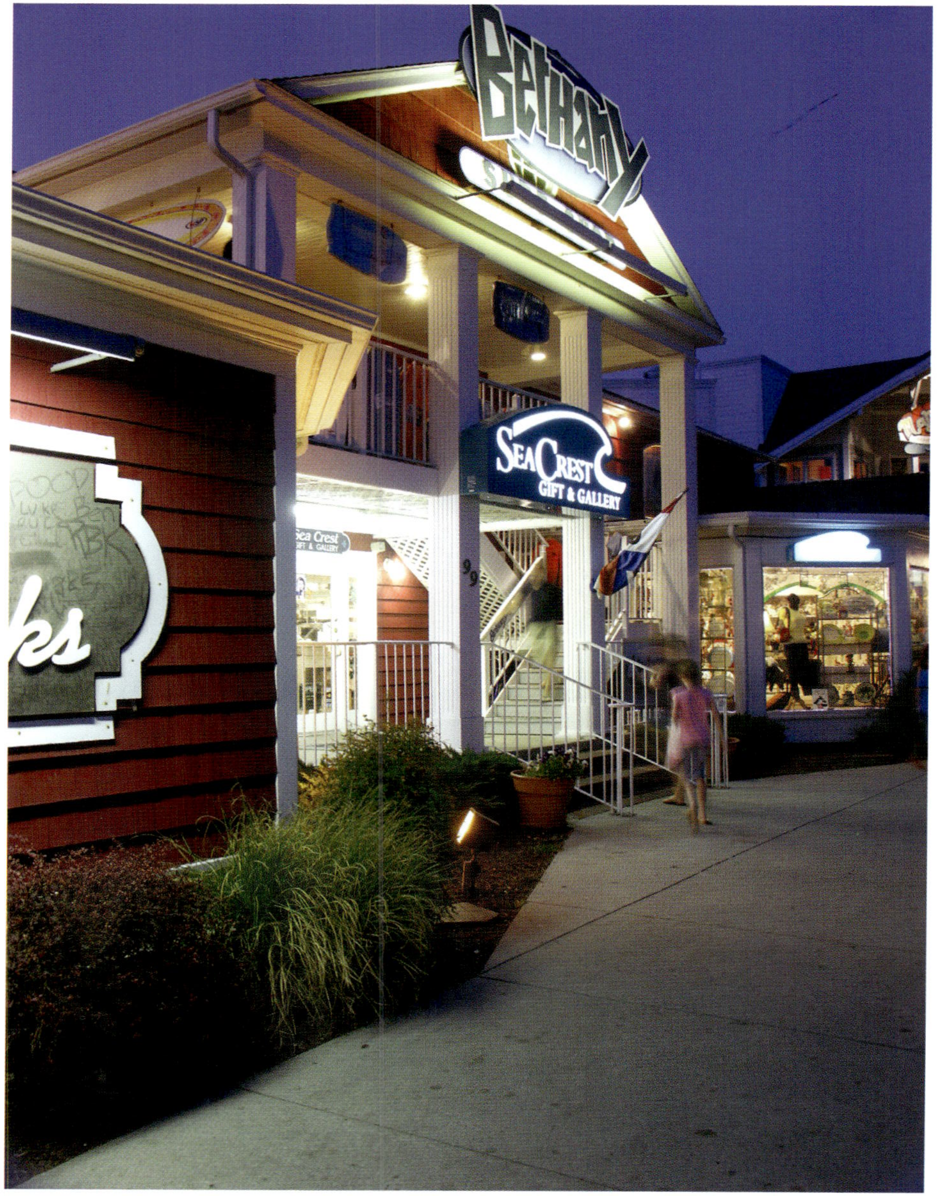
Bethany
SeaCrest
GIFT & GALLERY
99

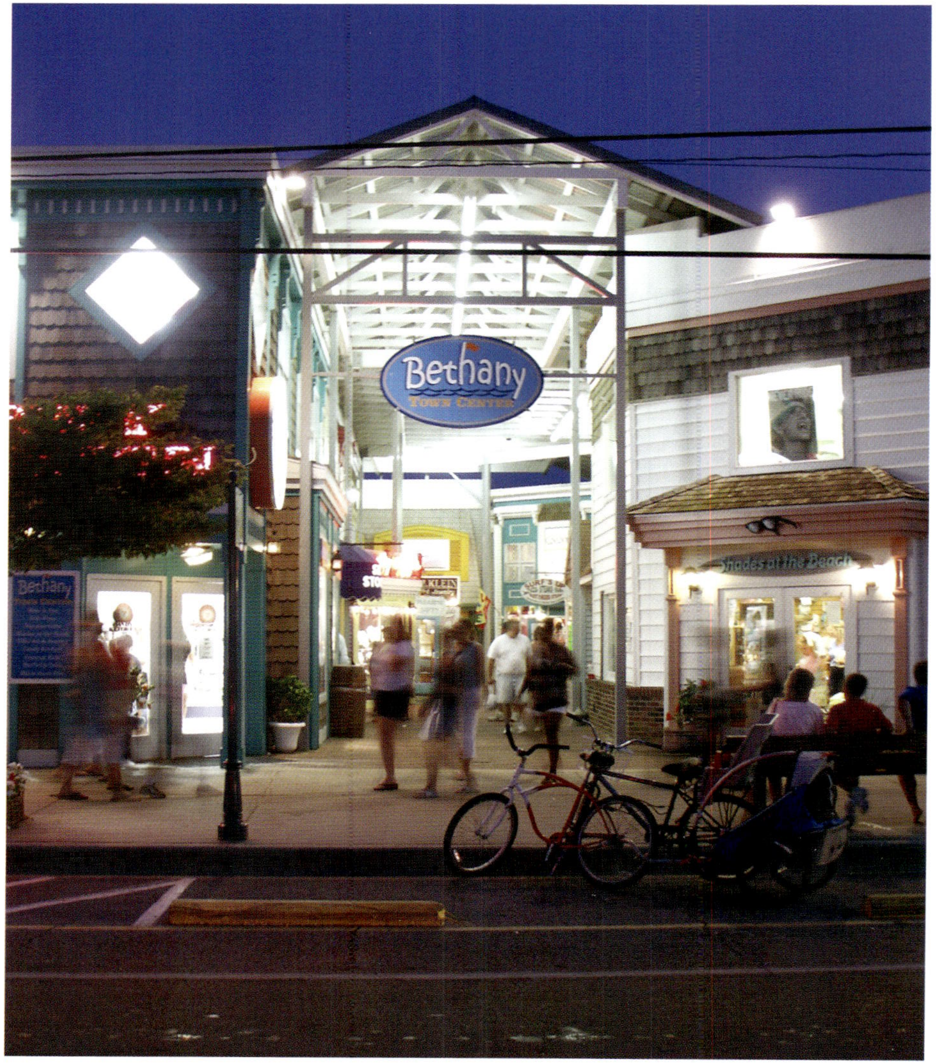
Bethany
TOWN CENTER
Shades at the Beach

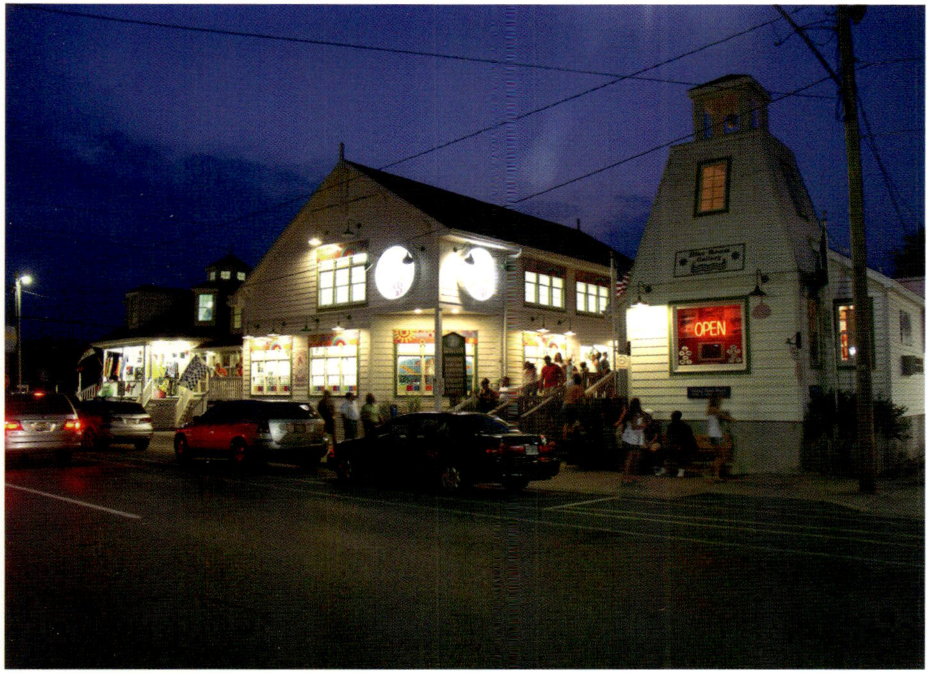
OPEN

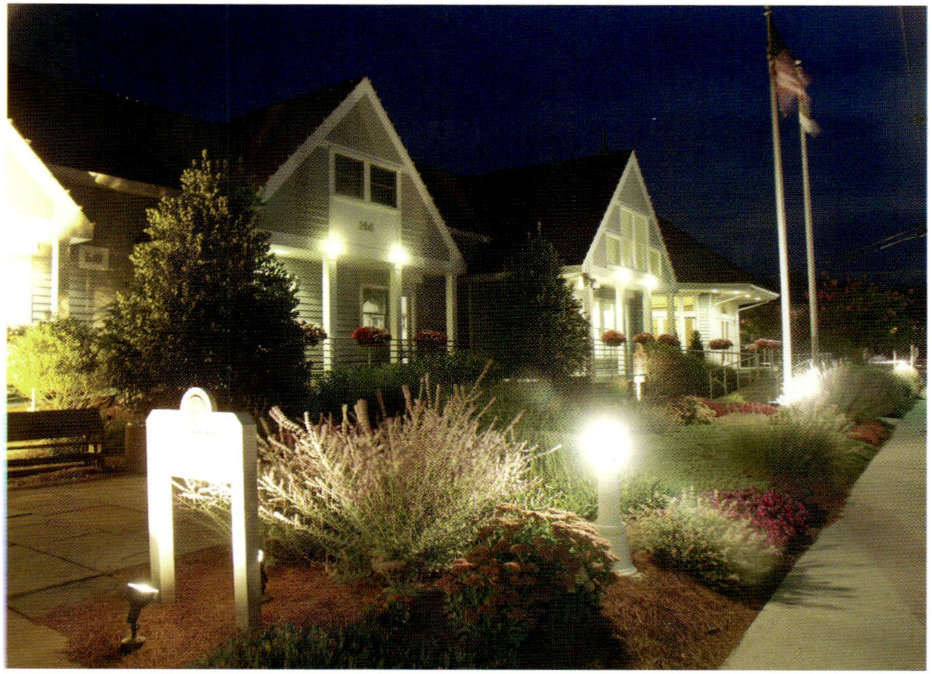

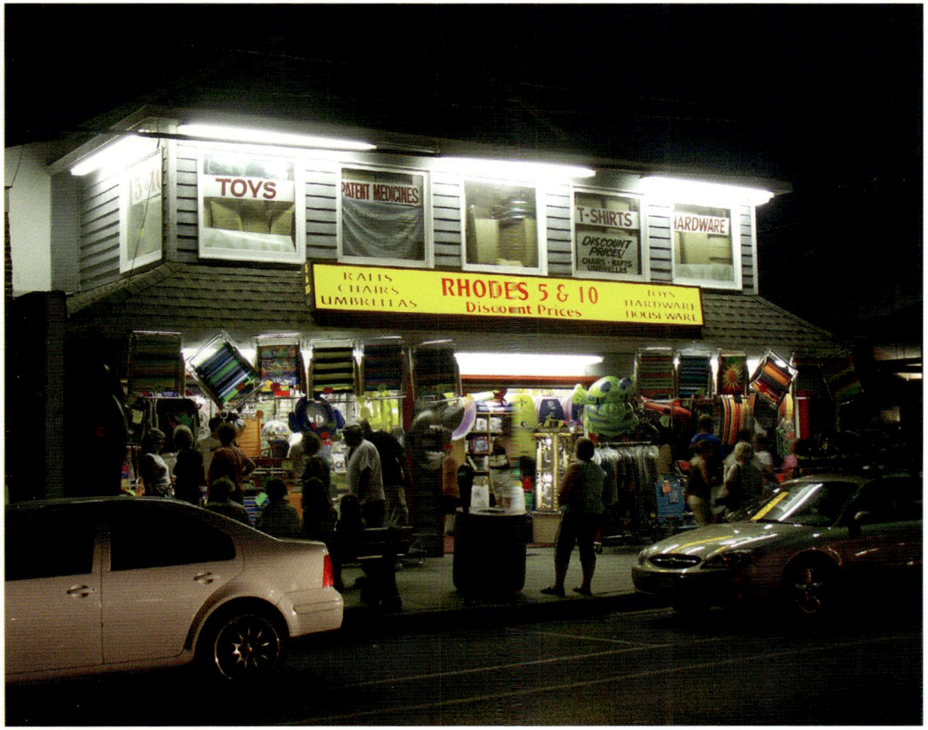
TOYS
PATENT MEDICINES
T-SHIRTS
DISCOUNT PRICES!
HARDWARE
RAFTS
CHAIRS
UMBRELLAS
RHODES 5 & 10
Discount Prices
TOYS
HARDWARE
HOUSEWARE

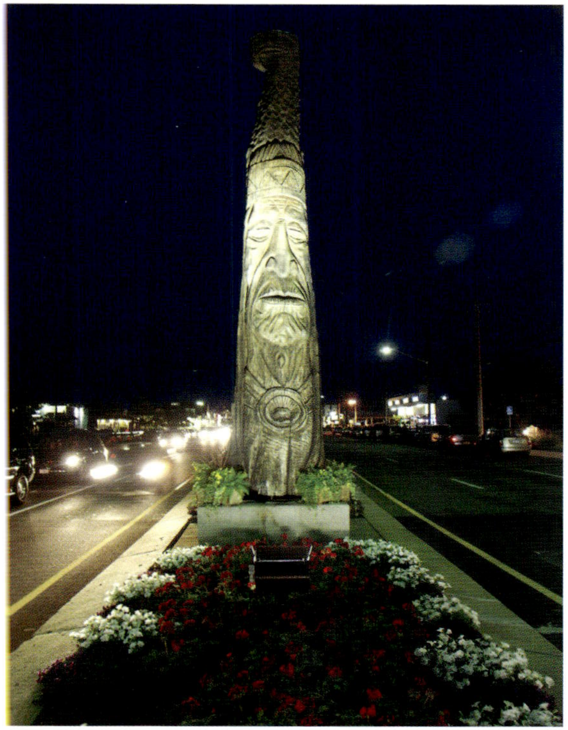

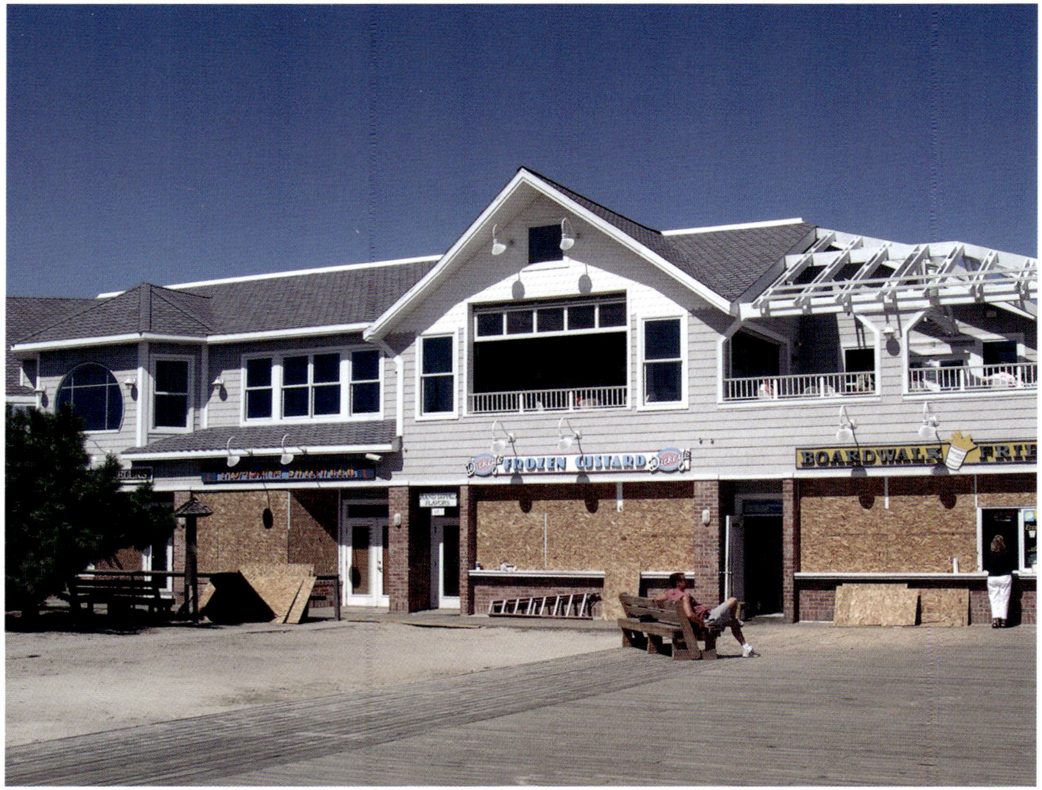

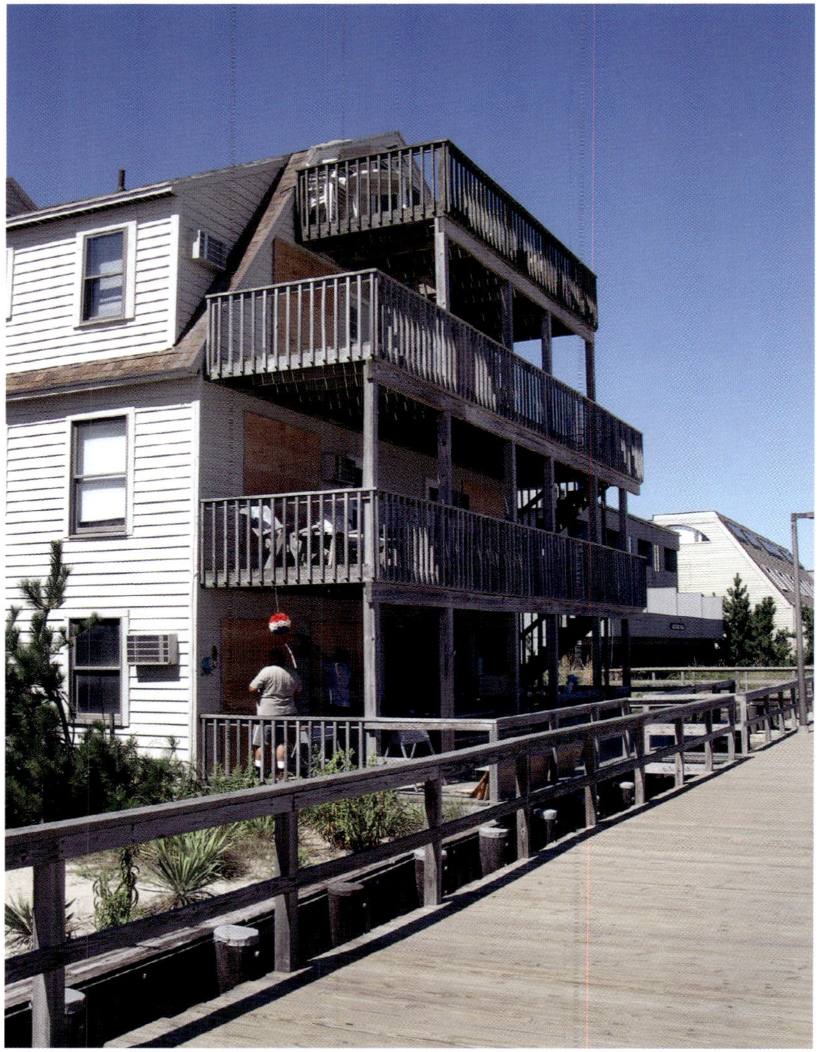

Though Bethany Beach is best known as a quiet resort, the cacophony of a furious sea occasionally rises in the distance, forcing property owners to ready their buildings in case tropical storms or hurricanes call upon the seaside resort.

The Bethany Beach Jazz Funeral is an annual tradition held every Labor Day. The New Orleans-inspired funeral includes a procession down the boardwalk, Dixieland music, and mourners dressed in black.

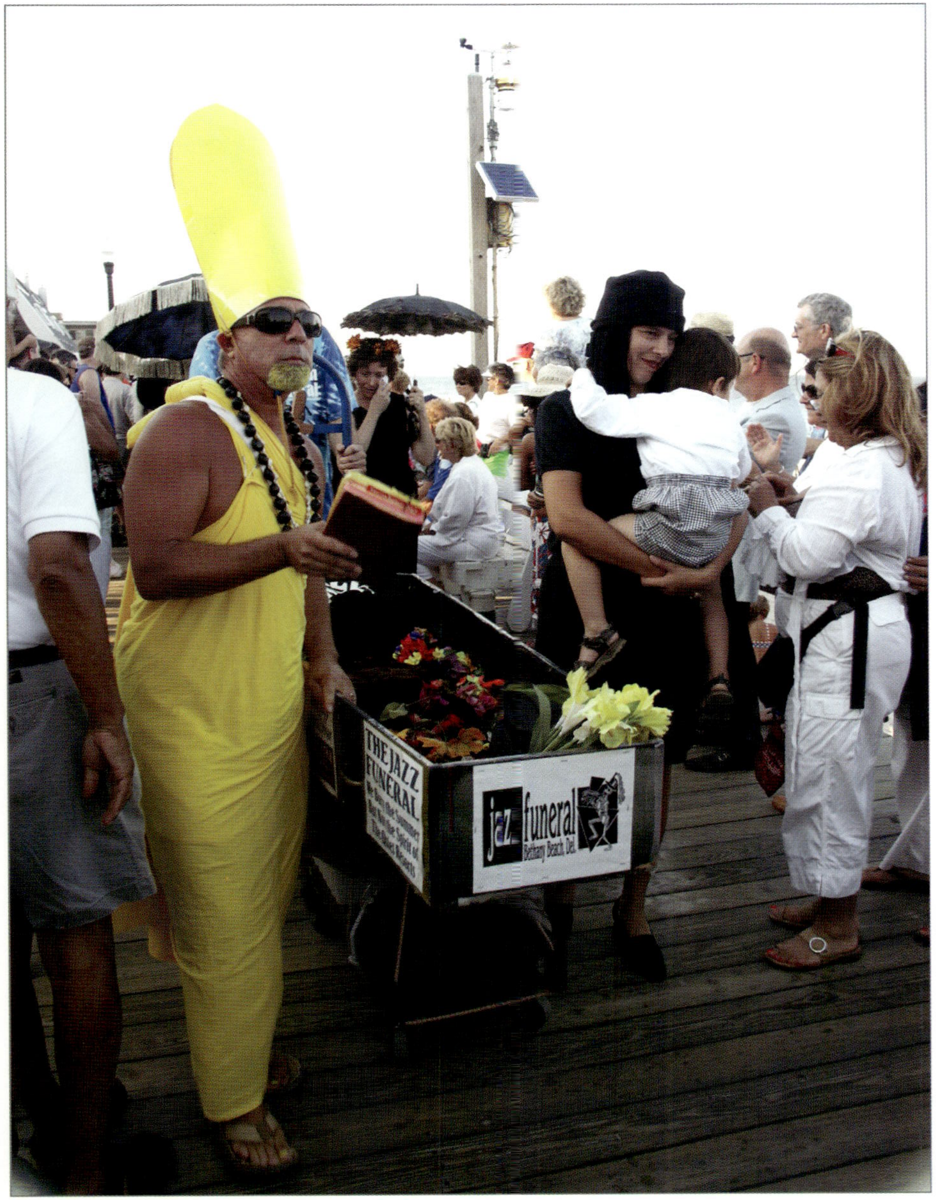

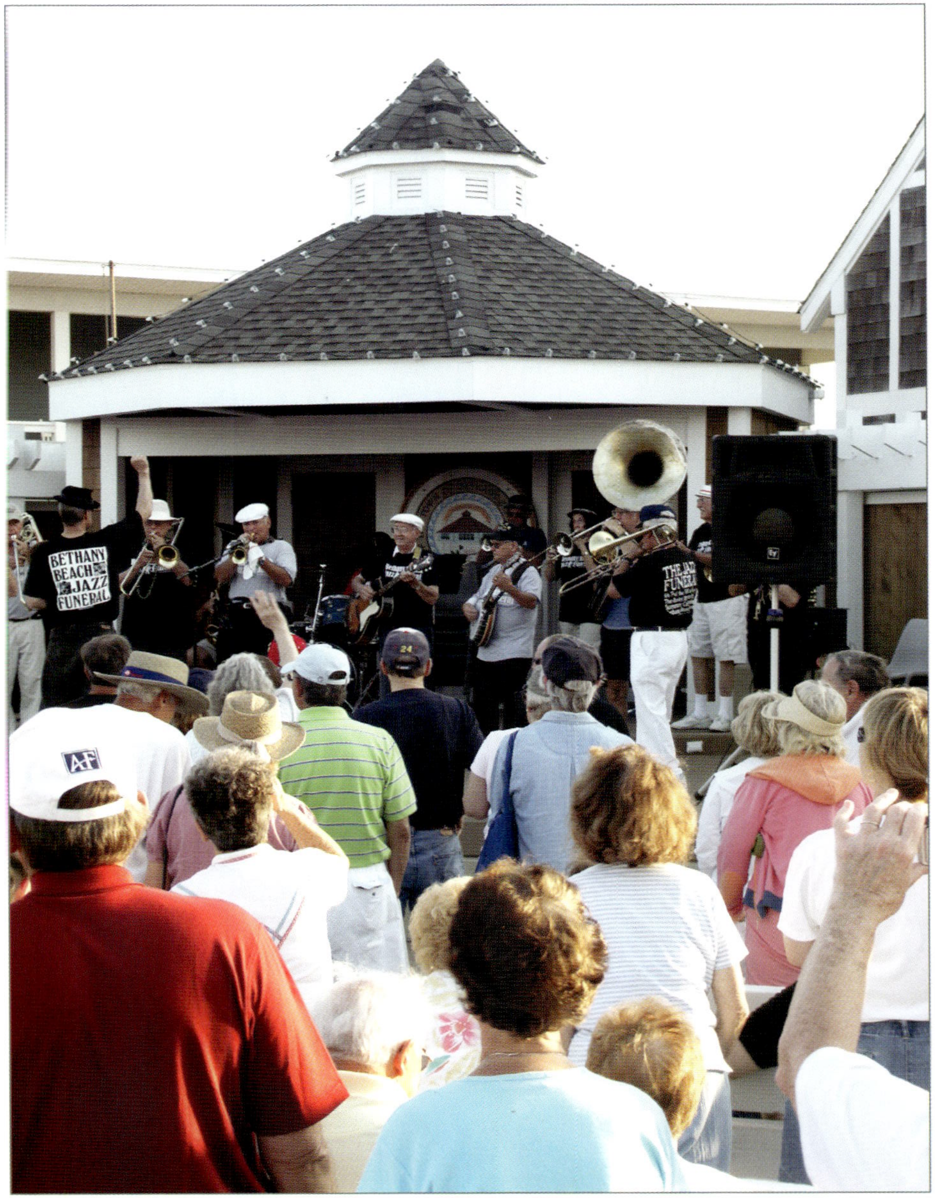

7

Fenwick Island & Fenwick Island State Park

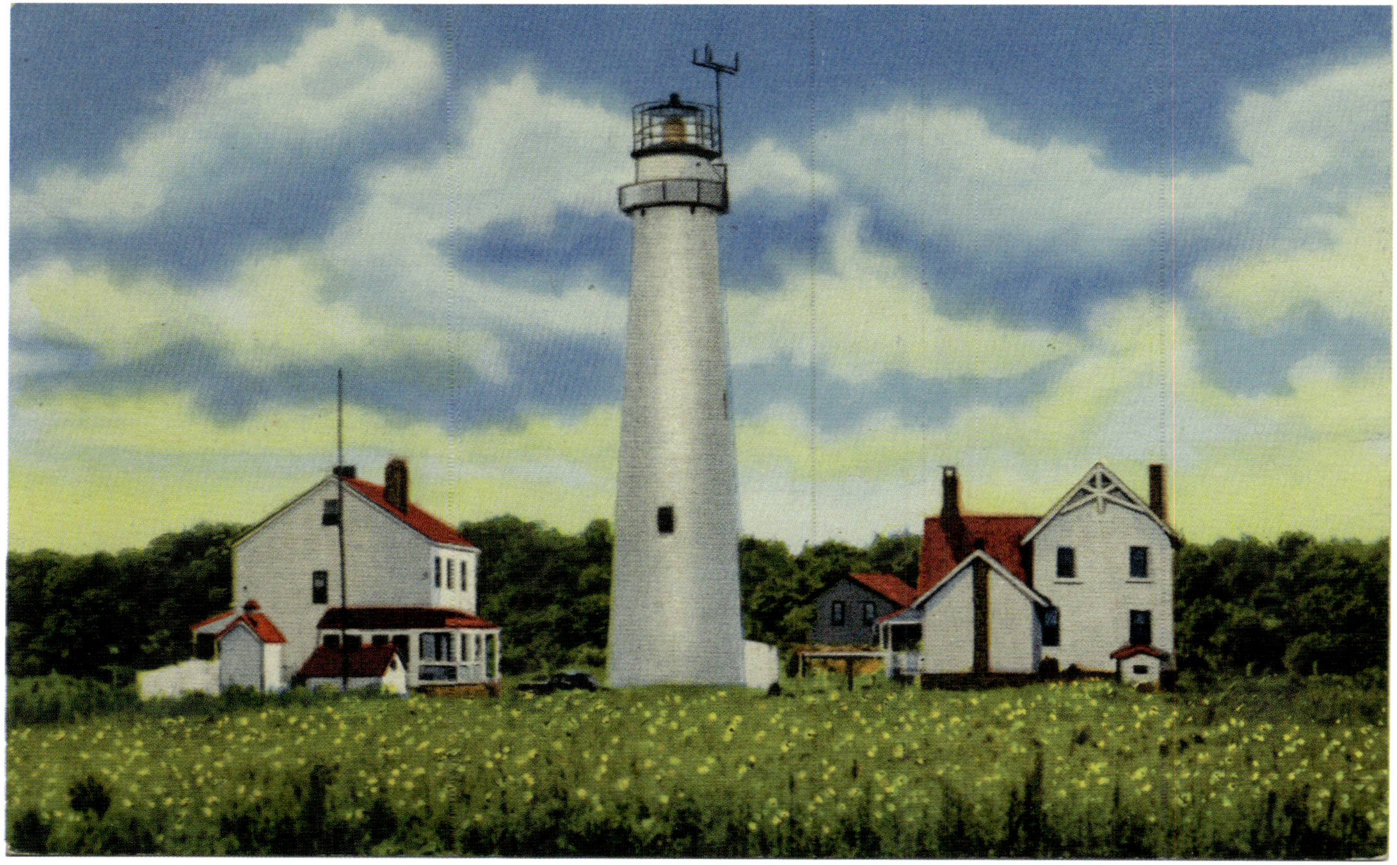

University of Delaware Library Postcard Collection, University of Delaware, Newark, Delaware

Fenwick Island is not your typical seaside resort. There aren't any high-rise hotels, nor is there an oceanfront boardwalk. You won't find a vibrant nightlife or entertainment pier. But what the town lacks in amenities it makes up for in quiet, pristine beaches.

Perhaps more so than any of the other "Quiet Resorts," Fenwick Island lives up to its name. To its immediate south lies Maryland and the neon lights of Ocean City. The two towns may be adjacent to one another, but they are worlds apart in personality.

Fenwick Island is named for Thomas Fenwick, who was granted the surrounding land from Lord Baltimore in 1682. He never actually lived on the land. The Trans-Peninsular Line, which separates Delaware from Maryland, was surveyed in 1750-1751 and begins in Fenwick. Prior to that, pirates roamed the Atlantic Coast off Fenwick Island as well as the nearby bays.

Fenwick Island is known for its historic lighthouse, which was constructed in 1858 and lit in 1859. The light tower is 87-ft. tall and was built by the U.S. Army Corps of Engineers on a ten-acre plot of land that cost $50. The total cost for the tower and keeper's house was under $24,000. The lighthouse, which was automated in 1940, still maintains its original lens.

In 1880, a bridge was constructed over "the ditch," linking the barrier island with the mainland. It was replaced by a new wooden pike drawbridge twelve years later, then replaced again in 1934. The current bridge dates from 1958.

Settlement on Fenwick Island didn't really occur until the 1930s when small cottages were constructed. In July 1953 the town was incorporated – in part to slow development that was occurring to the south in Ocean City.

Today, commercial establishments can be found; however, they are mostly limited to Coastal Highway. Retail offerings include local chains as well as a few eclectic stores. The Discoveries from the Sea Shipwreck Museum is a popular local attraction, and several restaurants cater to visitors from Ocean City to Bethany Beach.

To the north of the town is Fenwick Island State Park, a 344-acre park that features ocean and bay shoreline. To its east is the sometimes turbulent Atlantic Ocean; to its west the placid Little Assawoman Bay. The three mile barrier island was once part of the World War II coastal defenses, and a concrete observation tower from the war still stands. In 1966, the land became the southern extension of Delaware Seashore State Park, becoming Fenwick Island State Park in 1981. Today, it is a popular destination for surfing and surf fishing, and it features a guarded beach during the summer months.

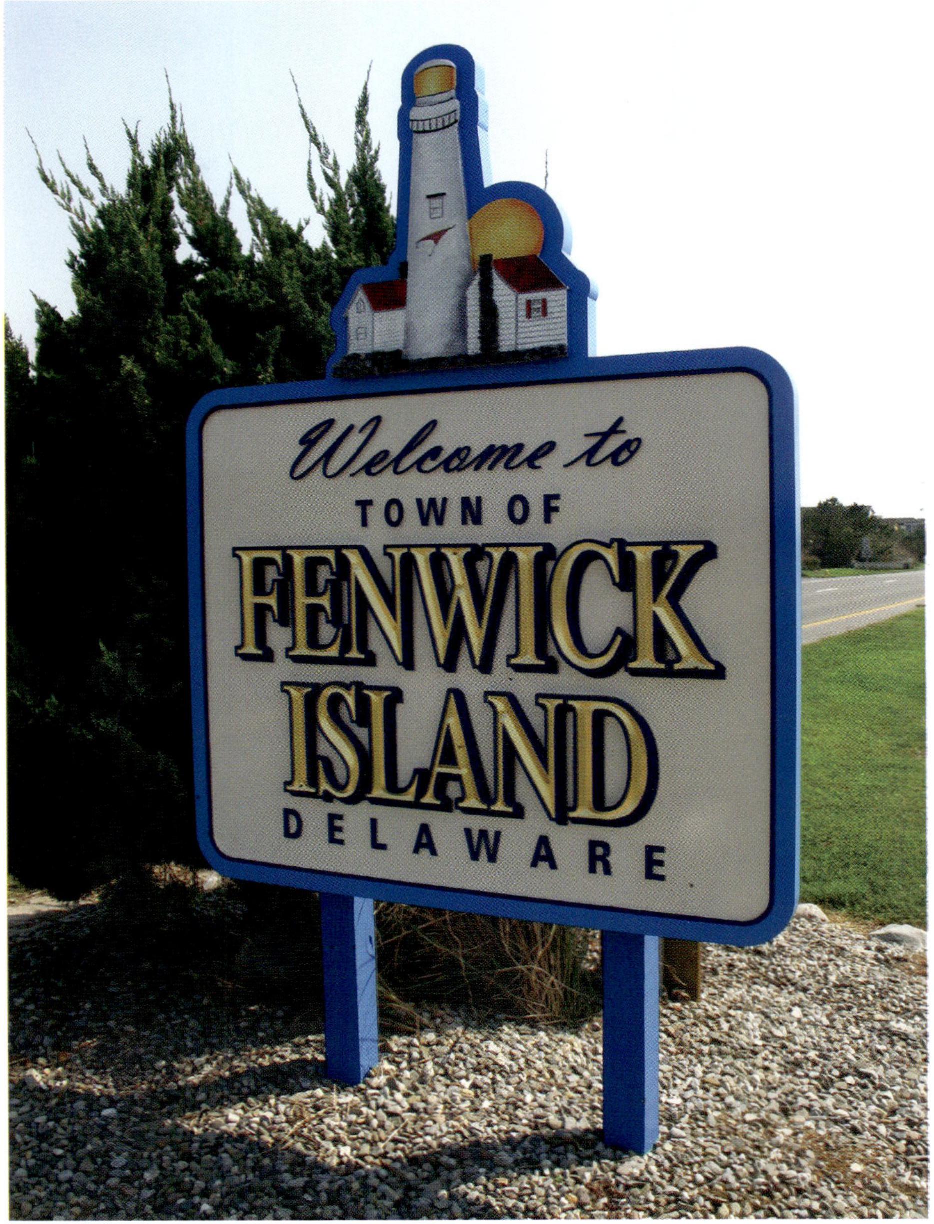

Fenwick Island is known as much for its historic lighthouse as for being one of Delaware's "Quiet Resorts."

Dawn over the Little Assawoman Bay – the true embodiment of a "quiet resort."

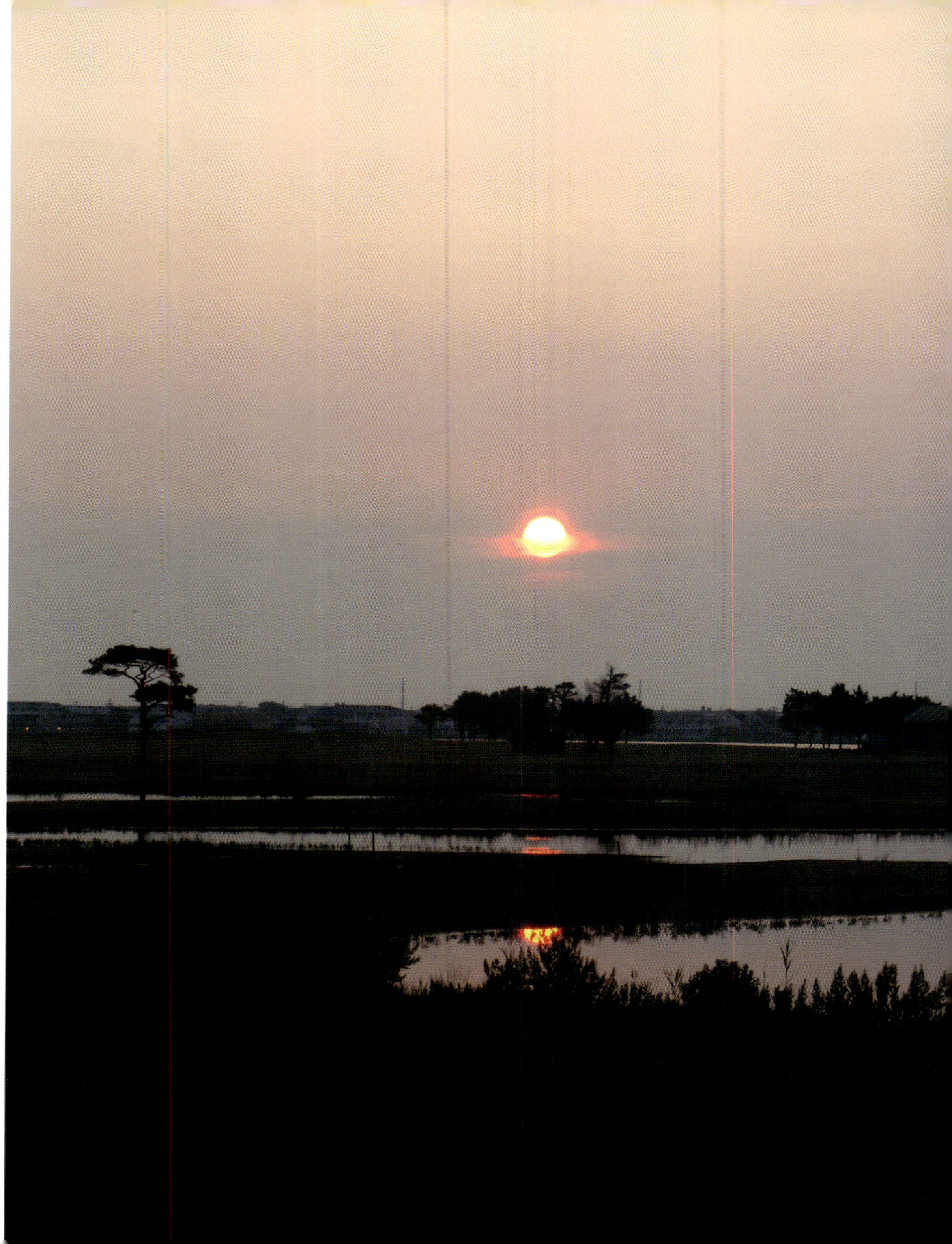

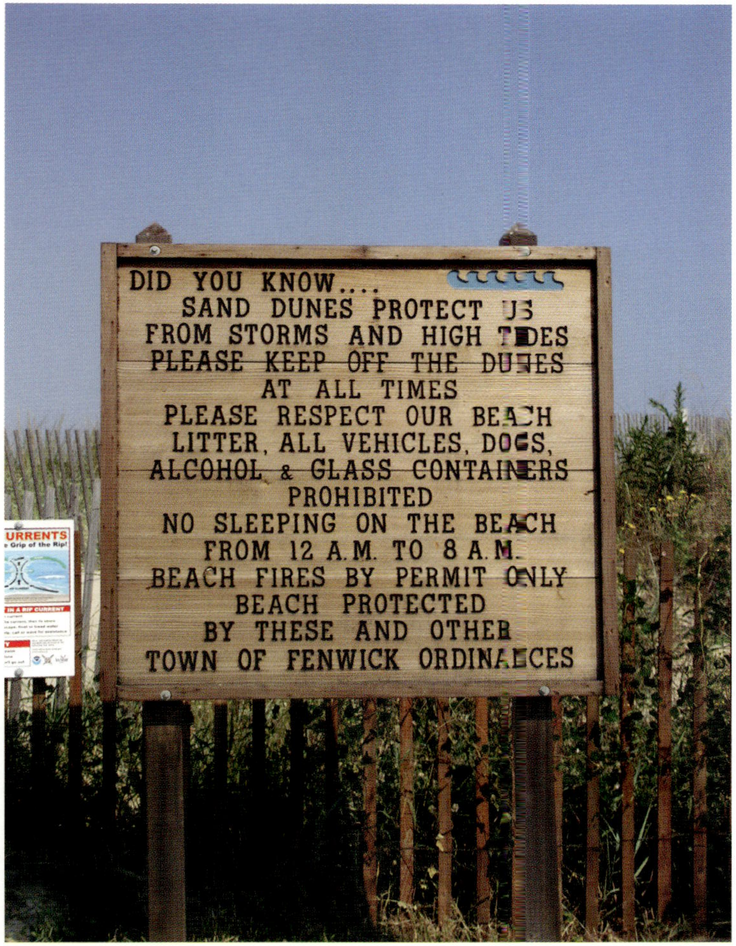

The wide beaches of Fenwick Island are known for being quiet and family-oriented, which is an atmosphere for which the community is quite proud.

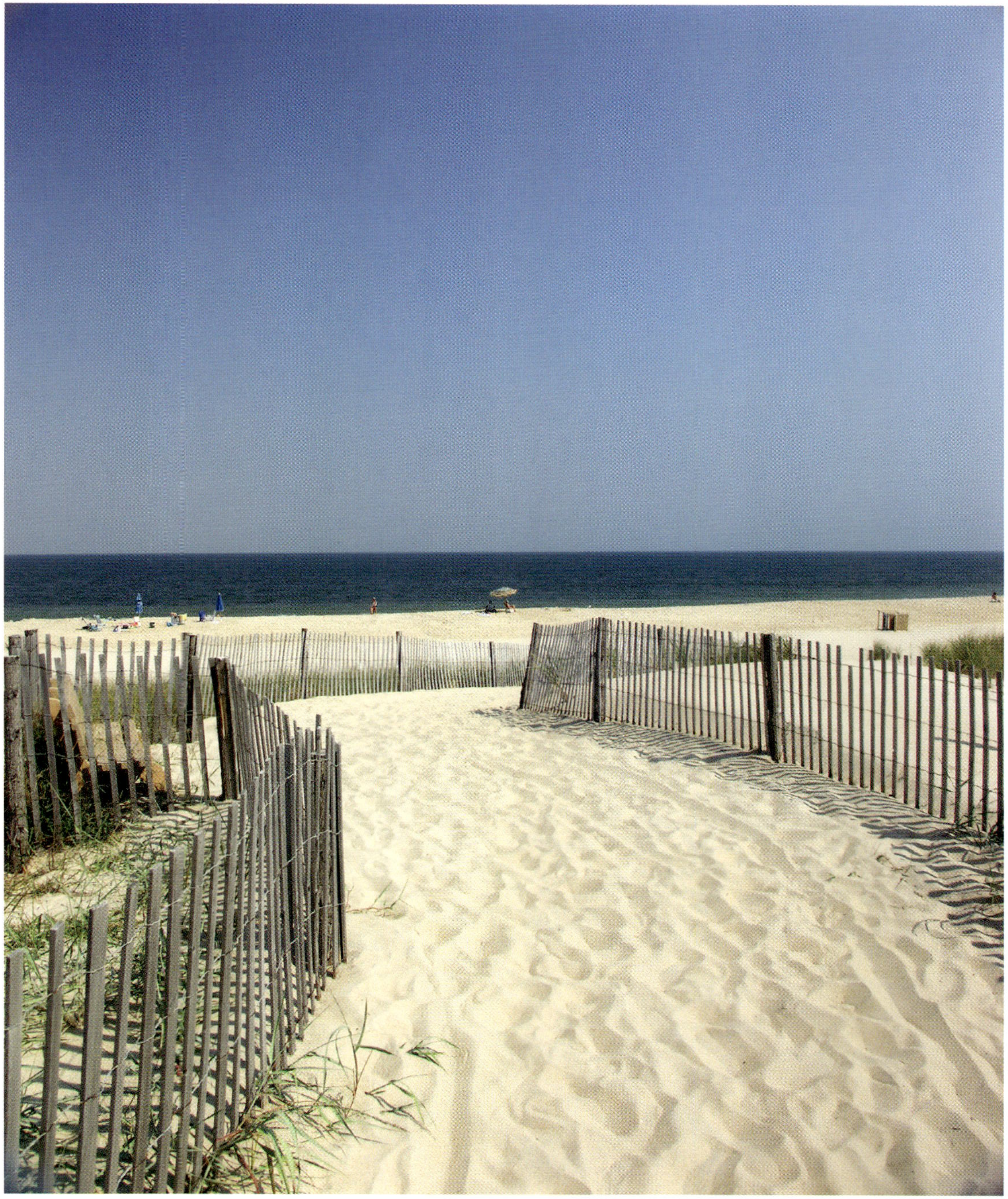

Fenwick Island's Pottery Place is one of the most curious and exotic stores on the Delaware coast, offering everything from a cup of hot coffee to goods imported from Asia and Africa.

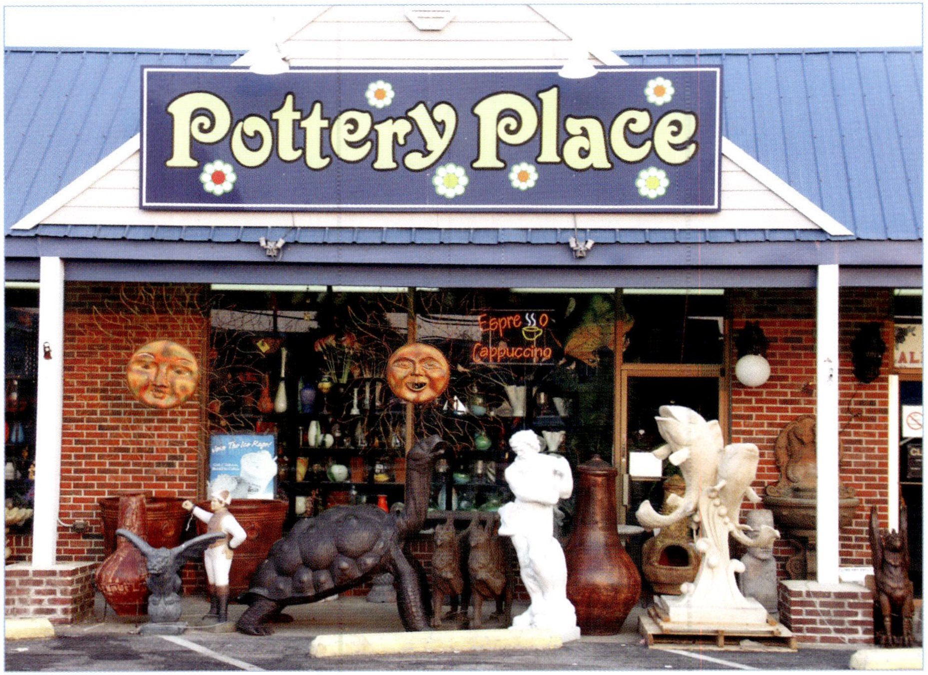

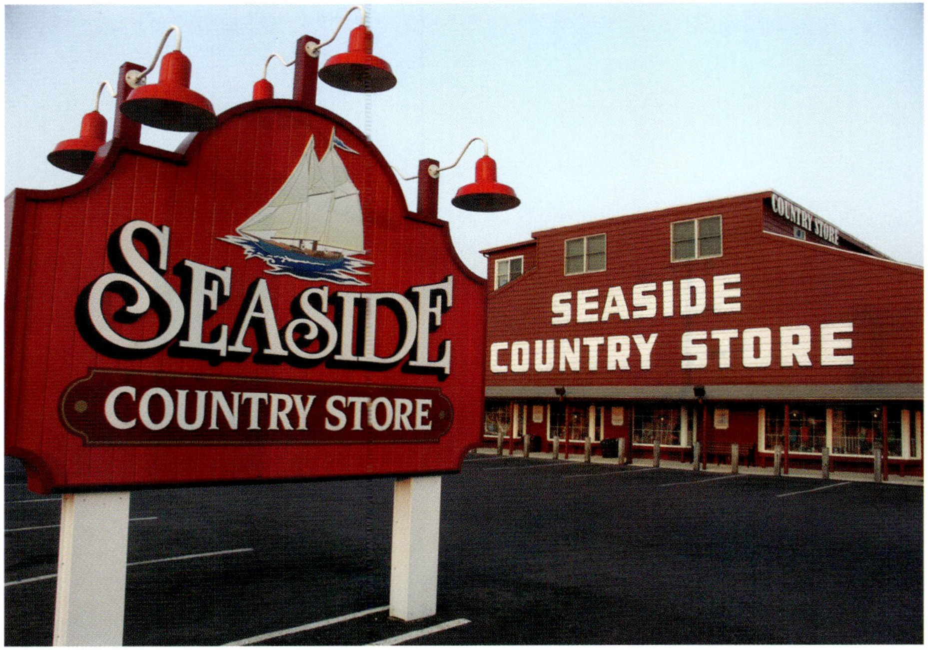

Seaside Country Store bills itself as "The Most Unusual Store on the Shore." It has been a popular attraction since 1969, offering a wide assortment of gifts. However, it is the scrumptious fudge and delectable cheese spreads – including the ever-popular horseradish cheddar – that keeps people coming back time and again.

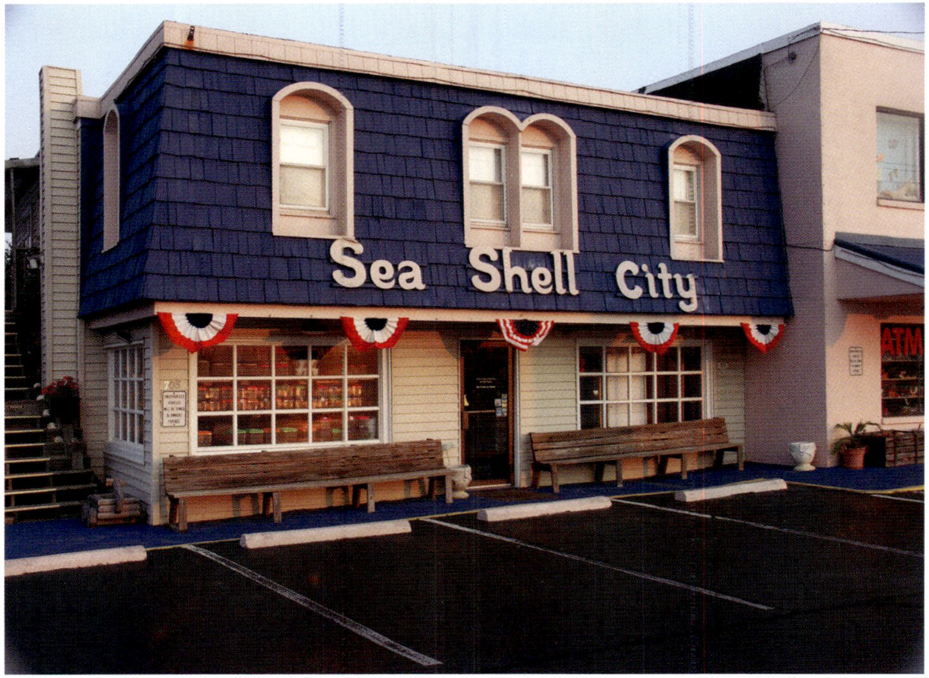

As its name suggests, Sea Shell City is the place in town to stop for a wide assortment of sea shells collected throughout the world. The shop offers an eclectic mix of beach décor, gifts, and apparel. Located above Sea Shell City is the Discoveries from the Sea Shipwreck Museum, which opened in 1995 and contains approximately 10,000 shipwreck and recovered artifacts.

Located along Coastal Highway, Sunsations is a popular purveyor of everything and anything needed for a day at the beach.

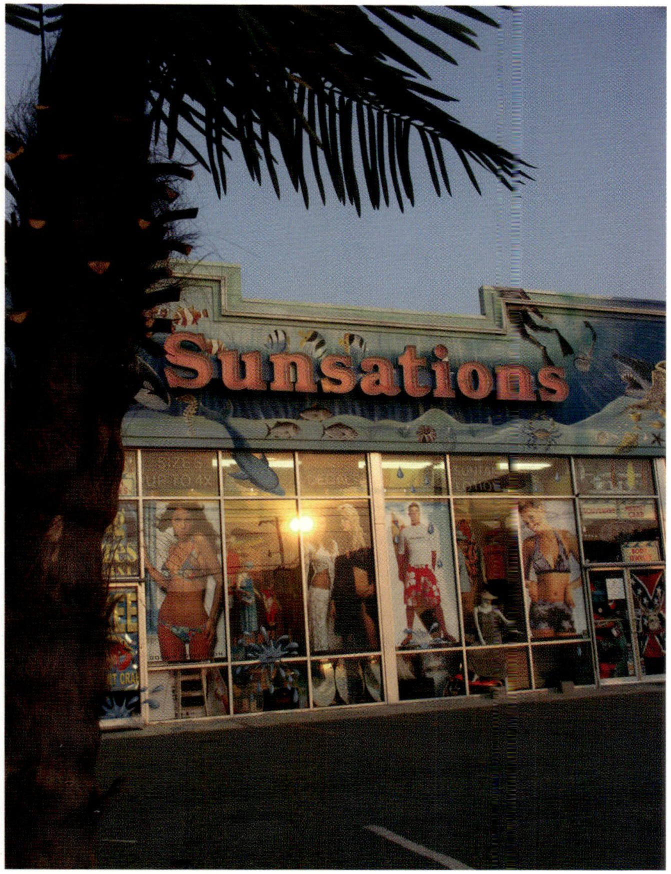

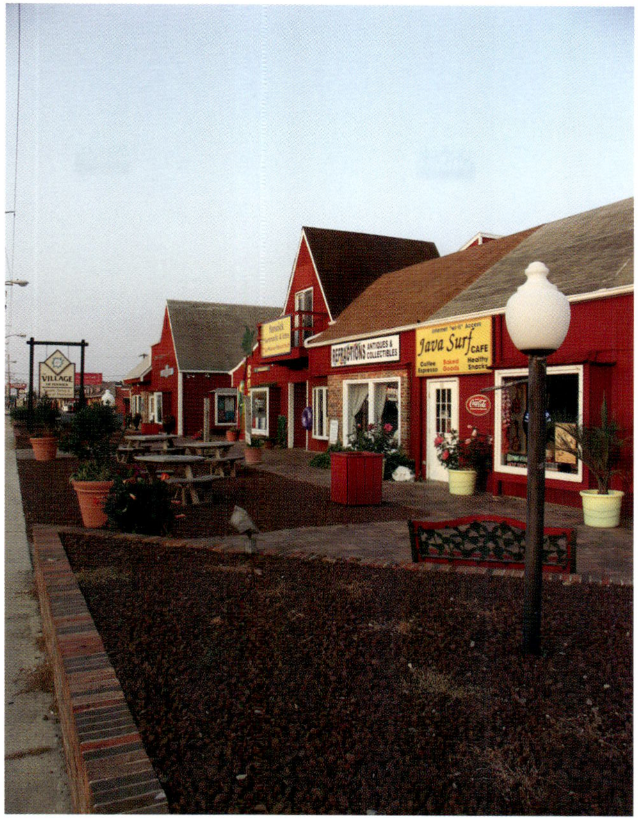

The Village of Fenwick is perhaps Fenwick Island's version of a seaside boardwalk, with fifteen stores clustered together.

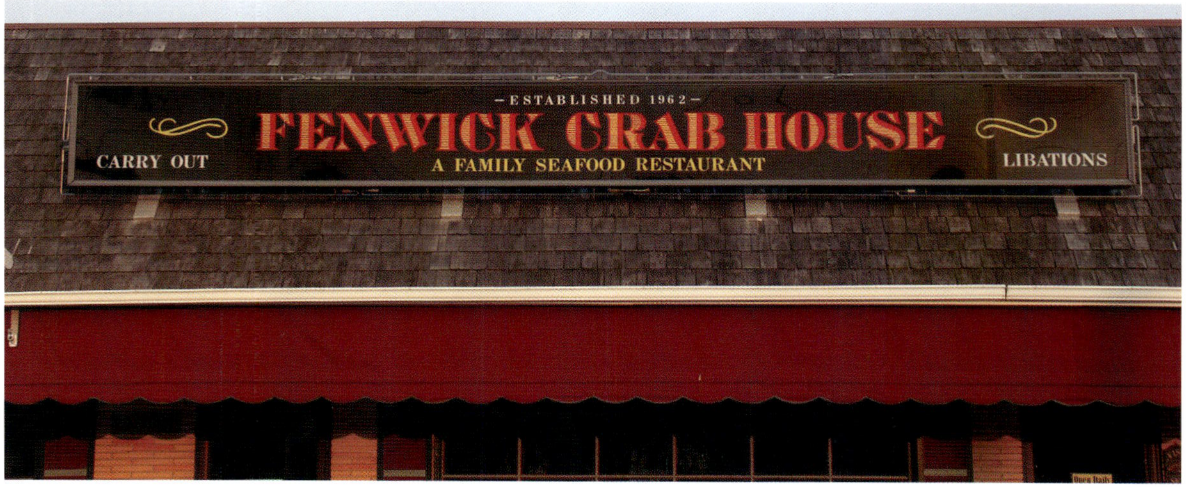

Fenwick Crab House is a popular hangout and a "must-visit" destination for many annual beachgoers. Once recognized by *Washingtonian Magazine* for having the best steamed crabs, today the Fenwick Crab House is known far and wide for their sumptuous crab cakes.

The Bethany-Fenwick Area Chamber of Commerce operates a spacious Information Center on Coastal Highway just north of the town of Fenwick Island.

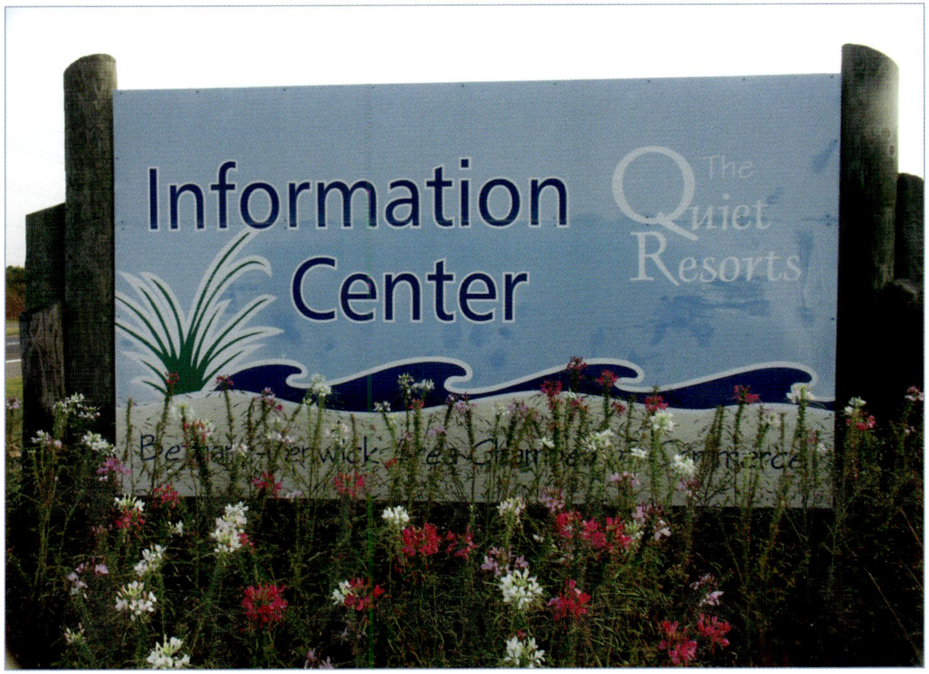

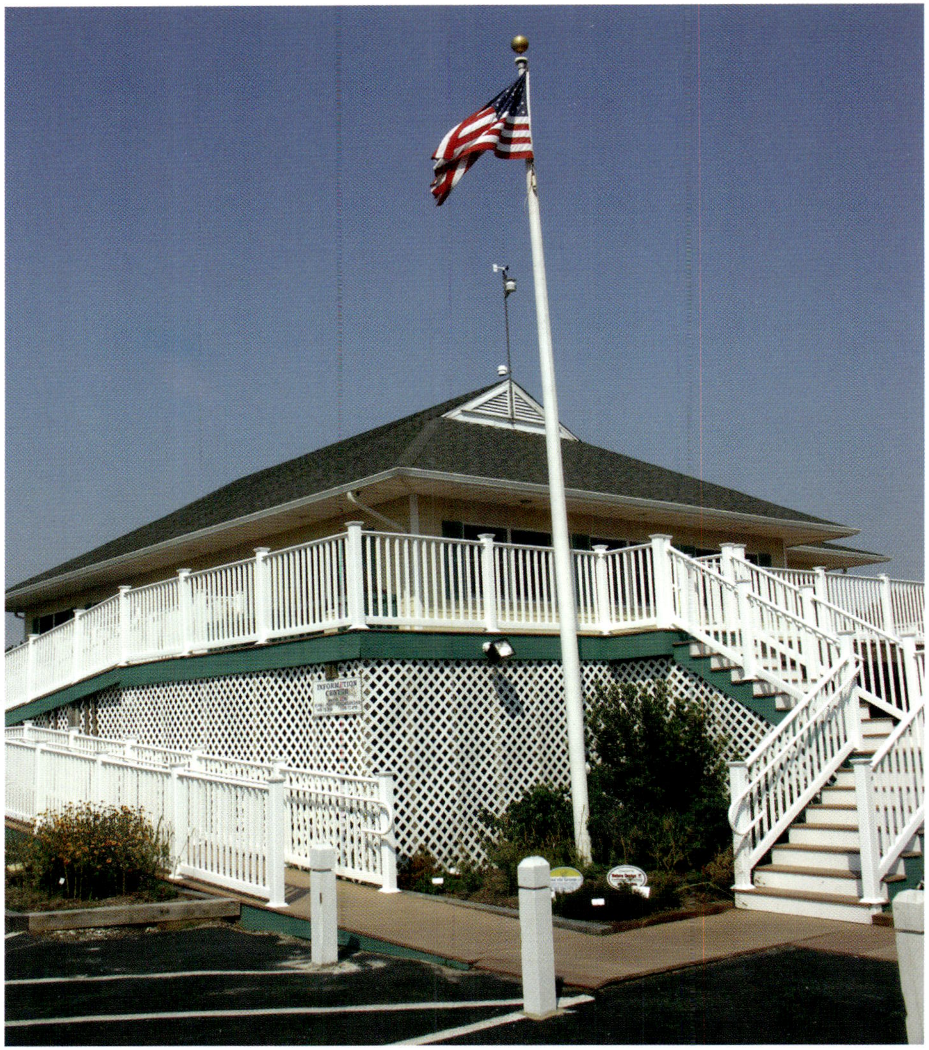

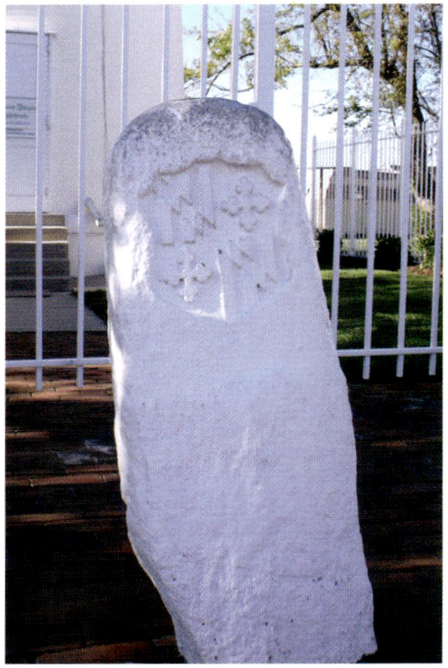

The Transpeninsular Line was surveyed in 1750-1751 to settle a boundary dispute. On one side was the Penn family; on the other was Lord Baltimore and the Calvert family. The line created a boundary between the Lower Counties on Delaware – which fell under the province of William Penn and his heirs – and Maryland. The line begins in Fenwick Island and continues 69 miles west to Taylor's Island. This marker, beside the Fenwick Island Lighthouse, denotes the line and features the Penn coat of arms on the north side and Calvert coat of arms on the south side.

Fenwick Lighthouse was built in response to a need to have a light between lighthouses at Cape Henlopen and Assateague Island. In 1856, $25,000 was appropriated by the U.S. Congress for construction of the lighthouse, which was completed in 1858 and lit one year later. A two-story frame house was also built and featured a 2500-gallon cistern in the basement to collect rain-water.

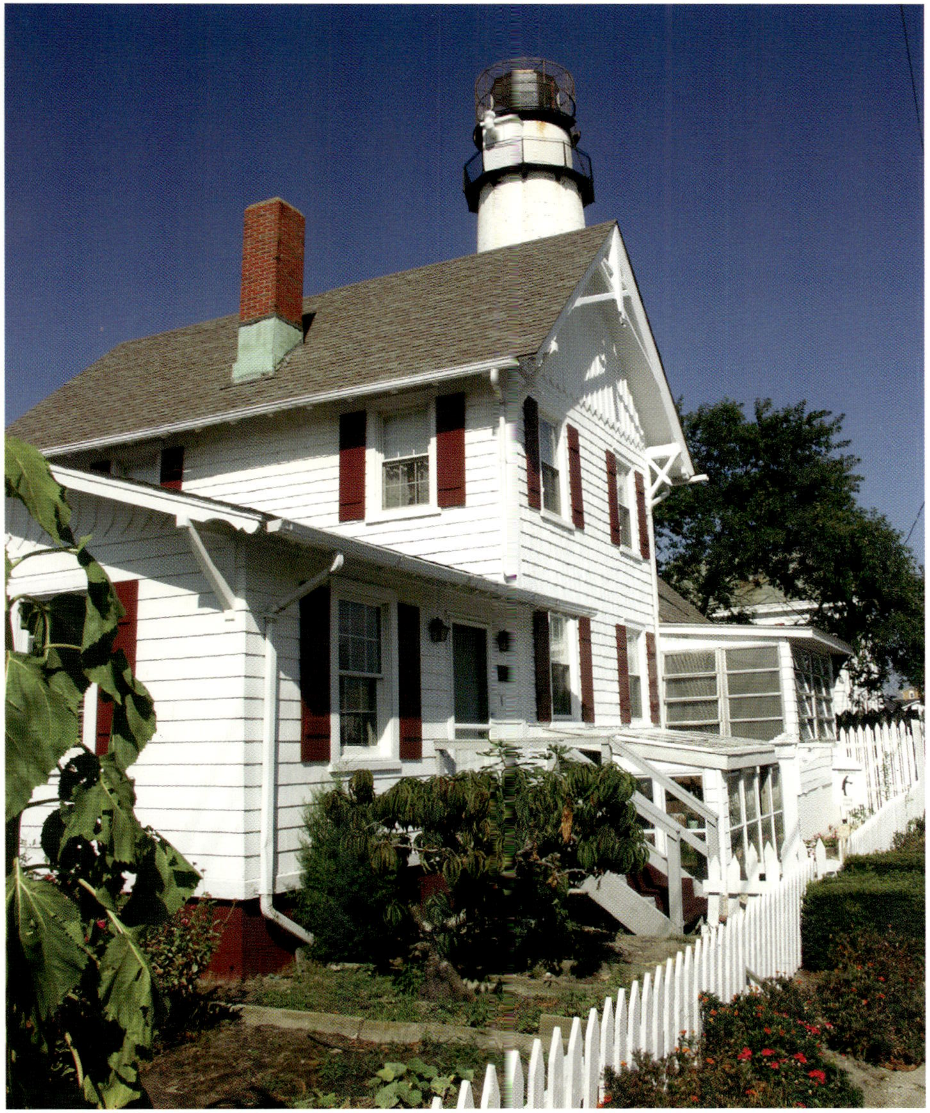

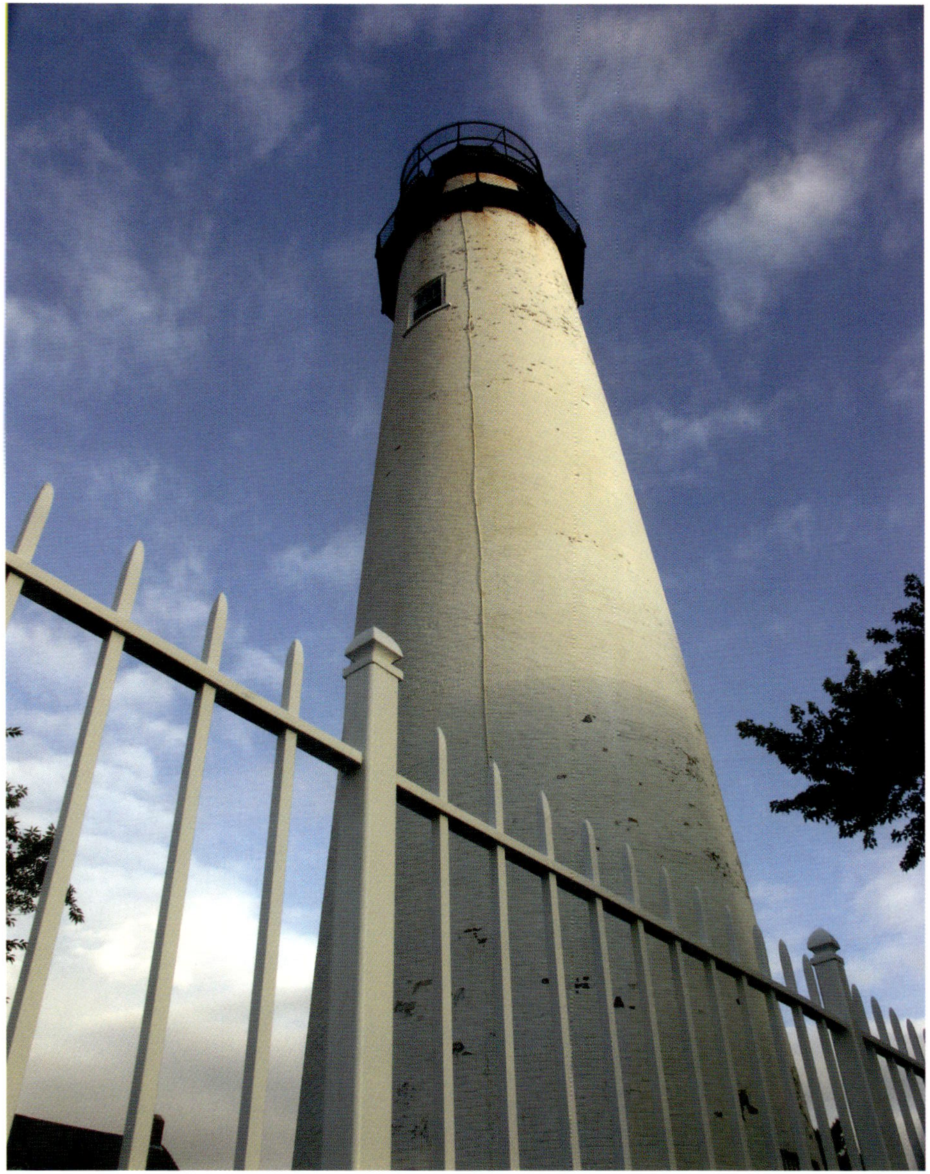

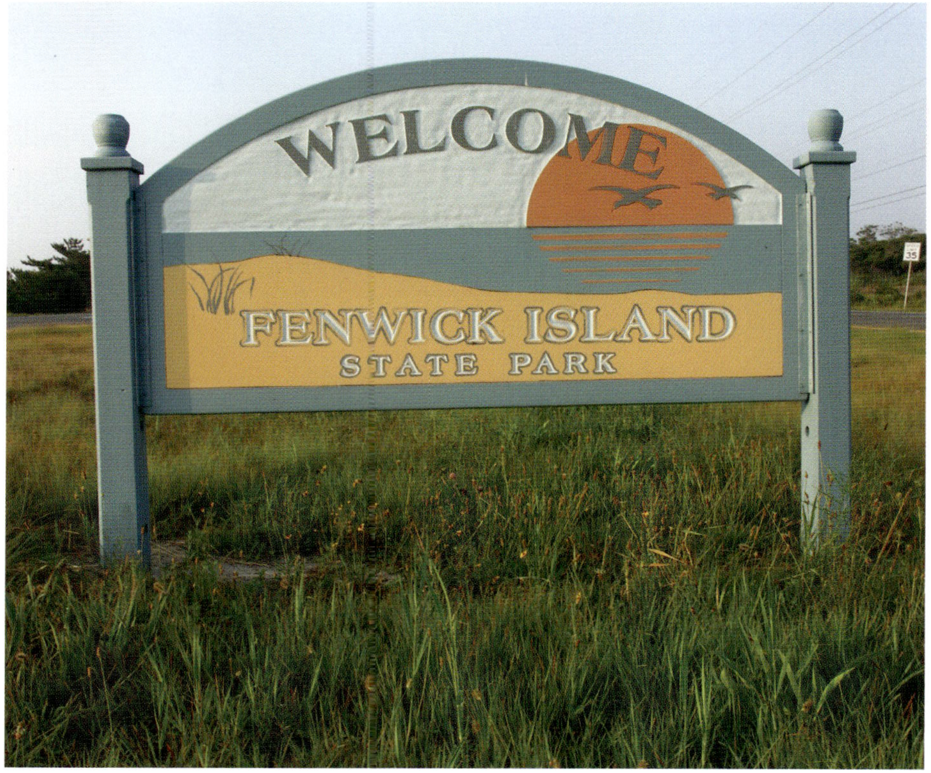

Fenwick Island State Park is situated on 344 acres of ocean and bay shoreline along a three-mile stretch of barrier island between South Bethany and Fenwick Island. The park has a designated surf area, guarded beaches, modern bathhouse, and lots of white sand.

One of thirteen artillery control towers constructed along the Delaware Bay and Atlantic Ocean during World War II. Eleven towers are located in Delaware, two in New Jersey. Each tower is slightly different as they were constructed using sand from the immediate surroundings in order to expedite construction.

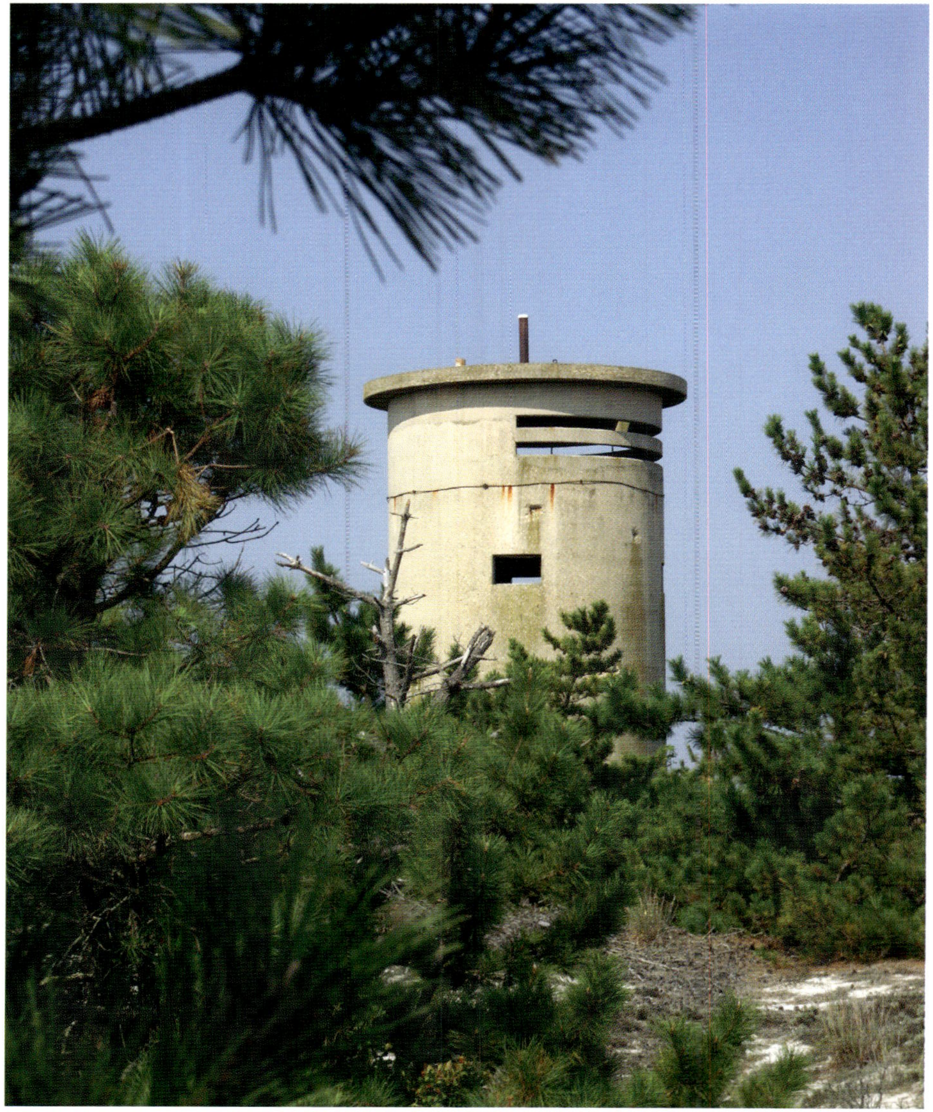

A quiet sunset over Assawoman Bay is a perfect way to end a day of fun in the sun.

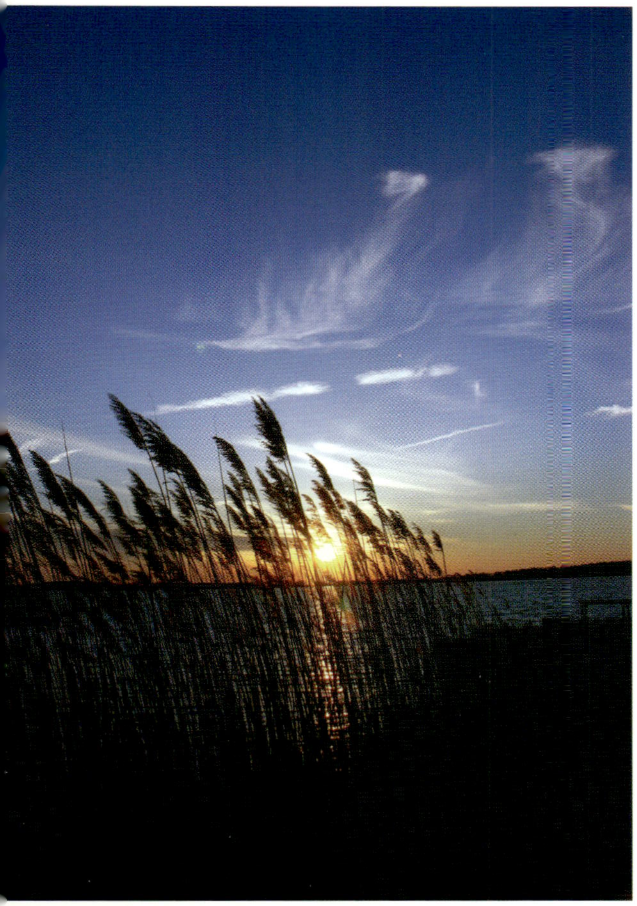

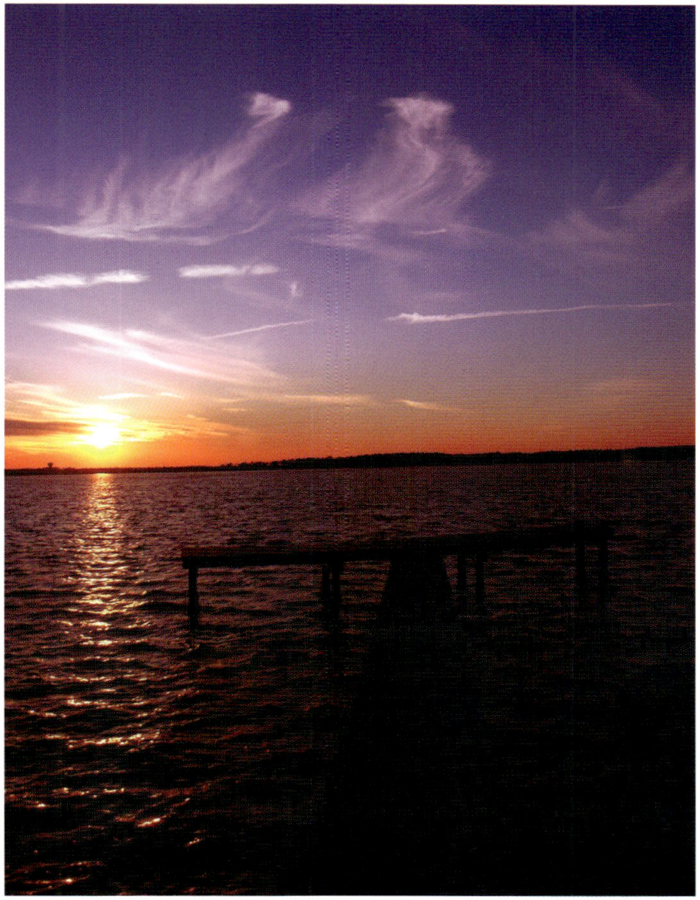

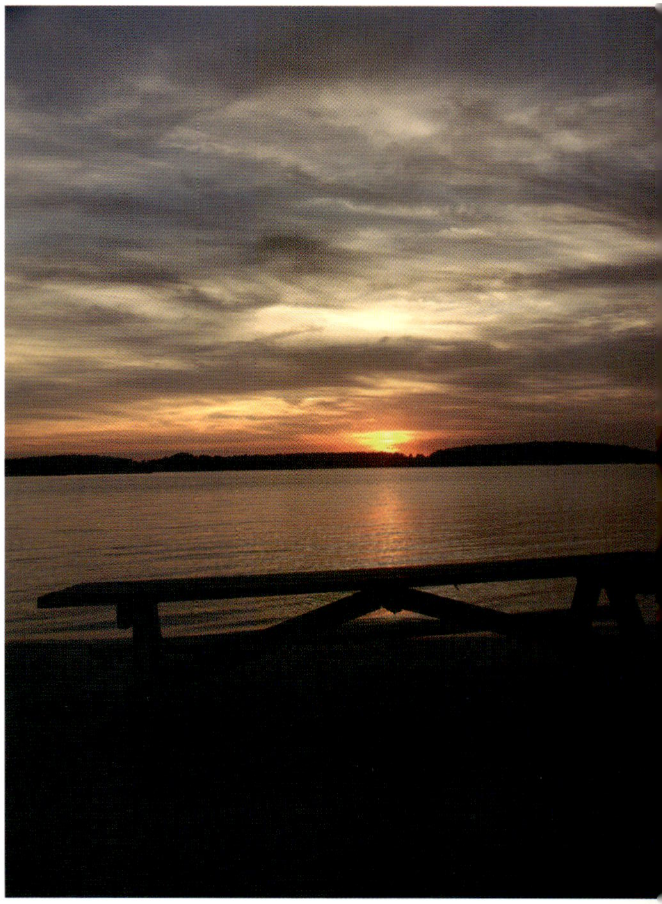

8 Beyond the Beach & Bay

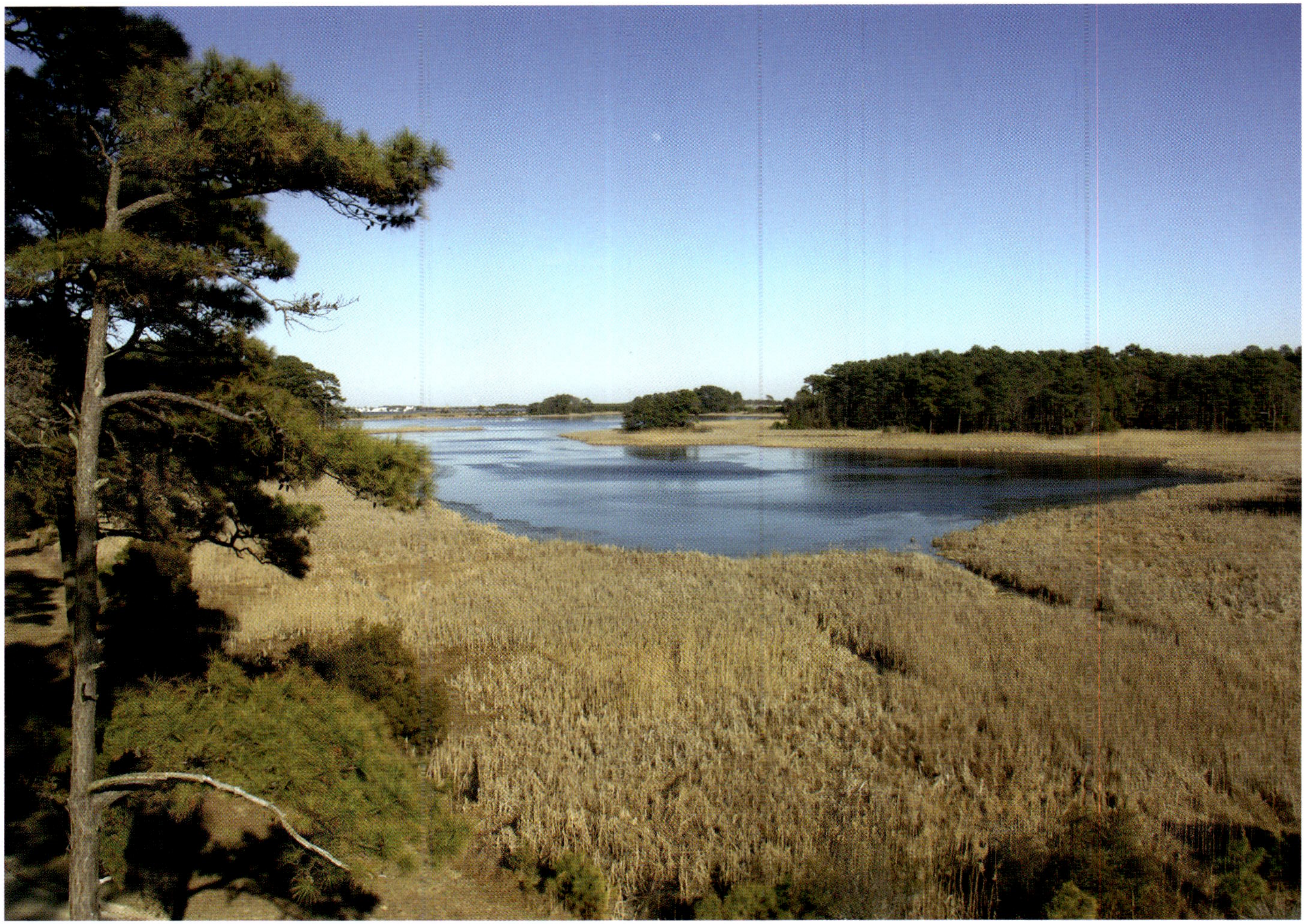

In addition to the resorts and parks of the Delaware coast, there are many excursions near and far to occupy a sun-filled day beyond the beach.

Historic Milton is one such location. The alluring small town was settled along the Broadkill River in 1763 by English colonists. It went by several names until 1807, when it was named for English poet John Milton, author of "Paradise Lost." A small Town Centre serves as the commercial district, offering antique stores, dining, and the Milton Theatre.

Millsboro sits along the Indian River, which connects the historic town with the Indian River Bay and Atlantic Ocean beyond. The town dates from the late 18th century and has a small commercial district with several antique stores.

Not far from Millsboro near Oak Orchard can be found the Nanticoke Indian Museum. Located in a former one-room schoolhouse, the museum houses a collection of artifacts that interprets the history of the "People of the Tidewaters" – the Nanticoke Indian Tribe.

Assawoman Wildlife Area offers a completely different coastal experience. The secluded refuge is located to the west of Fenwick Island State Park on almost 1700 acres of land adjacent to the Little Assawoman Bay. Here you'll find various species of waterfowl, white tailed deer, grey and red fox, bald eagles, ospreys, hawks, and many other species.

In recent years the Delaware coast has emerged as a destination for championship golf courses. Three notable courses are the "Augusta of the North," Baywood Greens in Long Neck; the Rick Jacobson designed Bear Trap Dunes in Ocean View; and the Jack Nicklaus Signature Golf Course at the Bayside Resort Golf Club in Selbyville, which was recognized by Golfweek Magazine as a "Top 50 Best New Course."

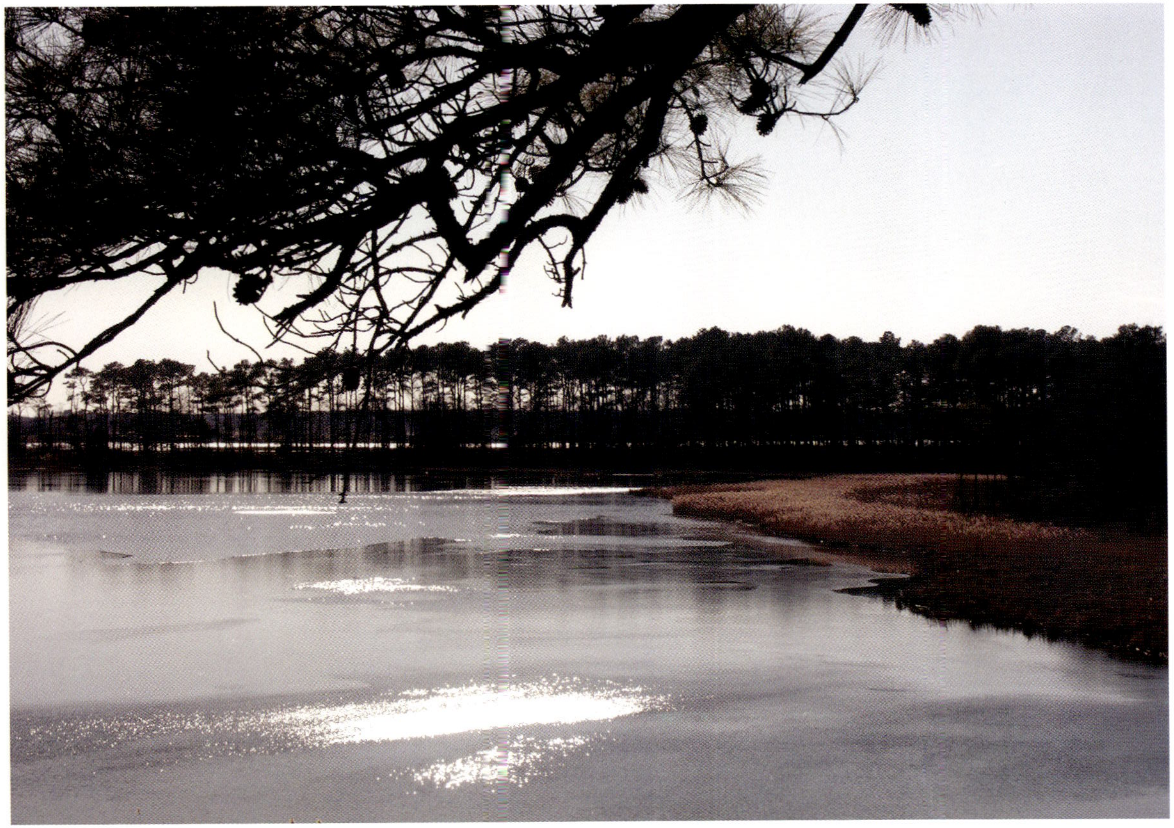

The Assawoman Wildlife Area comprises almost 1700 acres along the Little Assawoman Bay. Administered by Delaware Department of Natural Resources and Environmental Control, the preserve is located off-the-beaten-path and provides a great location for observing waterfall, deer, and even bald eagles.

Several championship caliber golf courses have been constructed along the Delaware coast in recent years, including Baywood Greens, which has been nicknamed "Augusta of the North."

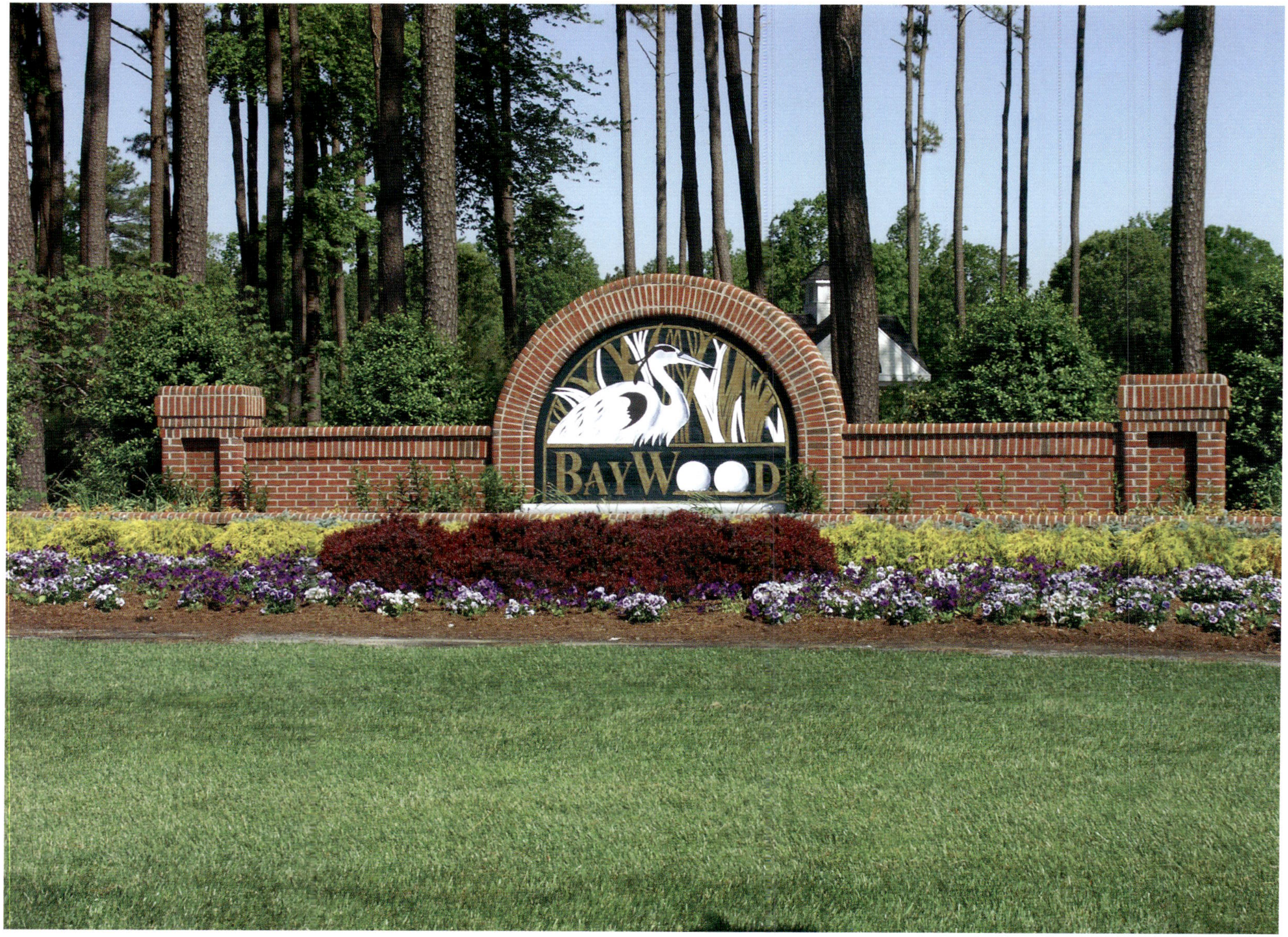

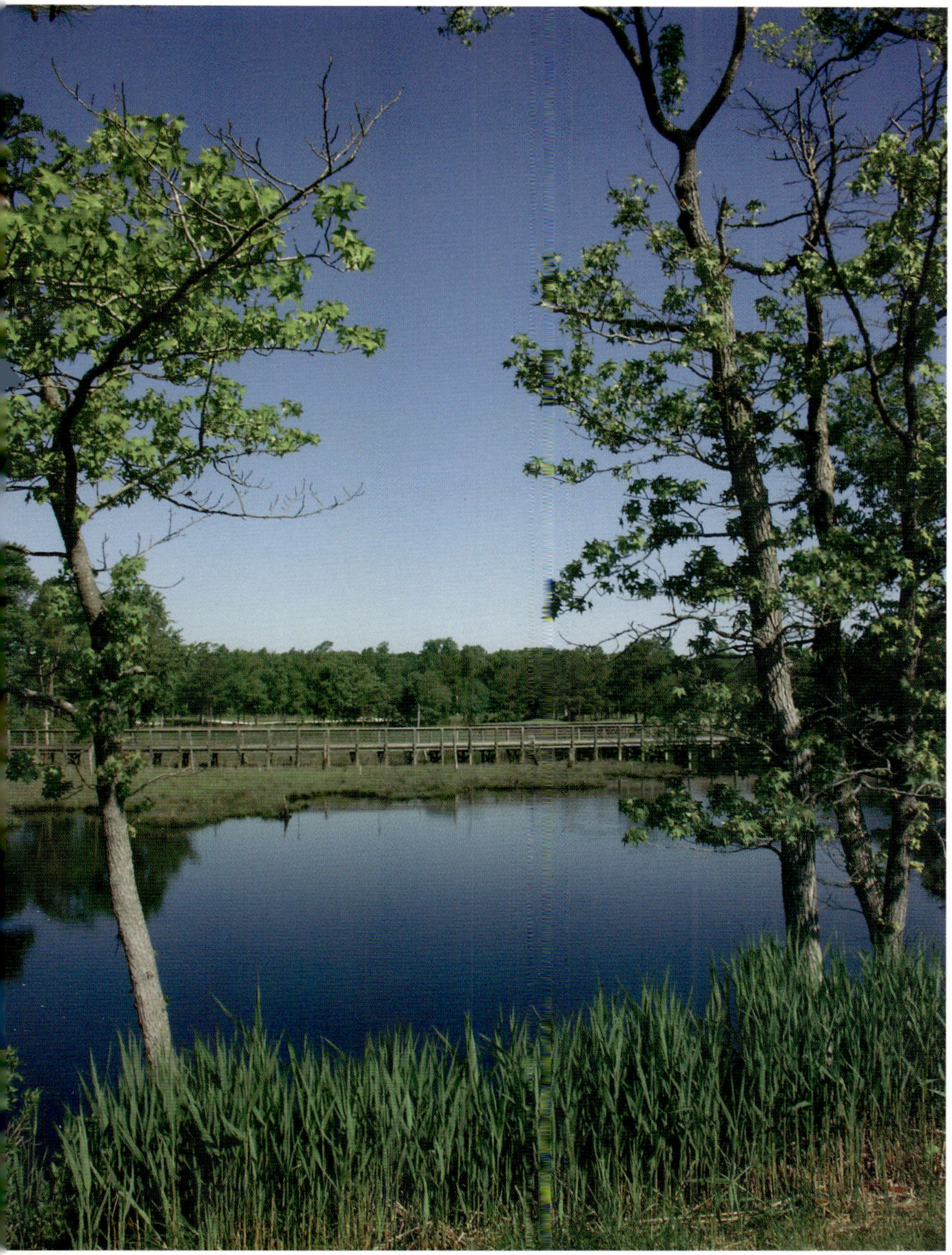

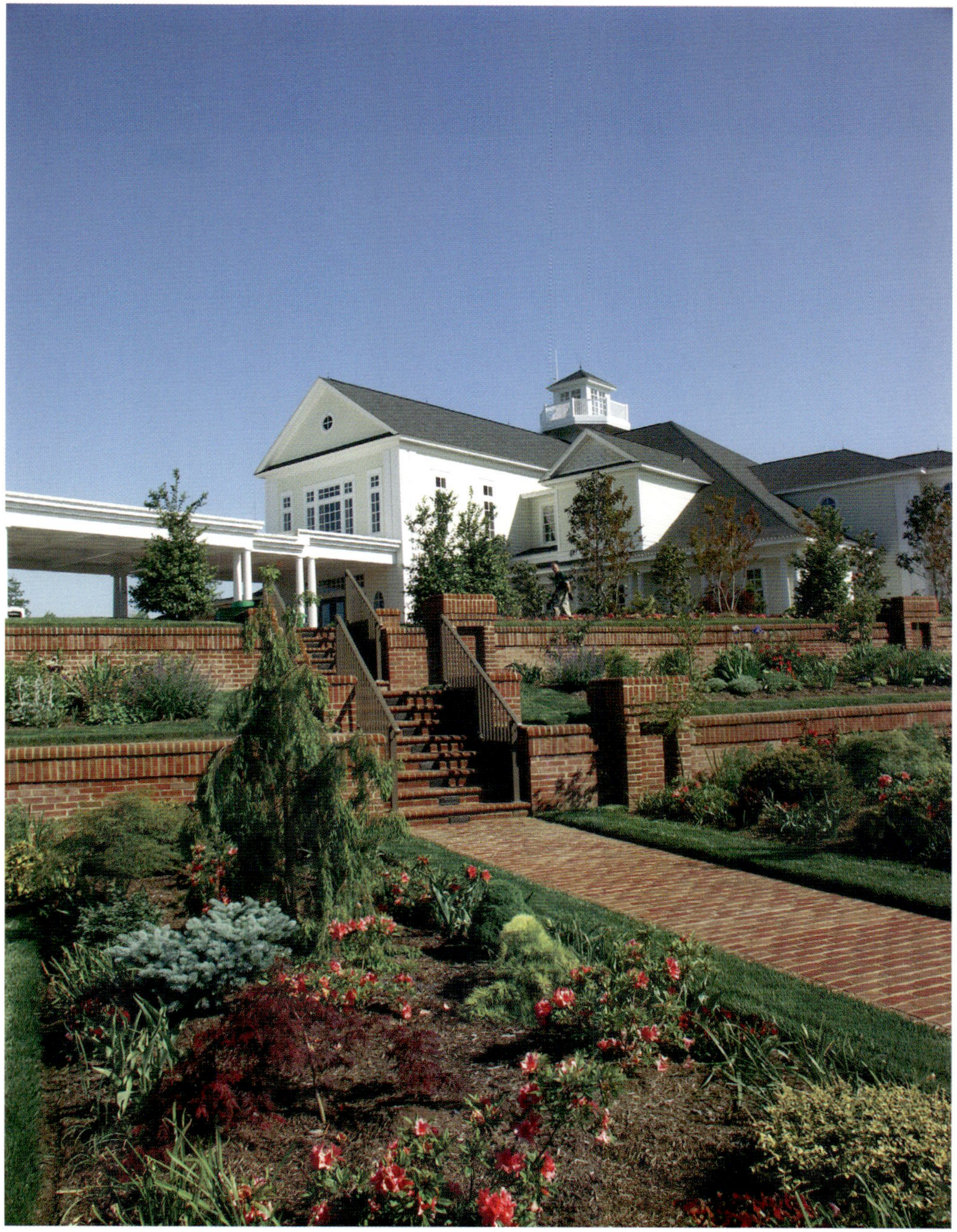

Nanticoke Indian Museum is located near Oak Orchard in a former one-room school house. The Nanticoke Indian Tribe is native to Sussex County and is today perhaps best known for its annual pow-wow event.

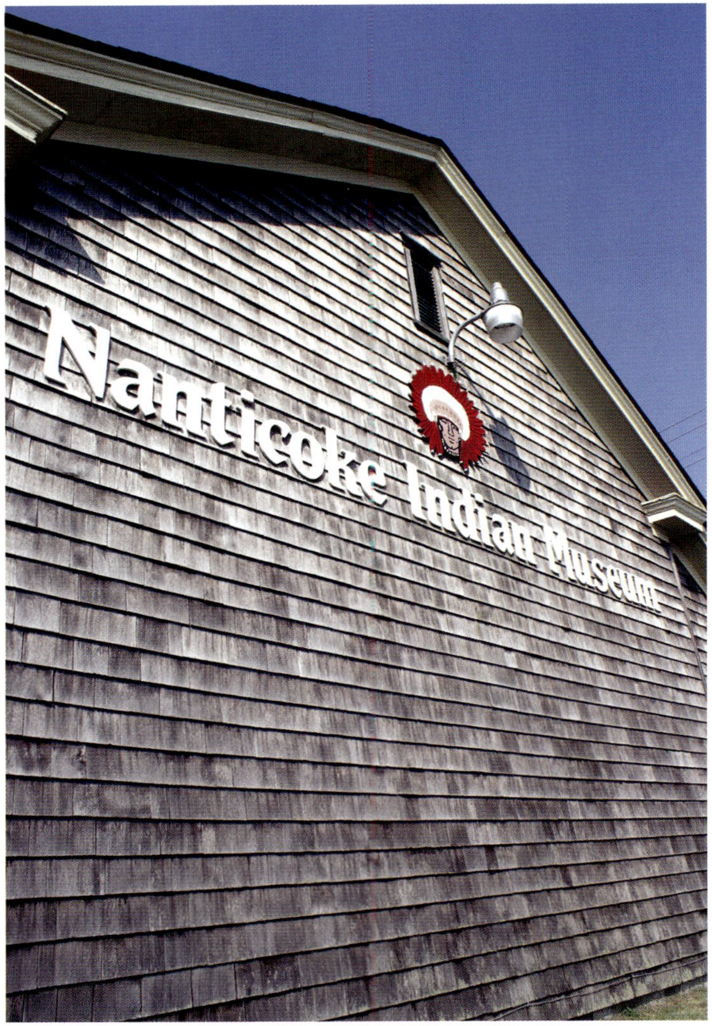

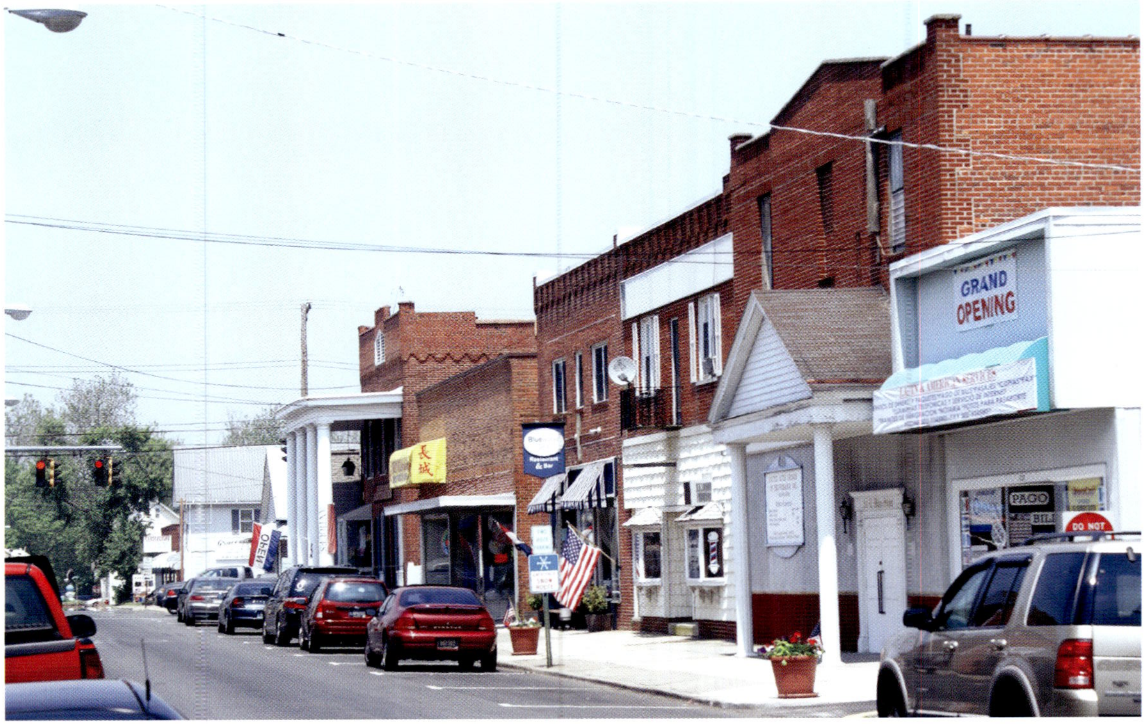

Millsboro, which sits at the first point on the Indian River, was established in the late 18th century.

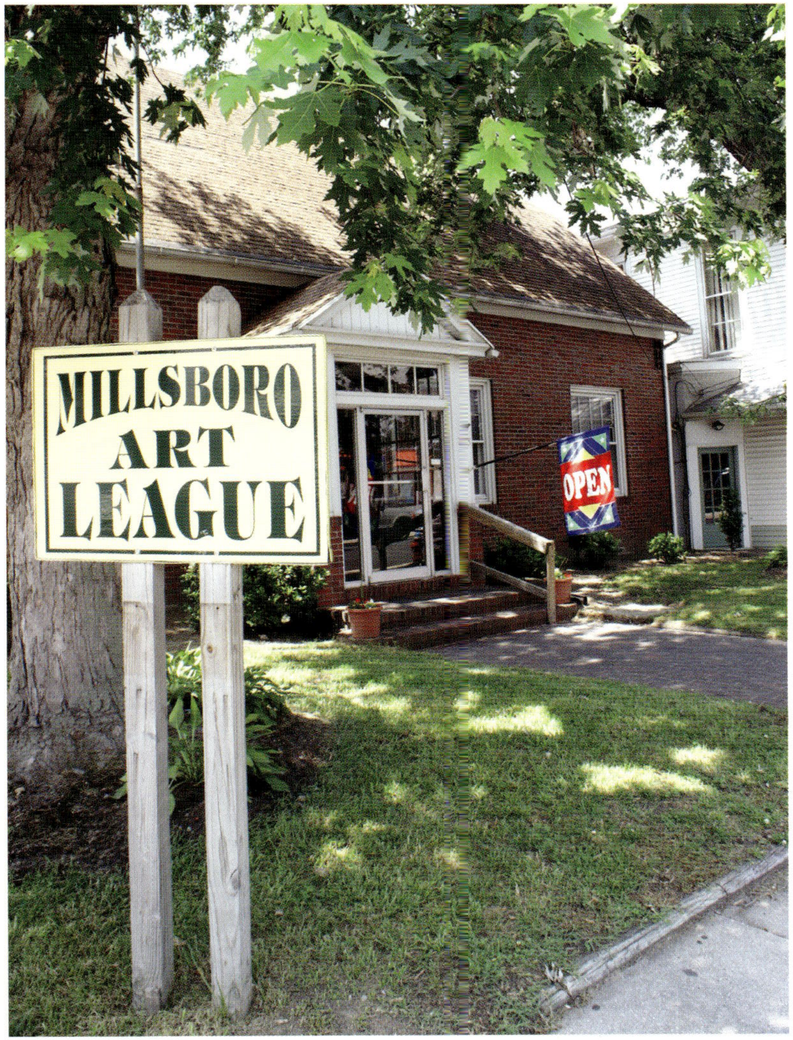

Millsboro Art League was founded in 1988 by local citizens devoted to promoting the visual and cultural arts. The non-profit organization is located in the former Millsboro Library building, which is where they had their first showing.

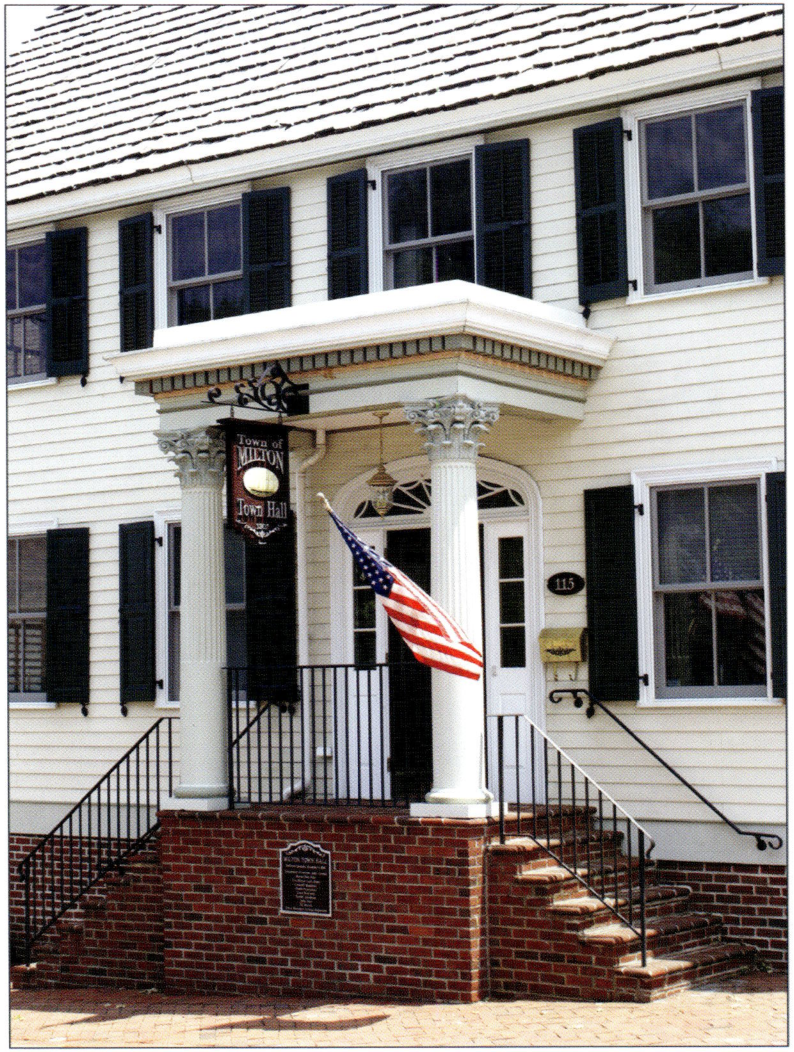

The town of Milton dates from 1763 and is rich in history as a center for shipbuilding. Today, a National Register of Historic Places historic district includes over 200 buildings.

Milton's business district includes antique stores, eateries, and the historic Milton Theater.

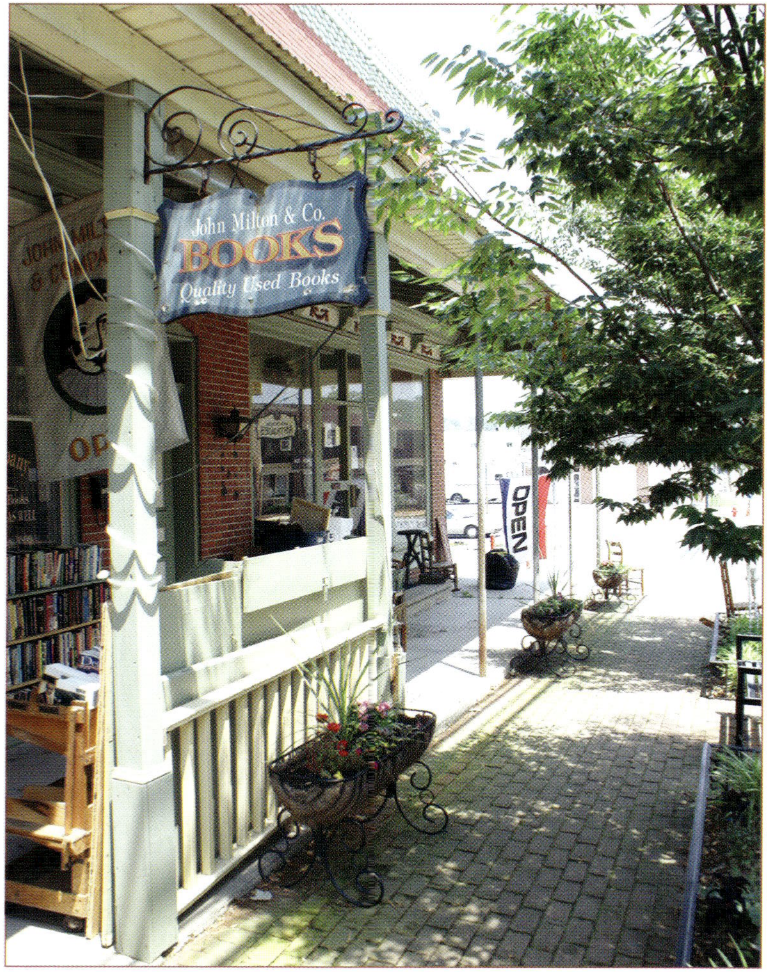

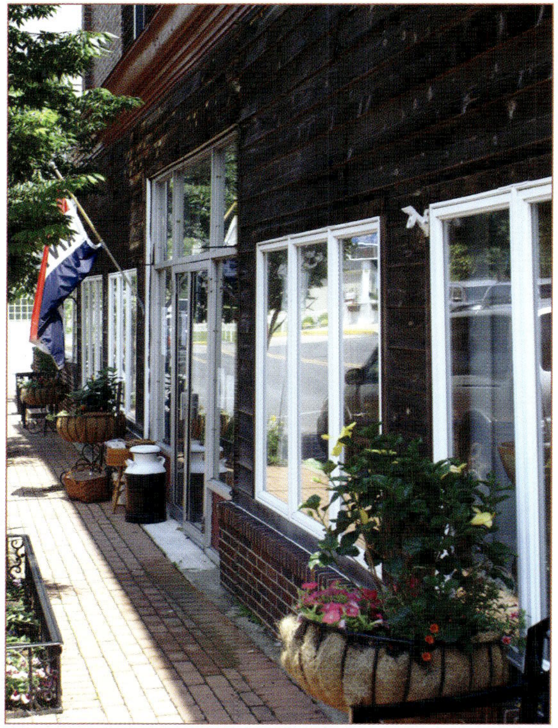

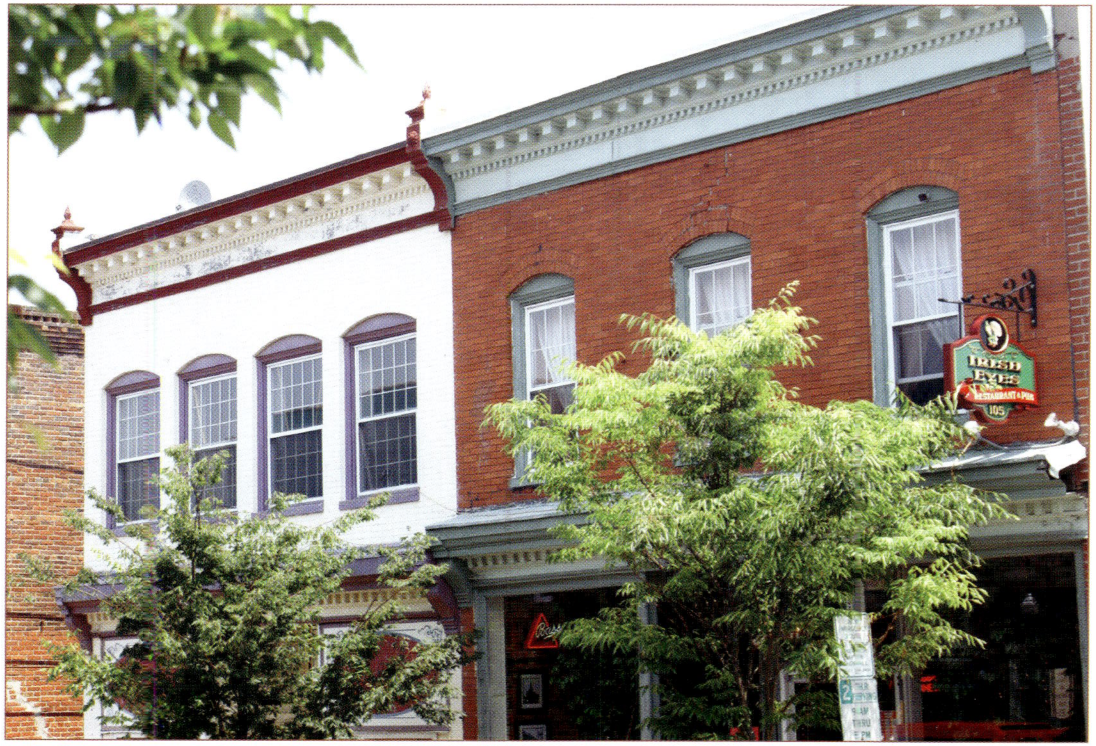

N. W. McGee House in Milton, constructed in 1850 by a local shipbuilder.

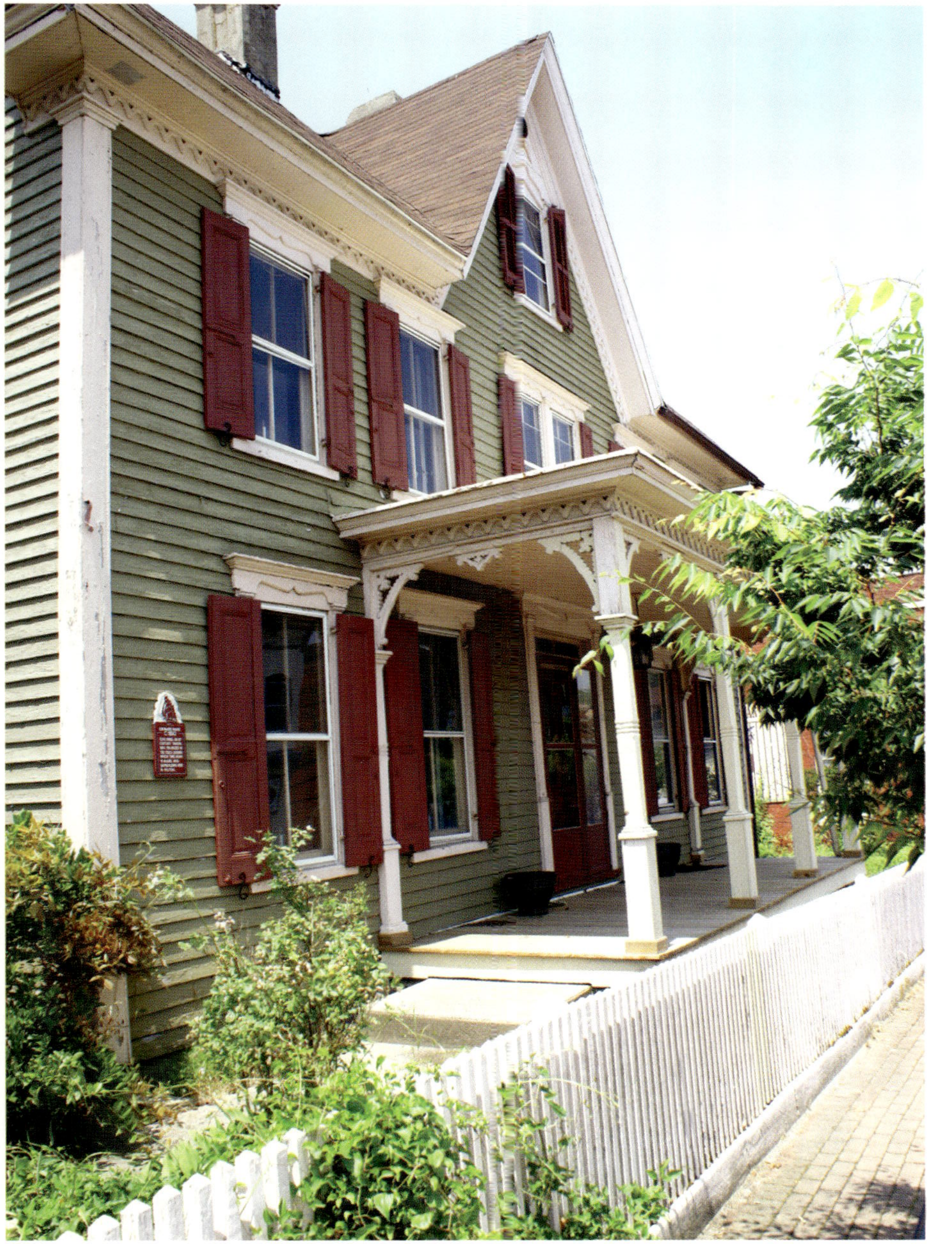

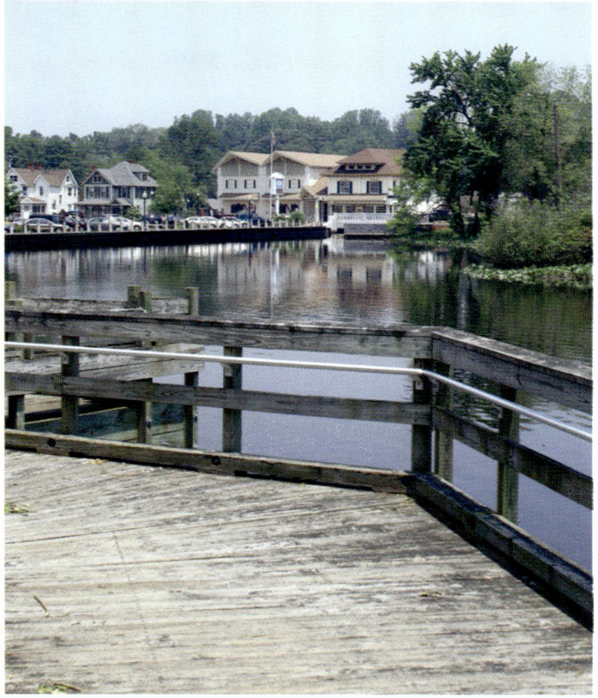

Wagamon's Pond in Milton features a new Fishing Pier and spillway.

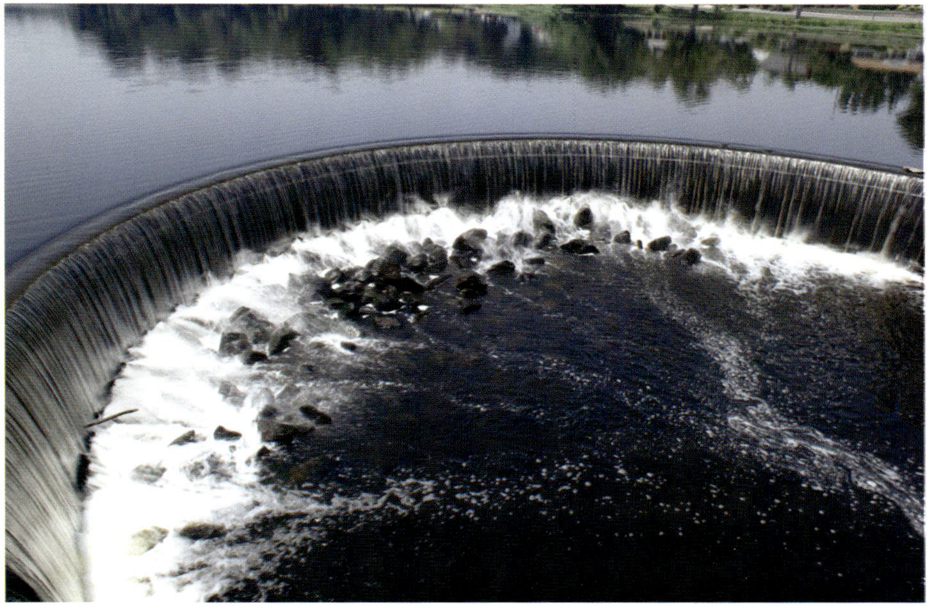

Bibliography

Books

Grayson, William C. *Delaware's Ghost Towers*. Bloomington, IN: Authorhouse, 2005.

Haden, Amy et al. *Victorian Lewes and Its Architecture*. Lewes, DE: The Lewes Historical Society and The Preservation Trust, 1986.

Pamphlets

2007 Visitors Guide. Lewes, DE: Lewes Chamber of Commerce, 2007.

Bethany-Fenwick Area Community Guide. Elgin, IL: VillageProfile.com, Inc., 2006.

Delaware Beaches Visitors Guide. Virginia Beach, VA: VistaGraphics, Inc., 2008.

Historic Milton – A Charming Experience. Milton, DE: Milton Chamber of Commerce.

Southern Delaware Official Visitors Guide & Vacation Planner. Georgetown, DE: Southern Delaware Tourism.

The Quiet Resorts 2007-2008 Official Visitors Guide. Fenwick Island, DE: Bethany-Fenwick Area Chamber of Commerce, 2007.

Welcome to Lewes. Lewes, DE: Lewes Chamber of Commerce, 2007.

Web sites

http://archives.delaware.gov
http://bethanybeachnews.com
www.addysea.com
www.baltimoresun.com
www.beach-fun.com
www.beach-net.com
www.bethany-beach.net
www.bethanybeachbooks.com
www.bethany-fenwick.org
www.bethanysurfshop.com
www.butteryrestaurant.com
www.cafelocal.com
www.census.gov
www.ci.milton.de.us
www.cmlf.com
www.coastalpoint.com
www.d3stores.com/candykitchen/
www.delawarebaylights.org
www.delawarenationalguard.com
www.delawareonline.com
www.deldot.gov
www.delmarvakayak.home.comcast.net
www.delmarvanow.com
www.destateparks.com
www.deweybeachclub.com
www.deweybeachlife.com
www.discoversea.com
www.dnrec.delaware.gov
www.dnrec.state.de.us
www.dolles-ibachs.com
www.dspf.net
www.fenwickisland.org
www.frommers.com/destinations/lewes/
www.grottopizza.com
www.historiclewes.org
www.jazz-funeral.com
www.kohrbros.com
www.lewes.com
www.leweschamber.com

www.lewesde.com
www.lewespresbyterianchurch.org
www.lighthousefriends.com
www.millsborochamber.com
www.msbusinessreport.com
www.myspace.com/bottleandcork
www.newszap.com
www.nps.gov
www.oceanretreatdayspa.com
www.overfalls.org
www.potteryplaceperks.com
www.rbsa.org
www.rd.com
www.rehoboth.com
www.rehobothartleague.org
www.rehobothbandstand.com
www.ruddertowneusa.com
www.savethetower.org
www.seacolonyrecreation.org
www.seacolonyreunion.com
www.seacrestgifts.com
www.seashellcity.com
www.seasidecountrystore.com
www.southbethany.org
www.stateparks.com
www.stpeters.episcopaldelaware.org
www.theinnatcanalsquare.com
www.townofbethanybeach.com
www.travel.yahoo.com
www.tripsandgetaways.com
www.TRUTV.com
www.visitdelaware.net
www.washingtonpost.com
www.wikipedia.org

Index

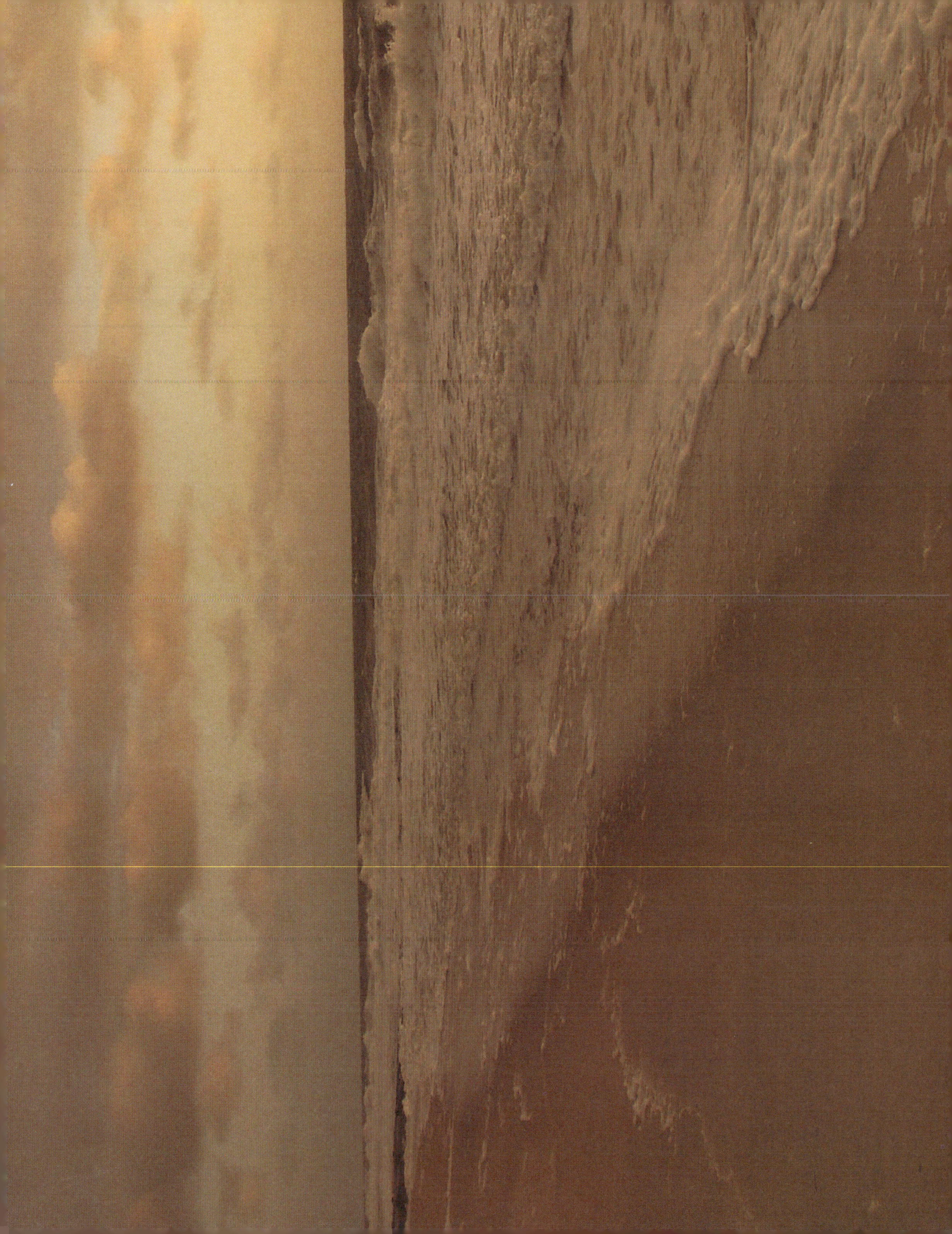